SCENES OF
SUBJECTION

SCENES OF
SUBJECTION

Terror,
Slavery, and
Self-Making in
Nineteenth-Century
America

SAIDIYA HARTMAN

Foreword by Keeanga-Yamahtta Taylor
Afterword by Marisa J. Fuentes and Sarah Haley
Notations with Cameron Rowland
Compositions by Torkwase Dyson

W. W. NORTON & COMPANY
Independent Publishers Since 1923

Copyright © 2022, 1997 by Saidiya V. Hartman
Notations © 2022 by Saidiya V. Hartman and Cameron Rowland
Cosmogram drawing © 2022 by Saidiya V. Hartman and Samuel Miller

All rights reserved
Printed in the United States of America
Revised and Updated Edition

First published by Oxford University Press, Inc. in 1997, revised and updated paperback issued in 2022 by W.W. Norton & Company, Inc.

For information about permission to reproduce selections from this book, write to Permissions, W. W. Norton & Company, Inc., 500 Fifth Avenue, New York, NY 10110

For information about special discounts for bulk purchases, please contact W. W. Norton Special Sales at specialsales@wwnorton.com or 800-233-4830

Manufacturing by Lakeside Book Company
Book design by Chris Welch
Production manager: Julia Druskin

ISBN: 978-1-324-02158-2

W. W. Norton & Company, Inc., 500 Fifth Avenue, New York, N.Y. 10110
www.wwnorton.com

W. W. Norton & Company Ltd., 15 Carlisle Street, London W1D 3BS

1 2 3 4 5 6 7 8 9 0

For those who made the way

CONTENTS

I
FORMATIONS OF TERROR AND ENJOYMENT

II
THE SUBJECT OF FREEDOM

FOREWORD

Keeanga-Yamahtta Taylor

In the United States, we like to discuss the distortions of the nation's history as amnesia, when it is more appropriate to understand our affliction as selective memory clotted with omissions intended to obscure the raw truth about our society. A few years ago, I traveled to New Orleans for a family vacation after a semester of teaching about slavery in the United States. I was anxious to visit the city knowing that by the time the United States ended its role in the transatlantic slave trade, New Orleans had become the center of a robust, internal marketplace for enslaved labor. Today, Americans think of New Orleans as a cultural capital known for its street parties and its Cajun and Creole cuisine, and some may even be familiar with its history of jazz and other Black artistic creations. But there is almost no trace of its vital role in the history of American slavery.

There have been more recent efforts in New Orleans to place a plaque here or there, near areas where tourists traverse, but only to be found by the most adroit. Today, Jackson Square, located in the French Quarter, is at the heart of local tourist attractions and restaurants, but there is hardly any mention or marker of its former function as an open-air marketplace for buying and selling enslaved men, women, and children. There is no public memory of it as the site of the public execution of slaves who participated in an 1811 slave rebellion, the largest in American history. Nor is there any recollection that in its grisly aftermath, the heads of executed slaves were hoisted upon the pikes of the wrought iron gates adorning the park.

New Orleans is hardly unique as a site of selective memory when it comes to the public reckoning with its local history of slavery. From the local to the national, our history of slavery has been recast as part of our narrative of forward progress. Where slavery is depicted as our founding "national sin," it is as quickly dispatched as having been exorcized through the carnage of the Civil War, setting the United States upon its essential course toward a more perfect union. Slavery's essential role in building the nation's treasure that would, in turn, facilitate its rise as the most powerful nation on earth has been minimized, if not wholly ignored. As have been the roots of slavery to the nation's enduring crisis of racism and its attendant impacts within the lives of Black people thereafter.

Saidiya Hartman's powerful exploration of slavery and freedom in the United States, *Scenes of Subjection: Terror, Slavery, and Self-Making in Nineteenth-Century America*, first appeared in print in 1997, during the last period of spoiled "race relations" in the twentieth century. Just a few years prior to its publication, the United States had experienced the Los Angeles rebellion, the largest urban insurrection in American history. In response to the uprising, the American state rallied its political forces around crime legislation and a prison-building bonanza. The draconian response provoked the unprecedented outpouring mobilized in the form of the Million Man March, organized by Louis Farrakhan and led by the Nation of Islam. The march was not conceived of as a protest, but became a massive gathering of Black men dejected and marginalized within an increasingly repressive United States. The mounting instability of racial politics in the late 1990s precipitated then-president Bill Clinton's poorly conceived "conversation on race," to be facilitated by a new commission to study "race relations" in the United States.

Shortly after its formation, that commission produced a dubiously titled report called, the "One America Initiative." The remedies that emerged for healing the "racial divide" in the United States included a heated debate over whether the president should apologize for slavery. In 1998, when Bill Clinton traveled to Africa, the intensifying debate over the apology continued, even as his spokesperson assured the American public, "He certainly is going to talk about the legacy of slavery and the scar that it represents on America," but an apology would be, "extraneous and off the point." In lieu of an apology, he eventually conceded the painfully obvious: "Going back to the time before we were even a nation, European Americans received the fruits of the slave trade, and we were wrong in that."

Twenty-five years later, the United States is embroiled in new turmoil in its latest iteration of a national reckoning about the continuing role of racism in American society. In the summer of 2020, the cumulative weight of the Trump presidency's embrace of white supremacy, coupled with the horrific carnage produced by the unprecedented onslaught of a novel coronavirus chewing its way through Black communities, gave way to unprecedented protests, when an explosive video captured a modern-day lynching of George Floyd at the hands of a white police officer. It provoked the latest national awakening about the continued power of racism within American society, which has returned us to old and unresolved discussions about the role of slavery in American history as a way of understanding the longevity of racism in the United States. This has included a renewed discussion about reparations for African Americans as compensation for a history of unpaid labor. To that end, the only federal legislation to emerge from the rebellions and protests of the summer of 2020 has not been for police reform or in the establishment of new programs intended to improve the life chances of Black people; it has been the establishment of Juneteenth, a new national holiday to commemorate when federal troops arrived in Texas and freed the enslaved.

This kind of national celebration of the symbolic, while leaving undisturbed the architecture of oppression that has made African Americans disproportionately vulnerable to premature death and a "travestied" freedom, has been a hallmark of the Black experience since the abolition of slavery. This is not to say that the national recognition of the end of slavery is unimportant, but it does serve to reinforce what formally concluded, while paying almost no attention to what carried on after slavery. Instead, the celebrations of the abolition of slavery and the misassumption that it inaugurated Black people into personhood and then citizenship have served to mute other conversations about the ways that one form of bondage gave way to new coercive relationships. This is less about cynicism concerning the immutability of racism or even anti-Blackness than it is an expression of extraordinary pessimism about American liberalism and all of its haughty conceits about its universalism, autonomy, and justice.

Neither a historian nor social scientist, Saidiya Hartman is a scholar of criticism, law, cultural history, and slavery. *Scenes* was a pioneering achievement of interdisciplinary scholarship just as such work was being called upon to provide differing insights while applying varied methodological applications as a means to invoke different kinds of interventions. Here, Hartman's work breathed new life into scholastic understanding of performance studies, as well as prescient analyses of racial capitalism in cultural studies and criticism. Indeed, *Scenes* should be considered among the texts that have spelled out the mutually constitutive relationship between racism and capitalism in American history. Hartman has become a master at cracking through disciplinary and genre roadblocks and facades that for years have acted as gatekeepers around specific bodies of knowledge. Yet *Scenes* and subsequent work from

Hartman upholds scholarly standards of rigor based in evidence and command of scholarly debates, including where one fits and departs from the conversations. Indeed, *Scenes of Subjection* does not retell the history of slavery and emancipation; instead Hartman is asking us to think differently about these events. Not as part of the narrative arc of justice and progress in American history, but as affirmation of a kind of deeply constrained and compromised conception of democracy and liberty in the first place, which inevitably then gave way to constrained and compromised visions of freedom in slavery's aftermath. Hartman is challenging the assumption that the continued forms of subjugation endured by ordinary Black people after slavery's end are only the result of ongoing patterns of exclusion from the governing and financial institutions of the country, leaving inclusion as the solution. Instead, Hartman has asked us to consider different questions, namely, what is meant by *freedom*? If freedom is simply the opposite of bondage, while affording nothing other than the right to compete with other free people in a human scrum for income, food, clothing, and housing, then it is an exceedingly thin and narrow conception of liberty. If, however, we think of freedom as a right to move through life with genuine self-possession that can only be rooted in the satisfaction of basic human needs and desires, then Black emancipation in the United States was something altogether different. Indeed, how could a conception of freedom that was so intimately conjoined with enslavement produce any other outcome, when the only thing separating slavery from freedom was the declaration that it was over? With no effort to address the past, to heal the deformation cast unto Blackness that had been used to rationalize and legitimize slavery, and with no effort to ease the transition from property to person with freedom dues, then, as Du Bois lamented, the freedpeople enjoyed an ever-brief moment in the sun only to return to a condition as near to slavery as slavery itself.

It is also important to convey that the historical omissions and the occurrences of unfreedom that shape the Black entry into personhood in the United States and that have been perpetuated thereafter, are not simply oversights, unfortunate slips, or other kinds of accidental erasures born of ignorance and, essentially, innocence. They are contrived, mean-spirited, and deliberate. The United States' self-idealization as an "exceptional" country in its democratic founding and promises of unfettered social mobility *necessarily* diminishes the centrality of slavery and racism in the country's ascendance as a world power. Indeed, the country's periodic return to slavery as a metaphorical "original sin" not only creates an origin story for racism in the United States, but it also explains its persistence after slavery as a hangover or vestige in an otherwise narrative arc bending toward progress. Where racism does reoccur, it is the work of backward individuals who see color. Where disparities in jobs, housing, education, and beyond exist, the problem is with the individual unable to assimilate into the affluence that America has to offer. The notion of "systemic racism" is rejected, while lapsed personal responsibility is assumed. And where white poverty is hidden, and thus exoticized upon discovery, Black poverty is ubiquitous, expected, and ultimately, paradigmatic.

Hartman is suggesting that instead of thinking of America's persisting crises of racial inequity, domination, and subjugation as the accumulated toll of missed opportunities, failed programs, and policy conundrums, that perhaps we consider a deeper, existential problem with American democracy itself. American freedom, liberty, justice, and ultimately democracy came into being through slavery, genocide, rape, dispossession, murder, and terror. Indeed, it was the actual existence of slavery that crystalized the moral valence of liberty and freedom for the founders. It is well known that the leading lights of the American Revolution compared their status as colonial subjects of the British Parliament to enslavement. The founders invoked slavery as a rallying cry to marshal their forces.

It was part rhetoric and metaphor, but it was also buttressed by a reality that, in fact, they intimately understood that slavery meant an abject absence of freedom and total subordination to another person's will. The deep understanding of slavery, as slaveholders, formed their understanding of freedom and liberty. Moreover, the enslaved embodied abject Blackness, thus providing a negative mirror for white men to imagine their lives in sharp contrast to. Consider the insights of a white lawyer from South Carolina who wrote in 1775, "Liberty ... is a principle which naturally and spontaneously contrasts with slavery. In no country on earth can the line of distinction ever be marked so boldly.... Here there is a standing subject of comparison, which must be ever perfect and ever obvious.... The constant example of slavery stimulates a free man to avoid being confounded with the blacks.... Slavery, so far from being inconsistent, has, in fact, a tendency to stimulate and perpetuate the spirit of liberty." It is not only that slavery provided a negative meaning for American liberty, but its realization within private property, possessive individualism, and its eventual glorification of the so-called free market, narrowed its benefits to an even smaller number, initially to be shared among wealthy white men with land and eventually to white men of any standing.

Given the symmetry between slavery and freedom, then, for Hartman, the persistence of unfreedom in the aftermath of slavery was predictable. The voices of those African Americans who lived within and then after slavery could attest to this confounding reality as clearly as anyone. In 1937, a woman who had lived in slavery and was later interviewed in the controversial Works Progress Administration project that recorded survivors of slavery could speak to these continuities. Her name was Patsy Mitchner, and she perfectly captured the riddle of American freedom in Black hands. She said, "Slavery was a bad thing, and freedom, of the kind we got, with nothing to live on, was bad. Two snakes full of poison. One lying with his head pointing north, the other with his head pointing south. Their names was slavery and freedom. The snake called slavery lay with his head pointed south, and the snake called freedom lay with his head pointed north. Both bit the nigger, and they was both bad."[1]

It is important to note that Hartman's examination is not a new tributary feeding the larger pools of critical race theory that have examined the ways that American law has been a tool in stripping the meaning and substance out of Black achievement of civil rights. As she writes in her endnotes:

> Legal liberalism, as well as critical race theory, has examined issues of race, racism, and equality by focusing on the exclusion and marginalization of those subjects and bodies marked as different. . . . The disadvantage of this approach is that the proposed remedies and correctives to the problem—inclusion, protection, and greater access of opportunity—do not ultimately challenge the economy of racial production or its truth claims or interrogate the exclusions constitutive of the norm, but instead seek to gain equality, liberty, and redress within its confines.

In other words, by simply examining the regime of exclusions that has been at the heart of liberal critiques of the American state, the *nature* of the state has gone underexamined. This is especially true of mid-twentieth-century racial liberalism, which held the assumption that the central problem in the United States was that of exclusion, as opposed to extraction, accumulation, and dispossession as organizing principles for the American state and the political class that facilitates its function. In other words, the racial liberals assumed that the inclusion of Black Americans into the American mainstream would produce a large Black middle class, as had been done among white Americans. While it is undoubtedly true that some portions of Black Americans were incorporated into the mainstream of American society, different modes of inclusion also included new opportunities for economic exploitation, dispossession, and extraction from African Americans as well. It was a well-rehearsed pattern, even if in different eras, different intentions motivated the rhetoric of inclusion. For example, after Emancipation, the inclusion of African Americans into contract-making—a document joining together parties based on their own will and volition—did not only create new opportunities for autonomy, but also for new forms of coercion as the elite of the white South raced to reconstitute their labor force under conditions as close to slavery as they could legally finagle.

It is the nature of the liberal American state to which Hartman returns, and its particularly pernicious effects in the lives of Black people. But the absence of self-determination afforded to freedpeople meant that even when they were formally accepted into the body politic or civic society, inclusion existed within a web of coercive inducements masquerading as sovereign individualism. Capitalist societies like the United States proselytized the virtues of autonomy and self-possession, while simultaneously organizing an economic order that produced class differences that impaired unfettered access to rights, property, and other forms of wealth and possession. As Hartman points out, after slavery, there were two freedoms in the United States: freedom from bondage and the freedom to starve. Freedoms correlated with the market produced enormous wealth and power for some, but immiserating poverty for others, and in the process, undermined the autonomy, liberty, and self-possession of the poor and working classes. In other words, post-Emancipation American freedom was imagined as consistent and the fulfilment of a market-based economy, thus valorizing individualism and autonomy as products of personal success, in contrast to what historian Thomas Holt observed: "Throughout most of human history the highest value or good has been to achieve a sense, not of autonomy, but of belonging, that psychic and physical security of incorporation into the group." Nevertheless, these were the conditions of freedom into which Black freedpeople were liberated. Their situation was then compounded by color and utter dispossession, thereby heightening the coercive measures undertaken to compel Black people to return to the work that had previously defined their existence.

Hartman is also suggesting something beyond the deficiencies of the American state to understand the continuing patterns of subjugation that define the Black experience. Part I of *Scenes* is dedicated to interrogating the ways that the Black subject is constructed and how this construction contributes to their marginalization in the aftermath of slavery. Indeed, the insistence that Black freedpeople could simply slip into the garments of American citizenship with no trace of the "badges or incidents" of slavery as garish adornments upon their person, was to ignore the ways that Blackness had been cast as abject in the hands of buyers and sellers of Black bodies. This blind spot obscured the ways that slavery, race, and racism marked the Black body, then ignored how those etchings placed the Black subject outside of and beyond the rationale and logic of universalism, including the legal frameworks that had been built to govern a republic conceived of as only for white men. Within the regime of slavery, slave subjectivity did not exist in any formal capacity beyond the ways that the state could define the crimes of the enslaved and enumerate punishment against the enslaved. But with no punishment by the nineteenth century for the rape or murder of the enslaved, Black women, men, and children were effectively excluded from the liberal framework of personhood and all its attendant rights and responsibilities.

The absence of legal protections made the enslaved vulnerable to the forms of depraved violence that pervaded the institution of slavery. The display of violence against the enslaved to engender sympathy or empathy as a means to gather opposition to slavery called upon white sympathizers to put themselves in the place of the slave to form an opposition to slavery. In doing so, the experience of the enslaved person is lost again, while the emotional drama of the white sympathizer is the action that must be assuaged. The result may, in fact, be the end of slavery, but nothing has been done to repair or restore the harm done to the enslaved. In fact, the experiences of the enslaved have barely been attended, because the focus has been trained on the emotional experience of white witnesses. It is also an example of the ways that, within the liberal framework, even abolitionists were complicit in reinforcing conceptions of abject Blackness while decrying slavery. For Hartman this is not a morality play; it is simply to say that slavery was so closely sutured to freedom in America that it was impossible to imagine the social relations of Black and white outside of its paradigm.

Hartman argues for a different approach in distilling the brutality of slavery. By looking at what she describes as the "quotidian routines of slavery," Hartman suggests that we can see something even more insidious about the institution. In this way, she examines the demand of slaves as entertainment for white audiences as a potentially more fruitful place to understand slavery as a site of domination. Here, Hartman's delve into performance and the multiple meanings of "embodiment" in her discussion of Blackness as an invention of white society not only draws attention to a different kind of brutality during this period, but it also prefaces the extraordinary complexity of Black freedom after slavery. The forced jocularity created through the command of white audiences, but also as deception deployed by the enslaved, in both cases as a means to dissimulate either terror or disobedience, was also evidence of the brutality of slavery. Whether making the enslaved dance through the Middle Passage, charm on the auction block, or minstrel to brighten the doldrums of white workers, Blackness is construed as irrevocably joyful, carefree, lascivious, and impervious. Even where enslaved people slipped into the affectations of Blackness to comfort an owner with their submission, there was no greater evidence of subjection.

But the misunderstanding of Black participation within these formal and informal routines could also be touted as evidence of volition, will, and agency within the framework of slavery. These perceptions reinforced ideas that remained popular about American slavery well into the twentieth century, namely that the institution was familial and pastoral, thereby assuming the complicity of the enslaved, albeit with periodic eruptions of patriarchal violence. Where those ideas don't necessarily prevail, we still find their trace. Consider the school of the new social historical studies of slavery that emerged in the 1960s and '70s. A feature of the new social history was the search for slaves' resistance to their condition as evidence to challenge the perception that slaves were so dominant that they had no conceivable lives outside of the direction of their owners. The new social historians, many of whom had been influenced by the social movements of the 1960s, wanted to show that slaves had their own lives independent of slavery, where examples of their autonomy and self-possession could be identified. Hartman, in anticipation of Walter Johnson's later and well-known and critical essay "On Agency," cautions against the easy invocation of "slave's agency" as a means of capturing "slave humanity."[2] If agency is an expression of free will and volition—the very essence of liberal self-making and self-possession—then how do we locate these expressions in the actions of human property? The notion of the consent or autonomy of slaves to opt in or out of anything essentially "neutralizes the dilemma of the object status and pained subject constitution of the enslaved and obscures the violence of slavery." Well-intended efforts to "humanize" the enslaved by pointing to disparate moments of activity can assume consent with enslavement elsewhere. Conflating agency with activity imposes a kind of autonomy and freedom in the choices made by the enslaved that obfuscates the conditions of subjection and abjection understood in a system of slavery. As Hartman argues, "If agency is simply about the capacity to act, it does not tell us nearly enough about the conditions within which one is acting, the material makeup of the forces that one is acting against, or the wider contexts within which these actions take place." Implied in the hunt for slave agency is an implicit representation of slavery as a negotiated relationship where the enslaved could haggle over the terms of their bondage. In the end, the notion that slaves wielded choice or had agency in their daily negotiations within slavery softens our perceptions of the system while humanizing its architects. This, of course, doesn't mean that the enslaved did not resist their enslavement. As Hartman points out: "Strategies of domination don't exhaust all possibilities of intervention, resistance, escape, refusal, or transformation." The question is how to understand the constraints shaping resistance without reinscribing enslavement as a normative condition.

The domination and subordination at the core of American enslavement shaped the afterlife of Black Americans as freedpeople. The continuation of abuse and recurring efforts across the South to reimpose the conditions of slavery on the freed were enshrined into law with the Black Codes in slavery's immediate aftermath. The codes were ultimately abolished and replaced with a new federal law, the 1866 Civil Rights Act, which along with the Reconstruction Amendments, was passed to allow for African Americans to become citizens of the United States. Black people were no longer formally excluded from the rights endowed by citizenship, but they were also freed with almost no discernible means to create new lives outside of bondage. Their newfound poverty was now mapped onto an existing antipathy of Blackness that had not only built up over two centuries of legal enslavement, but that had also been reinforced by new expertise and pseudoscience that elocuted the inferiority and social and scientific deformation of Black people. Moreover, not only had conceptions of freedom like autonomy and possessive individualism only ever been imagined as quintessentially white, the 1866 Civil Rights Act used whiteness as the baseline standard for understanding the rights available to Black people. In the legislation, the enumeration of the rights of citizenship is followed by the phrase "as is enjoyed by white citizens." The efforts to base new laws, rights, and citizenship on a concept of *white* universalism obscured more than it clarified. It created the conditions where specific Black demands for redress, repair, or standing could only be construed as "special rights." The law performed colorblindness in a country where the color-conscious subordination of Black people had been a core feature since its eighteenth-century founding.

In this sense, the modern United States came into formation when the U.S. Supreme Court, in the 1883 *Civil Rights Cases*, hollowed out the Civil Rights Act of 1875, which had relied upon an expansive reading of the Thirteenth Amendment as abolishing slavery and all of its requisite "badges and incidents," invariably including the private sector, where racism could rage like wildfire. The *Civil Rights Cases* ruling was the final wedge necessary to separate the laws governing the supposed public sphere from the private. The ruling declared the private sphere to be free from the legal requirements to recognize the rights of Black citizens, effectively reconstituting Black citizenship to an exceedingly small set of locations. The justices wrote:

> The XIIIth Amendment relates only to slavery and involuntary servitude (which it abolishes); . . . yet such legislative power extends only to the subject of slavery and its incidents; and the denial of equal accommodations in inns, public conveyances and places of public amusement (which is forbidden

by the sections in question), imposes no badge of slavery or involuntary servitude upon the party, but at most, infringes rights which are protected from State aggression by the XIVth Amendment.

Justice Joseph P. Bradley continued:

When a man has emerged from slavery, and by the aid of beneficient legislation has shaken off the inseparable concomitants of that state, there must be some stage in the progress of his elevation when he takes the rank of a mere citizen, and ceases to be the special favorite of the laws, and when his rights as a citizen, or a man, are to be protected in the ordinary modes by which other men's rights are protected. There were thousands of free colored people in this country before the abolition of slavery, enjoying all the essential rights of life, liberty and property the same as white citizens; yet no one, at that time, thought that it was any invasion of his personal status as a freeman because he was not admitted to all the privileges enjoyed by white citizens, or because he was subjected to discriminations in the enjoyment of accommodations in inns, public conveyances and places of amusement. Mere discriminations on account of race or color were not regarded as badges of slavery. If, since that time, the enjoyment of equal rights in all these respects has become established by constitutional enactment, it is not by force of the Thirteenth Amendment (which merely abolishes slavery), but by force of the Thirteenth and Fifteenth Amendments.

With the court abdicating any legal responsibility for the defense and protection of Black citizens, while preserving a socially permissible private sphere of racism, the eventual *Plessy v. Ferguson* ruling

in 1896 was inevitable. This is not the discourse of fatalism, but it is
at the core of the actual reckoning we must grapple with. The legal
tools inscribed by the most powerful court in the country reflected
the deteriorated status of Black people, while also working to further degrade their condition. The lack of power inherent in not even
being able to accurately define your social position is an affront to
any notion of self-determination, self-possession, autonomy, and
is certainly not liberty. It is a state of subjection, different from
enslavement, but unfree, nonetheless.

   Scenes of Subjection is not a dour lament on the fixity of this condition, but it is an unrelenting argument that these conditions cannot
be changed by tinkering with laws that never address the root of the
affliction in the first place. We must look at the totality of the society and the foundation upon which it was built to understand why,
even more than one hundred and fifty years after slavery, ordinary
Black people continue to suffer from the vicious entrapments of racism. Twenty-five years after this spectacular book first appeared, a
twenty-first-century social movement evincing the most elemental
recognition of humanity calls itself Black Lives Matter in hope to
make it so. It is a centuries-long quest that may only be recognized
with the realization that it may require a completely different society, where inclusion and humanity are understood expansively and
broadly, where freedom is the absence of coercion, and human need
and fulfilment are the bottom upon which our lives can be rebuilt.

The Hold of Slavery

The conviction that I was living in the world created by slavery propelled the writing of this book. I could feel the force and disfigurement of slavery in the present. The life of the captive and the commodity certainly wasn't my past, but rather the threshold of my entry into the world. Its grasp and claim couldn't be cordoned off as what happened then. For me, the relation between slavery and the present was open, unfinished.

In rereading *Scenes of Subjection*, I am struck by the breathlessness of the prose, by its ardent desire to say it all, to say everything at once. If it were possible, I might have written it as a 345-page-long sentence. This sentence would be written in the past, present, and future tense. Temporal entanglement best articulates the still open question of abolition and the long-awaited but not yet actualized freedom declared over a century and a half ago. The hold of slavery was what I sought to articulate and convey. The category crisis of human flesh and sentient commodity defined the existence of the enslaved and this predicament of value and fungibility would shadow their descendants, the blackened and the dispossessed.[1] I also hoped to change the terms in which we understood racial slavery, by attending to its diffuse terror and the divisions it created between life and not life. The scenes of subjection I endeavored to unpack were not those of spectacular violence—the thirty-three

lashes at the whipping post, the torture, rape, and brutality ubiquitous on the plantation, the public rituals of lynching and dismemberment, the vast arsenal of implements employed to harm and
maim, the Sadeian pursuits, the endless variations of humiliation
and dishonor, and the compulsive displays of the broken and violated body—all of which were endemic to slavery and key to the
cultivation of antislavery sentiment and pedagogy. My interest lay
elsewhere. To be subjected to the absolute power of another and to
be interpellated as a subject before the law were the dimensions of
subjection that most concerned me. I intended to bring into view
the ordinary terror and habitual violence that structured everyday
life and inhabited the most mundane and quotidian practices. This
environment of brutality and extreme domination affected the most
seemingly benign aspects of the life of the enslaved and could not be
eluded, no matter the nature of one's condition, whether paramour,
offspring, dutiful retainer, or favored nursemaid. The shift from the
spectacular to the everyday was critical in illuminating the ongoing
and structural dimensions of violence and slavery's idioms of power.

No less important was the domain of practice. In creating an
inventory of ways of doing and a genealogy of refusal, I tried to
account for extreme domination *and* the possibilities seized in practice. Black performance and quotidian practice were determined
by and exceeded the constraints of domination. This dimension has
received less attention in the reception of the book. The focus on its
arguments about empathy, terror and violence, subjection and social
death has overshadowed the discussion of practice. *Scenes* endeavored to illuminate the countless ways in which the enslaved challenged, refused, defied, and resisted the condition of enslavement
and its ordering and negation of life, its extraction and destruction
of capacity. The everyday practices, the ways of living and dying,
of making and doing, were attempts to slip away from the status of
commodity and to affirm existence as not chattel, as not property, as

not wench. Even when this other state could not be named, because incommensurate or untranslatable within the conceptual field of the enclosure, the negation of the given was ripe with promise. The wild thought and dangerous music of the enslaved gave voice to other visions of the possible and refused captivity as the only horizon, opposed the framework of property and commodity, contested the idea that they were less than human, nurtured acts of vengeance, and anticipated divine retribution.

This subjugated knowledge or speculative knowledge of freedom would establish the vision of *what might be*, even if unrealizable within the prevailing terms of order. It explains why a commodity might describe themself as human flesh, or a fugitive trapped in a garret write letters describing a free life in the North, or a hand laboring in the field read the signs and take note of "the drops of blood on the corn as though it was dew from heaven" and in the woods discern in the arrangement of leaves a hieroglyph of freedom coming, or an ex-slave prove capable of imagining "an auspicious era of extensive freedom," as does Olaudah Equiano in *The Interesting Narrative*: "May the time come—at least the speculation is to me pleasing—when the sable people shall gratefully commemorate the auspicious era of extensive freedom."[2] It is a curious and prescient formulation. How does one commemorate what has yet to arrive?

In the context of social death, everyday practices explored the possibility of transfigured existence and cultivated an imagination of the otherwise and elsewhere, cartographies of the fantastic utterly antagonistic to slavery. The enslaved refused to accept the order of values that had transformed them into units of currency and capital, beasts and crops, breeders, incubators, lactating machines, and sentient tools. At secret meetings and freedom schools, hidden away in loopholes of retreat and hush arbors, gathered at the river or dwelling in the swamp, the enslaved articulated a vision of freedom that far exceeded that of the liberal imagination. It enabled them to conceive other ways of existing, flee the world of masters and invite its fiery destruction, anticipate the upheaval that would put "the bottom rail on top," nurture a collective vision of what might be possible when no longer enslaved, and sustain belief in the inevitability of slavery's demise. A messianic vision of the last days and the end of world was articulated in a range of quotidian practices, from work songs to the ring shout, a circle dance of worship and divine communion. Such practices shaped the contours of the day-to-day. An expansive register of minor gestures, ways of sustaining and creating life, caring for one another, undoing slavery by small acts of stealth and destruction, communal dreaming, sacred transport, acts of redress, and faith in a power greater than master and nation made it possible to survive the unbearable while never acceding to it. The arrangement of stars in the night sky, the murmur and echo of songs traveling across a river, the revered objects buried near a prayer tree, the rumors of fugitives in the swamp or maroons in the hills nourished dreams of a free territory, or an existence without masters, or a plot against the plantation, or reveries of miraculous deliverance.

———

In the archive of slavery, I encountered a paradox: the recognition of the slave's humanity and status as a subject extended and intensified servitude and dispossession, rather than conferring some small measure of rights and protection. The attributes of the human— will, consciousness, reason, agency, and responsibility—were the inroads of discipline, punishment, and mortification. This foreshadowed the subject of freedom and the limits of personhood bound indissolubly to property. The recognition of the formerly enslaved as a newly endowed subject of rights was not the entry to the promised land. This should not have been a surprise. Western humanism was born in the context of the Atlantic slave trade and racial slavery. It became apparent that being a subject was not the antidote to being a slave, but rather that these figures were intimate, twinned. I wanted for some other end: a true abolition of property, a leveling of the vertical order of life, a messianic cessation, a way of keeping terror at bay, a rampart against devastation and the dangers of what lived on.

Any certainty about the historical divide between slavery and freedom proved to be increasingly elusive. The exclusion and hierarchy constitutive of the discourse of rights and man and the racism of the white republic and the settler nation were robust and not to be eradicated by acts or proclamations or field orders or amendments. The movement from slave to "man and citizen" would be impeded, thwarted. The restricted vision of freedom offered by the liberal imagination, a vision even more attenuated and hollowed out by counterrevolution, economic predation, antiblack violence, and white supremacy, would not transform the plantation, or abolish racial slavery and its badges or indices, or eradicate caste, or negate the legacy and stigma of having been chattel.

With the advent of Emancipation, only the most restricted and narrow vision of freedom was deemed plausible: the physical release from bondage and the exercise and imposition of the contract—this and little more. In the aftermath of slavery's formal demise, the old relations of servitude and subordination were recreated in a new guise. The signs of this were everywhere apparent: The enslaved failed to be compensated for centuries of unremunerated labor. They never received the material support or resources necessary to give flesh to words like "equality" and "citizen." The gulf between blacks, marked and targeted as not human or as lesser humans and social inferiors, and white citizens only widened. A wave of revanchism and counterrevolution engulfed the nation.

Racist violence intensified and white citizens committed a series of massacres with the goal of returning the newly freed to their proper place. The "gift of freedom" gave birth to the landless tenant and the indebted worker. The enslaved were transformed into a new kind of property—alienable labor or property in the self; but in all other ways they were without resources. This property in the self was to be sold and exchanged, at least as an ideal. Again, one entered the world of objects and social relations congealed as the circulation of goods and things. The contract enabled the transition from slavery to involuntary servitude, and the much-lauded exercise of choice was shored up by the threat of punishment and imprisonment. The liberty to sell one's labor resulted in sharecropping, peonage, and immiseration, and the failure to exercise this liberty led to the chain gang or being leased as a convict. Coercion rather than consent defined the free market and free labor. Equality was interpreted and adjudicated to enforce segregation, the regime of separate but equal, and the hierarchy of racially differentiated life. The enormity and tragedy of this stopped me in my tracks.

It was not hindsight but the restricted scope of freedom, especially when contrasted with what might or could be, that made me pause and question: What, exactly, were the social arrangements envisioned and desired after Emancipation? Was captivity the prevailing schema, not by default but design? Could an idea of freedom fundamentally bound to property do anything other than reproduce dispossession and confirm the alienability and disposability of life and capacity? Could democracy built on racial slavery and settler colonialism ever sustain freedom, repair what has been broken, return what has been stolen, release land to earth, provide to each according to their needs, and enable all to thrive? The answer remains a resounding "no." As many ex-slaves remarked, freedom without material resources was another kind of slavery. So, when my attention turned to freedom and its philosophical and legal

foundations, I realized how formative and enduring the hold of slavery continued to be. The liberal conception of freedom had been
built on the bedrock of slavery.

With striking ease and facility, new modalities of involuntary
servitude emerged to replace and replicate the old one. Abolition
remained an aspiration, rather than a feat realized and completed. I
didn't yet have the language of the "afterlife of slavery" to describe
the structural hold of racial slavery. Yet, it is clear I was writing
toward this concept, which would be developed in *Lose Your Mother*
and "Venus in Two Acts."[3]

If the conventional narrative "from slavery to freedom" failed to
capture the temporal entanglement of racial slavery as our past and
our present, the lasting effects of the slave's exile from and precarious belonging to the category of the human, the recursive character
of violence and accumulation, and the long duration of unfreedom,
then how might I frame and approach such matters? How might
I interrupt the traditional account, revise historical chronology,
cast doubt on the progressive arc and telos of narrative, and blast
open the time of slavery? I searched for a critical lexicon that would
elucidate slavery and its modes of power and forms of subjection,
and challenge the prevailing understanding of the enslaved as a
constricted or impaired version of the worker and the individual,
terms which seemed to obscure the state and condition of enslavement rather than clarify it. This framework, even as amended for
the black worker and newly minted subject, failed to perceive or
comprehend the modes of domination, the distribution of death, the
role of reproductive labor, and the forms of gendered and sexual
violence that sustained racial slavery.[4] So how best to describe this
anomalous existence distributed between the category of subject
and object, person and thing? Or the figurative capacity that enabled the captive to fulfill any and every need, from cotton production to fellatio. The plantation was hell, factory, killing ground, and

Sodom. In attempting to explicate the violence of slavery and its idiom of power, *Scenes* moved away from the notion of the exploited worker or the unpaid laborer toward the captive and the fungible, the commodity and the dominated, the disposable and the sexually violated, to describe the dynamics of accumulation and dispossession, social reproduction and social death, seduction and libidinal economy, and to highlight the vexed relation of the enslaved to the category of the human.

In striving to describe the context of racial slavery, what quickly became apparent was the insufficiency of the prevailing concepts of power, subjection, exploitation, and politics. Slavery was the blind spot in critical theory.[5] I was determined to name and articulate the character of power, which was an assemblage of extreme domination, disciplinary power, biopower, and the sovereign right to make die. The dimensions of subjection traversed the categories of human, animal, and plant. The modes of accumulation and exploitation failed to be explained by precapitalist modes of production or the factory floor. The character of gendered and sexual difference, and negated maternity and severed kinship, bore no resemblance to the intimate arrangements of the white bourgeois family and cast out the enslaved from the nomenclature of the human.

Scenes of Subjection was a radical departure from the extant historical literature. Conservative scholarship had minimized the role of racial slavery in the making of capitalist modernity, failed to theorize race, characterized slavery as a premodern mode of production, denied the magnitude of the violence required to produce the human commodity and reproduce the relations of master and slave, and replicated the assumptions of romantic racialism and the plantation pastoral by describing slavery as a paternal institution characterized by reciprocity and consent, an approach which has been characterized as "Aunt Jemima in Dialectics."[6] The work of radical historians and intellectuals was devoted to refuting such assertions and celebrating slave agency, excavating slave culture, demonstrating black humanity and resilience in the face of dehumanization, recognizing the enduring totality of African beliefs and values despite the rupture of the Middle Passage, and fundamentally challenged the idea of the damaged person or psyche produced by centuries of enslavement. They did so by emphasizing the vitality of black culture, the autonomous zones created in the slave quarters and the provision grounds, and the strength of the black family. The goal of these radical scholars was to affirm black humanity in the confines of racial capitalism and the plantation's brutality. *Scenes* was indebted to the work of these radical scholars, but mine was a different task. I set out to detail the entanglement of humanity and violence, liberal philosophy and racial reason, the human and its devalued others.

The matters engaged in *Scenes*—the domain of practice, the everyday forms of making and doing, black performance, the imagination of freedom, social death and the afterlife of slavery, the violence of the archive and methods for transposing its statement, involuntary servitude and the longstanding struggle to elude and defeat it, the antagonism to capitalist discipline, the refusal of work, the movement of the unsovereign, dispossession and racialized enclosure, transfiguration, and a language for black existence not bound to property or the subject—would preoccupy me for two decades.

In *Scenes*, I first wrestled with questions of the archive—what it enabled and what it prevented us from knowing or discerning. Could I use its statements, yet destroy the master's tools? It was in these pages that I initially used the term "fabulation," but the term was latent, not yet emergent. Even then, I wanted to use the archive to create another order of statements, to produce a different account of what had happened and what might be possible. Here the work of novelists and poets provided a model.[7] I sought to create a method that acknowledged and comprehended the violence of the archive and the forms of silence and oblivion it produced, and yet endeavored to use the archive for contrary purposes. It was an engagement that reckoned with the power of the archive but dared attempt to exceed the limits imposed and render a radically different account of black existence. For the archive is also a repository of practices, a textual trace of the repertoire that transforms and refuses the given.

I feel extremely fortunate that the contribution of *Scenes* has been significant enough to merit its republication on its twenty-fifth anniversary. My peers as well as a generation of younger scholars have embraced *Scenes* and extended and elaborated its critical vocabulary: empathy, fungibility, subjection, black performance, the property of enjoyment, the attenuation of consent and agency, the figurative capacities of blackness, sexual violence and negligible injury, redress, the violence of reciprocity and mutuality in the context of extreme domination, the ruses of power, the nonevent of Emancipation, infidelity to the timeline of history or embrace of temporal entanglement, affirming other ways of knowing or subjugated knowledge. It is impossible for me to read the book today without hearing these other voices, without reading between the lines for the contributions of my interlocutors.

The freighted last paragraph of the book attempted to underscore the incompleteness of freedom and the hold of slavery. What did it mean to exist between the "no longer" enslaved and the "not yet" free? What awaited us was another century of extreme domination, precarious life, dispossession, impoverishment, and punishment. What awaited us were centuries of struggle animated by visions that exceeded the wreckage of our lives, by the avid belief in what *might* be.

SCENES OF
SUBJECTION

a gesture toward other planes

Introduction

The "terrible spectacle" that introduced Frederick Douglass to slavery was the beating of his Aunt Hester. It is one of the most well-known scenes of torture in the literature of slavery, perhaps second only to Uncle Tom's murder at the hands of Simon Legree. By locating this "horrible exhibition" in the first chapter of his 1845 *Narrative of the Life of Frederick Douglass*, Douglass establishes the centrality of violence to the making of the slave and identifies it as an original, generative act equivalent to the statement "I was born."[1] The passage through the bloodstained gate is an inaugural moment in the formation of the enslaved. It is a primal scene. By this I mean that the terrible spectacle dramatizes the origin of the subject and demonstrates that to be a slave is to be under the brutal power and authority of another.[2]

I have chosen not to reproduce Douglass's account of the beating of Aunt Hester to call attention to the ease with which such scenes are usually reiterated, the casualness with which they are circulated, and the consequences of this routine display of the slave's ravaged body. Rather than inciting indignation, too often they inure us to pain by virtue of their familiarity—the oft-repeated or restored character of these accounts and our distance from them are signaled by the theatrical language usually resorted to in describing these instances—and especially because they reinforce the spectacular character of black suffering. What interests me are the ways we are called upon to participate in such scenes. Are we witnesses who confirm the truth of what happened in the face of the world-destroying capacities of pain, the distortions of torture, the sheer unrepresentability of terror, and the repression of the dominant accounts?[3] Or are we voyeurs fascinated with and repelled by exhibitions of terror and suffering? What does the exposure of the violated body yield? Proof of black sentience or the inhumanity of the "peculiar institution"? Or does the pain of the other merely provide us with the opportunity for self-reflection? At issue here is the precariousness of empathy and the uncertain line between witness and spectator. Only more obscene than the brutality unleashed at the whipping post is the demand that this suffering be materialized and evidenced by the display of the tortured body or endless recitations of the ghastly and the terrible. In light of this, how does one give expression to these outrages without exacerbating the indifference to suffering that is the consequence of the benumbing spectacle, or contend with the narcissistic identification that obliterates the other, or the prurience that too often is the response to such displays? This was the challenge faced by Douglass and other foes of slavery, and this is the task I take up here.

Rather than try to convey the routinized violence of slavery and its aftermath through invocations of the shocking and the terrible, I have chosen to look elsewhere and consider those scenes in which terror can hardly be discerned—slaves dancing in the quarters, the outrageous darky antics of the minstrel stage, the constitution of humanity in slave law, and the fashioning of the self-possessed individual. By defamiliarizing the familiar, I hope to illuminate the terror of the mundane and quotidian rather than exploit the shocking spectacle. The terror and the routine violence of racial slavery were perpetrated under the rubric of pleasure, property, and personhood.

The scenes of subjection examined here entail the enactment of subjugation and the constitution of the subject; and they include the
blows delivered to Topsy and Zip Coon on the popular stage, the
obligatory revels of slaves in the marketplace, the simulation of will
in slave law, the fashioning of identity, and the processes of individuation and normalization.

Human Flesh

When Charlie Moses reflected on his years of slavery, the "preach-
er's eloquence" noted by the Works Progress Administration
interviewer who recorded his testimony did not blunt his anger.
In recounting the harsh treatment received by colored folks, he
emphasized that the enslaved were used like animals and handled
as if they existed only for the master's profits: "The way us niggers
was treated was awful. Marster would beat, knock, kick, kill. He
done ever' thing he could 'cept eat us. We was worked to death. We
worked Sunday, all day, all night. He whipped us 'til some jus' lay
down to die. It was a poor life. I knows it ain't right to have hate in
the heart, but, God almighty!" As if required to explain his animos-
ity toward his former owner who "had the devil in his heart," Moses
exclaimed that "God almighty never meant for human beings to be
like animals. Us niggers has a soul an' a heart an' a min'. We ain'
like a dog or a horse."[4]

In some respects, Tom Windham's experience of enslavement
was the opposite of that described by Charlie Moses; he reported
that his owner had treated him well. Nonetheless, like Moses, he
too explained the violation of slavery as being made a beast of burden. While Moses detailed the outrages of slavery and highlighted
the atrocity of the institution by poignantly enumerating the essential features of the slave's humanity—a soul, a heart, and a mind—
Windham, in conveying the injustice of slavery, put the matter

simply: "I think we should have our liberty 'cause us ain't hogs or horses—us is human flesh."[5]

The flesh, existence defined at its most elemental level, alone entitled one to liberty. This basic assertion of colored folks' claim to freedom implicitly called into question the rationales that legitimated the exclusion of blacks from the purview of universal rights and entitlements. As Moses and Windham were well aware, the discourse of humanism, at the very least, was double-edged, since the life and liberty they held in esteem were racial privileges formerly denied them. In short, the selective recognition of humanity that undergirded the relations of chattel slavery had not considered them men deserving of rights or freedom. In taking up the language of *human* being and *human* flesh, they seized upon that which had been used against and denied them.

However, suppose that the recognition of humanity held out the promise not of liberating the flesh or redeeming one's suffering, but rather of intensifying it? Or what if this acknowledgment was little more than a pretext for punishment, dissimulation of the violence of chattel slavery and the sanction given it by the law and the state, and an instantiation of racial hierarchy? What if the presumed endowments of man—conscience, sentiment, will, and reason—rather than assuring liberty or negating slavery acted to yoke slavery and freedom? Or what if the heart, the soul, and the mind were simply the inroads of discipline rather than that which confirmed the crime of slavery and proved that blacks were men and brothers, as Charlie Moses had hoped.

I am interested in the ways that the recognition of humanity and individuality acted to tether, bind, and oppress. For instance, although the captive's bifurcated existence as both an object of property and a person (whether understood as a legal subject formally endowed with limited rights and protections, or as a submissive, culpable, or criminal agent, or as one possessing restricted capacities for self-fashioning) has been recognized as one of the striking contradictions of chattel slavery, the constitution of this humanity (or legal personhood) remains to be considered. The law's recognition of slave humanity has been dismissed as ineffectual and as a volte-face of an imperiled institution. Or, worse yet, it has been lauded as evidence of the hegemony of paternalism and the integral relations between masters and slaves. The violence part and parcel of personhood and the recognition of the slave as a subject (we might even say the imposition of being made a subject) are the heart of my concern. It is a matter that largely has escaped scrutiny.

I approach these issues from a different vantage point and consider the outrages of slavery not only in terms of the object status of the enslaved as commodity, beast of burden, and chattel, but also as they involve notions of slave humanity. Rather than dismiss paternalism as ideology, understood in the orthodox sense as a false and distorted representation of social relations, I engage seriously its premises. My intent is to illuminate the savage encroachments of power that take place through notions of reform, consent, reciprocity, and protection. Contrary to our expectations, sentiment, enjoyment, affinity, will, affection, and desire facilitated domination and terror precisely by preying upon the flesh, the heart, and the soul. The mutuality of social relations and the expressive and affective capacities of the subject augmented and fortified violence. It was often the case that benevolent correctives and declarations of slave humanity intensified the brutal exercise of power upon the captive body rather than ameliorating the chattel condition.

Metamorphosis

The metamorphosis of chattel into man and citizen was the promise of abolition. The failure of Reconstruction made it impossible to achieve and secure this desired end. This failure was not only a matter of policy or weak implementation or evidence of a flagging commitment to black rights, which was undeniably the case; the limits of emancipation, the ambiguous legacy of universalism, the exclusions constitutive of liberalism, and the blameworthiness of the freed individual were no less decisive in producing new forms of involuntary servitude and inequality. The rights of contract and the wage failed to disestablish fundamental aspects of slavery; emancipation made the lives of the formerly enslaved more precarious: rights facilitated relations of domination, and new forms of bondage were enabled by proprietorial notions of the self. The pedagogical and legislative efforts aimed at transforming the formerly enslaved into rational, acquisitive, dutiful, and responsible individuals required coercion and the regular threat of arrest, punishment, and death. From this vantage point, emancipation appears less the grand event of liberation than a point of transition between modes of servitude and racial subjection. It also leads us to question whether the rights of man and citizen are realizable or whether the appellation "human" can be borne equally by all.[6]

The selective recognition of the humanity of the slave did not redress the abuses of the institution nor prevent the wanton use of the captive warranted by his or her status as chattel, since in most instances the acknowledgment of the slave as subject was a complement to the arrangements of chattel property rather than its remedy; nor did self-possession liberate the former slave from his or her bonds, but rather sought to replace the whip with the compulsory contract and the collar with guilty conscience. Put differently, the barbarism of slavery did not express itself singularly in the constitution of the slave as object but also in the forms of subjectivity and circumscribed humanity imputed to the enslaved. Nor can the failures of Reconstruction be recounted solely as a series of legal reversals or troop withdrawals; they also need to be located in the very language of persons, rights, and liberties. With this in mind, I

attend to the forms of violence and domination enabled by the recognition of humanity, licensed by the invocation of rights, and justified on the grounds of liberty and freedom.

I do not offer a comprehensive examination of slavery and Reconstruction or recover the resistances of the dominated, but critically
interrogate terms like "will," "agency," "individuality," and "responsibility." To do so requires questioning the formation of the subject
by dominant discourses as well as the ways in which the enslaved
and the emancipated grappled with these terms and endeavored to
reelaborate and refuse them in fashioning themselves as agents and
in striving to make a free life. The scenes of subjection at issue here
include the Manichaean identities constitutive of slave humanity—
that is, the contented subordinate and/or willful criminal, as well as
the calculation of humanity in increments of value, the fabrication
of the will, the performance of subjection, and the relation between
injury and personhood. While the calibration of sentience and
terms of punishment determined the constricted humanity of the
enslaved, the encumbered individuality of the emancipated resulted
largely from the equation of responsibility with blameworthiness,
making duty synonymous with punishment. The enduring legacy of
slavery was readily discernable in the travestied liberation, thwarted
agency, coerced labor, interminable servility and blameworthiness
of the free individual. The ubiquitous fun and frolic that suppos-
edly demonstrated slave contentment and the African's suitedness
for slavery were mirrored in the panic about idleness, intemperate
consumption, recalcitrance, and fanciful expressions of freedom,
all of which justified coercive labor measures and the constriction
of liberties. The entanglements of slavery and freedom were undeniable and everywhere apparent. Dutiful submission remained the
defining characteristic of black subjectivity, whether in the making
and securing of the captive as chattel personal (an item of moveable
personal property) or in the fashioning of individuality, cultivation

of conscience, training and discipline of free labor, and harnessing
of the will.

Figurative Capacities

In the economy of racial slavery, the enjoyment of property was
predicated on the figurative capacities of blackness—the ability to
be an object or animal or not-quite-human or guilty agent. The value
of blackness resided in this metaphorical aptitude, whether literally
understood as the fungibility of the commodity or as the imaginative surface upon which the master and the nation came to understand themselves. As Toni Morrison writes, "The slave population,
it could be and was assumed, offered itself up as surrogate selves for
meditation on problems of human freedom, its lure and its elusiveness."[7] Indeed, blackness provided the occasion for self-reflection
and for an exploration of terror, desire, fear, loathing, and longing.[8]

Figurative capacity is another way of describing the mutability
of the commodity and the paradox or conundrum of agency for the
oscillating subject-object of slave law. In the scene of subjection,
agency is produced or feigned by means of terror and violence; sentiment and reciprocal relations, or mutuality, secure the extreme
domination of slavery. The power of the weak, or servile love,
enhanced the enjoyment of property, albeit disguised as intimacy
or shared affection. The rhetoric of seduction crafted a story of intimacy and consent, willfulness and submission that dissimulated the
violence of rape and sexual assault. This distinctive meditation on
slavery and freedom encompassed and engulfed the domain of sexuality with ruthless effect.

The seeming polarities of terror and enjoyment frame this exploration of subjection. Calculations of socially necessary and socially
tolerable violence and the varied uses of property determine the
person fashioned in the law—an anomalous subject of restricted

sentience and qualified value—and the blackness conjured on the popular stage. The obliteration and engulfment of the slave and/or black occurred, as well, by slipping on blackness and stepping into the skin of the other; and by way of an empathic identification in which the self stands in for and subsumes the other.

The exercise of power is inseparable from its display. Domination depended upon demonstrations of the slaveholder's dominion and the captive's abasement. Representing power was essential to wielding it. A significant aspect of maintaining relations of domination, as James Scott notes, "consists of the symbolization of domination by demonstrations and enactments of power."[9] Such performances made the captive body the vehicle of the master's power and truth. What was demanded by the master was simulated by the enslaved. To "go before the master" required the enslaved to strike it up lively, or witness the beating, torture, and execution of fellow captives, or be subjected to necessary and gratuitous acts of punishments. A child's name might be changed on a whim or made the punchline of a joke to confirm that the slaveholder, not the parents, decided the child's fate, or the community forced to gather and listen intently as the gospel of slavery was recited with malice. The fulfillment of or compliance with these demands must be considered as pragmatism rather than resignation, since one either yielded or risked brutal punishment. It is difficult if not impossible to establish an absolute and definitive division between "going before the master" and other amusements. This accounts for the ambivalent pleasure afforded by such recreations. At the same time, these performances constituted acts of defiance conducted under the cover of nonsense, indirection, and seeming acquiescence. By virtue of such tactics, these performances were sometimes turned against their instrumental aims. The reliance on masquerade, subterfuge, and indirection also obscured the small acts of resistance conducted by the enslaved. This opacity enabled them to flourish and made them illegible and uncertain.

After all, how does one determine the difference between dissemblance or "puttin' on ole massa"—the simulation of compliance for covert aims, the yes'm to death and destruction—and the grins and gesticulations of Sambo indicating the repressive construction of contented subjection? At the level of appearance, these contending performances often differed little. At the level of effect, however, they diverged radically. One performance aimed to reproduce and secure the relations of domination and the other to manipulate appearances in order to challenge these relations and create a space for action not generally available. Since acts of resistance exist within the context of relations of domination and are not external to them, they acquire their character from these relations, and vice versa. At a dance, holiday fete, or corn shucking, the line between dominant and insurgent orchestrations of blackness could be effaced or fortified in the course of an evening, either because the enslaved utilized instrumental amusements for contrary purposes or because surveillance necessitated cautious forms of interaction and modes of expression.

The simulation of agency and the enactment of willed submission unfolded along lines no less brutal in the domain of law, especially as it concerned matters of intimacy and sexuality. The rhetoric of seduction licensed sexual violence by ascribing power to the dependent, the subordinate, the servile, and the violated. Carnality and reciprocal desire eclipsed rape; consent was taken for granted, indifferent to force of compulsion. To act or to want was to assent to violence or invite punishment. How could the always wanting and always willing utter "no"? The conflation of coercion and consent underscores the limits of will and capacity in a state of extreme domination. In such circumstances, was it possible to experience a condition or feeling "akin to freedom"? No one knew better the ambivalence of a free state than Harriet Jacobs. As she recounted in *Incidents in the Life of a Slave Girl*, the loophole of retreat is a space of freedom that is at the same time a space of captivity.[10] The difficulties experienced in trying to assume the role of the free and self-possessed individual prefigure the critique of emancipation advanced by the formerly enslaved.

The extended servitude of emancipation would trouble an absolute and certain divide between bondage and freedom. The constituent elements of slavery would endure despite the changes wrought by emancipation and the shifting registers of racial subjection. The duties and obligations that conscripted the masterless culminated in a new racial order no less brutal than the old regime. Notwithstanding the negative power of the Thirteenth Amendment, racial slavery was transformed rather than annulled. It was a state best described as "slavery in all but name."[11] Blackness recast in the guise of the wage laborer, contractual subject, blameworthy individual and (impaired) citizen refigured the relations of mastery and servitude. The shift from the legal-status ascriptions characteristic of the antebellum period to the regulatory power of a racial state obsessed with matters of blood, sexuality, population, and natural antipathy ultimately reproduced the status-race of chattel slavery. No less significant was the state-sanctioned and extrajuridical violence essential to the making of a "servile race" and disposable population. The encumbrances of emancipation and the unfree condition of the exslave, at the very least, lead us to reconsider the meaning of freedom, if they do not cast doubt on the narrative of progress.

A Note on Method

How does one tell the story of an elusive emancipation and a travestied freedom? Certainly, reconsidering the meaning of freedom entails looking critically at the production of historical narratives, since the very effort to represent the situation of the subaltern reveals the provisionality of the archive as well as the interests that shape it and determine the emplotment of history. For example, the imperative to construct a usable and palatable national past certainly determined the picture of slavery drawn in the testimonies gathered by the Works Progress Administration, not to mention the hierarchical relations between mostly white interviewers and black interviewees. Bearing this in mind, one recognizes that writing the history of the dominated requires not only the interrogation of the governing narratives and the exposure of their contingent and partisan character but also the reclamation of archival material for contrary purposes. As Gayatri Spivak remarks, "The 'subaltern' cannot appear without the thought of the 'elite.'"[12] In other words, there is no access to the subaltern consciousness outside dominant representations or elite documents. This examination of the cultural practices of the enslaved is possible only because of the accounts provided by literate black autobiographers, white amanuenses, plantation journals and documents, newspaper accounts, missionary tracts, travel writing, amateur ethnographies, songbooks, government reports, et cetera. Because these documents are "not free from barbarism," I have tried to read them against the grain to write a different account of the past, while realizing the limits imposed by employing these sources, the impossibility of fully recovering the experience of the enslaved and the emancipated, and the risk of reinforcing the authority of these documents even as I try to use them for contrary purposes.[13]

The effort to "brush history against the grain" requires excavations at the margins of monumental history for the ruins of the dismembered past to be retrieved and turning to forms of knowledge and practice not generally considered legitimate objects of historical inquiry or appropriate or adequate sources for history making.

I attend to the cultivated silence, exclusions, and forms of violence and domination that engender the official accounts and listen for other sounds, the ways of knowing disguised as jargon and non-sense. The documents, fragments, and accounts considered here, although retrieved for purposes divergent from those for which they were gathered, nonetheless remain entangled with the violence of racial slavery and its afterlife. The effort to reconstruct the history of the dominated is often discontinuous with the prevailing accounts or official history, and it entails a struggle within and against the constraints and silences imposed by the nature of the archive—the system that governs the appearance of statements and generates social meaning.[14]

My interest in reading this material is twofold: in interpreting these materials, I hope to illuminate the practice of everyday life—specifically, tactics of resistance and refusal, modes of self-fashioning, and figurations of freedom—and to investigate the construction of the subject and social relations contained within these documents. This effort is enmeshed with the relations of power and dominance it strives to write against; it resists, complies with, and exceeds the official narratives of slavery and freedom. My reliance on the interviews conducted by the Works Progress Administration raises a host of problems regarding the construction of voice, the terms in which agency is identified, the dominance of the pastoral in representing slavery, the political imperatives that shaped the construction of national memory, the ability of those interviewed to recall what had happened sixty years earlier, the use of white interviewers who were sometimes the sons and daughters of former owners in gathering the testimony, and so on. The transcription of black voice by mostly white interviewers through the grotesque representation of what they imagined as black speech, the questions that shaped these interviews, and the artifice of direct reported speech when, in fact, these interviews were paraphrased non-verbatim accounts make quite tentative all claims about representing the intentionality or consciousness of those interviewed, despite appearances that would encourage us to believe that we have gained access to the voice of the subaltern and located the true history after all.[15]

With all this said, how does one use these sources? At best with the awareness that a totalizing history cannot be reconstructed from these interested, selective, and fragmentary accounts and with an acknowledgment of the interventionist role of the interpreter, the equally interested labor of historical revision, and the impossibility of reconstituting the past free from the disfigurements of present concerns.[16] With all these provisos issued, these narratives, nonetheless, remain an important source for understanding the everyday experience of slavery and its aftermath. Bearing the aforementioned qualifications in mind, I read these documents with the hope of gaining a glimpse of black life during slavery and the postbellum period while remaining aware of the impossibility of fully reconstituting the experience of the enslaved. I don't try to liberate these documents from the context in which they were collected, but instead augment the surface of archival fragments and slave testimony to write histories at odds with the constellation of values undergirding racial slavery and regard the lives of the enslaved and the forms of practice created and enacted inside the enclosure. My attempt to read the archive against the grain is perhaps best understood as a combination of foraging and disfiguration—raiding for fragments upon which other narratives can be spun and transposing and deforming the testimony through selective quotation and amplification.

Of course, the WPA testimony is circumscribed and provisional, and it is characterized by lapses of forgetting, silences, and exclusions, but what sources are immune to such charges? John Blassingame has detailed the difficulties inherent in using the WPA

narratives because of the power differential between white interviewers and black interviewees, the editing and rewriting of these
accounts, and the time lapse between the interview and the experience of slavery; yet he concedes that they are an important source
of information about slavery.[17] I agree with Blassingame's assessment and would add that there is no historical document that is not
interested, selective, or a vehicle of power and domination; and it
is precisely the matter of power and domination that I bring to the
fore in assessing everyday practices, both the restricted confines in
which they exist and flourish and the terms in which they are represented. Besides, contemporaneous narratives and interviews are
no less selective or partisan in their representations of slavery. The
WPA testimony is an overdetermined representation of slavery, as
are all of the accounts. The work of reconstruction and fabulation
I have undertaken highlights the relation between power and voice
and the constraints and closures that determine not only what can
be spoken but also (the identity of) who speaks. My reading of slave
testimony is not an attempt to recover the voice of the enslaved but
an attempt to consider specific practices in a public performance of
slavery that ranges from slaves on the auction block to those sharing
their recollections decades later.[18] The gap between the event and its
recollection is bridged not only by the prompting of interviewers,
but also by the censored context of self-expression and the uncanny
resonance between the dissemblance of the enslaved and the tactics of withholding aimed at not offending white interviewers and/
or evading self-disclosure.

The effort to examine the event of emancipation is no less riddled
with inescapable ironies, the foremost of these being the discontinuity between substantial freedom and legal emancipation. Inevitably
one is forced to confront the discrepant legacy of emancipation and
the decidedly circumscribed possibilities available to the freed. How
does one adequately convey the double bind of emancipation—that

is, acknowledge the illusory freedom and travestied liberation that succeeded chattel slavery without gainsaying the minor triumphs of Jubilee? Certainly, one must contend with the enormity of emancipation as both a breach with slavery and a point of transition to what looks more like the reorganization of the plantation system than self-possession, citizenship, or liberty for the "freed." In the place of the grand narrative of freedom, with its decisive events and incontrovertible advances, I offer an account that focuses on the ambivalent legacy of emancipation and the undeniably truncated opportunities available to the freed. Lacking the certitude of a definitive partition between slavery and freedom, and in the absence of a consummate breach through which freedom might unambivalently announce itself, there is at best a transient and fleeting expression of possibility that cannot ensconce itself as a durable temporal marker. If periodization is a barrier imposed from above that obscures the involuntary servitude and legal subjection that followed in the wake of slavery, then attempts to assert absolutist distinctions between slavery and freedom are untenable. Fundamentally, such assertions involve distinctions between the transient and the epochal, underestimate the contradictory inheritance of emancipation, and diminish the reign of terror that accompanied the advent of freedom. Put differently, does the momentousness of emancipation as an event ultimately efface the continuities between slavery and freedom and occlude the dispossession inseparable from becoming a "propertied person"?

If one dares to "abandon the absurd catalogue of official history," as Édouard Glissant encourages, then the violence and domination perpetuated in the name of slavery's reversal come to the fore.[19] From this vantage point, emancipation seems a double-edged and perhaps obfuscating label. It discloses as well as obscures since involuntary servitude and emancipation were synonymous for a good many of the formerly enslaved. This is evidenced in "common-sense" observations that black lives were more valuable under slavery than under freedom, that blacks were worse off under freedom than during slavery, and that the gift of freedom was a "hard deal." I use the term "common sense" purposely to underline what Antonio Gramsci described as the "chaotic aggregate of disparate conceptions" that conform with "the social and cultural position of those masses whose philosophy it is." It is a conception of world and life "implicit to a large extent in determinate strata of society" and "in opposition to 'official' conceptions of the world."[20] Common sense challenges the official accounts of freedom and stresses the similarities and correspondences of slavery and freedom. At a minimum, these observations disclose the disavowed transactions between slavery and freedom as modes of production and subjection.

The abolition of chattel slavery and the emergence of man, however laudable, long awaited, and cherished, did not yield such absolute distinctions; instead fleeting, disabled, and short-lived practices stand for freedom and its failure. Everyday practices, rather than traditional political activity like the abolition movement, black conventions, the struggle for suffrage, and electoral activities, are the focus of my examination because I believe that these pedestrian practices illuminate inchoate and utopian expressions of freedom that are not and perhaps cannot be actualized elsewhere. The desires and longings that exceed the frame of civil rights and political emancipation find expression in quotidian acts labeled "fanciful," "exorbitant," and "excessive" primarily because they express an understanding or imagination of freedom quite at odds with bourgeois expectations. Paul Gilroy, after Seyla Benhabib, refers to these utopian invocations and the incipient modes of friendship and solidarity they conjure up as "the politics of transfiguration."[21] He notes that, in contrast to the politics of fulfillment, which operate within the framework of bourgeois civil society and occidental rationality, "The politics of transfiguration strives in pursuit of the sublime, struggling to repeat the unrepeatable, to present the unpresentable. Its rather different hermeneutic focus pushes towards the mimetic, dramatic and performative." From this perspective, stealing away, the breakdown, moving about, pilfering, and other everyday practices that occur below the threshold of formal equality and rights gesture toward an unrealized freedom and emphasize the stranglehold of slavery and the limits of emancipation. In this and in other ways, these practices reveal much about the aspirations of the dominated and the contestations over the meaning of abolition and emancipation.

This intervention is an attempt to recast the past, guided by the conundrums and compulsions of our contemporary crisis: the hope for social transformation in the face of seemingly insurmountable obstacles, the quixotic search for a subject capable of world-historical action, and the despair induced by the lack of one. I hope that the instances of insurgency and contestation narrated herein and the relentless proliferation of small acts of resistance perhaps offer some measure of encouragement and serve to remind us that the failures of Reconstruction still haunt us. In part, it explains why the grand narratives continue to hold sway over our imagination. While I acknowledge history's "fiction of factual representation," to use Hayden White's term, I also recognize the political utility and ethical necessity of historical fiction. As Walter Benjamin remarked, "Only that historian will have the gift of fanning the spark of hope in the past who is firmly convinced that *even the dead* will not be safe if the enemy wins."[22]

Part I

FORMATIONS OF TERROR
AND ENJOYMENT

unforeseen passage in the labyrinth of forms

Innocent Amusements

THE STAGE OF SUFFERING

Innocent amusements, when under proper regulations and when partaken of with moderation, conduce to morality and virtue.... Negroes are naturally prone to gaiety, and I conceive it a duty to ourselves as well as them not to change this inclination in them, but rather to promote it by every prudent and allowable means.

—Nicolas Herbemont, *On the Moral Discipline and Treatment of Slaves*

Everything like rational enjoyment was frowned upon, and only those wild and low sports peculiar to semicivilized people were encouraged.

—Frederick Douglass, *Life and Times of Frederick Douglass*

In an epistle to his brother, John Rankin illumined the "very dangerous evil" of slavery in a description of the coffle, detailing the obscene theatricality of the slave trade: "Unfeeling wretches purchased a considerable drove of slaves—how many of them were separated from husbands and wives, I will not pretend to say—and having chained a number of them together, hoisted over the flag of American liberty, and with the music of two violins marched the woe-worn, heart-broken, and sobbing creatures through the town."[1] Rankin, aghast at the spectacle and shocked by "seeing the most oppressive sorrows of suffering innocence mocked with all the light-ness of sportive music," decried: "My soul abhors the crime." The violation of domesticity, the parody of liberty, and the callous defi-ance of sorrow define the scene in which crime becomes spectacle. The "very dangerous evil" of slavery and the "agonizing groans of suffering humanity" had been made music.[2]

Although Rankin conceded that the cruelty of slavery "far exceed[ed] the power of description," he nonetheless strove to ren-der its horrors. And in so doing, Rankin makes apparent that the crimes of slavery are not only witnessed but staged. Terms like "stage," "spectacle," and "scene" convey these horrors, and, more important, the "abominations of slavery" are disclosed through the reiteration of secondhand accounts and circulating stories from "unquestionable authorities" to which Rankin must act as surro-gate witness. In the effort to "bring slavery close," these circulating reports of atrocity, in essence, are reenacted in Rankin's epistles. The grotesqueries enumerated in documenting the injustice of slav-ery are intended to shock and to disrupt the comfortable remove of the reader/spectator. By providing the minutest detail of maca-bre acts of violence, embellished by his own fantasy of slavery's bloodstained gate, Rankin hoped to rouse the sensibility of those indifferent to slavery by exhibiting the suffering of the enslaved and facilitating an identification between those free and those enslaved: "We are naturally too callous to the sufferings of others, and con-sequently prone to look upon them with cold indifference, until, in imagination we identify ourselves with the sufferers, and make their sufferings our own. . . . When I bring it near, inspect it closely, and find that it is inflicted on men and women, who possess the same nature and feelings with myself, my sensibility is roused" (56–57). By bringing suffering near, the ties of sentiment are forged. In let-ter after letter, Rankin strove to recreate this shared experience of horror in order to transform his slaveholding brother, to whom the letters were addressed, as well as the audience of readers. In his letters, pain provides the common language of humanity; it extends humanity to the dispossessed and, in turn, remedies the indifference of the callous.[3]

The shocking accounts of whipping, rape, mutilation, and suicide assault the barrier of indifference, for the abhorrence and indignity roused by these scenes of terror, which range from the mockery of the coffle to the dismemberment and incineration of a slave boy, give rise to a shared sentience between those formerly indifferent and those suffering. So intent and determined is Rankin to establish that slaves possess the same nature and feelings as himself, and to demonstrate the common humanity of all men on the basis of this extended suffering, that he narrates an imagined scenario in which he, along with his wife and child, is enslaved. The "horrible scenes of cruelty that were presented to [his] mind" as a consequence of this imagining aroused the "highest pitch of indignant feeling." In this scenario Rankin speaks not only for, but literally in the place of the enslaved. By believing himself to be and by phantasmically becoming the enslaved, he creates the scenario for shared feelings:

> My flighty imagination added much to the tumult of passion by persuading me, for the moment, that I myself was a slave, and with my wife and children placed under the reign of terror. I began in reality to feel for myself, my wife, and my children—the thoughts of being whipped at the pleasure of a morose and capricious master, aroused the strongest feelings of resentment; but when I fancied the cruel lash was approaching my wife and children, and my imagination depicted in lively colors, their tears, their shrieks, and bloody stripes, every indignant principle of my bloody nature was excited to the highest degree. (56)

The nature of the feelings aroused here is complex. While this flight of imagination enables a vicarious firsthand experience of the lash, excoriates the pleasure experienced by the master in this brutal exercise of power, induces tears, and unleashes Rankin's fiery indignation and resentment, the phantasmic vehicle of this identification is complicated, unsettling, and disturbing. Although Rankin's fantasy culminates in indignant outcries against the institution of slavery and, clearly, the purpose of this identification is to highlight the crimes of slavery, this flight of imagination and slipping into the captive's body unlatches a Pandora's box; surprisingly, what comes to the fore is the difficulty and slipperiness of empathy. Properly speaking, empathy is a projection of oneself into another to better understand the other or "the projection of one's own personality into an object, with the attribution to the object of one's own emotions."[4] Yet empathy in important respects confounds Rankin's efforts to identify with the enslaved because in making the slave's suffering his own, Rankin begins to feel for himself rather than for those whom this exercise in imagination presumably is designed to reach. By exploiting the vulnerability of the captive body as a vessel for the uses, thoughts, whims, and feelings of others, the humanity extended to the slave inadvertently confirms the expectations and desires definitive of the relations of chattel slavery. In other words, the ease of Rankin's empathic identification is as much due to his good intentions and heartfelt opposition to slavery as to the fungibility of the captive body.

By making the suffering of others his own, has Rankin ameliorated indifference or only confirmed the difficulty of understanding the suffering of the enslaved? Can the white witness of the spectacle of suffering affirm the materiality of black sentience only by feeling for himself? Does this not only exacerbate the idea that black sentience is inconceivable and unimaginable but, in the very ease of possessing the enslaved body and slipping into the skin of the other, ultimately elide an understanding and acknowledgment of the slave's pain? Beyond evidence of slavery's crime, what does this exposure of the suffering body of the bondsman yield? Does this not reinforce the "thingly" quality of the captive by reducing the body to evidence in the very effort to establish the humanity of the enslaved? Does it not reproduce the hyperembodiedness of the powerless? Does it not exacerbate the gulf or severance between "human flesh" and the captive body? The purpose of these inquiries is not to cast doubt on Rankin's motives for recounting these events but to consider the precariousness of empathy and the thin line between witness and spectator. In the fantasy of being beaten, Rankin must substitute himself and his wife and children for the black captive in order that this pain be perceived and experienced. So, in fact, Rankin becomes a proxy and the other's pain is acknowledged to the degree that it can be imagined, yet by virtue of this substitution, the object of identification threatens to disappear. In order to convince the reader of the horrors of slavery, Rankin must volunteer himself and his family for abasement.

The effort to counteract the habitual indifference to black suffering requires that the white body be positioned in the place of the black body in order to make this suffering visible and intelligible. Yet if this violence can become palpable and indignation fully aroused only through the masochistic fantasy, then it becomes clear that empathy is double-edged, for in making the other's suffering one's own, this suffering is occluded by the other's obliteration. The slave remains an object to be animated by human feelings. Given the litany of horrors that fill Rankin's pages, this recourse to fantasy reveals an anxiety about making the slave's suffering legible. This anxiety is historically determined by the denial of black sentience and exacerbated by the slave's status as object of property, the predicament of witnessing given the legal status of blacks, and the repression of counterdiscourses on the "peculiar institution."

Rankin must supplant the black captive in order to give expression to black suffering, and as a consequence, the dilemma—the denial of black sentience and the obscurity of suffering—is not attenuated but instantiated. The ambivalent character of empathy—more exactly, the repressive effects of empathy—can be located in the "obliteration of otherness" or the facile intimacy that enables identification with the other only as we "feel ourselves into those we imagine as ourselves." And as a result, empathy fails to expand the space of the other but merely places the self in its stead.[5] This is not to suggest that empathy can be discarded or that Rankin's desire to exist in the place of the other can be dismissed as a narcissistic exercise, but rather to highlight the dangers of a too-easy intimacy, to note that the attention to the self occurs at the expense of the slave's suffering, and that identification yields to violence of another order.[6]

We need to ask why the site of suffering so readily lends itself to inviting identification. Why is pain the conduit of identification? This question may seem to beg the obvious, given the violent domination and dishonor constitutive of enslavement, the acclaimed transformative capacities of pain in sentimental culture, the prevalence of public displays of suffering inclusive of the pageantry of the trade, the spectacle of punishment, circulating reports of slavery's horrors, the runaway success of *Uncle Tom's Cabin*, and the passage through the "bloodstained gate," which was a convention of the slave narrative, all of which contributed to the idea that the feelings and consciousness of the enslaved were most available at this site. If the scene of beating readily lends itself to an identification with the enslaved, it does so at the risk of fixing and naturalizing this condition of pained embodiment and, in complete defiance of Rankin's good intention, increases the difficulty of beholding or reckoning with black suffering. The endeavor to bring pain close exploits the spectacle of the body in pain and oddly confirms the spectral character of suffering and the inability to witness the captive's pain. This suffering remains indescribable and occluded when embodied in the slave. On one hand, pain extends humanity to the dispossessed and the ability to sustain suffering leads to transcendence; on the other, the spectacular character of this suffering effaces and restricts black sentience.

As Rankin himself states, in order for this suffering to induce a reaction and stir feelings, it must be brought close. Yet if sentiment or morality are "inextricably tied to human proximity," observes Zygmunt Bauman, the problem is that in the very effort to "bring it near" and "inspect it closely" it is dissipated. "Morality conform[s] to the law of optical perspective. It looms large and thick close to the eye."[7] So, then, how does suffering elude or escape us in the very effort to bring it near? It does so precisely because it can only be brought near by way of a proxy and by way of Rankin's indignation and imagination. If the black body is the vehicle of the other's power and pleasure, status and value, then no less true is the fact that the white or near-white body makes the captive's suffering visible and discernible.[8] Indeed, the elusiveness of black suffering can be attributed to racist optics in which black flesh is itself identified as the source of opacity, as a surface inscribed by violence, yet unreadable. The denial of black humanity is the outcome of this effacement of sentience, this inability to bring the black close.[9] This is further complicated by a moral perspective that insists upon the other as a mirror of the self and that recognizes suffering only by substituting the self for the other.

While Rankin attempts to ameliorate the insufficiency of feeling before the spectacle of black suffering, this insufficiency is, in fact, displaced rather than remedied by his standing in. This attempt exacerbates the distance between the readers and those suffering by literally removing the slave from view. We, too, need to consider whether the identification forged at the site of suffering confirms black humanity at the peril of reinforcing racist assumptions of

limited sentience, in that the humanity of the enslaved and the violence of the institution can only be brought into view by extreme
examples of incineration and dismemberment or by placing white
bodies at risk. What does it mean that the violence of slavery or the
pained existence of the enslaved, if discernible, is only so in the most
heinous and egregious examples and not in the quotidian routines of
slavery?[10] As well, is not the difficulty of empathy related to both the
devaluation and the valuation of black life?

Empathic identification is complicated further by the fact that
it cannot be extricated from the economy of chattel slavery with
which it is at odds, for this projection of one's feeling upon or into
the object of property and the phantasmic slipping into captivity,
while it is distinct from the pleasures of self-augmentation yielded
by the ownership of the slave and the expectations fostered therein,
is nonetheless entangled with this economy and identification facilitated by a kindred possession or occupation of the captive body,
albeit on a different register. What I am trying to isolate are the
kinds of expectations and the qualities of affect distinctive to the
economy of slavery. The relation between pleasure and the possession of slave property, in both the figurative and literal senses, can
be explained in part by the fungibility of the slave—that is, the joy
made possible by virtue of the replaceability and interchangeabil-
ity endemic to the commodity—and by the extensive capacities
of property; the augmentation of the master subject through his
embodiment in external objects and persons.[11] Put differently, the
mutability of the commodity makes the captive body an abstract
and empty vessel vulnerable to the projection of others' feelings,
ideas, desires, and values; and, as property, the dispossessed body of
the enslaved is the surrogate for the master's body since it guarantees his disembodied universality and acts as the sign of his power
and dominion. While the beaten and mutilated body presumably establishes the brute materiality of existence, black suffering

regularly eludes (re)cognition by virtue of its replacement by other signs of value, as well as by other bodies.

The desire to don, occupy, or possess blackness or the black body as a sentimental resource and/or locus of excess enjoyment is both founded upon and enabled by the material relations of chattel slavery. In light of this, is it too extreme or too obvious to suggest that Rankin's flight of imagination and the excitements aroused by suffering might also be pleasurable? Certainly this willing abasement confirms Rankin's moral authority, but what about the pleasure made possible by this embrace of pain? Are the tumultuous passions of the flightly imagination stirred by this fantasy of being beaten? Rankin's imagined beating is immune neither to the pleasures to be derived from the masochistic fantasy nor to the sadistic pleasure to be derived from the spectacle of suffering. My intention is not to shock or exploit the perverse but to consider critically the dense nexus of terror and enjoyment by examining the obviated and debased diversions of the capricious master; the pleasure of indignation yielded before the spectacle of extreme violence; the instability of the scene of suffering; and the confusion of song and sorrow typical of the coffle, the auction block, performing before the master, and other popular amusements.

By slipping into the black body and figuratively occupying the position of the enslaved, Rankin plays the role of captive and attester, and in so doing articulates the crisis of witnessing determined by the legal incapacity of slaves or free blacks to act as witnesses against whites. Since the veracity of black testimony is in doubt, the crimes of slavery must not only be confirmed by unquestionable authorities and other white observers, but they must also be made visible, whether by revealing the scarred back of the slave—making the body speak—or, better yet, by enabling reader and audience member to experience vicariously the "tragical scenes of cruelty."[12] If Rankin as a consequence of his abolitionist sentiments was willing to occupy the "unmasterly" position, sentimentalism prescribed the terms of his identification with the enslaved, and the central feature of this identification was suffering. For Rankin, the pageantry of the coffle and sportive music failed to disguise "the sorrows of suffering innocence." However, for others who also possessed antislavery sentiments, the attempt to understand the inner feelings of the enslaved only effaced the terror of slavery and further circumscribed the captive's presumably limited capacity for suffering. For many eyewitnesses of the coffle, the brutality and enmity of slavery were dissipated by song, and violence was transformed into a display of agency and good cheer.

Black suffering is perceived or registered only in the most spectacular circumstances of violence, and, conversely, the exaggeration and theatricality of spectacle conceals and diminishes suffering. In one respect, the combination of imagined scenes of cruelty with those culled from unquestionable authority evidences the crisis of witnessing that results from the legal subjection of slaves and the barring of their testimony. Yet, the extravagant display of extreme violence exacerbates this crisis of witnessing, since only the most horrific instance will suffice to convey the brutality of slavery. A cynical formulation might question whether black suffering exists or is of any import or consequence in the absence of a white witness or observer. To the degree that the body speaks, it does so as the vehicle of abolitionist fantasy; just as it is made to speak the master's truth and augments his power through the imposition and intensification of pain.[13] The illegibility or incoherence of black suffering is its failure to register as pain at all. The impasse, the inability to perceive or discern black suffering, is made more difficult by the overdetermined reading of the sounds of slavery. The "half-articulate" and "incoherent song" confound the transparency of testimony; uncertainty and complexity characterize the depiction of slavery. Does the extension of humanity to the enslaved ironically reinscribe their subjugated status? Do the figurative capacities of blackness enable white flights of fantasy while increasing the likelihood of the captive's disappearance? Can the moral embrace of pain extricate itself from the pleasures borne by subjection? In other words, does the scene of the tyrannized slave at the bloodstained gate delight the loathsome master and provide wholesome pleasures to the upright and the virtuous? Is the act of "witnessing" a kind of looking no less entangled with the wielding of power and the extraction of enjoyment? Does the captive's dance allay grief or articulate the fraught and impossible character of agency? Or does it exemplify the use of the body as an instrument against the self?

The scenes of subjection—the coerced spectacles orchestrated to encourage the trade in black flesh; scenes of torture and festivity; the tragedy of virtuous women and the antics of outrageous darkies—all turn upon the simulation of agency and the excesses of black enjoyment. The affiliation of performance and blackness can be attributed to racist conceptions of Negro nature as carefree, infantile, hedonistic, and indifferent to suffering, and to a purposeful misreading of the interdependence of labor and song common among the enslaved.[14] The constitution of blackness as an abject and degraded condition and the fascination with the other's enjoyment went hand in hand. In the logic of a slaveholding world, blacks were envisioned fundamentally as vehicles for white enjoyment, in all of its sundry and unspeakable expressions; this was as much the consequence of the chattel status of the captive as it was of the excess enjoyment imputed to the other, for those forced to dance on the decks of slave ships crossing the Middle Passage, step it up lively on the auction block, sing and fiddle as if your life depended on it, and amuse the master and his company were seen as the purveyors of pleasure. The amazing popularity of the "darkies" of the minstrel stage must be considered in this light. The variants of racist discourse, ranging from the proslavery plantation pastoralism to the romantic racialism of abolitionists, similarly constituted the African as childish, primitive, contented, and endowed with great mimetic capacities. Essentially, these characteristics defined the infamous and renowned Sambo. This history is of central importance when evaluating the politics of pleasure, the uses of slave property, the formation of the subject, and the tactics of resistance. Indeed, the convergence of terror and enjoyment cannot be understood outside it.

The pageantry of the coffle, stepping it up lively on the auction block, going before the master, and the blackface mask of minstrelsy and melodrama all evidenced the enmeshing of terror and enjoyment. Above all, the simulated jollity and coerced festivity of the slave trade and the instrumental recreations of plantation management document the investment in and obsession with "black enjoyment" and the significance of these orchestrated amusements as part of a larger effort to dissimulate the extreme violence of the institution and disavow the pain of captivity. The transubstantiation of abjection into contentment suggested that the traumas of slavery were easily redressed and, likewise, the prevalence of black song confirmed blacks' restricted sentience and immunity to sorrow. Enjoyment defined the relation of the dominant race to the enslaved. The boundless and unspeakable uses of the captive licensed by the legal and social relations of slavery articulated the nexus of pleasure and possession and bespoke the critical role of diversion in securing the relations of bondage. In this way, enjoyment disclosed the sentiments and expectations of the "peculiar institution."

The Property of Enjoyment

From the vantage point of the everyday relations of slavery, enjoyment, broadly speaking, defined the parameters of racial relations, since in practice all whites were allowed a great degree of latitude in

regard to uses of the enslaved. Before proceeding to limn the important features of antebellum enjoyment, a gloss on enjoyment and its
relation to use and possession would be helpful here.[15] *Black's Law
Dictionary* defines the term "enjoy" as "to have, possess, and use
with satisfaction; to occupy or have the benefit of." While enjoyment encompasses these rudimentary features, it also denotes more
extensive capacities. It entails "the exercise of a right; the promise and function of a right, privilege or incorporeal hereditament.
Comfort, consolation, contentment, ease, happiness, pleasure and
satisfaction. Such includes the beneficial use, interest, and purpose
to which property may be put, and implies rights to profits and
incomes therefrom." At the outset, it is clear that to take delight in,
to use, and to possess are inextricably linked and that enjoyment
entails everything from the use of one's possession to the value of
whiteness, which can be considered an incorporeal hereditament or
illusory inheritance of chattel slavery.

Since the subjection of the slave to all whites defined his condition in civil society, effectively this made the enslaved an object of
property to be potentially used and abused by all whites; however, to
speak at all of the civil condition of the slave, as George M. Stroud
remarked, is a kind of solecism.[16] It is a tricky matter to detail the
civil existence of a subject who is socially dead and legally recognized as human only to the degree that he or she is criminally culpable. Yet it is the anomalous status of the enslaved that determines
the specific uses of the slave as object of property and the relation
between citizens and those who can be identified as civil subjects in
the most circumscribed and tentative fashion. What is striking here
are the myriad and unrestricted uses of slave property, and the ways
in which the slaves become the property of all whites given their
status in civil society. In this effort, let us turn to William Goodell's *American Slave Codes* and Stroud's *A Sketch of the Laws Relating
to Slavery in the Several States of the United States of America.* Stroud

examines the condition of the slave as a member of civil society. The
notable features of this anomalous civil condition are: the slave cannot be a witness against a white person, either in a civil or criminal
cause; the slave cannot be a party to a civil suit; the benefits of education are withheld from the slave; the means for moral or religious
education are not granted to the enslaved; submission is required of
the slave, not to the will of his master only but to that of all other
white persons; the penal codes of the slave-holding states bear much
more severely upon slaves than upon white persons; and slaves are
prosecuted and tried upon criminal accusations in a manner inconsistent with the rights of humanity.[17]

Here, I want to focus on a singular aspect of the slave's existence in civil society—the submission of the slave to all whites. The
great concession to the power of the master and to all whites was
evidenced by laws that prohibited the slave from defending himself
from the master to avoid vindictive punishment or from striking any
white in self-defense. Such laws not only exacted strict submission
extending to bloodshed and murder but also "furnish[ed] a pretext"
and an inducement to oppress and tyrannize the enslaved. As a
consequence, the enslaved were forced to "patiently endure every
species of personal injury, which a white person, however brutal or
ferocious his disposition . . . may choose to offer."[18] After review-
ing state statutes that prohibited the slave from defending himself
against the assault of any white person and punished such offenses
by cropping ears, inflicting thirty lashes on a bare back, or bringing about death, Goodell concluded that "if civil government were
designed for human demoralization and torture, it is not easy to see
how its ends could be more effectually reached."[19]

To be sure, the laws of slavery subjected the enslaved to the absolute control and authority of any and every member of the dominant
race. The relations of chattel slavery served to enhance whiteness
by racializing rights and entitlements, designating inferior and

superior races, and granting whites' dominion over blacks. In light of such considerations, the contours of antebellum enjoyment reveal less about "the nature of the Negro" than the terms of interracial interaction and coexistence. It made blackness a material to be utilized and exploited for whatever ends. The myriad uses of the captive as tool, implement, prosthetic, and amusement cultivated and reinforced the idea of black excess, blackness as excess, as surfeit. Given this, let me suggest that not only were the rights and privileges of white citizens undergirded by the subjection of blacks but, moreover, that enjoyment in turn defined the meaning of subjection. The interdiction against self-defense and the inability of a slave to testify against whites permitted the slave to be used in any capacity that pleased the master or his surrogates. And as Goodell notes in a rather indirect fashion, the uses of property also included the sexual violation of the enslaved. The few restrictions placed upon the uses of slave property concerned only the master's rights regarding the use of his property by others.[20] Indeed, the dissolute uses of slave property marked the identity of the captive and hence the nature of the Negro. These actual or imagined usages established the parameters of interracial association.

There was no relation to blackness outside the terms of this use of, entitlement to, and occupation of the captive body, for even the status of free blacks was shaped and compromised by the existence of slavery. As I have argued, enjoyment was predicated on the wanton uses of slave property; yet this boundless utility, this capacity to be everything and nothing was attributed to the slave and believed to be an essential or inherent feature of blackness; and in this way, it served to minimize and disavow the violence of slavery and the terrible things done to human flesh. As a result, in spectacles like the coffle, it appeared not only that the enslaved were indifferent to their wretched condition, but as well that they had achieved a measure of satisfaction with their condition. The efficacity of violence was indicated precisely by its invisibility or transparency and in the copious display of slave agency. Just as the imputation of lasciviousness condoned and erased the sexual violation of the enslaved, and the punitive recognition of will and responsibility justified punishment while denying the slave the ability to forge contracts, testify, or sustain natal and conjugal relations, enjoyment registered and effaced the violence of property relations.

The fixation on the slave's "good times" conceals the affiliations of white enjoyment and black subjection and the affective dimensions of mastery and servitude. From this perspective, the seemingly casual observations about black fun and frolic obscure this violent use and the incorporation of the captive body in realizing the extensive and sentient capacities of the master subject. Fantasies about the other's enjoyment are ways for us to organize our own enjoyment. "Does not the Other's enjoyment exert such a powerful fascination because in it we represent to ourselves our own innermost relationship toward enjoyment?"[21] What is revealed about this innermost relationship toward enjoyment? An indifference to suffering or a keen investment in it? Whose unease was allayed by the dance? If the excess of enjoyment imputed to the enslaved displaced what we would think of as disturbing circumstances, it did so only by obscuring violence and conflating it with pleasure.

(In)sufferable Pleasures

Rankin was not alone in his desire to slip into blackness and experience the suffering of slavery "firsthand," so to speak. To the contrary, the popularity of Uncle Tom's Cabin and The Octoroon indicates the willingness of others to suffer, too. The elasticity of blackness and its capacious affects enabled such flights and becomings. In this case, the figurative capacities of blackness and the fungibility of the commodity are directly linked. The abstractness

and immateriality of the commodity, the ease with which it circu-
lates and changes state, shifting from one incarnation of value to
another, extends to the black body or blackface mask enabling it
to serve as the vehicle of white self-exploration, renunciation, and
enjoyment.[22] The ability to put on blackness must be considered in
the context of chattel slavery and the economy of enjoyment that
subtends it. Antebellum formations of pleasure, even those of the
North, need to be considered in relation to the affective dimensions
of racial slavery, since enjoyment is virtually unimaginable without
recourse to the black body and the subjection of the captive, the
pleasures yielded by dispossession, the delirium of the old plantation, and the libertine fantasies launched by the myriad uses of the
sentient object. Every pound of flesh, every organ and orifice afford
opportunity. For these reasons, the formal features of this economy
of pleasure and the politics of enjoyment are explicated in regard
to the literal and figurative occupation and possession of the body.
This reading attempts to elucidate the means by which the wanton
use of and the violence directed toward the black figure come to be
identified as *its* pleasure and danger; the expectations and demands
of slave property are ontologized as the innate capacities and inner
feelings of the enslaved, and in turn, the ascription of excess and
enjoyment to the African conceals and enchants the violence perpetrated against the enslaved.

The schematic analysis of minstrelsy and melodrama that follows explores the convergence of violence and pleasure, which is
one of the primary attributes of this economy of enjoyment, rather
than providing a close reading of the texts of minstrelsy and melodrama. Scant attention is paid to the white spectator's identification with blackface characters. Instead, the major issue explored is
the relation between pleasure and violence: the facility of blackness
in the other's self-fashioning and the role of pleasure in securing
the mechanisms of racial subjection. This economy of enjoyment is

questioned through a consideration of the dynamics of possession and close scrutiny of the object of property and its uses.

Despite differences between their respective conventions and stylistic devices, the uses made of the black figure established continuities between minstrelsy and melodrama that surpassed their generic differences.[23] While the ethical valence of such violence differed, it nonetheless delivered a significant pleasure. Blows caused the virtuous black body of melodrama to be esteemed and humiliated the grotesque black body of minstrelsy. Uncle Tom's tribulations were tempered by the slaps and punches delivered to Topsy. The body's placement as ravaged object or as the recipient of farcical blows nonetheless established a corporeal language that marked Zoe, Tom, and Topsy as identifiably black and exposed the affiliations between the auction block and the popular theater.[24] Affect, gesture, and a vulnerability to violence constituted blackness. Even in the antislavery blackface of *Uncle Tom's Cabin*, the violation of the ersatz black body incited great pleasure, whether a monopathic wholeness generated by the Manichaean struggle of good or evil, or the bawdy pleasures of Topsy's comic antics and the brutish response to them.[25] Torture and agony both generated enjoyment.

Injury and punishment defined the personhood of these characters, not unlike the legal interpellation of slave humanity. Whether venerated as an opportunity for Christian endurance or legitimated by darky pretensions and trespasses, violence engendered blackness. The virtuous suffering and ethical submission of sentimentalism and the social transgression enacted and punished in farce conspired to make the corporeal enactment of blackness a pained one.[26] Melodrama presented blackness as a vehicle of protest and dissent, and minstrelsy made it the embodiment of unmentionable and transgressive pleasures. In both instances, the fashioning of blackness aroused pity and fear, desire and revulsion, terror and pleasure. This ambivalent complex of feelings describes not only the emotional appeals of the popular stage but also the spectacle of the auction block.[27]

Black characters rarely appeared as heroes or heroines in melodrama, except in the moral drama of antislavery plays. As dictated by convention, slavery was staged as the clash of villainy and virtue. "The very dangerous evil" of slavery and, in particular, the crimes of the slave trade were well-suited to the stage of melodrama. The crime of the trade was seen as a crime of the heart—"the outrages of feelings and affection." (For example, Professor E. A. Andrews, in his treatise on the slave trade, argued for the abolition of the trade on the grounds that "domestic relations [were] the foundation of all virtue, and consequently of all the happiness of society, and everything inconsistent with the perpetuity of these relations ought at once, everywhere, and forever, to cease."[28] The offense against virtue perpetuated in the sundering of families offended sentiment and easily transformed slavery's crimes into the stuff of melodrama. When one is considering the crimes of slavery, the popular theater is as central as the courthouse.) Virtue, imperiled and unrecognized, positioned slaves as innocents held captive by the pernicious institution, and blackness was the emblem of this tortured innocence. Melodrama provided the dramatic frame that made the experience of slavery meaningful in the antinomian terms of the moral imagination. The emotional power of melodrama's essential language of good and evil armed antislavery dissent with the force of moral right and might. Abolitionist discourse shared melodrama's obsession: virtue, virginity, and the sanctity of the family. After all, what was the coffle but a drama of moral life accompanied by the music of violins? The descriptions of Rankin and other nineteenth-century observers rendered the trade and the coffle in the style of the melodramatic tableau—the frozen moment in which gestures and attitudes take the form of moral emblems.[29] Woe-worn, "loaded with chains," and driven by "unfeeling wretches," the slaves are mute while their music conveys the message of anguish. Song became the emblem of oppression, and in these songs, sorrow was as palpable as the chains that bound the flesh, and yet it was ineffable, too.

Melodramas were also replete with minstrel fare. The antics of plantation darkies provided levity amid catastrophe. Generally, representations of blackness were restricted to stock "darky" characters or low-comedy types, with the exceptions of the tragic mulatto and the dignified, pathetic, and suffering slave.[30] In antislavery dramas, beleaguered slave heroes and heroines supplemented rather than replaced darky fanfare. Ironically, the maintenance of racial boundaries occurred through the donning of the blackface mask or the display of tragically bifurcated racial bodies. For example, in the case of *Uncle Tom's Cabin*, the grammar of sentiment and the rhetoric of minstrelsy set the stage for a performance of slavery that wed cruelty and festivity.[31] Abolitionists' politics allied with blackface techniques created an ambivalent portrait of slavery that denounced the institution as it supplemented minstrelsy's range of darky fare.

Blackness was a masquerade in melodrama no less so than in minstrelsy, since the roles of the black subjects of melodrama were usually performed by white actors in blackface.[32] Akin to the mask of blackness on the minstrel stage, melodrama's black mask was ambivalent and contradictory. Truth and virtue were manifested in gesture, expression, and comportment, and the body was to be read as an ethical allegory; yet melodrama too manipulated the disparity between substance and surface. The pleasures of duplicity were inextricably linked with its dangers. Melodrama explored the pleasures and dangers of racial travesty in tales of distressed quadroons and octoroons. Mulatto figures, who were usually women, represented a crisis of racial legibility, and, at the same time, they made blackness more palatable. The disparity between identity and appearance contributed to the hero's or heroine's affliction and his or her usually tragic end. In these moral dramas, the battle of good and evil was waged at the site of the tortured and chaste black body: suffering announced virtue. Tom's chained and beaten body proclaimed his saintliness; Zoe's self-immolation conveyed her great love and humility. Meanwhile, black characters bearing a striking resemblance to Zip Coon, Jim Crow, and Coal Black Rose, the bumbling, loyal, and childish Sambos and wenches of minstrel fare, provided the comic b(l)ackdrop of virtue's triumph.

Blackness in *Uncle Tom's Cabin*, *The Escape*, *Dred*, and *The Octoroon* was also delineated by darky antics—lying, loafing, stealing, and breakdown dancing. Even saintly Tom's performance was embellished with minstrelsy.[33] The convergence between abolitionism's sentimental structure of feeling with that of proslavery discourse was evidenced in the stage productions of *Uncle Tom's Cabin*. Uncle Tom sang a rendition of "Old Folks at Home," a popular minstrel song written by Stephen Foster, and even "Uncle Tom's Religion" resembled a minstrel air. The lyrics to "Old Folks at Home" clearly make the case:

Way down upon de Swanee ribber,
Far, far away
Dere's wha my heart is turning ebber,
Dere's wha de old folks stay.
All up and down de whole creation,
Sadly I roam,
Still longing for de old plantation,
And for de old folks at home.
All de world am sad and dreary,
Ebry where I roam,
Oh! darkeys how my heart grows weary,
Far from de old folks at home.[34]

Dissembling tricksters, fools, and wenches also populated the stage of melodrama. Fancy footwork, sexual flourishes, tomfoolery, and deceit were accompanied by the blows that grounded the body and returned the trespasser/dissembler to his place. On stage, Topsy was as great an attraction as Tom. The audience enjoyed scenes of suffering innocence, terrifying villainy, heart-rending deaths, and the triumph of virtue, and they enjoyed the bawdy and outrageous acts of minstrelsy as much, if not more. Tearful episodes were followed by raucous laughter. The imperiled and suffering figure of melodrama and the dangers of the lower bodily realms gratified the audience's desire to witness and experience the prohibited and the repressed. The indiscriminate use of the black body made possible the pleasure of terror and the terror of pleasure. Within this framework, suffering and shuffling were complementary.

The convergences between the bodily politics of minstrelsy and those of melodrama might be said to center on the redemptive and recreational use of violence.[35] Certainly, the disciplinary vengeance of farce exercised in minstrelsy reproduced black subjection, albeit accompanied by laughter.[36] On the minstrel stage, the comic inversions, bawdy humor, and lampooning of class hierarchies nonetheless operated within the confines of the tolerable, particularly since this transgression of order occurred by reproducing the abject status of blackness. While the dynamics of "romance and repulsion," to borrow Eric Lott's terms, enabled acts of transgression licensed by the blackface mask, blackness was also policed through derision, ridicule, and violence. In the end, the white flights of imagination and transgressive exploits facilitated by donning blackface ultimately restored the racial terms of social order.[37] The transgressions and the loosened strictures of identity enabled by the blackface mask in turn fortified a repressive and restrictive reception of blackness, one that was elastic enough to permit white self-exploration, but unwilling to trespass the parameters established to maintain racial hierarchies. Minstrelsy flouted high culture and cultivated a common sense of whiteness only as it reinforced the subjugated status of blacks. Minstrelsy articulated a white working-class consciousness, writes David Roediger, "by racializing conflict more than directly articulating class grievances."[38] The Manichaeanism at the heart of minstrelsy was the division between the races. The seeming transgressions of the color line and the identification forged with the blackface mask through aversion and/or desire ultimately served only to reinforce relations of mastery and servitude. "Far from being a failed union of black and white workers," observes Michael Rogin, "minstrelsy realized the Jacksonian dream of allying the northern popular classes with slave labor."[39] It is no surprise that the relations of mastery and servitude, which determined the meaning of white identity, the character of citizenship, the notion of personhood, and the scope of rights and entitlements, were also essential to antebellum formations of pleasure.[40]

Minstrelsy's plantation nostalgia returned Jim Crow to his happy home and affirmed the institution of slavery in happy scenes of the plantation and carry-me-back-to-the-old-plantation songs of ex-slaves. Only punishment awaited those who entertained foolish aspirations of being like white men.[41] Songs like "Away Down Souf," "My Old Kentucky Home," and "Old Folks at Home" all celebrate the glories of the South and the desire to return to the plantation home where "de corn-top blossom and de canebrake grow." Stephen Foster's renowned "Massa's in de Cold Ground" was replete with the sentimentalism of plantation nostalgia:

Massa made de darkeys love him, cayse he was so kind
Now de sadly weep above him, mourning cayse he leave dem
behind.
I cannot work before tomorrow, cayse de tear drops flow
I try to drive away my sorrow, pickin on de old banjo.[42]

The most famous of these Southern pastorals was Dan Emmett's "I Wish I Was in Dixie's Land," which was written in the spring of 1859. Years later, Emmett, clarifying the origin and authorship of the tune, stated that "Dixie" "is nothing but a plain simple melody with plantation words, the purport of which is that a negro in the north feels himself out of place, and thinking of his old home in the south, is made to exclaim, in the words of the song—I wish I was in Dixie."[43] The longing and substance of this simple tune, as succinctly outlined by Emmett, was to return the Negro to his proper place, which brings to mind George Fredrickson's observation that in the antebellum world, the "good negro" was always in his place and the "bad nigger" outside it.[44] By extension, this logic of return and suitable placement can also be applied to tunes like "Loozyanna Low Grounds," "De Ole Jaw Bone," "De Floating Scow of Ole Virginia," and other "carry-me-backs" that recollect the good old days on the plantation, lament the separation from family and home as a result of the move north, and proclaim a fervent desire to return to the slave quarters.[45] The sentiment of the carry-me-backs is illuminated by the following stanzas of "I'm Going Home to Dixie," written by Dan Emmett in 1858.

> There is a land where cotton grows, a land where milk and
>   honey flows
> I'm going home to Dixie! Yes! I'm going home.
> I've got no time to tarry, I've got no time to stay.
> 'Tis a rocky road to travel, to Dixie far away.
> I've wander'd far both to and fro'
> But Dixie's heaven here below
> I'm going home.
> O list to what I've got to say
> Freedom to me will never pay!
> I'm going home.

In Dixie Land the fields do bloom
And color'd men have welcome room
I'm going home.
I will proclaim it loud and long
I love old Dixie right or wrong.
I'm going home.[46]

The representations of slavery rendered in the minstrel show created a plantation pastoral in which "Gayly de Niggas Dance[d]."[47]
Even sentimental plays and tunes that explored issues of separation
implied that the loss of family and friends was the result of Cuff's or
Sambo's choice.

Minstrelsy dramatically resolved the tension between domination and intimacy by recourse to sentimental tropes of reciprocity,
domesticity, love, and kinship. Like the orchestrated amusements
of the master, minstrelsy elaborated and fixed blackness in a theatrical presentation both violent and celebratory. Whippings were to
minstrelsy what tears were to melodrama. If grotesque bodily acts
such as rolling eyes, lolling tongues, obscene gestures, shuffling,
and the like animated the body, blows invested it with meaning.
Thrashing and blows reestablished the proper place of those who
defied the boundaries of race and status. The vain displays of Zip
Coon and the inept self-promotion of would-be strivers like Jim
Dandy were the source of ridicule. Plays like *Oh, Hush!* and *Old Zip
Coon* and songs like "Dandy Jim from Caroline," "Pompey Squash,"
"Jim along Josey," and "High Daddy" mocked such pretensions.[48]
In the same vein, characters like Sambo Johnson, Doctor Quash,
or 'Meriky, a colored fashion plate, put on airs and, more important, strove to be something greater than they were and defied the
racist logic of suitable placement. In the end, however, these vain
aspirations were punished and blacks returned to their proper sta-
tions.[49] Whenever Zip Coon slipped out of place, he was brutally

returned there. When 'Meriky converted to Episcopalianism, she was beaten by her father until she regained her senses and declared that she was "a deep-water Baptist." Doctor Quash, the sham physician and mangler, is beaten, murdered, revived, and forced to run a gauntlet.[50] His name alone obviates the inextricable link between fashioning blackness and violence. (Quashie was the generic name for a black person or slave, "especially one considered credulous or insignificant.")[51] Sambo Johnson's pretense of literacy and buffoonish display of skill and learning are rewarded with a humiliating unmasking and whipping by Cuff. In this fashion, the duplicitous and the pretentious were herded into the acceptable confines of the social. These performances of blackness regulated the excess they conjured up with the threat of punishment and humiliating exposure.

The pretensions of high culture and the society of manners were lampooned by focusing on black buffoonery and the ridiculously impossible aspirations of blacks trying to improve themselves—that is, putting on airs and trying to be white. According to the tenets of minstrelsy, the only ambition fitting for blacks was "showing de science of his heels."[52] "High Daddy" mocked the aspirations to be white and, in this case, free, in a more direct fashion:

I know a darkie and his name it was Joe,
I met High Daddy in the morning.
I know'd it was, for he once told me so;
I met High Daddy and I wont go home any more, any more.
He used to hoe and dig up all the land,
I met High Daddy in the morning.
But now he says that work is contraband.
I met High Daddy and I wont go home any more, any more.
He drank skimm'd milk from morn 'till night,
I met . . .

Somebody said that it would make him white;
I met . . .
But let him drink until he gets his fill,
I met . . .
He always bound to be a darkie still!
I met . . . [53]

"Bound" to be a darky, still, whether slave, contraband, or free, delineates the very nexus of this economy of enjoyment. The bound black body, permanently affixed in its place, arouses pleasure not only ensuant to the buffoonery and grotesqueries of Cuff, Sambo, and Zip Coon but, above all else, from the very mechanisms of this coercive placement; it is a pleasure obtained from the security of place and order and predicated upon chattel slavery. Blackface restaged the seizure and possession of the black body for the other's use and enjoyment. The culture of cross-racial identification facilitated in minstrelsy cannot be extricated from the relations of chattel slavery.

Overwhelmingly, the donning of the blackface mask reiterated racial subjection, however much this subjection might provide a liberating vehicle for white working-class consciousness or a sense of white integrity and wholeness produced by the policing of racial boundaries.[54] In blackface, as elsewhere in antebellum society, the fashioning of whiteness in large measure occurred by way of the violent domination and humiliation of blacks. The illusory integrity of whiteness was facilitated by attraction and/or antipathy to blackness and ultimately dependent on the use and possession of the black body. The appropriation of Sambo's affect, the sport and swagger of blackface, and the audience's consequent identification with the minstrel mask provided whiteness with a coherence and illusory integrity dependent upon the relations of mastery and servitude (and the possession of a figurative body of blackness), whether to incite abolitionist passions or cultivate white working-class consciousness.

Both minstrelsy and melodrama (re)produced blackness as an essentially pained expression of the body's possibilities. Paradoxically, racial subterfuge and artifice reiterated absolute and repressive definitions of blackness. The punitive pleasures yielded through the figurative possession of blackness cannot be disentangled from the bodily politics of chattel slavery. Blackness permitted if not encouraged prohibited explorations, tabooed associations, immodest acts, and bawdy pleasures. The terror of pleasure—the violence that undergirded the comic moment in minstrelsy—and the pleasure of terror—the force of evil that propelled the plot of melodrama and fascinated the spectator—filiated the coffle, the auction block, the popular stage, and plantation recreations in a scandalous equality. At each of these sites of performance, suffering was transformed into wholesome pleasures. As Zoe, the heroine of *The Octoroon*, imagined it: "Our race has at least one virtue—it knows how to suffer!"[55]

The Coffle

Upon observing a mournful procession of slaves "loaded with chains," singing a "little wild hymn of sweet and mournful melody," and headed to market, George Tucker could only wonder: "What is their crime? And what is to be their punishment?"[56] Astonished by the incongruence of the display, we are also left to ponder how sweet wild hymns and crime coexist, whether the origin of American theater is to be found in a no-longer-remembered primal scene of torture, and whether song bears the trace of punishment. The pageantry of the trade, the unabashed display of the market's brutality, the juxtaposition of sorrow and mirth, and the separation of families accounted for the trade's declared status as the most horrible feature of the institution of slavery.[57] The coffle was described by nineteenth-century observers as a domestic Middle Passage, piracy, a momentous evil, and, most frequently, a crime. George W. Featherstonhaugh, though revolted by the coffle, could not help but exclaim that it was "the most striking spectacle ever witnessed." The unseemliness of those shackled and bound for market being cajoled to sing "Old Virginia Never Tire," a minstrel tune, no less, to the accompaniment of a banjo inspired his incredulity and amazement. Although the procession of the coffle, in Featherstonhaugh's words, was "disgusting" and "hideous," the march of despair was obviously not without its festivities. As Featherstonhaugh observes, the slave drivers, aware of the slaves' disposition to mutiny, "endeavor to mitigate their discontent by feeding them well on the march, and by encouraging them to sing 'Old Virginia never tire,' to the banjo." Given that the "poor negro slave is naturally a cheerful, laughing animal, and even when driven through the wilderness in chains, if he is well fed and kindly treated, is seldom melancholy," the lively stories, oranges, and sugar to be had achieved their ends and effected a singular docility.[58]

Although this "melancholy spectacle" aroused Featherstonhaugh's revulsion and sympathy, what is interesting for my purposes is the movement from the "disgusting" and "hideous" display to the cheerful laughing Negro, who seems conjured up rather than situated within the spectacle, or from repulsion to romance. While Featherstonhaugh definitely recognizes the driver's instigation of song and provides ample details of the hideous scene, he nevertheless suggests that the enslaved are cheery and contented, based upon his musings about black character and the slave's minimal longing for animal comforts—sufficient food, kind treatment, and warmth. The incongruence first attributed to the spectacle is no less marked in Featherstonhaugh's divergent assessments. He both decries the revolting and the hideous and projects comfort and cheer, and as a

result the ghastly scene is itself detached from the characters shackled within it. Despite the initial revulsion that the coffle induced,
the melancholy spectacle remains at an emotional and contempla-
tive distance, and musings about Negro character displace the hideous with the entertaining. This is all the more disturbing precisely
because this scene gives expression to Featherstonhaugh's abolitionist sentiments. The fixation on comfort and gratification is not
indifferent to suffering, and Featherstonhaugh winds up reconciling
the two by way of speculations about Negro character and animal
comforts. The gaze shifts from the spectacle to the inner recesses
of feeling and desire, as he probes the emotional substrate residing
within the "poor slave," yet this entrée mutes the shock of the scene
and mitigates its ghastly incommensurability with the suggestion of
contentment.

The association of song and suffering raises a host of issues that
exceed the fascination or disapprobation incited by the apparently
unsettling juxtaposition of the festive and the obscene. Foremost
among these issues is the thorny status of pleasure, given such
instrumental uses, the instability or ambivalence of agency, and
the merging/melding of pain and pleasure at various sites of amusement, inclusive of slaves striking it smart on the auction block, the
popular stage, and the breakdown performed in the quarters. The
affiliations between these diverse sites of performance outline the
problematic of enjoyment in which pleasure is inseparable from subjection, will conflated with submission, and bodily integrity bound
to violence. The observations of Tyrone Power, an Irish traveler jour-
neying through the United States in the 1830s, are revealing in this
regard. Upon encountering a caravan of fifty to sixty slaves moving
southwest with their owners, Power surmised: "Judging fairly by
their deportment and loud merriment, despite the great fatigue and
constant exposure, the affair was taken in a sort of holiday spirit,
no way warranted by their half-naked miserable appearance."[59] If

the holiday spirit is, as Power asserts, unwarranted, judging by the miserable appearance and the wretched condition of the enslaved, it leads us to interrogate whose pleasure is being considered at the site of such encounters—the observers' or that of those in chains? What is the relation of song and suffering in this miserable parade?

When Abraham Lincoln encountered a slave coffle aboard the steamboat *Lebanon*, en route to St. Louis, he was prompted to consider "the effect of condition upon human happiness," not the crime of the trade or the distress of the slaves:

> A gentleman had purchased twelve negroes in different parts of Kentucky and was taking them to a farm in the South. They were chained six and six together. A small iron clevis was around the left wrist of each, and this fastened to the main chain by a shorter one at a convenient distance from the others; so that the negroes were strung together precisely like so many fish upon a trot-line. In this condition they were being separated from the scenes of their childhood, their friends, their fathers and mothers, and brothers and sisters, and many of them, from their wives and children, and going into perpetual slavery where the lash of the master is proverbially more ruthless and unrelenting than any other where; and yet amid all these distressing circumstances, as we would think of them, they were the most cheerful and apparently happy creatures on board. One whose offence for which he had been sold was an over-fondness for his wife, played the fiddle almost continually; and others danced, sung, cracked jokes, and played various games with cards from day to day. How true it is that "God tempers the wind to the shorn lamb," or in other words, that He renders the worst of the human condition tolerable, while He permits the best, to be nothing but tolerable.[60]

Lincoln's observations would suggest that song, dance, and game discredit any and all claims of suffering. The cheerful disposition of the enslaved not only established the suitedness of the slave's nature to the condition of slavery but provided the occasion on which to muse about the adequacy of the human condition. Lincoln surmises, based upon this scene, that the worst of the human condition mirrors the best in being simply bearable. What are the dimensions of this investment in and fixation with Negro enjoyment? Is the encounter with black suffering merely an opportunity for white self-reflection? More broadly speaking, the elasticity of blackness enables its deployment as a vehicle for exploring the human condition, although, ironically, these musings are utterly indifferent to the violated condition of the vessel of song.

The utility of what Toni Morrison has described as the "Africanist persona" resides in these reflexive or figurative capacities, which make possible such ruminations about existence as well as explorations of dread and desire.[61] It is not surprising or unusual that the wretchedness (and incongruous display) of the coffle prompted reflection on the human condition, but what is remarkable is the way violence becomes neutralized and the shocking readily assimilated to the ordinary, the everyday, the bearable, the tolerable. Reflection acts to normalize the presence of violence by characterizing it as within the context of the socially endurable and by shifting the scene from despair to one of contentment. Sufferance denotes the ability to endure the terrible situation patiently, to weather long suffering, to be unaffected by loss, to embrace a wretched condition, and, by all appearances, to celebrate in misery. Remarkably, the emotional resources, animal needs, and limited affections of the enslaved are made responsible for this shift.

The liberal extension of feeling to those shackled like a herd of cattle or strung together like a line of fish only serves to efface violence and circumscribe the captives' sentience through attributions of contentment or evaluations of the bearable. As reported, either their feelings seem unwarranted given their condition—holiday spirit incongruously paired with a half-miserable and wretched condition—or this proverbial cheer, inability to feel pain, and blunted sensibility especially suited them for enslavement. The very effort to engage the predicament of slavery culminates in a selective acknowledgment of sentience that only reinforces the tethers of subjection. Certainly, Lincoln's discernments of sentiment harmonize chattel slavery with the verities of the human condition. In order to understand the disposition of the enslaved, Lincoln basically likens them to himself to address the human condition. The assimilative character of empathy can be blamed in part for this, for identification overtakes the proximity or availability for others essential to ethical conduct and the violence of this obliteration and assimilation is no less great, albeit of a different character, than the racist antipathy that can only envision the enslaved as object and dehumanized other. Those shackled to one another do not document the disparities of the human condition or, most obviously, the violation of natural liberty or cause Lincoln to reflect on the liberties and entitlements that he enjoys, but merely provide an opportunity for self-reflection and a narrative digression within an otherwise "most dull and silly" letter. The separation of fathers and children, the lash, the small irons attaching the enslaved like so many fish upon a trotline, ruthless masters, and the rest, although distressing conditions as "we" might imagine them, appear to have little effect on these apparently happy creatures. Songs, jokes, and dance transform wretched conditions into a conspicuous, and apparently convincing, display of contentment. This circumscribed recognition of black humanity itself becomes an exercise of violence.

For the moment, suffice it to say that such indulgence in song, often prompted by the sting of the whip, reflected neither an embrace of slavery nor a unity of feeling, but was a veiled articulation of the extreme and paradoxical conditions of slavery, often mistaken for nonsense or joy. As Frederick Douglass remarked, these seemingly meaningless and incoherent songs, though difficult for those outside and within the circle of slavery to understand, revealed more about the horrors of the institution than did volumes of philosophy.

While I will undertake a more extensive discussion of the politics of cultural production later, here let me stress the complexity and opacity of black song and the difficulty of clarifying, with any degree of certainty or assuredness, the politics of slave song and performance when dissolution and redress collude with each other and terror is yoked to enjoyment. My engagement, following the path laid by Douglass and W. E. B. Du Bois, turns upon the veiled and half-articulate messages contained in song, or, to quote Paul Gilroy, the politics of a lower frequency and the "unsayable claims to truth" that can never be communicated.[62] The task is neither to unearth the definitive meaning of song or dance nor to read song as an expression of black character, as was common among nineteenth-century ethnographers, but to give full weight to the opacity of these texts composed in the confines of terror and brutality and in fleeting moments of reprieve. Rather than consider black song as an index or mirror of the slave condition, this examination emphasizes the significance of opacity as precisely that which enables something in excess of the orchestrated amusements of the enslaved and troubles the distinctions between joy and sorrow and toil and leisure. For this opacity, the subterranean and veiled character of slave song, must be considered in relation to the imposition of transparency and the degrading hypervisibility of the enslaved. By the same token, such concealment should be considered a form of resistance, a refusal of legible forms of address. As Glissant advises, "The attempt to approach a reality so hidden from view cannot be organized in terms of a series of clarifications."[63] The right to obscurity or opacity must be respected, for the "accumulated hurt," the "rasping whispers deep in the throat," the wild notes, and the screams lodged deep within confound simple expression and, likewise, withstand the prevailing ascriptions of black enjoyment.

Disavowing the Claims of Pain

For those forced to "step it up lively," the festivity of the trade and the pageantry of the coffle were intended to shield the violence of the market and deny the sorrow of those sold and their families. These extravagant displays elided the distinction between submission and willfulness in the denial of pain. This disavowal of the captives' pain operates on a number of levels, from simple denial to the stipulation of an excessive enjoyment.[64] The terms of this disavowal are something like: *No, the slave is not in pain. Pain isn't really pain for the enslaved, because of their limited sentience, tendency to forget, short-lived attachments, and easily consolable grief. Most important, the slave is happy and, in fact, his happiness exceeds "our" own.* The outcome of this line of thought: the initial revulsion and horror induced by the sight of shackled and manacled bodies gives way to reassurances about black pleasure.

Sellie Martin, who was sold at age six along with his mother and ten-year-old sister, described the "heart breaking scene" when the coffle departed for market: "When the order was given to march, it was always on such occasions accompanied by the command, which slaves were made to understand before they left the 'pen,' to 'strike up lively,' which means they must sing a song. Oh! what heartbreaks there are in these rude and simple songs! The purpose of the trader in having them sung is to prevent among the crowd of negroes who usually gather on such occasions, any expression of sorrow for those who are being torn away from them; but the negroes, who have very little hope of ever seeing those again who are dearer to them than life, and who are weeping and wailing over the separation, often

turn the song demanded of them into a farewell dirge."[65] By turning
the song into a farewell dirge, the coerced performance becomes a
veiled articulation of the sorrow denied the enslaved.

Martin's account of his experiences was echoed by William
Wells Brown. As a speculator's assistant, Brown prepared the slaves
held in the pen for inspection and sale. In effect, he set the scene for
the buyers' entry: "Before the slaves were exhibited for sale, they
were dressed and driven out into the yard. Some were set to dancing,
some to jumping, and some to playing cards. This was done to make
them appear cheerful and happy. My business was to see that they
were placed in those situations before the arrival of the purchas-
ers, and I have often set them to dancing when their cheeks were
wet with tears."[66] Brown's account of the rituals of the marketplace,
like that of Martin, frames the ersatz merriment of the enslaved as
an inducement to exchange. Stephen Dickinson remembered being
paraded about the streets for an hour by an auctioneer who compelled one slave to carry a red flag and the other to ring a bell.[67] Joy
from this perspective is not an index of the expressive capacities of
the enslaved but rather a means toward the enhancement of value
and an incident of fungibility.

Contrary to our expectations, gaiety articulates the brutal calculations of the trade. The self-betrayal enacted by stepping it lively
and enthusiastically assisting in one's sale underscores the affiliations of spectacle and suffering. And, accordingly, "fun and frolic"
become the vehicles of the slave's self-betrayal and survival.[68] By
stepping it lively and "acting smart," the captive was made the
agent of his or her dissolution.[69] The body of the slave, dancing
and on display, seemingly revealed a comfort with bondage and a
natural disposition for servitude. Those observing the singing and
dancing and the comic antics of the auctioneer seemed to revel
in the festive atmosphere of the trade, and it attracted spectators not intending to purchase slaves. According to Cato Carter,

"They used to cry the niggers off just like so much cattle and we didn't think no different of it. . . . Everybody liked to hear them cry off niggers. The cryer was a clown and made funny talk and kept everybody laughing."[70] Catherine Slim remembered seeing a coffle of slaves chained together, going south; some were singing and some were crying.[71] Mary Gaffney ironically described the "fun" of the trade as "all the hollering and bawling."[72] Others, like James Martin, remarked upon the coerced theatricality of the trade: "And we sees others sol[d] on the auction block. They're put in stalls like pens for cattle and there's a curtain, sometimes just a sheet in front of them, so the bidders can't see the stock too soon. The overseer's standin' just outside with a big black snake whip and a pepper box pistol in his hand. Then they pulls the curtain up and the bidders crowd 'round. The overseer tells the age of the slaves and what they can do. . . . Then the overseer makes 'em walk across the platform. He makes 'em hop, he makes 'em trot, he makes 'em jump."[73] Polly Shine recalled being driven with others like cattle to the marketplace: "Our master would put us in the road ahead of them and they would be on horses behind us as we traveled and they would follow and we had to travel pert, no laggin behind if we did, he always had whip that he would tap us with boy! when he hit us across the legs we could step real lively and I don't mean maybe either."[74] True to form, this theater of the marketplace wed festivity and the exchange of captive bodies. The distribution of rum or brandy and slaves dancing, laughing, and generally "striking it up lively" entertained spectators and gave meaning to the phrase "theater of the marketplace." James Curry noted the disparity between the journey to market and the "studied nicety" of the slave. When the coffle is being driven, "no attention is paid to the decency of their appearance. They go bare-headed and bare-footed, with any rag they can themselves find wrapped around their bodies. But the driver has clothing prepared for them to put on, just before they reach the market, and they are forced to array themselves with studied nicety for their exposure at public sale."[75]

The lubricating effects of intoxicants, the simulation of good times, and the to-and-fro of half-naked bodies on display all acted to incite the flow of capital. The centrality of amusement to the slave trade is confirmed by an article in the *New Orleans Daily Picayune:* "Amusements seldom prove attractive here unless music is brought to the aid of other inducements to spend money. So much is this the custom and so well is this understood, that even an auctioneer can scarcely ra[lly] a crowd without the aid of the man with the drum. We do not feel called upon personally to be responsible for the character of all the music, but it is a solemn fact, that to rise in the world it is necessary to make a big noise."[76] The range of lewd pleasures on offer were as standard to the trade as greasing black bodies to create an enhanced and youthful appearance. This spectacle reconciled the self-evident truths of a liberal social order—liberty, equality, and property—with the existence of racial slavery through the coerced enactment of indifference and the orchestration of diversions. As L. M. Mills stated, "When a negro was put on the block he had to help sell himself by telling what he could do. If he refused to sell himself and acted sullen, he was sure to be stripped and given thirty lashes."[77] By the same token, these displays of excess enjoyment seemed to suggest that the same natural law that established the liberty of all men also authorized slavery, since the natural inclination of the enslaved was good cheer and they seemingly endured horrendous circumstances with ease.

Counterpoised to the intensity of this laughter were the lamentations of the enslaved. Dave Bryd recalled that "when one of them buyers bought a slave you never did hear such bawling and hollering in your life that would take place because they did not want to leave each other [and] probably would not see them again."[78] The shame and humiliation experienced in being paraded and sold like cattle at the market, in addition to being disrobed publicly, provide a stark contrast to the festive goings-on of the traders. Ethel Dougherty noted that at the sales, women were forced to stand half-naked for hours while crowds of rough-drinking men bargained for them, examining their teeth, heads, hands, and other parts at frequent intervals to test their endurance.[79] According to Edward Lycurgas, enslaved women "always looked so shame[d] and pitiful up on dat stand wid all dem men standin' dere lookin' at em wid what dey had on dey minds shinin' in they eyes."[80] Shining in their eyes and expressed in "indecent proposals" and "disgusting questions" was the power, acquired and enjoyed by the owner, to use slave women as he pleased.[81] Millie Simpkins stated that before they were sold, they had to take all their clothes off, although she refused to take hers off, and roll around to prove that they were physically fit and without broken bones or sores.[82] Usually any reluctance or refusal to disrobe was met with the whip.[83] When Mattie Gilmore's sister Rachel was sold, she was made to pull off her clothes. Mattie remembered crying until she could cry no more, although her tears were useless.[84]

The simulation of consent in the context of extreme domination was aimed at making the captive body speak the master's truth and intent on disproving the misery of the enslaved. A key aspect of the manifold uses of the body was its facility as a weapon used against the enslaved. It can only be likened to torture, which, as noted by Elaine Scarry, destroys the integral relation of body and belief.[85] Here, I would like to underline the disarticulation of body and belief, without presupposing an a priori integral relation, by exploring the denotative capacities of the captive body. In *Slave Life in Georgia*, John Brown, in his as-told-to narrative, addresses this chasm between truth and the body by elaborating the role of violence and ventriloquy in enhancing slave value. In order to disenchant the simulated revelry of the trade, he painstakingly described the New Orleans slave pen in which he was held:

> The slaves are brought from all parts, are of all sorts, sizes, and ages, and arrive in various states of fatigue and condition; but they soon improve in their looks, as they are regularly fed, and have plenty to eat. As soon as we were roused in the morning, there was a general washing, and combing, and shaving, pulling out of grey hairs, and dyeing the hair of those who were too grey to be plucked without making them bald. When this was over—and it was no light business—we used to breakfast, getting bread, and bacon, and coffee, of which a sufficiency was given to us, and that we might plump up and become sleek. Bob would then proceed to instruct us how to show ourselves off. . . . The buying commenced at about ten in the morning, and lasted till one, during which time we were obliged to be sitting in our respective companies, ready for inspection. . . . After dinner we were compelled to walk, and dance, and kick about in the yard for exercise; and Bob, who had a fiddle, used to play up jigs for us to dance to. If we did not dance to his fiddle, we used to have to do so to his whip, so no wonder we used our legs handsomely, though the music was none of the best. . . .
>
> As the importance of "looking bright" under such circumstances may not be readily understood by the ordinary run of readers, I may as well explain that the price a slave fetches depends, in great measure, upon the general appearance he or she presents to the intending buyer. A man or woman may be well made, and physically faultless in every respect, yet their value be impaired by a sour look, or dull, vacant stare, or a general dullness of demeanor. For this reason the poor wretches who are about to be sold, are instructed to look

"spry and smart": to hold themselves up, and put on a smiling, cheerful countenance.

When spoken to, they must reply quickly, with a smile on their lips, though agony is in their heart, and the tear trembling in their eye. They must answer every question, and do as they are bid, to show themselves off; dance, jump, walk, leap, squat, tumble, and twist about, that the buyer may see they have no stiff joints, or other physical defect. . . . Not a word of lamentation or anguish must escape from them; nor when the deed is consummated, dare they bid one another good-bye, or take one last embrace.[86]

An entire chapter of the narrative is dedicated to detailing the activities of the slave pen. For the most part, this enormous effort is expended in demystifying the ruses of the trade, attuning the reader to the difference between the apparent and the actual, narrating the repression of the "real" that occurs by way of this costuming of the contented slaves—hair dyed, faces greased, preening, primping, smiling, dancing, tumbling. By now what is familiar in Brown's account is the use of the body against the captive to enhance the value of the commodity and deny anguish. This conspiracy of appearances acts to repudiate the claims of pain. Brown challenges the legitimacy of slavery, particularly as it is grounded in such compulsory displays of good cheer; each detail of the chapter counters the "disposition for slavery" argument and anxiously unmasks the captive's pleasure as the trade's artifice.

Slave Life in Georgia "dare[d] not—for decency's sake—detail the various expedients that are resorted to by dealers to test the soundness of a male or female slave." Soundness was a shorthand for male and female captives as incubators and breeders; as implements of pleasure, they were to be tested in a similar manner. There were no limits to what the marketplace encouraged and permitted. Brown preferred to settle for understatement and indirection in outlining the "horrible picture" of those who lived intimately the extraction and sale of their capacities. The WPA testimony is replete with the details of these tests for soundness. As one former slave recounted, the woman displayed on the block "would have just a piece around her waist; her breast and thighs would be bare. De seller would turn her around and plump her to show how fat she was and her general condition. Dey would also take her breasts and pull dem to show how good she was built for raisin' chillun."[87] The sexual dimensions of the enjoyment of slave property were expressed in regard to issues of breeding and in the prices fetched for "fancy girls."[88]

The sale of Sukie, as recounted by Fannie Berry, a fellow slave, illuminates the sexual dimensions of possession. On the auction block, Sukie calls attention to the gaze—the power exercised in looking that opens the captive body to the desires and pecuniary interests of would-be owners. By defying the studied nicety of the trade, Sukie underscores the violence of the spectacle, issuing a threat of her own to those so intent on looking and probing. As Fannie Berry tells it:

> Sukie was her name. She was a big strappin nigger gal dat never had nothin' to say much. She used to cook for Miss Sarah Ann, but ole Marsa was always tryin' to make Sukie his gal. One day Sukie was in the kitchen making soap. Had three gra' big pots o' lye just comin' to a bile in de fireplace when ole Marsa come in for to git arter her 'bout somep'n. He lay into her, but she ain't never answer him a word. Den he tell Sukie to take off her dress. She tole him no. Den he grabbed her an' pulled it down off'n her shoulders. When he done dat, he fo'got 'bout whippin' her, I guess cause he grab hold of her an' try to pull her down on de flo.' Den dat black girl got mad. She took an push ole Marsa an' made him break loose an' den she gave

him a shove an' push his hind parts down in de hot pot o' soap. Soap was near to boilin,' an it burnt him near to death. He got up holdin' his hind parts an' ran from the kitchen, not darin' to yell, 'cause he didn't want Miss Sarah to know 'bout it.

Well, few days later he took Sukie off an' sol' her to de nigger trader. An' dey 'zamined her an' pinched her an' den dey opened her mouf, an' stuck dey fingers in to see how her teeth was. Den Sukie got awful mad, and she pult up her dress an' tole de nigger traders to look an' see if dey could find any teef down dere.[89]

The assault that led to Sukie's sale and the event staged on the auction block raise a number of issues critical to the scene of subjection: will, agency, submission, and consent. The master's attempted rape is framed as seduction, as "trying to make Sukie his gal," which documents the conflation of rape and concubinage in the sexual economy of slavery. Sukie's threatening striptease is an interdiction, a refusal, ironically issued as invitation, as I dare you. A related set of issues concerns the capacities of the performative in doing (as in making) and undoing the subject and the status of the enslaved as a curious hybrid of person and property.

In one respect, Sukie's performance can be understood as an arrogation of the will that undermines her social existence as an object of property. This dramatic seizure of the will figuratively expropriates the power of the (would-be) master to animate and annex the captive body. Sukie's actions place her outside the law because she defies the fundamental tenet of slavery: the slave is subject to the master's will in all things. This breach of law enacted in the insolence and disregard of the block's decorum, interestingly enough, provides the only possibility for the emergence of the subject, because criminality is the only form of slave agency recognized by law. The fashioning of the subject must necessarily take place in violation of the law, so that will, criminality, personhood, and punishment are inextricably linked. Sukie's performance exploits the charged nexus of possession and sexuality, challenges the willlessness or passivity of the object, and induces a category crisis for the spectators whose enjoyment is defined by the promiscuous uses of property.

This performance on the auction block defies the tricks of the trade and, by extension, the related practices that secure and reproduce the relations of mastery and servitude through a parodic enactment of the auction's devices. By staging this rebellion in the domain of sexuality, Sukie fills in the details of the "horrible picture" that dare not be spoken without the risk of breaching decency; she does so in service of contesting the uses of slave property. The subversive reiteration of the potential buyer's splaying of the body, specifically Sukie's gesture to the "teeth down there," makes plain the violence of the exhibition. It was common practice for bidders to feel between women's legs, examine their hips, and fondle their breasts.[90]

By contrast, Sukie's gesture to the teeth down there launched a threat and explicitly declared the dangers that awaited further probing and pulling. The *vagina dentata* and the threat of castrating genitals transpose the captive body in its dominated and ravaged condition into a vehicle to be used against the would-be slave owner, rather than in the service of his interests and appetites. This threat of castration echoes the foiled attempt of her former master, whose "hind parts" were also placed in jeopardy, and promises retaliation for those anticipating the sexual uses of property. By lifting her skirts, Sukie complies with the demand to expose herself and display her body to potential buyers, but she subverts this act of submission and compliance by alluding to the hazards that awaited the buyer or trader who would venture to "make her his gal." The gesture to the teeth down there calls attention to the obscene display of black bodies in the market and to the libidinal economy of slavery, sexual violence thrives at the intersection of enjoyment and terror. This revolt staged at the site of enjoyment and the nexus of production and reproduction exposes the violence of the trade's spectacle in what merits being called a deconstructive performance. In this instance the infamous propensity of the Negro for mimicry and imitation is tantamount to insurgency.

What is being staged in these varied renderings of the coffle and the auction block is nothing less than slavery itself, whether in the effort to mute the extreme violence that enabled this sale of flesh through the coerced performances of the enslaved or the clownish antics of the auctioneer, or reconcile subjugation and natural law, or document the repressive totality of the institution, or enact refusal, or undo the terms of debasement. An anxiety about enjoyment distinguishes the site of exchange. This can be seen in assurances to buyers about the contentment of the slaves on display and the intensity of abolitionist efforts to prove the commonplace—slaves were neither happy nor indifferent to being sold like cattle and separated from their families.[91] The fear that black suffering would remain unnoticed bespeaks abolitionist anxieties about the deficit of black grief and the surfeit and complicity of pleasure.

The Pleasant Path

The parade of shackled bodies to market captured not only the debasements of slavery but also its diversions. The convergence of pleasure and terror so striking in the humiliating exhibitions and defiling pageantry of the trade was also present in "innocent amusements." The slave dancing a reel at the big house or stepping it up lively in the coffle similarly transformed subjugation into a pleasing display for the master, albeit disguised, to use Pierre Bourdieu's term, by the "veil of enchanted relationships."[92] These "gentler forms" extended and maintained the relations of domination through euphemism and concealment. Innocent amusements constituted a form of symbolic violence—that is, a "form of domination which is exercised through the communication in which it is disguised."

When viewed in this light, the most invasive forms of slavery's violence lie not in these exhibitions of "extreme" suffering or in what we see, but in what we don't see. Shocking displays too easily obfuscate the more mundane and socially endurable forms of terror.[93] In the benign scenes of plantation life (which comprised much of the Southern and, ironically, abolitionist literature of slavery) reciprocity and recreation obscure the quotidian routine of violence. The bucolic scenes of plantation life and the innocent amusements of the enslaved, contrary to our expectations, succeeded not in lessening terror but in assuring and sustaining its presence.

Rather than glance at the most striking spectacle with revulsion or through tear-filled eyes, we do better to cast our glance at the more mundane displays of power and the border where it is difficult to discern domination from recreation. Bold instances of cruelty are too easily acknowledged and forgotten, and cries quieted to an endurable hum. By disassembling the "benign" scene, we confront the everyday practice of domination, the daily routine of terror, the nonevent, as it were. Is the scene of slaves dancing and fiddling for their masters any less inhumane than that of slaves sobbing and dancing on the auction block? If so, why? Is the effect of power any less prohibitive? Or coercive? Or does pleasure mitigate coercion? Is the boundary between terror and pleasure clearer in the market than in the quarters or at the "big house"? Are the most enduring forms of cruelty those seemingly benign? Is the perfect picture of the crime the one in which the crime goes undetected? If we imagine for a moment a dusky fiddler entertaining at the big house, master cutting a figure among the dancing slaves, the mistress egging him on with her laughter, what do we see?

"Dance you damned niggers, dance," Epps would shout. Usually his whip in his hand, ready to fall about the ears of the presumptuous thrall, who dared rest a moment, or even to stop to catch his breath. When he himself was exhausted, there would be a brief cessation, but it would be very brief. With a slash, crack and flourish of the whip, he would shout again, "Dance, niggers dance," and away they would go once more, pell-mell, while I, spurred by an occasional sharp touch of the lash, sat in a corner, extracting from my violin a marvelous quick stepping tune. . . . Frequently, we were thus detained until almost morning. Bent with excessive toil—actually suffering for a little refreshing rest, and feeling rather as if we would cast ourselves upon the earth and weep, many a night in the house of Edwin Epps have his unhappy slaves been made to dance and laugh.[94]

This passage from Solomon Northup's *Twelve Years a Slave* exemplifies the permeability of pleasure and punishment in the ceremonies of slavery. The humiliations delivered the conscripts of Master Epps's terrorizing bacchanals and the harsh command to merrymaking suggest that the theatricality of the Negro emerges only in the aftermath of the body's brutal dramatic placement—in short, after the body has been made subject to the will of the master.[95] The uproarious behavior of Epps, slashing limbs with his whip while gaily dancing a quick step with the slaves, casts a different light on the dusky fiddler in the golden days of Southern glory. And the spree, as narrated by Northup, resonates with the evil of twice-told tales about fiddlers abducted by Satan and the fiendish revels of hell.

Behind the facade of innocent amusements lay the violence the master class assiduously denied; but what else could jigs danced in command performances be but the gentle indices of domination? It was as much the duty of slaves "to devote themselves to the pleasure of their masters" as to work for the master's benefit, commented Jacob Stroyer.[96] He noted rather cryptically that "no one can describe the intense emotion in the negro's soul on these occasions when they were trying to please their masters and mistresses."[97] Such performances cast the slave as contented bondsman and elide the difference between volition and violation. However, as Northup's narrative indicated, the contented slave appeared only after she or he had been whipped into subjection. In short, Sambo did not design the stagecraft of slavery, as apologists would have it, but was one of its effects.

In the effort to cultivate docile and dutiful slaves, slaveholders promoted "natural gaiety" by "all allowable means." Innocent amusements were designed to promote gaiety by prudent means, ameliorate the harsh conditions of slavery, make the body more productive and tractable, and secure the submission of the enslaved by the successful harnessing of the body. In effect, plantation ceremony endeavored to make discipline a pleasure, and vice versa.[98] Innocent amusements supplemented other methods of managing the slave body. These ostensibly benevolent forms of management, according to Douglass, were designed to better secure "the ends of injustice and oppression."[99] In fact, such diversions were an important element of plantation management, as the internalization of discipline and reward was considered essential to the good order of the plantation, for the ideal model of plantation management stressed humanity and duty. Prizewinning essays on the tenets of management held that "industry and good conduct should be encouraged [and] the taste for innocent amusements gratified."[100] These designs for mastery troubled distinctions between leisure and labor and employed an extensive notion of discipline that included everything from the task system to the modes of singing allowed in the field. As one planter commented, "When at work, I have no objection to their whistling or singing some lively tune, but no drawling tunes are allowed in the field, for their motions are almost certain to keep time with the music."[101] It is clear that musical diversions enhanced productivity and were also a means of cultivating particular forms of conduct. In this case, power extended itself in the form of recreation.

By encouraging entertainment, the master class sought to cultivate hegemony, harness pleasure as a productive force, and regulate the modes of permitted expression. Slave owners managed amusements as they did labor, with a keen eye toward discipline. Promoting fun and frolic could alleviate unrest: "One South Carolina planter who was having trouble disciplining his slaves supplied his people with fiddle and drums and 'promoted dancing.' To his gratification the ill temper of the slaves disappeared and the peace was once more established on the plantation."[102] Nonetheless, the diversions the planter considered as placating ill temper created conflicts no less unsettling. When the enslaved were required to perform before the master and even when they eagerly partook of entertainment, such pleasures were tempered by their fettered condition and the ever-threatening exercise of the master's power.

Despite the forethought given to and the energy expended in orchestrating such diversions, proponents of these paternal forms of management nonetheless insisted that Africans' natural propensity for song did, in fact, reflect a disposition for servitude. A Georgia physician who fancied himself a physiologist of culture remarked that Negroes possessed a sixth sense—a musical sense—and that despite their kinship with hogs in nature and habit, the Negro has music in his soul. This physician described the enslaved as without regrets for the past or anxieties about the future and "full of fun and frolic," which were the standard assessments of black character shared by proslavery discourse and romantic racialism.[103] Whether this was the result of nature or condition was difficult for him to discern: "Our Southern negroes seem to have a natural gift for music, and such a thing as a non-singing negro is almost unknown. Now, whether this is peculiar to the negroes of the Southern states, and as a result of the happifying influences of slavery, we are not prepared to say; but certainly it does appear that music—and that, too, of a cheerful kind—would not be likely to become a passion, a very second nature, with a people so debased and downtrodden as Southern slaves are represented in certain quarters."[104] The physician therefore advised planters to encourage music because it added to the enjoyment and fitness of the slave. Put simply, music was the antidote to black sloth and torpidity.

In the June 1851 edition of *De Bow's Review*, a Mississippi planter recommended a management plan that he thought would contribute to the happiness of both master and slave. After offering suggestions regarding the arrangement of the quarters, meals, clothing, et cetera, he noted that he had "few sour looks and as little whipping" as was possible on a plantation of his size. Attributing the good-naturedness of his slaves to more than adequate care, he confessed that in addition to providing for the basic needs of his slaves, he literally "fiddled" them into contented submission: "I must not omit to mention that I have a good fiddler, and keep him well supplied with catgut, and I make it his duty to play for the negroes every Saturday night until 12 o'clock. They are exceedingly punctual in their attendance at the ball, while Charley's fiddle is always accompanied with Ihurod on the triangle, and Sam to 'pat' [patting juba]."[105] According to the planter, the whip used sparingly, the fiddle, and the Bible formed the holy trinity of plantation management.

Even though "church brethren might think hard of it," a small-farm owner also confessed that he encouraged the playing of the fiddle in his quarters. He bought the fiddle and encouraged slaves to play it "by giving the boys [fiddlers] occasionally a big supper."[106] Plantation management plans clearly demonstrated that within the confines of the plantation and slaveholding society there were no "innocent" amusements. The hours from sundown to sunup were as important as those spent in the field in cultivating the productivity of the plantation household and maintaining social control. Slaveholders' managing of slave "leisure," surveillance of parties and dances, and financial investment in slave amusements (which were important enough for slave owners to provide fiddles for their slaves, teach them to play, and purchase enslaved musicians), document the value of pleasure. The testimony of the enslaved also confirms this emphasis on diversion. Adeline Jackson's master bought a slave just because he could fiddle: "Master Edward bought a slave in Tennessee just 'cause he could play de fiddle. Named him 'Tennessee Ike' and he played long wid Ben Murray, another fiddler. Sometime all of us would be called up into de front yard to play and sing and dance and sing for Miss Marion, de chillun and visitors."[107] Gary Stewart's owner taught his slaves to play the fiddle.[108] Henry Bland's owner furnished him with a fiddle, which he played at square dances, the chief form of entertainment on the plantation, and at weddings, frolics, and other special occasions.[109]

The master's role in these revels, whether as an observer, manager, or participant, is mentioned repeatedly in slave narratives. D. Davis's owner arranged Saturday frolics for the slaves where he filled the role of fiddler. Davis described the occasion as "going before the king": "Every person on de place, from de littlest child to de oldest man or woman, would clean deyselves up and put on dey best clothes for to 'go before de king.' Dat's what us called it. All would gather in back of de big house under de big oak trees and Marse Tom, he would come out with a fiddle under he arm . . . and set himself down in de chair what Uncle Joe done fetched for him. . . . Den Marse Tom, he start dat fiddle playin' right lively and all dem niggers would dance and have de best kind of frolic. Marse Tom, he get just as much fun oten de party as de niggers themselves."[110] The slave's good times were at the same time a performance for the slaveholder. To go before the king demonstrated the master's power and hinted at the affinities of pleasure and mortification—the day of judgment. With each step of the Virginia reel, domination was extended and reproduced, although on occasion, the reel was turned to contrary purposes.

It was not uncommon for slave owners to participate in the frolics they organized. They indulged the slaves with whiskey, sang and danced with them, served as musicians, and were frequently spectators. Slave owners loved to watch their slaves performing. Ed Shirley recalled that at Saturday dances "some old negro would play the banjoes while the young darkies would dance and sing. The white folks would set around and watch; and would sometimes join in and dance and sing."[111] Ann Thomas observed that the master's son played the music for slave frolics: "He played the fiddle and liked to see the slaves dance 'cutting the pigeon wing.'"[112] According to Marinda Jane Singleton, anyone who could dance and sing well was taken to the big house to entertain the master's guests.[113] These performances pleased not only because of the abilities of those who performed but also because they served to display the owner's power and property. The captive body was an extension of the imperial body of the master and the prized object of his enjoyment. The master's gaze served as a reminder that diversion could not be extricated from discipline or domination. In this regard, the owner's pleasure in looking was without question a form of surveillance and a way of policing the slave population.

Essays in *De Bow's Review*, *Southern Planter*, and other agricultural journals unanimously concurred on the importance of docile and contented slaves to the successful management of the farm or plantation. These essays enumerated the responsibilities of slaveholders and methods for promoting slave productivity. Plantation journals, espousing paternalism and anxious about the image of the institution of slavery, particularly in light of mounting opposition to slavery, not surprisingly were much more forthright about the use of rewards and recreation rather than violence to achieve submission. The kindly master cognizant of his duty to slaves need not make recourse to the whipping post but instead fostered docility via the pleasant path. Herbemont opined that guiding the pleasures of the slave was a task equivalent to the sovereign's direction of his subjects. Attending to the recreation of slaves was for their general good and therefore not beneath the dignity of the master, since the path of pleasantness was "much more likely to be followed willingly" than the path covered with thorns and briars.[114]

Yet when the less thorny road was pursued, the enslaved had little difficulty discerning in "beneficial recreations" another form of coercion. Eda Harper described her owner's promotion of song as malevolent: "My old master mean to us. He used to come to the quarters and make us chillum sing. He make us sing Dixie. Seems like Dixie his main song. I tell you I don't like it now. But have mercy! He make us sing it."[115] The ironies of the pleasant path are highlighted in Harper's case. Forcing the enslaved to sing "Dixie," a tune from the minstrel stage adopted for the cause of Confederate nationalism, discloses the collusion of coercion and recreation. "The adoption of 'Dixie' as the emblematic Confederate song underlined the emotional centrality of these pseudo slave performances as affirmations of the Confederate national mission and the master-class's cherished self-image of benevolent paternalism," writes Drew Gilpin Faust.[116] The self-representation of the slaveholding South depended upon such performances of blackness. Conceivably, this explains why minstrelsy reached its zenith in the South during the Civil War.

Despite the general consensus regarding the efficacy of slave amusements, slaveholders' discussions of "slave culture" were tautological and fraught with contradictory assertions about nature and culture. On one hand, slave culture or, more aptly, managed amusements, demonstrated the inferior and slavish nature of the

African. Moreover, this "sixth sense" ill-equipped blacks for free-dom. On the other, the necessity of encouraging forms of benefi-cial recreations revealed planter anxiety about restlessness, if not rebellion. After all, if the slave was naturally predisposed to song, why the need to dictate merrymaking? At whatever cost, nature and condition were to be made compatible, and innocent amusements, in concert with combined forms of torture, punishment, and disci-pline, were to affect this union. Indeed, the slave would be made to appear as if born to dance in chains.

Fraught Pleasures

The slaveholder's instrumental use of entertainment was duly criti-cized by abolitionists. Douglass, at the forefront of such criticism, argued that the abjection of slave amusements "appeared to have no other object than to disgust the slaves with their temporary free-dom, and make them as glad to return to work as they had been to leave it."[117] Although he was speaking specifically of the holiday period between Christmas and New Year's, his condemnation of these diversions for cultivating submission and debasement is no less relevant to the routine amusements addressed above.[118] His criticisms were not unlike those of Henry Bibb and others. Abo-litionists emphasized the degraded character of these celebrations and stressed the confluence of brutality and merrymaking in such activities. Bibb held slaveholders responsible for prompting demean-ing sport: "When they wish to have a little sport of that kind, they go among the slaves, to see them dance, 'pat juber,' sing and play on banjo."[119] If slaves, unfortunately, participated in these debased amusements, their condition, not their nature, was to blame. Theo-dore Parker was less certain in this regard: "If the African be so low that the condition of slavery is tolerable in his eyes and he can dance in chains, then it is all the more a sin in the cultivated and strong, in the Christian, to tyrannize over the feeble and defenseless."[120] The permeable, shifting, and elusive boundary between instrumental amusements and the expressive culture of the enslaved was troubled and unsettling. For those like Parker, the ability of Africans to dance at all was unfathomable.

Douglass's searing criticism of these amusements concentrated on their function as "safety-valves to carry off the explosive elements inseparable from the human mind when reduced to the condition of slavery," and apparent in this condemnation is the longing for a culture of resistance.[121] In order to disentangle longing and disapprobation, Douglass's searing observations regarding slave holidays need to be considered alongside his commentary on slave song. For the most part, his objections to these holidays pertain to the derailing of "dangerous thought" by diversion. In other words, instrumental pleasures thwart the emergence of an oppositional consciousness: "To enslave men successfully and safely it is necessary to keep their minds occupied with thoughts and aspirations short of the liberty of which they are deprived. . . . These holidays served the purpose of keeping the minds of the slaves occupied with prospective pleasures within the limits of slavery. . . . A certain degree of attainable good must be kept before them. . . . But for these the rigors of slavery would have been forced to a dangerous desperation. . . . Not the slave's happiness but the master's safety was the end sought."[122] What Douglass yearns for is dangerous music and dangerous thought. The relentlessness of the critique and its broad strokes are intent upon destroying the discourse on servility and contentment that licensed the institution. Yet, even in the context of this eviscerating analysis of the pleasures afforded within the confines of slavery, Douglass manages to catch hold of glimmerings of opposition—in this case "the sharp hits against slaveholders" in "jubilee patting."

This search for an oppositional culture, or a symbolic analogue of Douglass's physical confrontation with Covey, the overseer and "nigger breaker," alights on slave song:

> They would sing...words which to many would seem unmeaning jargon, but which nevertheless, were full of meaning to themselves. I have sometimes thought that the mere hearing of these songs would do more to impress some minds with the horrible character of slavery, than the reading of whole volumes of philosophy on the subject could do. I did not when a slave, understand the deep meaning of those rude and apparently incoherent songs. I was myself within the circle; so that I neither saw nor heard as those without might see and hear. They told a tale of woe which was then altogether beyond my feeble comprehension; they were tones loud, long and deep; they breathed the prayer and complaint of souls boiling over with the bitterest anguish. Every tone was a testimony against slavery, and a prayer to God for deliverance from chains. The hearing of those wild notes always depressed my spirit, and filled me with ineffable sadness. I have frequently found myself in tears while hearing them. . . . To those songs I trace my first glimmering conception of the dehumanizing character of slavery.[123]

Yet these songs insufficiently meet the requirements of an oppositional culture, one capable of combating ostensibly beneficial diversions and poised to destroy these designs for mastery. While every tone testifies against slavery, sorrow rather than resistance characterizes such songs; as well, they are emblems of the "soul-killing effects of slavery." The mere hearing of these songs impresses one with the horrible character of slavery. The songs are valued as dirges expressive of the social death of slavery and inchoate expressions of a latent political consciousness. In this regard, they belie popular portraits of happiness and contentment. The opacity of these sorrowful and half-articulate songs perplexes and baffles those within and without the circle of slavery. When a slave, Douglass was unable to see and hear as those without might have, yet those without too often misinterpreted these songs as evidence of satisfaction. Anticipating Du Bois's assessment of the sorrow songs as "the music of an unhappy people, of the children of disappointment; they tell of death and suffering and unvoiced longing toward a truer world, of mist wanderings and hidden way," Douglass emphasized the singularity of sorrow, hoping to establish an absolute line of division between diversion and the awakening of protest.[124] This distinction could not be sustained, for the promiscuous exchanges of culture and the fraught terms of agency muddled the lines of opposition, and as Douglass himself recognized, on rare occasions the pleasures available within the confines of slavery indeed possessed glimmerings of insurgency and transformation.

ON BEING THE OBJECT OF PROPERTY

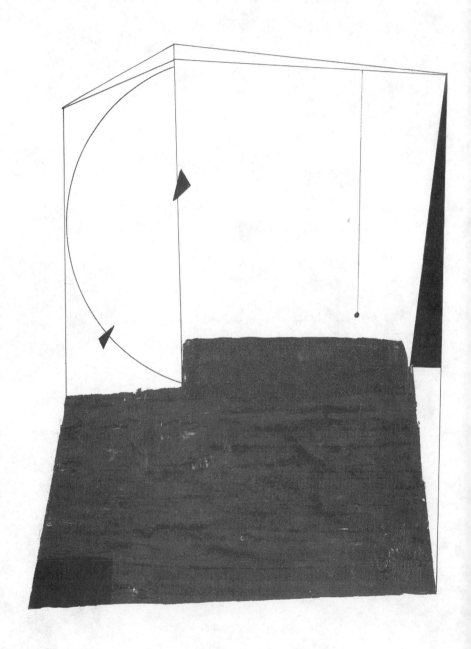

places that exist because we remember and imagine

2

Redressing the Pained Body

TOWARD A THEORY OF PRACTICE

> History is what hurts, it is what refuses desire and sets inexorable limits to individual as well as collective praxis, which its "ruses" turn into grisly and ironic reversals of their overt intention.
>
> —Fredric Jameson, *The Political Unconscious*

Lu Lee's owner encouraged the enslaved to have Saturday night dances, even though he was a religious man and thought it wrong to dance. Lee remembered him saying, "Seek your enjoyment, niggers got to pleasure themselves someway." The promotion of harmless pleasures was a central strategy in the slave owner's effort to cultivate contented subjection. Yet the complicity of pleasure with the instrumental ends of slaveholder domination led those like Mary Glover to declare emphatically, "I don't want [that] kind of pleasure." The response of the enslaved to the management and orchestration of "Negro enjoyment," on the whole, was more complex than a simple rejection of "innocent amusements." Rather, the sense of operating within and against the master's designs made the experience of pleasure decidedly ambivalent. If "good times," or amusements intended to placate and distract, were a scheme for the owner's profit and dominion, what possibilities could pleasure yield? For those like John McAdams, pleasure was less a general form of dominance than a way of naming, by contradistinction, the consumption and possession of the body and black needs and pos-sibilities. It was more than a tendency for understatement that led McAdams to characterize his experience and that of other slaves as "no pleasure, as we had to work just as soon as [we] got large enough to work."[1]

The contrast between labor and pleasure was tentative and unsustainable. The ambivalence of pleasure was to be explained by the yoking the captive body to the ambitions, whims, fanta-sies, and exploits of the owner and by the constancy of the slave's unmet yearnings, whether for food or for freedom. Yet McAdams's remarks also suggest that "lack" insufficiently describes the vexed state of pleasure, since the enslaved also lived for Saturday night dances. The opportunity to gather and assemble was valued above all else, and having a good time facilitated collective identification: "We made good use of these nights as that was all the time the slaves had together to dance, talk, and have a good time among their own color."[2] Pleasure was ensnared in a web of domination, abjection, resignation, and possibility. It was nothing if not cunning, mercurial, treacherous, and indifferently complicit with quite divergent desires and aspirations, ranging from the instrumental aims of slave-owner designs for mastery to the promise and possibility of releasing the body from constraint and redressing the pain of captivity.

The struggles waged against domination and enslavement in everyday life took a variety of forms, including opportunities seized in the domain of permissible and regulated amusements. If these occasions were designed, as Frederick Douglass argued, to "bet-ter secure the ends of injustice and oppression," they also provided a context in which power was challenged and claims made in the name of pleasure, need, want, and desire.[3] Pleasure was fraught with these contending investments. As Toby Jones noted, the Satur-day night dances permitted by the master were refashioned and used for their own ends by the enslaved: "The fun was on Saturday night when massa 'lowed us to dance. There was a lot of banjo pickin' and tin pan beatin' and dancin' and everybody talk bout when they lived in Africa and done what they wanted."[4] Within the confines of surveillance and nonautonomy, the resistance to subjugation proceeded by stealth: one acted furtively, secretly, and imperceptibly, and the enslaved seized any and every opportunity to slip off the yoke.

In these pages, I outline the clandestine forms of resistance, popular illegalities, and "war of position" conducted under the cover of fun and frolic. I do not mean to suggest that everyday practices were strategies of passive revolution but merely to emphasize that peregrinations, surreptitious appropriation, assembly, and moving about were central features of resistance or what could be described as the subterranean "politics" of the enslaved or as ways of doing and making recalcitrant to the values of the world made by slavery. With this in mind, I endeavor to illuminate the social struggle waged in "the Negro's enjoyment" and the challenges to domination launched under the rubric of pleasure. In order to do this, we must, first, situate performance within the context of everyday practices and consider the possibilities of practice in regard to specific forms of domination; second, defamiliarize fun and frolic or the performance of blackness to make visible the challenges that emerge in this arena; and, third, liberate the performative from the closures of sentiment and contented subjection to engage the critical labor of redress.[5]

The Centrality of Practice

Exploiting the limits of the permissible and creating transient zones of freedom were central features of everyday practice. Practice is, to use Michel de Certeau's phrase, "a way of operating" defined by "the non-autonomy of its field of action," internal manipulations of the established order, and ephemeral victories. The tactics that comprise the everyday practices of the dominated have neither the means to secure a territory outside the space of domination nor the power to keep or maintain what is won in surreptitious and necessarily incomplete victories.[6] The refashioning of permitted pleasures in the effort to undermine and redress the condition of enslavement was consonant with other forms of everyday practice. These efforts generally focused on the object status and chastened personhood of the slave, the depleted and ravished body, severed affiliations and natal alienation, and the assertion of denied needs. These practices sought to achieve the impossible: to reanimate the dead, to tend to the object of property as human flesh, to care for the exhausted and the damaged, to call the names of those gone, to repair the bruised and the shattered, to announce collectively we are the chosen, to plot and to study, to dream freedom. Practice is not simply a way of naming these efforts, but, as well, a way of thinking about the character of resistance, the precariousness of the assaults waged against domination, the fragmentary character of these efforts and the transient battles won, and the characteristics of a politics without a proper locus.

The everyday practices of the enslaved encompassed an array of tactics, such as work slowdowns, feigned illness, unlicensed travel, the destruction of property, theft, self-mutilation, dissimulation, physical confrontation with owners and overseers, that document the resistance to slavery.[7] These small-scale and everyday forms of resistance interrupted and defied the constraints of everyday life under slavery and exploited openings in the system for the use of the enslaved. What unites these varied tactics is the effort to redress the condition of the enslaved, restore the disrupted affiliations of the socially dead, challenge the authority and dominion of the slaveholder, and alleviate the pained state of the captive body. However, these acts of redress are undertaken with the acknowledgment that conditions will most likely remain the same. This acknowledgment implies neither resignation nor fatalism, but a recognition of the enormity of the breach instituted by slavery and the magnitude of domination.

Redressing the pained body encompasses operating in and against the demands of the system, negotiating the disciplinary harnessing of the body, and counterinvesting in the body as a site of possibility. Pain must be recognized in its historicity and as the articulation of a social condition of brutal constraint, extreme need, and constant violence; it is the perpetual state of managed depletion, of broken bodies and shattered persons, of soul murder and kinlessness. It is the embodied experience of stolen life and social death. Pain is a normative condition that encompasses the legal subjectivity of the enslaved, which is constructed along the lines of injury and punishment, the violation and suffering inextricably enmeshed with the pleasures of minstrelsy and melodrama, the operation of power on black bodies, and the life of property in which the full enjoyment of the slave as thing supersedes the admittedly tentative recognition of slave humanity and permits the intemperate uses of chattel. This pain might best be described as the history that hurts—the still-unfolding narrative of captivity and dispossession that engenders the black subject in the Americas.

If this pain has been largely unspoken and unrecognized, it is due to the sheer denial of black sentience rather than the inexpressibility of pain. The purported immunity of blacks to pain is absolutely essential to the spectacle of contented subjection or, at the very least, to discrediting the claims of pain.[8] The black is both insensate and content, indifferent to pain and induced to work by threats of corporal punishment. These contradictions are explained in part by the ambiguous and precarious status of the black in the "great chain of being," by pathologizing the black body, and this aberrant condition then serves to justify acts of violence that exceed normative standards of the humanely tolerable, though within the limits of the socially tolerable as concerned the black slave. Pain is essential to the making of productive slave laborers. The sheer enormity of this pain overwhelms or exceeds the limited forms of redress available to the enslaved. In light of this, the significance of the performative lies not in the ability to overcome this condition or provide remedy but in creating a context for the collective enunciation of this pain, transforming need into politics and cultivating pleasure as a limited response to need and a desperately insufficient form of redress.

The Closures of Sentiment

It is impossible to imagine the enslaved outside a set of associations in which the captive dancing in literal or figurative chains, on the deck of a ship, on the way to the marketplace, on the auction block or before the master does not figure prominently. This indelible image of a prostrate yet perky Sambo conjures up an idealized and fetishized state of servitude, in which the imputed consciousness of the enslaved ensures submission and docility more effectively than either the whip or the chain. The figure reconciles infantilized willfulness with the abject status of the will-less object. Not only is this image paradigmatic, it is also so pervasive and repressive that it makes claims about the performative as a practice of resistance and redress quite tentative. For the "Pompey" of the missionary report somnambulantly reciting the catechism, the Jim Crow of the minstrel stage, and the contented slave singing for the master or dancing on the auction block conspire to eradicate the social experience of enslavement—its terror, suffering, captivity, exchange, objectification, and predation, to name just a few of the significant features in a possibly endless litany of violence—precisely as they appear to give voice to the slave. In the case of these anointed agents of the enslaved, the counterfeit effectively annuls any possibility of redress or resistance.

Is it possible to consider, let alone imagine, the agency of the performative when the black performative is inextricably linked with the specter of contented subjection, obscene display, and the violation and abuse of the body that is the condition of the other's pleasure? As well, how does one explicate the conditions of slave agency when the very expression seems little more than an oxymoron that restates the unyielding paradox of the object status and dire subject constitution of the enslaved? How is it possible to think agency when the slave's very condition of being or existence is defined as a state of determinate negation or social death? What are the constituents of agency when personhood is refigured in the fetishized and fungible terms of object of property?

Generally, the representation of the performative has been inscribed in a framework of consensual and voluntarist agency that reinforces and romanticizes social hierarchy. The pastoral has been the dominant mode of this discourse. In the social landscape of the pastoral, slavery is depicted as an "organic relationship" so totalizing that neither master nor slave could express "the simplest human feelings without reference to the other." The master and the slave are seen as peacefully coexisting, or, at the very least, enjoying a relationship of paternalistic dependency and reciprocity. Notions of paternalism and hegemony minimize the extremity of domination with assertions about the mutually recognized humanity of master and slave. Even the regime of production becomes naturalized as "the rhythms of work," as if slave labor were merely another extension of blacks' capacity for song and dance. The lure of the pastoral is in reconciling sentiment with the brute force of racial slavery. As a result, the brutality and antagonisms of the chattel condition are obscured in favor of an enchanting reciprocity. The pastoral renders the state of domination as an ideal of care, duty, familial obligation, gratitude, and humanity. The ruthless use of bonded labor and the extraction of profit are imagined as the consensual and rational exchange between owner and slave. This is accomplished by representing direct and primary forms of domination as coercive and consensual—in short, by representing slavery as a hegemonic social relation.

This repressive problematic of consent frames everyday practices in terms of mutual obligation and reciprocity between owners and the enslaved. In so doing, it stages the agency of the enslaved as a form of willed self-immolation in that what is "consented" to is a state of subjugation of the most extreme order. In this regard, the representations of slave agency have intensified the effects of subjection and dispossession in the guise of will and denied the abject and ambivalent personhood of the captive in the facile and spurious attempt to incorporate the slave into the ethereal realms of the normative subject through demonstrations of his consent and/or autonomy. But this tentative, hollowed-out figure collapses under scrutiny. Certainly, the notion of the autonomous self endowed with free will is inadequate and, more important, inappropriate to thinking through the issue of slave agency. The self-possessed subject with his inalienable attributes is quite unthinkable or unimaginable in this case. Nevertheless, by emphasizing complementarity, reciprocity, and shared values, this hegemonic or consensual model of slave relations neutralizes the dilemma of the object status and pained subject constitution of the enslaved and obscures the violence of slavery.[9] What do reciprocity, mutuality, and the recognition of the captive's humanity mean in the context of slavery? In other words, who is protected by such notions—the master or the slave?

This vision of mutuality and organic order finds expression in the pastoral.[10] As a mode of historical representation, the pastoral seizes upon the strains of song and story, invariably a part of slave life, as precious components in the depiction of the moral landscape of slavery and gives voice to the values of the social order in the appropriately simple and dulcet tones of the enslaved. Song, dance, and story become the emblems of an integral moral economy. The grotesque speaking of "de bes' story" is the sentimental disguise of domination. The reverential status of the slave's voice, and more generally his or her agency, effectively links the exercise of will and contented subjection. The nonsense orthography provides the illusion of direct testimony and authenticity, which only serves to (re)produce the master's text, even if costumed in the rags of the slave.[11] (This mode is dominant in much of the historiography of slavery and in the slave testimony collected by the Works Progress Administration and underlines the difficulty of representing the experience of the enslaved, even when one has access to "firsthand" accounts. The politics, interests, psychic investments, and relations of power that condition such representations must be taken into account, even as one tries to read this testimony against the grain; the pastoral as mode of inquiry and a frame of interpretation represses the relations of domination that make this knowledge of the past possible.)[12]

Within the enclosures of the avowedly total and reciprocal relations of master and slave in which the simplest expression of human feelings is impossible without reference to the other, the fetish or artifice of the slave's consent and agency weds the exercise of will with contented subjection.[13] Not surprisingly, song and dance and a range of everyday acts, seemingly self-directed but actually regulated and directed by the owner, are the privileged expressions of this consenting agency. The paternal endowments of will, voice, and humanity deny the necessary violence of racial slavery. The performative is rendered as little more than scenes of revelry and good times that lighten the burden of slavery, and bonded labor represented as an extension of leisure. Servitude acquires a festive and celebratory character.[14] Most often these practices, when not envisioned as concessions of slaveholders designed to "win over" or to debase the enslaved, have been rendered through the idyllic lens of the pastoral, in which the "off times"—not bondage and coerced labor—define slave life.[15] Certainly Douglass was aware of this double bind; it was responsible for the anxiety that accompanied his discussion of slave recreations. He negotiated it by identifying holiday amusements with abasement and stressing the importance of interpretation and contextual analysis in uncovering the critical elements or "implicit social consciousness" of slave culture.

The Character of Practice

How might we reconsider the performative to illuminate the social relations of slavery and the daily practices of resistance that traverse these relations; or represent the critical labor of these practices without reproducing the contented subject of the pastoral or the heroic actor of the romance of resistance? To render everyday practices with any complexity requires a disfigurement and denaturalization of this history of the subject as romance, even if it is a romance of resistance. This requires that we forgo simply celebrating slave agency and instead endeavor to scrutinize and investigate the forms, dispositions, and constraints of action and the disfigured and liminal status of the agents of such acts. In contrast to approaches that foreclose performance in the troubled frame of autonomy, arrogating to the enslaved the illusory privileges of the bourgeois subject or self-possessed individual, or invoke it as evidence of the harmonious order of slaveholder hegemony and the slave's consent to that order, or as a reprieve from the terror of racial slavery, I engage performance and other modes of practice as they are determined by and exceed the constraints of domination.

How do the forms, relations, and institutions of power condition the exercise of agency? The particular status of the slave as object and as subject requires a careful consideration of the notion of agency if one wants to do more than "endow" the enslaved with agency as some sort of gift dispensed by historians and critics to the dispossessed. The constraints of agency are great in this situation, and it is difficult to imagine a way in which the interpellation of the slave as subject enables forms of agency that do not reinscribe the terms of subjection. Although it has become commonplace in Foucauldian approaches to power relations to conceptualize agency as an enabling constraint or an enabling violation, the problem with this approach is that it assumes that all forms of power are normatively equivalent, without distinguishing between violence, domination, force, legitimation, hegemony, et cetera.[16] Slavery is characterized by direct and simple forms of domination, brutal asymmetry of power, regular exercise of violence, and denial of liberty that make it difficult, if not impossible, to direct one's own conduct, let alone the conduct of others. As Foucault remarks, "There cannot be relations of power [as opposed to domination] unless subjects are free. If one were completely at the disposition of the other and became his thing, an object on which he can exercise an infinite and unlimited violence, there would not be relations of power. In order to exercise a relation of power, there must be on both sides at least a certain form of liberty."[17] Certainly this account of power challenges facile assertions of slave agency and casts doubt on the capaciousness of transgression. In a state of extreme domination, the operations of power appear more repressive than productive and are directed toward the mortification of the self rather than its cultivation, and the attendant forms of subjection seem intent upon preventing the captive from gaining any measure of agency that is not met with punishment. The slave exists as the object of violence, as property in the flesh.

The question remains as to what exercise of the will, forms of action, or enactment of possibility is available to animate chattel or the socially dead or the excluded ones who provide the very ground of man's liberty.[18] The double bind, simply stated, is: How does one account for the state of extreme domination and the possibilities seized in practice? How does one represent the various modes of practice without reducing them to conditions of domination or romanticizing them as pure forces of resistance? To complicate the picture further, how does one make any claims about the politics of performance without risking the absurd when discussing the resistances staged by an unauthorized dance in the face of the everyday workings of fear, subjugation, and violence? How does one calculate or measure such acts in the scope of slavery and its reasoned and routinized terror, its calibrations of subjectivity and pain, and the sheer incommensurability of the force that it deploys in response to the small challenges waged against it? Ultimately, the conditions of domination and subjugation determine what kinds of action are possible or effective, though these acts can be said to exceed the conditions of domination and are not reducible to them.

If the forms of power determine what kinds of practice are possible within a given field, what are the prospects for calculated action given that the very meaning of slave property is "being subject to the master's will in all things" and that issues of consent, will, intentionality, and action are utterly meaningless, except in the instance of "criminal" acts. Bearing this in mind, what possibilities for agency exist that don't put the enslaved at risk of a greater order of pain and punishment since the slave is a legal person only insofar as she is criminal and a violated body in need of limited forms of protection? The assignation of subject status and the recognition of humanity expose the enslaved to further violence in the case of criminal agency or require the event of excessive violence, cruelty beyond the limits of the socially tolerable, to acknowledge and protect the slave's person. Is it possible that such recognition effectively forecloses agency and that as subject the enslaved is still rendered without will or reinscribed as the object of punishment? Or is this limited conferral of humanity merely a reinscription of subjection and pained existence? Does the designation of "criminal" or "damaged property" intensify or alleviate the onus of anguished and liable person?

What I am trying to hint at here is the relation of agent and act—in particular, the anomalous status of the slave as subject and the circumscribed action characteristic of this condition. The cleavage or sundering of the slave as object of property, pained flesh, and unlawful agent situates the enslaved in an indefinite and paradoxical relation to the normative category "person." One must attend to this paradox in order to discern and evaluate the agency of the enslaved because the forms of action taken do not transcend this condition, but rather they are an index of the particular figurations of power and modes of subjection.

It is also important to remember that strategies of domination do not exhaust all possibilities of intervention, resistance, escape, refusal, or transformation. So what possibilities exist given these determinants, the myriad and infinitesimal ways in which agency is exercised, the disposition or probability of certain acts, and the mechanisms through which these "ways of operating" challenge and undermine the conditions of enslavement. Is the agency of the enslaved to be located in reiterative acts that undermine and discursively reelaborate the conditions of subjection and repression?[19] Is it founded upon the desire to negate constraint, to restage and remember the rupture that produced this state of social death, to exceed this determinate negation through acts of recollection, and/ or to attend to the needs and desires of the pained body?

Performing Blackness

The difficulties posed in rethinking the relation of performance and agency are related primarily to the pervasiveness of the spectacle of black contentment and abjection, the problematic of will and voluntarism, the punitive and burdened constitution of the slave as subject, and the extreme and violent enactments of power.[20] The dominant performance of blackness thwarts efforts to reassess agency because it has so masterfully simulated black "will" only to reanchor subordination. How does one discern "enabling conditions" when the very constitution of the subject renders him or her socially dead or subversively redeploy an identity determined by violent domination, dishonor, and natal alienation? In this case, does redemption rather than repetition become the privileged figure of the performative? How might it be possible to dislodge performance and performativity from these closures and reevaluate performance in terms of the claims made against power, the interruption and undermining of the regulatory norms of racial slavery, a way of operating under duress and constraint, and as an articulation of utopian and transformative impulses?

The import of the performative, as indicated by those like Toby Jones or John McAdams, is in the articulation of needs and desires that radically call into question the order of power and its production of "cultural intelligibility" or "docile and legible bodies."[21] Issues of redemption and redress are central to these practices, and the intended or anticipated effect of the performative is not only the reelaboration of blackness, but also its affirmative negation. It is important to remember that blackness is defined here in terms of social relational and structural position rather than identity; blackness incorporates subjects normatively defined as black, the relations among blacks, whites, and others, and the practices that produce racial difference. Blackness marks a social relationship of dominance and abjection, and potentially one of redress and emancipation; it is a contested figure at the very center of social struggle.[22]

"Performing blackness" conveys both the cross-purposes and the circulation of various modes of performance and performativity that concern the production of social meaning and subjectivity: the nexus of race, subjection, and spectacle, the forms of racial and race(d) pleasure, enactments of white dominance and power, and the reiteration and/or rearticulation of the conditions of enslavement. It is hoped that "performing blackness" is not too unwieldy and, at the same time, that this unruliness captures the scope and magnitude of the performative as a strategy of power and tactic of resistance. The interchangeable use of performance and performativity is intended to be inclusive of displays of power, the punitive and theatrical embodiment of racial norms, the discursive reelaboration of blackness, and the affirmative deployment and negation of blackness in the focus on redress. I have opted to use the term "performing blackness" as a way of illuminating the entanglements of dominant and subordinate enunciations of blackness and the difficulty of distinguishing between contending enactments of blackness based on form, authenticity, or even intention.

These performances are in no way the "possession" of the enslaved; they are enactments of social struggle and contending articulations of blackness. The unremitting and interminable process of revision, reelaboration, mimicry, and repetition prevents efforts to locate an originary or definitive point on the chain of associations that would fix the identity of a particular act or enable us to sift through authentic and derivative performances, as if the meaning of these acts could be separated from the effects they yield, the contexts in which they occur, or the desires that they catalyze, or as if instrumental amusements could be severed from the prospects of pleasure or the performative divorced from scenes of torture. These performances implicitly raise questions about the status of what is being performed—the power of whiteness or the black's good time, a nonsensical slave song, or recollections of dislocation.

The emphasis on blackness, subjection, and spectacle is intended
to denaturalize race and underline its givenness—the strategies
through which it is made to appear as if it has always existed,
thereby denying the coerced and cultivated production of race.
(This is particularly the case in the antebellum period, in which
race was made an absolute marker of status or condition, and being
black came to be identified with, if not identical to, the condition
of enslavement.) The "naturalization" of blackness as a particular
enactment of pained contentment or patient suffering requires an
extremity of force and violence to maintain this seeming "givenness." The "givenness" of blackness results from the brutal capture
and harnessing of the body, the extraction of its capacity, and the
fixation on its constituent parts as indexes of truth and racial meaning. The construction of black bodies as phobogenic objects (inciting
fear and the threat of dissolution, contamination, or engulfment)[23]
estranged in a corporeal malediction and the apparent biological
certainty of this malediction attest to the power of the performative to produce the very subject which it appears to express.[24] The
point here is that the body does not exist prior to the discourses and
practices that produce it as such. What is particular to the discursive constitution of blackness is the inescapable prison house of the
flesh or the indelible drop of blood—the purportedly intractable
and obdurate materiality of physiological difference.

Despite the effort to contextualize and engage blackness as
a production and performance, the sheer force of the utterance
"black" seems to assert a primacy, quiddity, or materiality that
exceeds the frame of this approach. The mention of this force is not
an initial step in the construction of a metaphysics of blackness or
an effort to locate an essence within these performances, but merely
an acknowledgment of the sheer weight of a history of terror that
is palpable in the very utterance "black" and inseparable from the
tortured body of the enslaved. It acts as a reminder of the material

effects of power on bodies and as an injunction to remember that the performance of blackness is inseparable from the brute force that brands, rapes, and tears open the flesh in the racial inscription of the body. The seeming obstinacy or the "givenness" of "blackness" registers the "fixing" of the body by terror and domination and the way that fixing or arrest has been constitutive.

If, as I have argued, the dominant performances of blackness are about the spectacle of mastery and the enactment of a willed subjection, then can the instances in which the dominant is used, manipulated, remade, and challenged be read as disruptive or refigured articulations of blackness? What other modes are possible? Are there stylistic markers that distinguish the differential articulations of "blackness"? Are the performances considered here at all concerned with creating the sense of a coherent black identity? Or are the articulations of blackness primarily concerned with and inseparable from the desire for a cessation of the given, freedom, redress, and restored affiliations? Put differently, how are Saturday night dances articulations or reelaborations of racial meaning? Or do such performances only inadvertently give meaning or form to blackness? If blackness is reelaborated, then how, in what terms, and by what means? If the condition of bondage is by definition a racial and class ascription, then is any effort to address, critique, or undermine racial dominance and enslavement necessarily a performance of blackness? How is the object transformed and refigured in practice?

If blackness is produced through specific means of making use of the body, it is important to consider this "acting on the body" not only in terms of the ways in which power makes use of the body, but also in terms of the possibilities of the flesh. Pleasure is central to the mechanisms of identification and recognition that discredit the claims of pain; yet it is critical to a sense of possibility—redress, emancipation, transformation, and affiliation under the pressure of domination and the utter lack of autonomy. Much attention has been given to the dominant mode of white enjoyment, but what about forms of pleasure that stand as figures of transformation or, at the very least, refigure blackness in terms other than abjection? Particular ways of making use of the body are diacritically marked in practice as "black" or as self-conscious forms of group pleasure: "having a good time among our own color," to quote McAdams. These acts become productions of blackness focused on particular patterns of movements, zones of erotic investment, forms of expression, and notions of pleasure. Blackness is produced as an "imaginary effect" by a counterinvestment in the body and the identification of a particular locus of pleasure, as in dances like the snake hips, the buzzard lope, and the funky butt. This counterinvestment in all likelihood entails a protest or rejection of the anatomo-politics that produces the black body as aberrant. More important, it is a way of attending to the pained constitution and corporeal malediction that is blackness.

Defamiliarizing the "Negro's Enjoyment"

The sense of black community expressed by "having a good time among our own color" depends upon acts of identification, restitution, creation, and remembrance. The networks of affiliation enacted in performance, sometimes referred to as the "community among ourselves," are defined not by the centrality of racial identity or the selfsameness or transparency of blackness or merely by the condition of enslavement, but by the connections forged in the context of disrupted affiliations, sociality amid the constant threat of separation, and shifting sets of relation particular to site, location, belief, and action. In other words, the "community" or the networks of affiliation constructed in practice are not reducible to race—as if race a priori gave meaning to community or as if community was the expression of race—but are to be understood in terms of the possibilities for making and doing conditioned by relations of power and the very purposeful aspiration to build community, to foster mutuality.

Despite the "warmly persuasive" and utopian quality that the word "community" possesses, with its suggestion of a locality defined by common concern, reciprocity, unity, shared beliefs and values, it cannot be assumed that the conditions of domination alone were sufficient to create a sense of common values, trust, or collective identification.[25] The commonality constituted in practice depends less on presence or sameness than upon desired change—the abolition of bondage. Contrary to identity providing the ground of community, identity is figured as the desired negation of the very set of constraints that create commonality: the yearning to be liberated from the condition of enslavement facilitates the networks of affiliation and identification.

Relations among slaves were characterized as much by conflict, distrust, betrayal, and contending values and beliefs as by mutual cooperation and solidarity. As one ex-slave put it, "They taught us to be against one another and no matter where you would go you would always find one that would be tattling and would have the white folks pecking on you. They would [be] trying to make it soft for themselves."[26] Another example is the dangers posed by surreptitious gatherings, which if discovered by the owner or the patrollers were met with punishment. There was also the possibility that a fellow slave would betray the meeting. This internal dissension or strife is documented by the number of planned slave revolts and rebellions that were defeated by informers.[27] Acts of betrayal and collusion with slaveholders reveal the limits of community, in that they document the clash and discord within group life and, as well, the exclusions and lines of division that inevitably shape collective existence. As an episode recounted by a former slave illustrates, complicity and collusion were punished by exclusion from the boundaries of community:

> I 'member once he built a house for young master and he said
> he was gonna let the darkies have a dance there, and they
> thought he was sure 'nough; but he didn't so they decided
> to have a dance anyhow. It was a moonlight night, and they
> had this big dance in the field, and the padderollers come and
> caught one man and threw him right on me, and he come and
> got me and said "God damn you," and kept his hand right in
> my collar and held me and took me home to master. He told
> master that he had told me that if I would tell who all was
> there he wouldn't whip me, but if I didn't he would whip me
> all day light, and you ought to heard me telling! It was around
> the time when the niggers was rising, and they asked me did I
> hear them shooting? "Did you see any guns?" And I said, "No,
> I didn't see no guns, but I heard them shooting." I hadn't heard
> a thing, but I knowed what they wanted to hear, so I said that
> I did. . . . I couldn't go to none of the parties after that. The
> niggers would kick me out if they saw me; they wouldn't have
> me there.

Any invocation of community must take into account the differences among the enslaved, the significance of "community among ourselves" as a utopian figure of transformation, and the fact that most acts of everyday resistance usually were solitary or involved only one other person.[28] A collective assault on the law and the authority of the slave owner would be subject to greater scrutiny and more likely to be betrayed. Both the enslaved and slave owners recognized the possibility and the danger enabled by these collective gatherings.

The pleasure associated with surreptitious gatherings was due, in part, to the sense of empowerment and possibility derived from collective action and the precariousness and fragility of "community." What was valued about these gatherings was "company with others." As John McAdams recalled: "Of course us negroes just lived for them negro dances we had every Saturday night there on the farm—no one to bother or interfere with us and believe me son, we made good use of these nights as that was all the time the slaves had together to dance, talk and *have a good time among their own color.* The white people they never bothered us on these times at all unless we raised too much hell, then they would come and make us behave ourselves" [emphasis mine].[29] The intersubjective and collective identification facilitated in these contexts should not be overestimated. These practices were important because they were vehicles for creating supportive and nurturing connections, experiencing joy that was fleeting and short-lived. These moments of ordinariness facilitated a practice of dreaming together. They were enactments of community, not expressions of an a priori unity.

The language of community has been shaped by an organic vision of social relations, as contrasted with the instrumentalist, utilitarian, violent, and distanced relations of society or social order. As it is traditionally invoked, community offers us a romance in place of complex and contentious social relations. The romance of community fails to recognize both the difficulty and the accomplishment of collectivity in the context of domination and terror. This is not to minimize or neglect the networks of support and care that existed among the enslaved, but to keep in mind the limits and fractures of community precisely because of the routine violence of slavery. Domination, surveillance, terror, self-interest, distrust, conflict, envy, the regular loss of friends and family to the slave trade made community an achievement, not a given. It is as crucial to engage the issue of community through the dissension and difference that are also its constituents. Here, we might think about the significance of conjuring as an articulation of envy and contestation within the slave community and not simply as an African "survival."[30]

"Community among ourselves" is an articulation of an ideal and a way of naming the networks of affiliation that exist in the context of terror, severed relations, loss and death.[31] The significance of becoming or belonging together in terms other than those defined by one's status as property, will-less object, and the not-quite-human should not be underestimated. This belonging together endeavors to redress and nurture the broken body; it is a becoming together dedicated to establishing other terms of sociality, albeit transient, and offering a small measure of relief from the debasements constitutive of one's condition.[32] The production of these shared affiliations and interests are constantly refigured and negotiated and also fractured by differences and antagonisms rather than defined by stasis and continuity. Community is not homogeneity or selfsameness or even a shared set of values, but a making or becoming together across differences: *having a good time among their own color*. The networks of affiliation or evanescent forms of sociality, the "us" made inside the circle, are enacted in assembling and gathering; these practices traverse a range of differences and create fleeting and transient lines of relation and connection.

The affinity or shared feeling experienced in "having a good time among their own color" or "talking about when we were free in Africa" is not fixed, but ephemeral. These acts can neither be reduced to domination nor explained outside it. They exceed the parameters of resistance and create alternative visions and experiences for those gathered, they permit one to say "we" and "us' with intention and regard, and do indeed challenge the dominant construction of blackness. This shared set of identifications and affiliations is enacted in instances of struggle, shared pleasures, transient forms of solidarity, and nomadic, oftentimes illegal, forms of association.

Politics without a Proper Locus

Resistance and refusal are engendered in everyday forms of practice that are excluded from the locus of the "political proper."[33] Both aspects of this assessment are significant because too often the interventions and challenges of the dominated have been obscured when measured against traditional notions of the political and its central features: the unencumbered self, the citizen, the self-possessed individual, and the volitional and autonomous subject. The concept of practice enables us to discern the capacity to act (the agency of the dominated) and the limited and transient nature of that agency. The key features of practice central to this examination of the agency of the enslaved are: the nonautonomy of the field of action; provisional ways of operating within the dominant space; local, multiple, and dispersed sites of resistance that have not been strategically codified or integrated; and the anomalous condition of the slave as person and property. Everyday and ordinary practices have been barred from the political as traditionally conceived. This has consequences and effects that include the constitution of the subject, the feasibility and appropriateness of certain forms of action, the incommensurability of liberal notions of will and autonomy as standards for evaluating subaltern behavior, the inscription of agency as criminal or, at the very least, as deserving of punishment, and the incompleteness of redress.

When thinking about these practices as the "infrapolitics of the dominated," to use James Scott's term, or as a "politics of a lower frequency," to use Paul Gilroy's term, it is important to note both the effects yielded by the popular illegalities or intransigence or recalcitrance of the enslaved and their remove from the proper locus of the political.[34] This is especially important in the case of the enslaved if we are to engage the particularities of the subject constitution and object status of the enslaved. The bourgeois individual, the

unencumbered self, and the featureless person who give meaning
to the term "political" in its conventional usage, with all the attendant assumptions about the relation of the subject and the state,
cannot incorporate the enslaved, for how does one express an individual will when one is without individual rights, or even without
a person in the usual sense of the term? After all, the rights of the
self-possessed individual and the set of property relations that define
liberty depend upon, if not require, the black as will-less actant and
sublime object. If the values most revered—liberty, equality, self-
possession, and inviolable rights of personhood—were purchased
with slave labor, then what possibilities or opportunities exist for
the black captive vessel of white ideality?[35]

The slave is the object or the ground that makes possible the
existence of the bourgeois subject and, by negation or contradistinction, defines liberty, citizenship, and the enclosures of the social
body. As Edmund Morgan has argued, the meaning and the guarantee of (white) equality depended upon the presence of slaves. White
men were "equal in not being slaves."[36] The slave is indisputably outside the normative terms of individuality and to such a degree that
the very exercise of agency is seen as a contravention of another's
unlimited rights to the object. (Even labor is not considered agency
because it is the property of another, extracted by coercive means,
and part of the brute capacities of the black; it simply personifies
the power and dominion of the owner.) Not surprisingly, the agency
of the enslaved is only intelligible or recognizable as crime and the
designation of personhood burdened with incredible duties and
responsibilities, which serve primarily to enhance the repressive
mechanisms of power, denote the limits of socially tolerable forms
of violence, and bound more tightly the sentient commodity in the
guise of protection, and punish through the recognition of slave
humanity. This official acknowledgment of agency and humanity, rather than challenging or contradicting the object status and

absolute subjugation of the enslaved as chattel, reinscribes it in the terms of personhood.

While this examination of slave agency primarily addresses issues of resistance, restitution, and redress, it is equally attentive to the constraints of domination and the brutal exercise of power that give form to resistance. Mindful of the aforementioned concerns regarding the subject, this exploration of agency and resistance is less concerned with issues of heroic action and oppositional consciousness than with the contingent, and submerged forms of contestation.[37] This approach emphasizes both the preponderance of resistance and the absence of a proper locus that would grant autonomy to these practices. These practices are significant in that they are local assaults and pedestrian challenges to slavery, the slave owner, the law, and the state, and, at the same time, they are provisional and short-lived and exploit the cleavages of the social order. The focus on the contingent and transient character of these practices is not an attempt to underestimate the magnitude of these acts, for they are fraught with utopian and transformative impulses that are unrealizable within the terms of the prevailing order precisely because of the scope of these far-reaching and allegorical claims for freedom, deliverance, redress, and restitution.

The plurality of resistances enacted in everyday life is produced by and details the relations and mechanisms of power. The dangers posed by these practices and the threats issued to the dominant order provide a map of the specific mechanisms of repression and power in antebellum social relations. For example, both the very incongruence or incommensurability of purported dangers posed by slave gatherings and the great force used to meet and crush them document the crisis of slavery and the attempt to manage it by a combined strategy of paternalism and brutal repression. In the context of crisis, infinitesimal assaults to the slave order acquire even greater significance. The import of these practices is evidenced not only in the testimony of the enslaved or the formerly enslaved and the terms in which they represent their experience, but in the power exercised both to encourage and manage slave amusements and to constrain, prohibit, and police such activities. The disruptions caused by a small act like sneaking off to a dance or attending a praise meeting catalyzed a chain of events that was disruptive, short-lived, and, to some degree, expected. The enslaved challenged and redefined their condition of absolute subjection in acts of minor transgression: movement without a pass to visit a loved one, stealing, and unpermitted gatherings.

Certainly it would be difficult to describe such acts as revolt or as a threat to destroy the plantocracy, yet the very excess of force with which they were met serves to illustrate the terror that is part and parcel of the everyday landscape of slavery and, more important, the difficulty of action in such circumstances. How is resistance registered in a context in which being found with a pen or pencil is almost as bad as having murdered your master, according to Elijah Green? Or being caught at a dance without a pass might result in being stripped and given twenty-five lashes, if you're lucky, or a life-threatening beating if you aren't? How does one enact resistance within the space of the permissible or exploit the "concessions" of slave owners without merely reproducing the mechanisms of dominance? What shape does resistance or rebellion acquire when the force of repression is virtually without limit, when terror resides comfortably within the necessary and the permitted, when the innocuous and the insurgent meet an equal force of punishment, or when the clandestine and the surreptitious mark an infinite array of dangers? In this context, might not a rendezvous at an unauthorized dance, attending a secret meeting, or sneaking off to visit your companion suddenly come to appear as insurgent, or, at the very least, as quite dangerous, even when the "threats" posed are not articulated in the form of direct confrontation, but expressed in quite different terms?

As Toby Jones recalled, such gatherings created a liberatory and utopian structure of feelings. Raymond Williams defines a structure of feelings as "a kind of feeling and thinking which is indeed social and material, but each in an embryonic phase before it can become fully articulate and defined exchange."[38] This inchoate and practical consciousness is expressed by Jones as the recollective anticipation of freedom and by others as an impulse or "instinct that we was going to be free."[39] Obviously, this structure of feeling existed in a troubled relation to slavery, for if a slave entertaining thoughts of freedom was discovered, she would be lucky to escape with a beating. Other slaves were forced to witness this beating and threatened with the same treatment if they were caught.[40] As one ex-slave commented, "Whipping darkies was the joy of the white man back in those days."[41]

Even small challenges to slavery could have disastrous effects. As John McAdams recounted, "The only way the slaves could go from one plantation to another was they had to have a pass from their Mas[t]er or Mistress; if they went without a pass, woe be unto that negro, for the mas[t]er of the place would ask us for our pass, and if we could not show one, it was just too bad. He would give us one of the worst whippings we ever got. Of course I use to slip off and go to see my girl on another farm, but I was very careful that I did not let anyone catch us."[42] Even a child's display of rebelliousness could be met with the threat of death. As a child, Susan Snow would "fight and scratch" with other children, black and white. In order to break her of this habit, her master forced her to look at the bodies of slaves who had been hanged for harming a white man.[43]

How does one survive the common atrocities of slavery yet possess a sensibility, a feeling, an impulse, an inexplicable, yet irrepressible, confidence in the possibilities of freedom? It is hard to imagine possibility, let alone freedom, within a world of such fatal incommensurability, a world in which the most innocuous gesture invites the threat of death. In slave testimony, extreme acts of violence are depicted matter-of-factly because of their regular occurrence. The recollections of Susan Snow and others catalog the coexistence of the mundane and the unimaginable and the diffusion and rationality of terror. The incongruence of act and punishment and the magnitude of violence that awaited even the smallest transgression document the provisional and restricted character of these practices or any claims that might be made on their behalf. Such instances demonstrate that even in circumstances where direct and primary forms of domination prevail, there are innumerable sites of confrontation and struggle, despite the great cost of such acts.

To illuminate the significance of performance and the articulation of social struggle in seemingly innocuous events, everyday forms of practice need to be situated within the virtually unbounded powers of the slave-owning class, and whites in general, to use all means necessary to ensure submission. It is no surprise that these everyday forms of practice are usually subterranean. I am reluctant to describe these practices as a "kind of politics," not because I question whether the practices considered here are small-scale forms of struggle or dismiss them as cathartic and contained.[44] Rather, my hesitation concerns the possibilities of practice as they are related to the circumstances of the enslaved as outside the "political proper," and it leads me both to question the appropriateness of the political to this realm of practice and to reimagine the political in toto. (As well, I take seriously Jean Comaroff's observations that "the real politik of oppression dictates that resistance be expressed in domains seemingly apolitical.")[45]

The contradictory status of the enslaved, their ambiguous relation to the state, and the nonautonomy of both their social status and their practice determine this limited and tentative use of the political and the effort to wrench it from its proper referent. Given the exclusion of the slave from the sphere of the political, what forms do the assertion of needs and desire acquire? What assumptions of the political are at all relevant or adequate to their social location? Slaves are not consensual and willful actors, the state is not a vehicle for advancing their claims, they are not citizens, and their status as persons is contested. Assimilating these practices into the normative frame of the political is less important than examining the dimensions of practice and whether practice requires a subject at all. What form does the political acquire for the enslaved? How might one best describe the politics of the object of property or the commodity? Is practice or performance better suited to explain how the broken body moves or the captive evades and inhabits the world? In what ways are the (im)possibilities of practice related to, if not determined by, the closures of politics? How are the claims of the dominated articulated or advanced and their needs addressed or accommodated? If the public sphere is reserved for the white bourgeois subject and the public/private divide replicates that between the political and the nonpolitical, then the agency of the enslaved, whose relation to the state is mediated by way of another's rights, is invariably relegated to the nonpolitical side of this divide. This gives us some sense of the full weight and meaning of the slaveholder's dominion. In effect, those subjects removed from the public sphere are formally excluded from the space of politics.

The everyday practices of the enslaved generally fall outside direct forms of confrontation; they are not systemic in their ideology, analysis, or intent, and, most important, the slave is neither civic man nor free worker, but excluded from the narrative of "we the people" that effects the linkage of the modern individual and the state. The enslaved were neither envisioned nor afforded the privilege of envisioning themselves as part of the "imaginary sovereignty of the state" or as "infused with unreal universality."[46] Even the

Gramscian model, with its reformulation of the relation of state and
civil society in the concept of the historical bloc and its expanded
definition of the political, maintains a notion of the political inseparable from the effort and the ability of a class to effect hegemony.[47]
By questioning the use of the term "political," I hope to illuminate
the possibilities of practice and the stakes of these dispersed resistances. All of this is not a preamble to an argument about the "prepo-
litical" consciousness of the enslaved, but an attempt to point to the
limits of the political and the difficulty of translating or interpreting
the practices of the enslaved within that framework. The everyday
practices of the enslaved occur in the default of the political, in the
absence of the rights of man or the assurances of the self-possessed
individual, and perhaps even without a "person," in the usual meaning of the term.

Stealing Away, the Space of Struggle, and the Nonautonomy of Practice

When the enslaved slipped away to have secret meetings, they
would call it "stealing the meeting," as if to highlight the appropriation of space and the expropriation of the object of property
necessary to make these meetings possible.[48] Just as runaway slaves
were described as "stealing themselves," so, too, even short-lived
"flights" from captivity were referred to as "stealing away." Stealing
away designated a wide range of activities, from praise meetings,
quilting parties, and dances to illicit visits with lovers and family on
neighboring plantations. It encompassed an assortment of popular
illegalities focused on contesting the authority of the slave-owning
class and contravening the status of the enslaved as possession.
The very phrase "stealing away" played upon the paradox of property's agency and the idea of property as theft, alluding to the captive's condition as a legal form of unlawful or amoral seizure, what

Hortense Spillers describes as "the violent seizing of the captive body from its motive will, its active desire."[49] Echoing Pierre-Joseph Proudhon's "property is theft," Henry Bibb put the matter simply: "Property can't steal property." It is the play upon this originary act of theft that yields the possibilities of transport, as one was literally and figuratively carried away by one's desire.[50] The appropriation of dominant space in itinerant acts of defiance contests the spatial confinement and surveillance of slave life and, ironically, redefines the meaning of property, theft, and agency. Despite the range of activities encompassed under this rubric, what these events shared was the centrality of contestation. Stealing away was the vehicle for the redemptive figuration of dispossessed, and for reconstituting kin relations, contravening the object status of chattel, transforming pleasure, and, investing in the body as a site of sensual activity, sociality, and possibility, it was an effort to redress an irreparable condition.

The activities encompassed in the scope of stealing away played upon the tension between the owner's possession and the slave's dispossession and sought to redress the condition of enslavement by whatever (limited) means available. The most direct expression of the desire for redress was the praise meeting. The appeals made to a "God that saves in history" were overwhelmingly focused on freedom.[51] For this reason, William Lee said that slaves "couldn't serve God unless we stole to de cabin or de woods."[52] West Turner confirmed this and stated that when patrollers discovered such meetings, they would beat the slaves mercilessly in order to keep them from serving God. Turner recounted the words of one patroller to this effect: "If I ketch you here servin' God, I'll beat you. You ain't got no time to serve God. We bought you to serve us."[53] Serving God was a crucial site of struggle, as it concerned matters regarding the style and intent of worship, and the very meaning of service, since the expression of faith was invariably a critique of the social conditions of servitude and mastery. As Turner's account documents, the threat embodied in serving God was that the recognition of divine authority superseded, if not negated, the mastery of the slave owner. Although by the 1850s Christianity was widespread among the enslaved and most owners no longer opposed the conversion or religious instruction of slaves, there was nonetheless an ethical and political struggle waged in religious practice that concerned contending interpretations of the word and styles of religious worship. Even those slaves whose owners encouraged religion or sent them to white churches found it important to attend secret meetings. They complained that at white churches they were not allowed to speak or express their faith in their own terms. "We used to slip off in de woods in de old slave days on Sunday evening way down in de swamps to sing and pray to our own liking. We prayed for dis day of freedom. We come from four and five miles to pray together to God dat if we don't live to see it, to please let our chillen live to see it, to please let our chillen live to see a better day and be free, so dat they can give honest and fair service to the Lord and all mankind everywhere. And we'd sing 'our little meetin's about to break, chillen, and we must part. We got to part in body, but hope not in mind. Our little meetin's bound to break.' Den we used to sing 'We walk about and shake hands, fare you well my sisters, I am going home.'"[54] These meetings held in "hush arbors" or covertly in the quarters illuminate the significant difference between the terms of faith and the import of Christianity for the master and the enslaved. For example, the ring shout, a form of devotional dance, defied Christian proscriptions against dancing. The shout made the body a vehicle of divine communication with God in contrast to the Christian vision of the body as the defiled container of the soul or as mere commodity. And the attention to the soul contested the object status of the enslaved, for the exchange of blacks as commodities and their violent domination were often described in terms of being treated as if one did not have a soul.[55]

The avid belief in an imminent freedom radically challenged and nullified the gospel of slavery, which made subordination a virtue and promised rewards in the "kitchen of heaven." Eliza Washington stated that ministers would "preach the colored people if they would be good niggers and not steal their master's eggs and chickens and things that they might go to the kitchen of heaven when they died." It was not uncommon for slave owners to impart a vision of Christianity in which the enslaved would also attend to them in the afterlife. As one mistress stated, "I would give anything if I could have Maria in heaven with me to do little things for me."[57] For the enslaved, the belief in a divine authority minimized and contained the dominion of the master. These meetings facilitated a sense of collective identification, creating an *us* and *we* through the invocation of a common condition as an oppressed people and of a shared destiny. Serving God ultimately was to be actualized in the abolition of slavery.

Stealing away involved unlicensed movement, collective assembly, and an abrogation of the terms of subjection in acts as simple as sneaking off to laugh and talk with friends or making nocturnal visits to loved ones.[58] Sallie Johnson said that men would often sneak away to visit their wives.[59] These nighttime visits to lovers and family were a way of redressing the natal alienation or enforced "kinlessness" of the enslaved; practices of naming, running away, and refusing to marry a mate not of one's choosing or to remarry after a husband or wife was sold away were efforts to maintain, if not reconstitute, these ties.[60] Dora Frank's uncle would sneak off at night to see his woman. On one occasion, he failed to return by daylight, and "nigger hounds" were sent after him. He was given one hundred lashes and sent to work with the blood still running down his back.[61] Dempsey Jordan recognized that the risks involved in such journeys were great but slipped off at night to see his girl in spite of them: "I was taking a great chance. I would go and see my girl lots of nights and one time I crawled 100 yards to her room and got in the bed with her and lay there until nearly daylight talking to her. One time I was there with her and them patter rollers come that night and walked all around in that room and this here negro was in her bed down under that moss and they never found me. I sure was scared."[62] The fact that the force of violence and the threat of sale did not prevent such actions illustrates the ways in which the mandates of property relations were defied in the course of everyday practices.

The consequences of these small-scale challenges were sometimes life threatening, if not fatal. Fannie Moore remembered the violence that followed the discovery of a secret dance. They were dancing and singing when the patrollers invaded the dance and started beating people. When Uncle Joe's son decided it was "time to die" because he couldn't sustain another beating and fought back, the patrollers beat him to death and whipped half a dozen others before sending them home.[63] If slaves had a party or a prayer meeting and they made too much noise, patrollers would beat them and sometimes would sell them. The patrollers took two of Jane Pyatt's brothers, and she never saw them again.[64] Generally, the punishment for unlicensed assembly or travel was twenty-five to fifty lashes.

Stealing away was synonymous with defiance because it necessarily involved seizing the master's property and claiming the self in transgression of the law. The trespasses that were invariably a part of stealing away were a source of danger, pride, and a great deal of boasting. Garland Monroe noted that the secret meetings he participated in were held in the open, not in huts or arbors. They were confident that they could outwit and defy patrollers. If the patrollers came, the slaves took advantage of a superior knowledge of the territory to escape capture or detection.[65] Physical confrontations with patrollers were a regular feature of these accounts, and a vine stretched across the road to trip the patrollers' horses was the most common method of foiling one's pursuers.[66] As James Davis bragged, "I've seen the Ku Klux in slavery times and I've cut many a grapevine. We'd be in the place dancin' and playin' the banjo and the grapevine strung across the road and the Ku Klux come ridin' along and run right into it and throw the horses down."[67] The enslaved were empowered by the collective challenge posed to power and the mutual reinforcement against fear of discovery or punishment. From this perspective, pastoral and folksy slave gatherings appear like small-scale battles with the slaveholders, local whites, and the law.

These day-to-day and routine forms of contestation operated within the confines of relations of power and simultaneously challenged those very relations as these covert and chameleonic practices both complied with and disrupted the demands of the system through the expression of a counter-discourse of freedom. In the course of such gatherings, even the span of the Potomac could be made a bridge of community and solidarity. As James Deane remembered, they would blow conch shells at night to signal a gathering. "We would all meet on the bank of the Potomac River and sing across the river to the slaves in Virginia, and they would sing back to us."[68]

Such small-scale infringements of the law also produced cleavages in the spatial organization of domination. The play on "stealing," "taking or appropriating without right or leave and with the intent to keep or make use of wrongfully" or "to appropriate entirely to oneself or beyond one's proper share," articulates the dilemma of the subject without rights and the degree to which any exercise of agency or appropriation of the self is only intelligible as crime or already encoded as crime.[69] It highlights the transgression of such furtive and clandestine peregrinations, since the very assertion of stealing away places emphasis on taking back what has been stolen and making visible the originary theft that produced the slave. The activity required to assemble at praise meetings and dances was nothing less than a fundamental challenge to and breach of the claims of slave property—the black captive as object and the ground of the master's inalienable rights, being, and liberty.

The agency of theft or the simple exercise of any claims to the self, however restricted, challenged the figuration of the black captive as devoid of will or force.[70] Stealing away ironically encapsulated the impossibility of self-possession as it exposed the link between liberty and slave property by playing with and against the terms of dispossession. The use of the term "play" is not intended to make light of the profound dislocation and rupture experienced by the enslaved or to imply that these tentative negotiations of one's status or condition attenuated the violence and brutality of slavery, but to highlight the performative dimension of these assaults as staged, repeated, and rehearsed—what Richard Schechner terms "twice-behaved behavior."[71] As well, might it be possible that dispossession entailed its own force and aspiration. Through stealing away, counterclaims about justice and freedom were advanced and the sanctity or legitimacy of rights of property refuted in a double gesture that played on the meaning of theft. Implicit within the appropriation of the object of property was an insistence that flew in the face of the law: liberty defined by inalienable rights of property was theft. Stealing away exploited the bifurcated condition of the black captive as subject and object by the flagrant assertion of unlicensed and felonious behavior and by pleading innocence, precisely because as an object the slave was the very negation of an intending consciousness or will. The disruptive assertions, necessarily a part of stealing away, contravened the law of property.

Stealing away defied and subversively appropriated slave owners' designs for mastery and control—the use of the captive body
as the extension of the master's power and the spatial organization
of domination and enclosure. Stealing away involved not only an
appropriation of the self but also a disruption of the spatial arrangements of domination that confined slaves to the policed location
of the quarters unless provided with written permission of the
slaveholder to go elsewhere.[72] The organization of dominant space
involved the separation of public and private realms; this boundary reproduced and extended the subordination and control of the
enslaved. If the public realm is reserved for the bourgeois citizen
subject and the private realm is designated by domestic or household relations, the sanctity of property ownership and contractual
transactions based upon free will, then in what space can the needs
and desires of the enslaved be articulated?[73] How does one contest
the limits of the political? Ultimately, the struggle against slavery
was waged in everyday practices, which appropriated and transfigured space in local and pedestrian acts, like holding a praise meeting in the woods, meeting a lover in the canebrake, or throwing
a surreptitious dance in the quarters. The negation and refusal of
one's status as transactable object or the vehicle of another's rights
was an essential aspect of this spatial practice. In these social
spaces, needs and desires were asserted, prayers offered, dreams
and counterclaims could be collectively aired, granting property a
social life and an arena of shared identification with other slaves.
Like de Certeau's walker who challenges the disciplinary apparatus of the urban system with his idle footsteps, these practices
also create possibilities within the space of domination, trespass
the policed space of subordination through unlicensed travel and
collective assembly, escape the isolation and division of plantation
households, and disrupt boundaries between the public and private
in the articulation of insurgent claims.[74]

Embodied Needs and the Politics of Hunger

The collective assertion of need and the radical longings of the enslaved rarely assumed a form recognized as politics. The vision and anticipation of a free life was nurtured in hush arbors and clearings and swamps and proceeded by stealth.[75] The assertion of black need has not been received as political, as Patricia Williams observes, but heard only "against the background of their erstwhile musicality."[76] It is the insistent and unceasing expression of black need that largely defines the critical labor of the performative and a subordinate politics characterized by the impossibility of decisive autonomy, or membership in the nation-state, or the entitlements of the subject in the normative terms of man and citizen. An example as commonplace as juba illuminates the way in which need provides a figure for radical transformation. A popular vernacular dance, juba, enabled and facilitated the counterinvestment in the body as a site of pleasure. In this body-drum song and dance, the depleted and hollowed-out captive body becomes the vehicle for the transfiguration of value.

Juba was a coded text of protest. It utilized rhythm and nonsense words as cover for social critique. The content of juba songs examined the dynamics of captivity, expropriation, and domination and addressed the needs of the enslaved. The attack on slavery centered on the use of the slave for the master's wealth and amusement and on the unmet longings of the violated and depleted body.[77] The consumption and extraction of the body's possibility and the constancy of hunger are at the center of juba's often witty commentary.[78] The most important characteristic of juba, besides "patting" or the rhythmic use of the body, was the songs. Even when the exact nature of its steps, whether jig, reel, or shuffle were uncertain, juba could be identified by the repertoire of juba songs that accompanied it.[79] Generally, the songs enacted resistance and aired dissent in the guise of play and sheer nonsense.[80] Solomon Northup mistakenly characterized them as "unmeaning songs, composed rather for [their] adaption to a certain tune or measure, than for the purpose of expressing any distinct idea."[81] And the guise of sheer play and nonsense led those like William Smith, after stumbling upon a performance of juba, to conclude that "slaves were the happiest of the human race."[82]

Douglass designated patting juba as "jubilee beating" to emphasize the revolutionary scope of redress and the possibilities of emancipation, sated needs, and nonpunitive embodiment. Although it was performed on the minstrel stage, he characterized juba as an exclusively Southern performance and claimed that every farm had its juba beater, because it "supplied the place of violin or other musical instrument." Juba also accompanied instrumental music.[83] Douglass's representation of juba emphasized the insurgent aspects of performance, the condemnation of slavery, and the yearnings for freedom: "The performer improvised as he beat the instrument, marking the words as he sang so as to have them fall pat with the movement of his hands. Once in a while among a mass of nonsense and wild frolic, a sharp hit was given to the meanness of slaveholders." The song details the cruelties of slavery, the exploitation of slave labor, and the appropriation of the slave's product by slave owners. Amid the seeming nonsense of the juba song was a bid for freedom:

> We raise de wheat,
> Dey gib us de corn;
> We bake de bread,
> Dey gib us de crust;
> We sif de meal,
> Dey gib us de huss;
> We peel de meat,

Dey gib us de skin;
And dat's de way
Dey take us in;
We skim de pot,
Dey gib us de liquor,
And say dat's good enough for nigger.
Walk over! Walk over!
Your butter and de fat;
Poor nigger, you can't get over dat!
Walk over![84]

Douglass's version of the juba song was similar to a version sung by Bessie Jones, a folk performer from the Georgia Sea Islands. Jones stated that the juba song she learned from her grandfather was a cryptic message about the abhorrent conditions of slave life, in particular the slop they were forced to eat.

Juba this and Juba that
Juba killed a yella cat
Get over double trouble, Juba.
You sift the meal,
You give me the husk.
You cook the bread,
You give me the crust
You fry your meat,
You give me the skin.
And that's where mama's trouble begin.[85]

The body of the song is almost identical to that recounted by Douglass. Jones interpreted this section of the song as follows: "The mother would always be talking to them about she wished she could give them some of that good hot cornbread, hot pies or hot what not.

But she couldn't. She had to wait and give that old stuff that was left over. And then they began to sing it and play it."[86] In both versions of the song, the lyrics give voice to resistance and foreground depletion and exploitation in the tacitly political content of coded language and covert acts of protest.

The form of redressive action at work in juba attends to unmet needs and cultivates pleasure while protesting the conditions of enslavement. The repertoire of songs addresses the condition of hunger and the unjust distribution of resources between the producers and the owners. In this case, the utilization of the body as a literal vessel of communication facilitates the expression of need and longing, as well as dissent. Beating the body like a drum and for one's own ends delivers a certain measure of pleasure, comforts the pained body, and offers a fleeting glimpse of autonomy. In this sense, juba can perhaps be seen as "a claim of one's body against power."[87] These forms of everyday practice entail the appropriation of space, the assertion of needs, the avowal of antagonism, railing against subordination, and the use of pleasure as a vehicle of dissent and transformation. The art of need is nothing less than a politics of hunger.

Memory and History

The space taken and remade in everyday practice enabled needs and desires to be aired and implicitly addressed the history of violence and dislocation that produced the captive, as well as the possibilities of redress that might undo this state. This appropriated space of social collectivity, in accordance with Henri Lefebvre's definition of representational space, is "redolent with imaginary and symbolic elements" that have their source in the violent history of the people.[88] The violence and dishonor and disaffiliation and loss constitutive of enslavement and the radical breach introduced by the Middle Passage are articulated within these everyday practices and determine the possibilities or the impossibility of redress. The dominant space is pilfered and manipulated in giving voice to need and in making counterclaims about freedom, human flesh, and the self (a reconstructed self that negates the dominant terms of identity and existence); it is transformed and remade as a sacralized and ancestral landscape so that it might shelter life, spirit, gods and ancestors. These sacralized and ancestral elements are created, imagined, and remembered in the use of prayer trees and inverted pots, performed in the shout, and called up in sacred gatherings. Devotional dances to ancestral spirits, remembering things they have not witnessed or experienced, like "when they lived in Africa and done what they wanted," and an insurgent nostalgia that expressed a longing for a home that most could only vaguely recall or that lived only in imagination transfigured the space of captivity into one inhabited by the revenants of a dismembered past.

The lived relations of domination and subordination did not simply coexist with the evocation of the ancestors and the recollection and anticipation of freedom; within these practices, the dislocation and displacement of enslavement were marked in varied and multifarious ways. The goal here is not to create an index of African survivals or retrievals of Kongo, Fon, Ibo, or Yoruba traces, but to consider the everyday historicity of these practices—the ways in which the quotidian articulates the wounds of history and the enormity of the breach instituted by the transatlantic crossing of black captives and the processes of enslavement: violent domination, dishonor, natal alienation, and chattel status. Everyday practices are texts of dislocation and transculturation that register in their "perversion of the original lines of descent" the violence of historical process and, in so doing, offer witness. This witnessing has little or nothing to do with the veracity of recollection or the reliability or fallibility of memory. What is most important here are the ways memory acts in the service of redress, not an inventory of the world lost.[89]

For example, the inverted pot used to evade detection during secret meetings and dances exemplifies the ways in which practices are sedimented with traces of a past, which perhaps are neither remembered nor forgotten but exist as a "memory of difference."[90] In the accounts of stealing to meetings, there is an emphasis on the methods used to prevent being detected by owners or patrollers. The inverted washtub or pot is the most frequently mentioned means of avoiding detection. Millie Simpkins stated that at quilting parties, while the older people worked on quilts and the young ones danced and had a good time, they would place a pot at the door to keep white people from hearing them. Mary Gladdy remembered gathering as often as two or three times a week to hold prayer and experience meetings. They placed a large iron pot against the door to keep their voices from escaping. After singing, praying, and sharing experiences all night long, they would leave believing that freedom was in the offing.[91]

The use of an overturned cooking or washpot to evade detection is mentioned throughout the narratives. According to Anderson and Minerva Edwards, "When we prayed by ourselves we daren't let the white folks know it and we turned a wash pot down to the ground to catch the voice. We prayed a lot to be free and the Lord done heared us. We didn't have no songbooks and the Lord done give us our songs and when we sing at night it jus' whispering to nobody. Nobody hear us."[92] "They would turn the kettle down outside the door, raised so that the sound can get under there and you wouldn't hear them. If they heard the women pray, the next morning they would hit them fifty lashes for praying."[93] Patsy Hyde said that the pot not only kept white folks from hearing what they said but also showed that God was with the slaves.[94]

This practice has been related to the use of sacred waterpots and drums in Africa.[95] Sidney Mintz has suggested that it may be an inversion that compensates for the prohibition of drumming, in that the overturned tub consumes or absorbs sound rather than producing it.[96] Albert Raboteau speculates it may be a fragmentary emblem of Eshu Elegba, because in orisha tradition, "it is obligatory to begin worship with an offering to Eshu Elegba in order to insure that the order and decorum of the service is not disturbed."[97] The use of the inverted pot is analogous to the placing of inverted flowerpots on African American gravesites to signify departed spirits. Robert Farris Thompson argues that in these gestures to the dead are traces of Kongo culture: "Inversion signifies perdurance, as a visual pun on the superior strength of the ancestors, for the root of *bikinda*, 'to be upside down, to be in the realm of the ancestors, to die' *is kinda*, 'to be strong,' because those who are upside down, who die, are strongest."[98]

Rather than locate the origins of these practices or classify Africanisms, I want to explore the way these practices witness and record the violent discontinuities of history introduced by the Middle Passage, the catastrophe of captivity and enslavement, and the experience of loss and affiliation. These traces of memory function in a manner akin to a phantom limb, in that what is felt is no longer there. It is a sentient recollection of connectedness experienced at the site of rupture, where the very consciousness of disconnectedness acts as mode of testimony and memory. The recognition of loss is a crucial element in redressing the breach introduced by slavery. This recognition entails a remembering of the broken body, not by way of a simulated wholeness but precisely through the recognition of the amputated body in its amputatedness, in the insistent acknowledgement of the violated body as human flesh, in the cognition of its needs, and in the anticipation of its release. The paradox is that the ravished body holds out the possibility of restitution, not the invocation of an illusory wholeness or the desired return to an originary plentitude.

The status of the past, whether figured as "life in Africa when we were free" or embodied by an African parent or grandparent or an unviolated natality (against the natal alienation of enslavement) or an understanding of the self in relation to the millions gone and/ or those on the other side of the Atlantic, is experienced most significantly in the terms of loss and discontinuity.[99] This past cannot be recovered, yet the history of the captive emerges precisely at this site of loss and rupture. In the workings of memory, there is an endless reiteration and enactment of this condition of exile and displacement. The past is untranslatable in the current frame of meaning because of the radical disassociations of historical process and the discontinuity introduced into the being of the captive as she is castigated into the abstract category of property. The Middle Passage, the Atlantic crossing, the way of death, the tear in the world, the great event of breach, engenders this discontinuity. The invocation of the past articulated in practice returns to this point of rupture. In this regard, memory is not in the service of continuity, but incessantly reiterates and enacts the contradictions and antagonisms of enslavement, the ruptures of history, and the severed and dispersed networks of kinship and affiliation. It is by way of this refrain or differential invocation of the past, by way of this memory of difference that everyday practices are redolent with the history of captivity and enslavement. This working through of the past, or recursive engagement with breach and rupture, is a significant aspect of redress.

Memory in black cultural practice has been interpreted most often through continuist narratives of tradition grounded in the foundational status of Africa. However, it is absolutely necessary to demystify, displace, and weaken the concept of Africa in order to address the discontinuities of history and the complexity of culture practice. As Paulin Hountondji argues, one must enfeeble the concept of Africanity "by dissipating the mystical halo of values arbitrarily grafted on this phenomenon by the ideologues of identity." In order to engage the complexity of history and tradition(s), "it [is] necessary to weaken resolutely the concept of Africa, to rid it of all its ethical, religious, philosophical, political connotations, etc., with which a long anthropological tradition overloaded it and the most visible effect was to close the horizon, to prematurely close history."[100] The very identification and cataloging of Africanisms is usually mired in a primitive and reductive metaphysics of Africanity that positions Africa as the temporal other of the West and the values of Africanity as little more than a shorthand for sensuousness, instinct, rhythm, superstition, improvisation, naturalness, and physical prowess.[101]

I have endeavored to attenuate the mystical and homogenizing Africanity of the discourse of "survivals" and instead emphasize the historicity of these practices by alternately describing the operation of memory and interrogating Africanity.[102] Contrary to the metaphysics of Africanity and the "submission to consanguinity," what is at stake here is precisely the *body* of memory—the dominated social collectivity of enslaved Africans and the brutal operation of power on these captive bodies.[103] History is illuminated not only by the recitation of the litany of horrors that characterized the "commercial deportation of Africans," but also by performance practices that serve as a means of redressing the broken body and restaging the event of rupture or breach that engendered "the other side." The constancy of unmet needs, routine violence, loss, wounded kinship, brutal and abundant death are articulated in the very endeavor to heal the flesh and to release the captive body. The transport and return enacted in performance offer a mode of remembering and redress.

The limits of an ethnological and continuist account of memory have been belabored to clear a space for considerations of memory that focus on rupture, breach, discontinuity, and crisis. From this vantage, let us again consider the example of juba as the conduit of subterranean and repressed histories, rather than a recollection of distant but retrievable origins or the eternal recurrence of essentialist particularisms within folksy and pastoral *milieux de mémoire*. This approach to memory confronts head-on the issues of dislocation, rupture, shock, and forgetting, as well as the fragmented texture of memory. The goal is to attend the loss inscribed in the social body and embedded in forms of practice, not to retrieve the prehistory of the captive, but to examine what Édouard Glissant describes as our nonhistory: "The experience of shock, contradiction, painful negation, and explosive forces which make a totalitarian philosophy of history an impossibility."[104] To call it a subterranean history is to underscore the millions of "unceremoniously buried" that mark the transatlantic crossing.[105] In this light, it is possible to describe juba as a practice of countermemory distinguished by rupture and dispersion. (Counter)memory disrupts the narrative of progress from ethnohistory or prehistory to history, or from *milieu* to *lieu*.[106] It attends to the breach instituted by the Middle Passage and to the violated, dismembered, captive body.

The Body of Memory

The subterranean history of death and discontinuity informs everyday practice in myriad ways.[107] Perhaps the most significant of these are the memory of difference and the role of repetition in performance. Repetition or iterability is what enables us "to regenerate ourselves through the continuing process of redefinition."[108] Yet the failure of full recovery or recompense, the inability to wholly occupy an imagined prior condition or to bridge the divide of the split subject, is what drives redress and deems it inadequate. It is this failure that necessitates repetition. If repetition "continually 'cuts' back to the start" or is homage to an "original generative instance or act," as James Snead argues, then what is returned to is the inevitable loss or breach that stands at the origin and engenders the black "New World" subject and "neo-African" forms like juba. The "cut" returns to denied and unmet needs.[109] The cut returns to shattered realms, to the womb abyss.

The event of rupture is articulated in a variety of ways. The discontinuity in juba's descent makes impossible the recuperation of origins: Was it an African circle dance, a jig, or a square dance? Isolated gestures insinuate the divergent lines of descent but refuse definitive classification. Mnemic traces of past practices cannot be followed to one site of origin. The impossibility of origins might also be conceptualized in relation to the sexual economy of slavery: the uncertainty of descent, the negation of maternity, the interdiction regarding the master-father's name, and the ambiguous legacy of inheritance and dispossession.[110] This approach to descent "fragments what was thought unified; it shows the heterogeneity of what was imagined consistent with itself."[111]

The very designation "juba" refers to a range of practices: the percussive use of the body, slapping out rhythms on chest, thighs, and knees while tapping or dancing a short step, shuffle, or jig; a circle dance of competition where the dancer pats or those in the circle keep time or create complex rhythms for the central dancer or couple; and a solo performance comprising mainly of patting chest, knees, and thighs.[112] It was commonly described as "a kind of reel with a calling leader" and as a jig, a designation that applied to the "Irish jig" and to an "impolite bacchanalian dance of grotesque manner" identified as "African."[113] The very term "juba" invokes this uncertainty and the submarine roots of the black Atlantic. The etymology of this revision or misrecognition has been traced to Bantu words like *juba*, *diuba*, or *guiba*.[114] Yet in the space of this revision and repetition emerges the subterranean history of rupture. Repetition is an outcome, a consequence, an accumulation of practice, and it also structures practice.[115] Repetition points to that which can never be fully recollected and to the impossibility of restoring that which has been breached. The constancy of repetition is catalyzed by the inadequacy of redress and unremitting domination and terror. These factors impel "rememory"; in other words, the compulsion or propensity for repetition is driven by the ungovernable processes of the social.[116] Breach triggers memory, and the enormity of the breach perhaps suggests that it can be neither reconciled nor repaired.

The forms of redress enacted in performance are a necessarily incomplete working through of the event of breach because of the relentless assault and the inability to transform social relations through such practices or generate an event that would result in the reversal of forces. While the breach can never be fully repaired or compensated, at the very least, the efforts to set things right would entail a revolution of the social order, an entirely new set of arrangements. Given this, the inadequacy of the redressive action undertaken in everyday practices does not signal the failure of these practices but serves to highlight the way pleasure or care or tending to the flesh serve as limited figures of social transformation.

Redress::How the Broken Body Moves

If redress does not or cannot restore or remedy loss, redeem the unceremoniously buried, or bridge the transatlantic divide, then what possibilities for relief or restitution does it provide? First, redress is a re-membering of the social body that occurs precisely in the recognition and articulation of devastation, captivity, and enslavement. The re-membering of the violated body must be considered in relation to the dis-membered body of the slave—that is, its segmentation and organization for purposes of work, reproduction, enjoyment, and punishment. This re-membering takes the form of attending to the body as a site of pleasure, eros, sociality, and articulating its violated condition. Second, redress is a limited form of action aimed at relieving the broken body through alternative configurations of the self or self-abandonment, and the redemption of the body as human flesh. Third, redress concerns the articulation of needs and desires and the endeavor to meet them. It is a way of making and doing directed toward the release of the captive, the reconstitution of severed natality, and the remembrance of breach. It is intended to minimize the violence of historical dislocation and dissolution—the history that hurts. Redressive action encompasses a heightened attention to the events that have culminated in the crisis and to the transfiguration of the body in shared ceremony, making it a vessel of communication, flesh to be loved, and a bridge between the living and the dead. The event of captivity and enslavement initiates the necessity of redress, the inevitability of its failure, and the constancy of repetition yielded by this failure.

The body is both the "eroding witness" to this history of terror and the object of redress. Certainly, the body broken by the regime of work, the regularity of punishment, the persistence of torture, and the violence of rape and sexual exploitation is in dire need of restitution. Yet the very conditions that have produced the broken and depleted body and the body as object, instrument, and commodity ensure that the work of restoration or recompense is necessarily incomplete. The limited means of redress available to the enslaved cannot compensate for the enormity of this loss; instead, redress is itself an articulation of loss and a longing for remedy and reparation. It is impossible to repair this violated condition or undo the catastrophe without the occurrence of an event of epic and revolutionary proportions—the abolition of property, the destruction of the racist order, recompense for stolen life and land, the trans-valuation of the given. The incompleteness of redress is related to the magnitude of the breach—the millions lost in the Middle Passage and the fifteen million and more captured and enslaved in the Americas—and to the inadequacy of remedy.[117]

I have adopted/adapted the term "redress" from Victor Turner's quadripartite schema of social drama, though my model of the social differs significantly from his with its social totality of schism and integration. In Turner's model, redressive action is about limiting or containing a breach. The need to contain or reconcile the breach is no less desperate because of its impossibility and inevitable failure, especially when the crisis is unceasing and acts of breach are endlessly perpetuated.[118] In the redressive phase of what Turner calls "disharmonic processes"—in my terms, the contradictions and antagonisms of the social—"pragmatic techniques and symbolic action reach their fullest expression."[119] Redress has liminal characteristics, the quality of being "betwixt and between"; it is poised between breach and mounting crisis and, as such, furnishes "a distanced replication and critique of the events leading up to and composing the crisis."[120] These techniques entail remedying disrupted affiliations, caring for the depleted and broken body, and reconstituting the terms of existence for the socially dead. The symbolic actions range from the redemptive "march to heaven," another way of describing the shout, to mundane activities like exchanging stories, staying up all night talking with your lover, or singing across the Potomac to slaves on the other side. The incompleteness of redress and the constancy of breach and crisis are primary determinants of the force of repetition in black performance and the ambivalent formation of pleasure.

These practices provide more than a reprieve from domination; they express the tensions, limits, fissures, wounds, and ravages inevitably a part of the centuries-long history of slavery. When Anna

Lee described Saturday night dances, she emphasized the fact that these dances provided the only occasion for collective gatherings and having fun: "We *had to have* some way to see the other sex and be together, and that was the only time that our master allowed us to be together just among ourselves, and we sure made the best of it cause we generally danced, hollered and had our fun all night long."[121] Rather than the dance providing an occasion for forgetting or escaping the "reality" of slavery, the pleasure such opportunities afforded were bittersweet, fleeting, and tempered by the perpetuity of bondage. The pleasure to be had was infused with despair, fear, dissatisfaction, melancholy, rage and the desire for freedom. These surreptitious gatherings were haunted by the threat of discovery and reprisal.

If through performance the enslaved "asserted their humanity," it is no less true that performance articulated their troubled relation to the category "human." As well, no absolute line could be drawn between the pleasant path of slave management and the collective articulation of needs, solidarity, and possibility. While the pleasures afforded within the confines of slavery were vulnerable to Douglass's critique of debased amusement and reactionary diversions, they also provided the occasion for small-scale assaults against slavery and opportunities for collective reflection on their shared condition. It is impossible to separate the use of pleasure as a technique of discipline from pleasure as a figuration of social transformation.[122] The confusion of the slave's good time and stealing away in these short-lived transports works against absolute assertions about pleasure. The claims made on behalf of pleasure are provisional and conflicting.

Pleasure was inseparable from the expenditure and breakdown of the body. As Celeste Avery recalled, at weekly frolics and dances, folks would get "broke down from so much dancing."[123] Parties were called "drag downs," "hoe downs," or "dig downs," according to Charles Anderson, because folks would "dig right into it, and give it all they got."[124] Without question, pleasure was inescapably ensnared with expenditure and dissolution—bodies exhausted and restored, broken and unsovereign, anguished and redressed. This state of expenditure, according to Victor Turner, is an integral part of the performance process, for in the "breakdown," the individual is "reduced or ground down in order to be fashioned anew."[125] The breakdown also illuminates the dilemma of pleasure and possession since the body broken by dance insinuates its other, its double, the body broken by the regimen of labor and (dis)possessed by the chattel principle.[126] This doubling of the body bespeaks the ambivalence of pleasure and illuminates the brutal and myriad uses of slave property and the infinitesimal and innumerable assaults posed in the expression of need and desire.

BLACK

The anomalous social
formation of cargo shapes
the field of action

Grief diminishes the value of the commodity

Healing the flesh/Releasing the body

Redress is a re-membering of the social body
that occurs precisely in the recognition and
articulation of devastation

The quotidian articulates the wounds of
history and the enormity of the breach

Insurgent claims transform need into politics

Politics without a proper locus

The art of cunning and dissemblance

The prerogative of no

Subterranean History

Her refusal culminates in the
death of the master

Infrapolitics of the dominated

The plurality of resistance enacted in
everyday life is produced by and details
the relations and mechanisms of power

Pleasure as a figure of
social transformation

Flight

PRACTICE

The nonautonomy
of practice

Assemb

The morality of free society
can have no application to
slave society

There are small acts, there are
loopholes, the attempts to sidest
the terror, the expected violence,
the anticipated death

Inadvertent, continge
and submerged forms
of contestation

ANTAGONISM

Juba

We raise de wheat,
Dey gib us de corn;
We bake de bread,
Dey gib us de crust;
We sif de meal,
Dey gib us de huss;

Transgression of the policed space of
subordination through unlicensed travel
and collective assembly

Counterinvestment in the body as a site
of pleasure and the articulation of needs
and desire

Ways of operating that undo the law
of property

Meeting a lover in the canebrake

The surreptitious dance

Stealing the meeting

Dangerous thought

The disruptive assertions,
necessarily a part of stealing
away, ultimately defy the
law of property

he Clearing

The Shout

Marronage

GATHERING

CRIMINALITY

Refusal

Stealing away is the vehicle
for the redemptive figuration
of the dispossessed

Crime

Insurgent claims. She
issues a threat to those
intent on looking and
groping

She threw the
baby away

Murder. Poison. Arson.

Celia's declaration of the limit
was an emancipatory articulation
of the desire for a different
economy of enjoyment

matrix of future increase

3

Seduction and the Ruses of Power

> In the very nature of things, he [the slave] is subject to despotism. Law as to him is only a compact between his rulers, and the questions which concern him are matters agitated between them.
>
> —Justice D. L. Wardlaw, *Ex parte Boylston*

> You never knew what it is to be a slave; to be entirely unprotected by law or custom; to have the laws reduce you to the condition of chattel, entirely subject to the will of another.
>
> —Harriet A. Jacobs, *Incidents in the Life of a Slave Girl, Written by Herself*

> The relation between legal interpretation and the infliction of pain remains operative even in the most routine of legal acts.
>
> —Robert Cover, "Violence and the Word"

In nineteenth-century common law, rape was defined as the forcible carnal knowledge of a female against her will and without her consent.[1] Yet the actual or attempted rape of an enslaved woman was an offense neither recognized nor punished by law. Rape was unimaginable because of purported black lasciviousness and carnality; the repression of rape as a category of injury or assault gave license to violence and displaced white culpability. Both the recognition of black humanity in slave law and the designation of the black subject as the originary locus of transgression and offense resulted in legal distributions of pain and death. To be recognized as a subject of law did not remedy subjection or position the captive outside the reach of slavery's terror, but, to the contrary, strengthened its clutch and enabled another order of violence to unfold.

The cases of *State of Missouri v. Celia, a Slave* and *George v. State* averred that the enslaved were not subjects of common law, thus not protected against rape.[2] Slaves were placed solely under the regulation of statutory law (slave codes) and not covered by the common law, though the rape of slave women was not a statutory offense either. The repression or effacement of rape cannot be explained completely by the inapplicability of common law to the enslaved. The erasure and negation of this act of violence is central not only to the pained constitution of blackness, but also to the figuration and deployment of sexuality in the context of captivity. The disavowal of rape most obviously involves issues of consent, agency, and will that are ensnared in a larger dilemma concerning the construction of person and the calculation of black humanity in slave law, since this repression of violence constitutes female gender as the locus of both unredressed and negligible injury.[3]

The dual invocation of person and property made issues of consent, will, and agency complicated and ungainly. Yet the law strove to contain the tensions generated by this seemingly contradictory invocation of the enslaved as property and person, as absolutely subject to the will of another and as actional subject by relying on the power of feelings or the mutual affection between master and slave and the "strength of weakness" or the ability of the dominated to influence, if not control, the dominant. The twinned existence of the slave as property and person was an effort to wed reciprocity and submission, intimacy and domination, the legitimacy of violence and the necessity of protection. The law's selective recognition of slave humanity nullified the captive's ability to give consent or act as agent and, at the same time, acknowledged the intentionality and agency of the slave, but only as it assumed the form of criminality.

The recognition and/or stipulation of agency as criminality served to identify personhood with punishment. Within the terms of the law, the enslaved was either a will-less object or a chastened agent.

If the definition of the crime of rape relies upon the capacity to give consent or exercise will, then how does one make legible the sexual violation of the enslaved when that which would constitute evidence of intentionality, and proof of the crime—the state of consent or willingness of the assailed—opens up a Pandora's box in which the subject formation and object constitution of the enslaved female are no less ponderous than the crime itself; or when the legal definition of the enslaved negates the very idea of "reasonable resistance"?⁴ We might also consider whether the wanton and indiscriminate uses of the captive body can be understood or grasped within the heteronormative framing of sexual violation as rape. If a crime can be said, in fact, to exist or is at all fathomable within the scope of any normative understanding of rape, perhaps it can only be apprehended or discerned precisely as it is entangled with the construction of person in slave law and the punitive stipulation of agency as servility or criminality. It is only by probing at the limits of the law and by examining issues of will and consent, subjectivity and injury, and instances of sexual violence that fall outside the racist and heteronormative framing of rape that the anomalous condition or the category crisis of the captive comes into view. The sexual exploitation of slave women cloaked as the legitimate use of property and the castration and assault of slave men fall outside the legal definition of rape. I feel it is warranted to look at this range of violence as sexual violation because enslaved men were no less vulnerable to the wanton abuses of their owners, although the extent of their sexual exploitation will probably never be known. The elusiveness or instability of gender in relation to the slave as property makes infinite the varieties of violence, which range from the terrible spectacle of Aunt Hester at the whipping post to the postbellum specter of lynching. The erotics of terror in the racist imaginary take hold of and inhabit the captive body, indifferent to the categories male and female. The aim is to make visible the "crimes" licensed and disavowed in the law by highlighting the violence of omission (the crimes of the state) and the categorization of negligible injury.

What Thomas Jefferson termed the boisterous passions of slavery, the "unremitting despotism" of slave owners, and the "degrading submissions" of the enslaved were curiously embraced, denied, inverted, and displaced in the law of slavery.[5] The boisterous passions bespeak the dynamics of enjoyment in a context in which joy and domination and use and violence could not be separated. As well, this language of passion expresses the essential conflation of force and feeling. The confusion between consent and coercion, feeling and submission, intimacy and domination, and violence and reciprocity constitutes what I term the *discourse of seduction* in slave law.[6] The discourse of seduction obfuscates the primacy and extremity of violence in master-slave relations and in the construction of the slave as both property and person. To paraphrase John Forrester, seduction is a meditation on liberty and slavery and will and subjection in the arena of sexuality.[7] Seduction makes recourse to the idea of reciprocal and collusive relations and engenders a precipitating construction of black female sexuality in which rape is unimaginable. As the enslaved is legally unable to give consent or offer resistance, she is presumed to be always willing.[8]

If the legal existence of the crime of rape depends upon evaluating the *mens rea* and *actus rea* of the perpetrator and, more important, the consent or nonconsent of the victim, then how does one grapple with issues of consent and will when the negation or restricted recognition of these terms determines the meaning of enslavement?[9] If the commonplace understanding of the "will" implies the power to control and determine our actions and identifies the expressive capacity of the self-possessed and intending subject, then certainly this is far afield of the condition or terms of action available to the enslaved. Yet the notion of the will connotes more than simply the capacity to act and to do; rather, it distinguishes the autonomous agent from the enslaved, the encumbered, and the constrained. Not only does the extremity of power and the absolute submission required of the slave render suspect or meaningless concepts of consent and will, but the sheer lack of limitations regarding the violence "necessary" to the maintenance of slave relations—that is, black submission—unmoors the notion of "force." What limit must be exceeded in order that the violence directed at the black body be made legible in the law? In the case of slave women, the law's circumscribed recognition of consent and will occurred only in order to intensify and secure the subordination of the enslaved, repress the crime, and deny injury. Before the law, the captive female was both will-less and always willing. The utter negation of the captive's will required to secure absolute submission was identified as *willful* submission to the master in the topsy-turvy scenario of onerous passions. Within this scenario, the constraints of sentiment were no less severe than those of violence. The purportedly binding passions of master-slave relations were predicated upon the inability of the enslaved to exercise her will in any way other than serving the master, and in this respect, she existed only as an extension or embodiment of the owner's rights of property. To act outside the scope of willful submission was to defy the law. The surety of punishment awaited such transgressions.

The Violence of the Law

I went to converse with Celia (defendant) at the request of several citizens. The object of my conversation was to ascertain whether she had any accomplices in the crime. This was eight

or ten days after she had been put into the jail. I asked whether
she thought she would be hung for what she had done. She
said she thought she would be hung. I then had her to tell the
whole matter. She said the old man (Newsome, the deceased)
had been having sexual intercourse with her. That he had told
her he was coming down to her cabin that night. She told him
not to come and if he came she would hurt him. She then got a
stick and put it in the corner. He came down that night. There
was very little fire in the cabin that night. When she heard
him coming she fixed the fire to make a little light. She said
his face was towards her and he was standing talking to her
when she struck him. He did not raise his hand when she went
to strike the first blow but sunk down on a stool towards the
floor. Threw his hands up as he sunk down. . . . The stick with
which she struck was about as large as the upper part of a . . .
chair, but not so long. . . . She said after she had killed him, the
body laid a long time, she thought an hour. She did not know
what to do with it. She said she would try to burn it.

In *State of Missouri v. Celia, a Slave*, Celia was prosecuted for the
murder of her owner, Robert Newsome. The first time Newsome
raped Celia was on the day he purchased her. He only stopped four
years later when she killed him. Celia was found guilty by the court
and sentenced to death by hanging. Although her attorney argued
that the laws of Missouri concerning crimes of ravishment embraced
slave women as well as white women and that Celia was acting to
defend herself, this argument was rejected by the court. *Missouri v.
Celia* raises critical questions about sexuality, agency, consent, and
subjectivity. Perhaps this is why the case was never reported or published. This case was neglected for over 145 years; it was not cited
in any legal index but abandoned in a file drawer at the Callaway
County Courthouse. Cases involving cruelty of a sexual nature were

often not reported or were omitted from the report of cases.[10] The few cases involving issues of rape and sexual violence that are available in legal indexes, not surprisingly, are civil cases concerned with the recovery of damages for the loss of slave property or criminal cases in which the enslaved and their "crimes," usually efforts to resist, defend, or flee from such violations, are on trial. For example, *Humphrey v. Utz*, a case in which a slave owner sued his overseer for the death of a slave who had been beaten brutally by the overseer and then subjected to a range of cruelties that included having his penis nailed to a bedpost, was also omitted from the state report of cases. These cases confirm and document the sexual violence routinely directed at the enslaved and the obscene way in which these atrocities entered the legal record as suits for damage to property or criminal charges made against the enslaved.

As *Missouri v. Celia* demonstrated, the enslaved could neither give nor refuse consent, nor offer reasonable resistance; yet they were criminally responsible and liable. The slave was recognized as a reasoning subject who possessed intent and rationality solely in the context of criminal liability. Ironically, the slave's will was acknowledged only as it was prohibited or punished. It was generally the slave's crimes that were on trial, not white violence or the ordinary brutality of the institution. Pain was inflicted by the most routine legal acts. In the effort to shift the locus of culpability from the captive, my attention turns of the crimes of the state and the white world, and to the inescapable violence that characterized the existence of the human commodity.[11] In positing the black as criminal, the state obfuscated its instrumental role in terror by projecting all culpability and wrongdoing onto the enslaved. The black body was simply the site on which the "crimes" of the dominant class and the violence of the state were externalized in the form of a threat. The criminality imputed to blacks disavowed white violence as a necessary response to the threatening agency of blackness. I employ

the terms *"white* culpability" and *"white* offense" because the absolute submission mandated by law was not simply that of slave to her
owner but the submission of the enslaved to all whites.[12]

The assignation of right and blame and privilege and punishment was a central element in the construction of racial difference
and the absolute distinctions of status between free white persons
and black captives. As the case of *State v. Tackett* made clear, "The
relation between a white man and a slave differs from that which
subsists between free persons." In this case, the Supreme Court of
North Carolina reversed a lower court ruling that convicted a non-
slave-owning white for the murder of a slave. (*State v. Tackett* also
involved the sexual arrangements of slavery and the conjugal relations of the enslaved, although they were considered incidental to
the case. Daniel, the murdered slave, had accused Tackett of "keeping his [Daniel's] wife," Lotty, and threatened to kill him if he did
not leave Lotty alone.) The court held that common-law standards
of provocation and mitigation were not applicable to the relation
between a white man and a slave: "The homicide of a slave may be
extenuated by acts, which would not produce a legal provocation if
done by a white person."[13] The extenuating circumstances included
arrogance, insult, trespass, and troublesome deportment. Acts of
homicide, battery, and mayhem were sanctioned if not deemed
essential to proper relations of free white persons and black captives
and the maintenance of black submission.[14]

White culpability was displaced as black criminality, and violence was legitimated as the ruling principle of the social relations of
racial slavery, just as Newsome's constant violations were eclipsed
by the criminal agency of Celia. *Missouri v. Celia* illustrates how difficult it is to uncover and articulate the sexual violation of enslaved
women exactly because the crime surfaces obliquely and only as the
captive confesses her guilt. Ultimately, the motive for Celia's act
was deemed inadmissible, and her voice was usurped and negated,

for her white inquisitors spoke for her during the trial. As neither slaves nor free blacks were allowed to testify against whites, the "crime" that precipitated the murder of Newsome was denied.

To assert that Celia was raped is to issue a provocation. It is a declaration intended to shift our attention to another locus of crime. It is to envision the unimaginable, excavate the repressed, and discern the illegible. It is to reveal sentiment and protection as the guise of violence in the legal construction of the captive person and, in particular, the slippage of desire and domination in the loosely constructed term "sexual intercourse." In the trial record, the "sexuality" of Celia was ensnared in the web of others' demands, and the trace of what I risk calling her "desire" was only discernible in the compliance with and defiance of these competing claims.[15] As the trial record stated, Newsome had been having "sexual intercourse" with Celia, he "forced her" on the day he purchased her, and, last, George, Celia's enslaved companion, "would have nothing to do with her if she did not *quit* the old man." "Coercion," "desire," "submission," and "complicity" are the circulating terms that come to characterize the sexuality of Celia, or the enslaved female, less than the way in which she is inhabited by sexuality and her body possessed.[16] Simply put, Celia embodied the vested rights of others.

The abjection of the captive body exceeds that which can be conveyed by the designation of or difference between "slave" women and "free" women. In this case, what is at issue is the difference between the deployment of sexuality in the contexts of white kinship—the proprietorial relation of the patriarch to his wife and children, the making of legitimate heirs, and the transmission of property—and black captivity—the reproduction of property, the relations of mastery and subjection, natal alienation and kinlessness, and the regularity of sexual violence—rather than the imputed "freedom" of white women or free black women. The engendering of race occurs within these different economies of constraint and by way of divergent methods of sexual control. Kinship and captivity designate radically different conditions of embodiment; and they reveal the determinacy of race in the deployment of sexuality and underline the particular mechanisms through which bodies are disciplined and regulated.

The (re)production of enslavement and the legal codification of racial subordination depended upon various methods of sexual control and domination: antimiscegenation statutes, rape laws that made the rape of white women by black men a capital offense, the sanctioning of sexual violence against slave women by virtue of the law's calculation of negligible injury, the negation of kinship, and the commercial vitiation of motherhood as a means for the reproduction and conveyance of property and black subordination.[17] *Alfred v. State* illuminates the convergence of these varied techniques in maintaining the domination of the enslaved and cultivating pained and burdened personhood. In *Alfred v. State*, Alfred, a slave, was indicted for the murder of his overseer, Coleman. A witness testified that Alfred admitted having killed the overseer: "The defendant wanted to introduce a witness on his behalf, a slave named Charlotte, who stated that she was the wife of the prisoner. . . . Prisoner's counsel then proposed to prove, by Charlotte, that about nine or ten o'clock in the morning . . . Coleman 'had forced her to submit to sexual intercourse with him'; and that she had communicated the fact to the prisoner before the killing."[18] Although the defense attempted to introduce Charlotte as a witness and thereby prove that Alfred's action was motivated by the rape of his wife, the district attorney objected to Charlotte's testimony. The court sustained the objection; the prisoner was convicted and sentenced to death by hanging.[19]

What is at issue here are the ways in which various mechanisms of sexual domination—the sanction and disavowal of rape, the negation of kinship, and the legal invalidation of slave marriage—act in concert. In this instance, sexuality is a central dimension of the power exercised over and against the slave population and entails everything from compulsory couplings to the right to manage life.[20] Charlotte's testimony was rejected because her relation to Alfred had no legal status, and thus it could not provide an alibi or motive for Alfred's action. The disallowance of the marital relation, in turn, rendered superfluous Charlotte's sexual violation.[21] In the rejection of Charlotte as witness, her status as wife and partner of Alfred was negated, her rape displaced as adultery and then dismissed, and the violence that precipitated the overseer's murder erased.

It is also significant that the rape of Charlotte is interpreted narrowly within the frame of "outrages of conjugal affections" and as adultery. The defense's argument focused on the violation of Alfred's rights as a "husband" rather than on the rape of Charlotte. Alfred's counsel unsuccessfully argued that "the humanity of our law . . . regards with as much tenderness the excesses of outraged conjugal affections in the negro as in the white man. The servile condition . . . has not deprived him of his social or moral instincts, and he is as much entitled to the protection of the laws, when acting under their influence, as if he were freed." The discussion of a husband's conjugal rights, even if that "husband" is a slave, supplants the rape of the "wife."[22] In all likelihood, the court denied Alfred the right to vindicate this outrage because the decedent was white. However, in cases of this nature involving other slaves, the court sometimes recognized the husband's exclusive sexual rights in his wife and "the sudden fury excited by finding a man in the very act of shame with his wife."[23] Ultimately, the motive for Alfred's act was deemed irrelevant because of the need to preserve black subordination and affirm the presumably negligible status of the injury.

Alfred v. State illuminates the legal mechanisms by which sexuality and subordination were yoked in securing the social relations of slavery. On the one hand, the management of slave sexuality indifferently translated the rape of slave women into adultery or sexual intercourse; on the other, it refused to recognize or grant any legitimacy to relations forged among the enslaved. The rape of black women existed as an unspoken but normative condition fully within the purview of everyday sexual practices, whether within the implied arrangements of the slave enclave or within the plantation household. This is evidenced in myriad ways, from the evasion and indirection that euphemized rape as ravishment or sex as carnal knowledge to the utter omission and repression of the crime in slave statute and case law. In this case, the normativity of rape is to be derived from the violence of the law—the identity or coincidence of legitimate uses of slave property and what Hortense Spillers terms "high crimes against the flesh." In this case, the normativity of sexual violence establishes an inextricable link between racial difference and sexual subjection.[24] As well, the virtual absence of prohibitions or limitations in the determination of socially tolerable and necessary violence sets the stage for the indiscriminate use of the body.

The legal transposition of rape as sexual intercourse shrouds this condition of violent domination with the suggestion of complicity. Sexual intercourse, regardless of whether it is coerced or consensual, comes to describe the arrangements, however violent, between men and enslaved females. (Enslaved women were also raped by enslaved men. Women and girls were not protected in these cases either.) What does sexuality designate when rape is a normative mode of its deployment? What set of effects does it produce? How can rape be differentiated from sexuality when "consent" is intelligible only as submission? How can we discern the crime when it is a legitimate use of property or when the black captive is made the originary locus of liability?[25] Does the regularity of violation transform it into an arrangement or a liaison from which the captive female can extract herself, if she chooses, as a lover's request or adultery would seem to imply?[26] Can she use or wield sexuality as a weapon of the weak? Do four years and two children later imply submission, resignation, complicity, desire, or the extremity of constraint?[27]

It is this slippage that Celia's act brings to a standstill through the intervention of her will or what inadequately approximates desire. To speak of will or desire broaches a host of issues that revolve upon the terms, dimensions, and conditions of action. Moreover, the term "will" is an overextended approximation of the agency of the dispossessed subject/object of property, or perhaps simply unrecognizable in a context in which act and intentionality are inseparable from the threat of punishment. It is possible to read Celia's act as a liberation of the captive body or as an escape from the master's hold, however transient this release, or as a decisive shift in embodiment, a movement from Newsome's Celia to Celia's body, though my intention is merely to underscore the act's complexity. The full dimensions of this act and the resignation, courage, or glimpse of possibility that might have fueled it defy comprehensive analysis since we have access to Celia's life only as it has been recorded by her interrogators and represented as crime. The fateful negotiation of autonomy at the site of the expended and exploited body affirms both the impossibility of consent and the struggle to mitigate the brutal constraints of captivity through an entitlement denied the captive—"no," the prerogative of refusal. Ultimately, Celia was hanged for this refusal. This effort to reclaim the body and experience embodiment as full, inviolate, and pleasurable, not as an extension of another's will or right or as a condition of expenditure or defilement, led Celia to construct a boundary at the threshold of her cabin that would shield her from the tacit violence seen as "befitting" the relation of slave owner and enslaved female. As A. Leon Higginbotham remarks, the Missouri court in pronouncing Celia's guilt "held that the end of slavery is not merely 'the [economic] profit of the master' but also the joy of the master in the sexual conquest of the slave."[28] In the end, Celia's declaration of the limit was a radical articulation of the desire for a different economy of enjoyment.

The Bonds of Affection

The effacement of rape in the context of enslavement is in service of the full enjoyment of the slave as thing. The eliding of rape must also be considered in relation to what is callously termed the recognition of slave humanity and the particular mechanisms of tyrannical power that converge on the black body. Tyranny is not a rhetorical inflation, but designates the absoluteness of power. Gender, if at all appropriate in this scenario, must be understood as indissociable from violence, the vicious refiguration of rape as mutual and shared desire, the wanton exploitation of the captive body tacitly sanctioned as a legitimate use of property, the disavowal of injury, and the absolute possession of the body and its "issue." In short, black *and* female difference is registered by virtue of the extremity of power operating on captive bodies and licensed within the scope of the humane and the tolerable.[29]

The sexual violence commensurate with the exercise of property rights and essential to the making of perfect submission was dissembled by black female "excesses"—immoderate and overabundant sexuality, bestial appetites and capacities that were most often likened to those of the orangutan, and an untiring readiness that was outstripped only by the extent of her willingness.[30] Lasciviousness made unnecessary the protection of rape law, for insatiate black desire presupposed that all sexual intercourse was welcomed, if not pursued. The state's crimes of omission and proaction—the failure to extend protection and the sanctioning of violence in the name of rights of property—disappeared before the spectacle of black concupiscence. The nonexistence of rape as a category of injury pointed not to the violence of the law but to the enslaved woman as a guilty accomplice and seducer. The omissions of law must be read symptomatically within an economy of bodies in which the full enjoyment of the slave as thing depended upon absolute authority and the exhaustive consumption of the body in its myriad capacities.[31]

The construction of black subjectivity as will-less, abject, insatiate, pained, and the instrumental deployment of sexuality in the reproduction of property and racial difference, usurped the category of rape. Sexuality formed the nexus in which black, female, and chattel were inextricably bound and acted to intensify the constraints of slave status by subjecting the body to another order of violation and whim.[32] The despotic exercise of power (the dominion of the slaveholder and all white persons) made violence indistinguishable from the full enjoyment of the thing. The tensions generated by the law's dual invocation of property and person, or by "full enjoyment" and limited protection to life and limb, were masked by the phantasmal allure of the carnal black.[33] Rape disappeared through the intervention of seduction—the assertion of the slave woman's complicity and willful submission. Seduction was central to the very making and imagination of the antebellum South, the erotic South, for it provided a way of masking the antagonistic fissures of the social by ascribing to the object of property an ensnaring and criminal agency. Black carnality provided the alibi and the cover for the barbarous forms of white enjoyment permitted within the law.

The discourse of seduction enabled those disgusted and enraged by the sexual arrangements of slavery, like Mary Boykin Chesnut, to target slave women as the culprits responsible for their husbands' downfall. The complicity of slave women displaced the act of sexual violence. According to Chesnut, decent white women were forced to live with husbands degraded by the lowliness of their enslaved "mistresses": "Under slavery, we lived surrounded by prostitutes, yet an abandoned woman is sent out of any decent house. Who thinks any worse of a Negro or mulatto woman for being a thing we can't name?"[34] The sexual exploitation of the enslaved female, incredulously, served as evidence of her collusion with the master class and as proof of her power, the power both to render the master weak and, implicitly, to be the mistress of her own subjection. The captive female not only suffered the responsibility for her sexual (ab)use but also was blameworthy because of her purported ability to render the powerful weak.

Even those like Fanny Kemble, who eloquently described the "simple horror and misery" that slave women regularly experienced, held enslaved females responsible for their abuse. When confronted with the inescapable constancy of rape and the "string of detestable details" that comprised the life of enslaved women, and after yet another woman, Sophy, shared her experience of violation, Kemble exclaimed: "Ah! but don't you know—did nobody ever teach any of you that it is a sin to live with men who are not your husbands?!"[35] Sophy, appropriately and vehemently, responded, "Oh, yes, missis, we know—we know all about dat well enough; but we do anything to get our poor flesh some rest from the whip; when he made me follow him into de bush, what use me tell him no? He have strength to make me."[36]

The equivocations that surround issues of consensual sexual relations under domination, the eliding of sexual violence by the imputation of the slave woman's sexual appetite or lack of virtue, and the presumption of consent as a consequence of the utter powerlessness of her "no" (the "no means yes" philosophy) are important constituents of the discourse of seduction. In a more expansive or generic sense, seduction denotes a theory of power that demands the absolute and "perfect" submission of the enslaved as the guiding principle of slave relations, and yet seeks to mitigate the avowedly necessary brutality of slave relations through the shared affections of owner and captive. What does mutuality or reciprocity mean at the threshold of Celia's cabin? What affection can be imagined after four years of abuse?

The doctrine of "perfect submission" reconciled violence and the claims of mutual benevolence between master and slave as necessary in securing the harmony of the institution. The presumed mutuality of feelings enchanted the brutal and direct violence of master-slave relations. Bearing this in mind, the term "seduction" is employed here to designate this displacement and euphemization of violence, for seduction epitomizes the discursive alchemy that shrouds direct forms of violence under the "veil of enchanted relations"—the reciprocal and mutual relations of master and slave.[37] This mining of the discourse of seduction attempts to illuminate the violence obscured by the veil by sifting through the language of power and feelings, specifically the manipulations of the weak and the kindheartedness and moral instruction of the powerful.

The benign representation of the paternal institution in slave law depicted the master-slave relationship as typified by the bonds of affection and this discursive alchemy transformed relations of violence and domination into those of affinity. Mutuality or relation depended upon a construction of the enslaved black as one easily inclined to submission, a skilled maneuverer wielding weakness masterfully and a potentially threatening insubordinate who could only be disciplined through violence. At stake in social fantasy is the representation of extreme violence and brutal use to whatever end by whatever means as a nonantagonistic, organic, and complementary relation. The ability of the South (and the nation) to imagine racial slavery as a paternal and benign institution and master-slave relations as bound by feelings depended on the specter of the obsequious and threatening slave. This Manichaean construction undergirded both the necessary violence and the bonds of affection set forth in slave law. As well, this fantasy enabled a vision of whiteness defined primarily by its complementary relation to blackness and by the desire to incorporate and regulate black excess.[38] Seduction provided a holistic vision of social order, not divided by antagonisms, but rather precariously balancing barbarism and civilization, violence and protection, mutual benevolence and absolute submission, brutality and sentiment. This harmonious vision of community, this fantasy, depended upon the exercise of violence and the bonds of affection. The consonance of the weak and the powerful, as presumed and elaborated in slave statute, made protection against violence unnecessary; and the consequences of this belief were devastating and often fatal.

How does seduction uphold perfect submission and, at the same time, assert the alluring, if not threatening force of the dominated? It does so by forwarding the strength of weakness. As a theory of power, seduction contends that there is an ostensible equality between the dominant and the dominated. The dominated acquire power based upon the identification of force and feeling. Seduction, as Jean Baudrillard writes, "play[s] triumphantly with weakness."[39] The artifice of weakness not only provides seduction with its power but also defines its essential character, for the enactment of weakness and the "impenetrable obscurity" of femininity and blackness harbor a conspiracy of power.[40] The dominated catalyze reversals of power, not by challenges presented to the system but by succumbing to the system's logic. Within this frame, power comes to be defined not by domination but by the manipulations of the dominated. The reversibility of power and the play of the dominated discredit the force of violence through the assertion of reciprocal and intimate relations. In this regard, the recognition of the power of the weak sustains subjection, while proclaiming the strength and influence of those in chains.

The proslavery ideologue George Fitzhugh celebrated the reversibility of power enacted through surrender. In *Cannibals All! Or, Slaves without Masters*, Fitzhugh argued that the strength of weakness disrupts the hierarchy of power within the family, as well as the master-slave relationship. Appearances conspire to contrary purposes; the seemingly weak slave, like the infant or (white) woman, exercises capricious dominion: "The dependent exercise, because of their dependence, as much control over their superiors, in most things, as those superiors exercise over them. Thus and thus only, can conditions be equalized."[41] Seduction appears to be a necessary labor, one required to extend and reproduce the claims of power, though advanced in the guise of the subaltern's control and disruptions: "The humble and obedient slave exercises more or less control over the most brutal and hard-hearted master. It is an invariable law of nature, that weakness and dependence are elements of strength, and generally sufficiently limit that universal despotism, observable throughout human and animal nature."[42] If, as Fitzhugh insists, the greatest slave is the master of the household, and the enslaved rule by virtue of the "strength of weakness," then, in effect, the slave is made the master of her subjection.

As Fitzhugh envisioned, kindness and affection undergirded the relations of subordination and dependency. As a model of social order, the patriarchal family depended upon duty, status, and protection rather than consent, equality, and civil freedom. Subjection was not only naturalized but consonant with the sentimental equality of reciprocity, inasmuch as the power of affection licensed the strength of weakness. Essentially, "the strength of weakness" prevailed due to the goodness of the father, "The armor of affection and benevolence." The generosity of the father enabled the victory claimed by the slave, the tyrannical child, and the brooding wife. The bonds of affection within the slaveholding family circle permitted the tyranny of weakness and supplanted the stranglehold of the ruling father. Ironically, the family circle remained intact as much because of the bonds of affection as the tyranny of the weak. Feeling bound the interests of the master and those of the slave in a delicate state of equilibrium, as one form of strength modified the other.[43] So we are to believe that the exercise of control by the weak softens universal despotism, subdues the power of the father by commanding his care, and guarantees the harmony of slave relations.

Seduction erects a family romance, papering over the kinlessness of the enslaved with a fiction of the plantation household bound by ties of affection (not blood). The elaboration of a racial and sexual fantasy transposes domination into mutual affection, subjection opens the pathway to equality, and perfect subordination is declared the means of ensuring great happiness and harmony. The patriarchal model of social order erected by Fitzhugh marries equality and despotism through an explicit critique of consent, possessive individualism, and contractual relations.[44] Feelings rather than contract are the necessary corrective to universal despotism; duty and reciprocity rather than consent become the basis for equality. The despotic and sovereign power celebrated by Fitzhugh could be abated only by the "bonds of affection," a phrase that resonates with the ambivalence attendant to the relation of owner and object.

If a conspiracy of power resides within seduction, then questions arise as to the exact nature of this conspiracy: Who seduces whom? Does the slave become entrapped in the enchanted web of the owner's dominion, lured by promises of protection and care? Does the guile and subterfuge of the dependent mitigate the effects of power? Are the manipulations and transgressions of the dominated fated to reproduce the very order presumably challenged by such actions? Or do such enactments on the part of the owner and the enslaved, the feigned concessions of power and the stylized performance of naïveté, effect any shifts or disruptions of force or compulsively restage power and powerlessness?

A Brutal Hand, a Yielding Heart

Seduction reifies the idea of submission by proclaiming it the pathway to ostensible equality, protection, and social harmony.

As expounded by proslavery ideologues like Fitzhugh or as a legal principle guiding master-slave relations, seduction professed that power and protection were acquired through surrender. To reiterate the tautology, the dominated exert influence over the dominant by virtue of their weakness, and therefore more formal protections against despotism or guarantors of mutuality are redundant. The insinuation that the enslaved were likewise invested in their subjugation recast violence in the ambiguous guise of affection and declared hegemony rather than domination the ruling term of order.[45] The assertion that coercion *and* consent characterized the condition of enslavement can be seen in the implied and explicit promises of protection extended by the law.

The necessity of submission—the slave must be subject to the master's will in all things—was upheld as the guiding principle of slave relations. Slave law ensured the rights of property and the absolute submission of the slave, while attending to limited forms of slave subjectivity. It granted slave owners virtually absolute rights and militated against the abuses of such authority by granting limited protection to slaves against "callous and coldblooded" murder, torture, and maiming, although procedural constraints, most notably the fact that a slave or free black could not serve as witness against a white person, acted as safeguards against white liability and made these laws virtually impossible to enforce. In the effort to attend to the interests of master and slave, the law elaborated a theory of power in which the affection of slave owners and the influence of the enslaved compensated for its failures and omissions. Mutual regard and influence were to bridge the shortcomings of law concerning the protection of black life. The ethic of perfect submission recognized the unlimited dominion of the slave owner yet tempered this dominion by invoking the centrality of affections in regulating the asymmetries of power in the master-slave relation.[46] The dual existence of the slave as property and person and the interests and absolute dominion of the slave owner were to be maintained in precarious balance by forwarding the role of attachment in mitigating brutality.

The case of *State v. Mann*, although it doesn't specifically involve issues of sexuality or rape, is important in considering the place of affection, violence, and surrender in the law. Mann was indicted for assault and battery upon Lydia, a slave of Elizabeth Jones whom he had hired for a year: "During the term, the slave had committed some small offence, for which the Defendant undertook to chastise her—that while in the act of so doing, the slave ran off, whereupon the Defendant called upon her to stop, which being refused, he shot and wounded her."[47] The lower court convicted Mann, finding him guilty of "cruel and unwarrantable punishment, and disproportionate to the offense committed by the slave." However, in an appeal to the North Carolina Supreme Court, the decision was reversed. While the liability of the hirer, Mann, to the owner for an injury presumably impairing the value of slave property was left to general rules of bailment (the transfer of possession, which in this case would be the delivery of the damaged slave and the amount equal to the diminution in value as a result of the injury), the charges of criminal battery were overturned. Even if the injury diminished the value of slave property, it was not indictable as cruel and unreasonable battery. The court held that the power of the master was absolute and not a subject for discussion.[48]

The higher court ruling held that the master had absolute power to render the submission of the slave perfect; yet it was also argued that the harshness of such a principle would be counterbalanced not by existing legislation but by feelings—the benevolence and affection between master and slave and the ruling moral code. In other words, the court considered affection to be an internal regulating principle of slave relations. The Supreme Court reversed the decision of the lower court on the following grounds: the power of the master had to be absolute in order "to render the submission of the slave perfect" although "as a principle of moral right, every person in his retirement must repudiate it. But in the actual condition of things it must be so." Yet the harshness implied by this difficult yet unavoidable decision would be mitigated by "the protection already afforded by several statutes (which made it illegal to murder a slave in cold blood), . . . the private interest of the owner, *the benevolence toward each other, seated in the hearts of those who have been born and bred together,* [and] the . . . deep execrations of the community upon the barbarian, who is guilty of excessive cruelty to his unprotected slave" [emphasis mine].

While the court acknowledged that the scope of such absolute rights of property left the enslaved open to violent abuses, it also recognized that the right to abuse had to be guaranteed to safeguard the institution, since the amorphous "public good" mandated the absolute subordination of the enslaved. The opinion amended this brutal admission with the assurance that the rights of ownership generally precluded such abuses because of self-interest, that is, pecuniary considerations. The rights of ownership, even temporary rights of possession, permitted any and all means necessary to render perfect submission; however, it was hoped that the use of excessive force was unnecessary because of the reciprocal benevolence of master-slave relations.

Rather than distinguish between implied relations and absolute dominance or separate affection from violence, the court considered them both essential to the maintenance and longevity of the institution of racial slavery. The ethic of submission embraced absolute power and human feeling, a brutal hand and the pull of the heartstring. The court, acknowledging the chasm between moral principle and the actual conditions necessary to sustain and reproduce slavery, stated plainly: the obedience of the slave was "the consequence only of uncontrolled authority over the body." How else could perpetual labor and submission be guaranteed? The services of one "doomed in his person and his posterity" and "without knowledge or the capacity to make anything his own, and to toil that another may reap the fruits" could only be expected of "one who has no will of his own" and "who surrenders his will in perfect obedience to that of another."[49] To be sure, the power of the master had to be absolute to produce this surrender of the will. For the "one doomed in his person and posterity," the law inflicted pain and death, offering it as remedy.

Perfect submission was an ordering principle of the social and to be accomplished by whatever violent means necessary; the only restraint on this extreme power depended upon feelings, not law, to guarantee basic protections to the enslaved. Submission not only encompassed the acquisition of power, but also explicitly addressed the power of affection in influencing relations between master and slave, although the court distinguished between the relationship of master and slave and other domestic relations with which it was frequently compared, like those of a parent and child, tutor and pupil, master and servant. The centrality ascribed to the role of feelings implicitly acknowledged the unrestricted violence the *Mann* opinion had licensed, yet minimized the consequences of this through an appeal to "moral right" rather than the actual condition of things. Feelings were to balance the use and role of force. As Judge Ruffin states: "I must freely confess my sense of the harshness of this proposition; I feel it as deeply as any man can; and as a principle of moral right every person in his retirement must repudiate it. But in the actual condition of things it must be so."

The importance attributed to the intimacies of domination illustrates the role of seduction in the law. As the opinion clearly stated, power resided not only in the title to slave property but also in the bonds of affection. Feelings repudiated and corrected the violence legitimated by law. Material interests and mutual benevolence would "mitigat[e] the rigors of servitude and ameliorat[e] the condition of the slave" and protect the slave from the ravages of abuse unleased by the ruling. In other words, the absolute and brutal dominion guaranteed by the law was to be adjusted by the influence of the enslaved—their pull on the heartstrings of the master. Slave law contradictorily asserted that absolute dominion was both necessary and voluntary. The intimacy of the master and the slave purportedly operated as an internal regulator of power and restrained the terror indispensable to unlimited dominion. In short, violence is displaced as mutual and reciprocal desire.

The significance attributed to feelings, attachment, reciprocity, and the familiarity of domestic slavery cast domination in a heartwarming light. The power of influence nurtured by the enslaved—the power of the weak to sway the powerful—and the place attributed to feeling in moderating the excesses of market relations refigured domination and exploitation as affection, and sometimes even love. Such reasoning held that violence was essential, while insisting that feelings determined the character of the master-slave relationship as well as social, familial, and political organization. In short, slave relations were dependent upon and determined by "the action taking place in individual hearts."[50]

The contradictory appeal to the public good contended that public tranquility required violence and, at the same time, served as the guarantee that this entitlement to virtually unlimited power need never be exercised. The invocation of the public good also established minimal standards for the recognition of slave humanity and required that certain provisions or protections be granted to the enslaved, like housing, clothing, food, and support for elderly and infirm slaves. Yet this concern for the welfare of the enslaved and the provisions granted them should not be mistaken for a dispensation of rights. As a judge commented in another case that hinged on determining degrees of necessary and excessive violence, although excessive violence "disturbed the harmony of society, was offensive to public decency, and directly tended to a breach of peace," the rights of the slave were extraneous to such considerations: "The same would be the law, if a horse had been so beaten. And yet it would not be pretended that it was in respect to the rights of the horse, or the feelings of humanity, that this interposition would take place."[51] The public good mandated absolute submission and minimal protections to sustain harmony and security. Even when the entreaty made in the name of the public good acted minimally on the behalf of the enslaved, it did so, not surprisingly, by granting these limited entitlements in a manner that "recognized" black humanity in accordance with minimal standards of existence. This truncated construction of the slave as person, rather than lessening the constraints of chattel status, enhanced them by making personhood conterminous with injury.

Although the public good served as the arbiter of care and coercion, the precarious status of the enslaved within this sphere raises questions about the meaning of the slave person, the protections advanced on her behalf, and the limitations of public decency. Contrary to pronouncements that sentiment would abate brutality, feelings intensified the violence of law and posed dire consequences for the calculation of black humanity, for the existence of the slave as object of property and person required that the feelings endowed to the enslaved be greatly circumscribed. While the slave was recognized as a sentient being, the degree of sentience had to be cautiously calibrated to avoid intensifying the antagonisms of the social order. How could property and person be reconciled on the ground of mutual benevolence and affection? How could the invocation of humanity and absolute submission be sustained, or the enslaved be protected, yet damned in her person and posterity?

The twofold existence of the slave as person and property can be traced to the forms of domination and coercion, accumulation and production which were integral to racial slavery.[52] The law attempted to manage this tension or conflict between the slave as subject of limited sentience and as implement of production by making more robust the language of person and human in slave statute. This effort was vital to maintaining the dominance of the slave-owning class, particularly in a period of national crisis concerning the institution. The increasing recognition of the slave person in the period 1830–1860 was an effort to combat the abolitionist polemic about the degradations of chattel status and the slave's lack of rights.[53] The double life of the slave was neither a matter of an essential ethical contradiction nor a conflict between bourgeois and slave relations (a viewpoint which assumes that racial slavery is not foundational to capitalism, but a precursor); it was an expression of the multivalence of subjection. The dual invocation quite easily accommodated the restricted recognition of the slave as person and the violence necessary to the creation of value and management of a captive population, since the figuration of the human in slave law was totally consonant with the domination of the enslaved. The acknowledgment of the slave as person was not at odds with her existence as a sentient object with a value in circulation or with the structural requirements of racial slavery, nor did it challenge the social relations of the antebellum world.

The dual invocation of law extended and constricted the rights of ownership as was necessary for the preservation of the institution. On one hand, there was increased liability for white violence committed against slaves; on the other, the law continued to decriminalize the violence thought necessary to the existence and reproduction of the institution. What never changed was the submission and obedience demanded of the slave. If anything, the prohibitions and interdictions designed to regulate the violent excesses of slavery extended this violence in the garb of sentiment. The recognition of the slave as subject and the figuration of the captive person in law served to explicate the meaning of dominion. To be subject in this manner was no less brutalizing than being an object of property.[54]

In the arena of affect, the body was no less vulnerable to the demands and the excesses of power. The bestowal that granted the slave a circumscribed and fragmented identity as person in turn shrouded the violence of this beneficent and humane gesture. Bluntly stated, the violence of subjection concealed and extended itself through the outstretched hand of legislated concern. The slave was considered a subject only insofar as she was criminal(ized), wounded body, or mortified flesh. This construction of the subject seems rather at odds with a proclaimed concern for the "total person."[55] However, it does not mean that the efforts to regulate the abuses of slavery were any less "genuine," but that in the very efforts to protect the enslaved from the ravages of the institution, a mutilation of another order was set in motion. Protection was an exemplary dissimulation, for it savagely truncated the dimensions of existence, inasmuch as the effort to safeguard slave life recognized the slave as subject only as she violated the law or was violated. In this restrictive frame, "person" signified little more than a maimed or damaged body, an increment of lost value and diminished capacity, or a recalcitrant in need of punishment.[56]

The designation of person was inescapably bound to violence, and the effort to protect embodied a degree of violence no less severe than the excesses being regulated. Despite the law's proclaimed concern for slave life or recognition of black humanity, minimal standards of existence determined personhood, *for the recognition of the slave as person depended upon the calculation of interest and injury.* The law constituted the subject as a wounded or damaged body or a trespasser to be punished; this acknowledgment of subjectivity certainly intensified the objectification of chattel status. Paradoxically, this recognition utterly negated the possibility of inhabiting the body or existing in a state other than one defined by tremendous vulnerability to violence and death. The black captive vanished in the chasm between object, criminal, pained body, and mortified flesh.[57] The law's exposition of sentiment culminated in a violent shuttling of the subject between varied conditions of harm, juggled between the plantation and the state and dispersed across categories of property, injury, and punishment.

The Measure of Humanity

In *Inquiry into the Law of Negro Slavery*, Thomas Cobb explicated the conditions in which the dominion of the master and the person of the slave were to be accommodated in the law. In examining the particular dimensions of personhood in common law and slave statutes, Cobb contended that the slave was recognized first as person and second as property, largely because in all slaveholding states "the homicide of a slave is held to be murder, and in most of them, [this] has been so expressly declared by law"; and even when not expressly declared by law, the principles of Christian enlightenment extend protection to life and limb.[58] Notwithstanding, he argued that slaves were not proper subjects of common law and proposed a minimal definition of protection of life and limb.

The calculation of slave existence was determined by base conditions necessary for functioning as an effective laborer and as producer of "future increase" or human commodities through childbearing or forced reproduction.[59] The extent of protection to life and limb was decided by diminutions in the value of capital. Within these boundaries, degrees of injury and magnitudes of value decided the meaning of the slave person. It is difficult to acknowledge this savage quantification of life and person as a recognition of black humanity, for this restricted stipulation of the human intensified the suffering of the enslaved. This scale of subjective value, this metric of lesser humanity, was a complement rather than a corrective to the violence that was the foundation of slave law.[60] While this acknowledgment of slave humanity was intended to establish criminal liability for acts of violence committed upon slaves, in the end it relied upon the diminutions in the value of property in determining and recognizing injury. In other words, the "corrective" resembled the ailment in that the effort to recognize humanity resulted in the reinscription of black life as property. The scale of subjective value was dictated by the use and value of property. The consequences of this construction of person intensified injury in the very name of redress. The selective inclusion of the slave into the web of rights and duties that comprised the common law demonstrated the tentativeness of this recognition of personhood.

Not surprisingly, Cobb's calibrations and the law's severely circumscribed dimensions of person constituted "woman" as a condition of negligible and unredressed injury in its dismissal of sexual violence as an "offense not affecting the existence of the slave."[61] Unlike other forms of violence, like maiming or battery, rape was not penalized by slave statute, nor were owners likely to pursue suits for "trespasses" on their property. This negligible injury, not like other forms of assault, might enhance the value of slave property rather than diminish it if children were the outcome. This simultaneously made the body prey to sexual violence and disavowed this violence and injury. The ravished body, the body violated by sexual assault, unlike a broken arm or leg, did not bestow any increment of subjectivity because it did not decrease productivity or diminish value—on the contrary, it might actually increase the captive's magnitude of value. Nor did it offend the principles of Christian enlightenment. It was declared to be inconsequential in the calculation of slave humanity and not within the rights and protections granted the enslaved:

If the general provision of the law against murder should be held to include slaves, why not all other penal enactments, by the same course of reasoning, be held to include similar offences when committed on slaves, without their being specifically named? ... The law, by recognizing the existence of the slave as person, thereby confers no rights or privileges except such as are necessary to protect that existence. All other rights should be granted specially. Hence, the penalties for rape would not and should not, by such implication, be made to extend to carnal forcible knowledge of a slave, that offense *not affecting the existence* of the slave, and that existence being the extent of the right which the implication of the law grants.[62]

While concerned with the neglect of sexual injury and the failure to protect slave women from rape in slave law, Cobb stated that "although worthy of consideration by legislators," it need not cause undue concern because "the occurrence of such an offense is almost unheard of; and the known lasciviousness of the negro, renders the possibility of its occurrence very remote."[63] As the black male's nature made "rape too often an occurrence," the black female's carnal appetite removed it entirely from consideration. It is not simply fortuitous that gender emerges in relation to violence—that is, the black female condition is constituted in terms of negligible and unredressed injury and the enhanced vulnerability to violence. Put differently, black and gendered difference is marked and determined by the capacity for sexual violence and/or the impossibility of such violence affecting one's existence. The engendering of race, as it is refracted through Cobb's scale of subjective value, entails the denial of sexual violation as a form of injury while asserting the prevalence of sexual violence due to the rapacity of the Negro. While Cobb's consideration of sexual violation initially posits gender differences within the enslaved community in terms of female victim and male perpetrator, ultimately the "strong passions" of the Negro annul such distinctions and concomitantly any concerns about "the violation of the person of a female slave." Since blacks were endowed less with sexuality than with criminality, according to Cobb, they were in need of discipline and management rather than protection. At first glance, it is tempting to say that black females were abandoned by the law, but the reality is far more complicated. The law determined the scope of existence by calibrating the vulnerability to violence and delimiting the kind of injury or offense that affected the life of the enslaved. Life in this frame was not an endowment, but the fine-tuning of managed depletion.[64] To be black and female was to be invulnerable or indifferent to sexual injury and capable of transmitting dispossession across generations. In simpler and starker terms, the sexual violation of black girls and women was not believed to have an impact on their existence. Yet, she is the figure most acutely marked by her status as a commodity, by her capacity to reproduce the condition of dispossession well into the future.

In *George v. State*, George, a slave, was indicted for rape under a statute making it a crime to have sex with a child under ten years of age. The Mississippi Supreme Court overturned a lower-court ruling that convicted George for the rape of a female slave under ten years old and sentenced him to death by hanging. The attorney for George cited Cobb's *Law of Slavery* in his argument before the court, declaring that "the crime of rape does not exist in this State between African slaves. Our laws recognize no marital rights as between slaves; their sexual intercourse is left to be regulated by their owners. The regulations of law, as to the white race, on the subject of sexual intercourse, do not and cannot, for obvious reasons, apply to slaves; their intercourse is promiscuous, and the violation of a female slave by a male slave would be mere assault and battery."[65] According to George's attorney, the sexual arrangements of the captive community were so different from those of the dominant order that they were beyond the reach of the law and best left to the regulation of slave owners. The Mississippi Supreme Court concluded that based on a "careful examination of our legislation on this subject, we are satisfied that *there is no act which embraces either the attempted or actual commission of a rape by a slave on a female slave.* . . . Masters and slaves cannot be governed by the same common system of laws: so different are their positions, rights, and duties" [emphasis mine]. The lower court's judgment was reversed, the indictment quashed, and the defendant discharged on the grounds that "this indictment cannot be sustained, either at common law or under our statutes. It charges no offence known to either system." The opinion held that slaves were not subject to the protection of common law and that earlier cases in which whites were prosecuted for the murder of slaves under common law were founded on "unmeaning twaddle . . . 'natural law,' 'civilization and Christian enlightenment,' in amending propio vigore, the rigor of the common law."

Rape and Other Offenses to Existence

If subjectivity is calculated in accordance with degrees of injury and sexual violation is not within the scope of offenses that affected slave existence, what are the consequences of this repression and disavowal in regard to gender and sexuality? Does this severe circumscription of black sentience define the condition of the slave female, or does it challenge the adequacy of gender as a way of making sense of the dispossession and use/exploitation of captive bodies? Put differently, what place does the enslaved female occupy within the admittedly circumscribed scope of black existence or slave personhood? Is her existence even more restricted and truncated? Does she exist exclusively as property? Is she insensate? Or is she the threshold or limit defining what violence is or is not, what a person is or is not? What are the repercussions of this construction of person for the meaning of "woman"?

The "too common occurrence of offence" and an "offence not affecting existence" differentiated what Cobb described as the strongest passion of blacks—lust—into gendered categories of ubiquitous criminality and negligible injury. Such designations illuminate the concerted processes of racialization, gender differentiation, domination, and sexual subjection. Here it is not my intention to reproduce a heteronormative view of sexual violence as only and always directed at women or to discount the "great pleasure in whipping a slave" experienced by owners and overseers or to eliminate acts of castration, sodomy, and genital mutilation from the scope of sexual violence, but rather to consider the terms in which gender—in particular, the category "woman"—becomes meaningful in a legal context in which subjectivity is tantamount to injury. The disavowal of sexual violence is specific not only to engendering "woman" in this particular instance, but also to the condition of enslavement in general. In cases like *Humphrey v. Utz* and *Werley v. State*, essentially what was being decided was whether acts of genital mutilation and castration (legally defined as acts of mayhem) were crimes when perpetuated against the enslaved or acts of just and reasonable violence. Obviously, the quotidian terror of the antebellum world made difficult the discernments of socially tolerable violence versus criminal violence. How did one identify "cruel" treatment in a context in which routine acts of barbarism were considered not only reasonable but also necessary?

The law's selective recognition of slave personhood was tethered to injury and diminished value in slave property. Protection failed to acknowledge the matter of sexual violation, specifically rape, and, as a result, defined the identity of the slave female by the negation of sentience, an invulnerability to sexual assault, and the negligibility of her injuries. However, it is important that the decriminalization of rape not be understood as dispossessing the enslaved of female gender, but in terms of differential production of gendered identity or, more specifically, the adequacy or meaning of gender in this context. What is at stake here is not maintaining gender as an identity category that is universal in its reach; rather, my intention is to examine gender formation in relation to extreme violence, dispossession, the sexual economy of racial slavery, and the calculation of injury and personhood.

Just as the weighing of person and property created a racially differentiated hierarchy of the human, so, too, did the omission of rape. The limited recognition of the slave as person, to the extent that it did not interfere with the full enjoyment of the slave as thing, endowed the enslaved with limited protections and made them vulnerable to injury, precisely because the recognition of person and the calibration of subjectivity were consonant with the imperatives of the institution. The protection of property (defined narrowly by work capacity and the value of capital), the public good (the maintenance of black subordination), and the safeguarding of the institution of slavery determined the restricted scope of personhood and the terms of recognition.[66] These concerns also governed "the regulation of their intercourse" and the negation of mothering, all of which stands in sharp contrast to the protections extended to white women to control their sexual conduct and produce legitimate heirs. Black subordination was consolidated by a variety of legal means.[67]

In the case of motherhood, the reproduction and conveyance of property decided the balance between the limited recognition of slave humanity and the owner's rights of property in favor of the latter. The maternal function was not enshrined with minimal or restricted rights but indistinguishable from the condition of enslavement and its reproduction. Motherhood was critical to the reproduction of property and black subjection, but parental rights were unknown to the law. This negation or wounding of kinship occurred in instances that ranged from the sale and separation of families to the slave owner's renaming of black children as a demonstration of his power and dominion. The issue of motherhood concerned the law only in regard to the disposition and conveyance of property and the determination and reproduction of subordinate status. The concept of "injury" did not encompass the loss of children, natal alienation, and enforced kinlessness. The law's concern with mothering exclusively involved questions of property: diminutions in the value of slave property if the slave female was unable to reproduce or disputes regarding the conveyance and loss of property—lest we forget, we are talking about children here. Motherhood, specifically, and parenting, in general, were social relations without legal recognition in terms of either positive or negative entitlements.[68]

The laws regarding miscegenation, seduction, and rape, as well as the protections extended white women reveal not only the indeterminacy of rights but also the way in which these entitlements are used to secure, if not intensify, subordination. In this case, "protection" secured racial and gender differences and was an instrument of social control. For example, the civil remedy for seduction required an action by the father in which the suit for damages was conducted under the guise of the master-servant relationship. Damages were awarded on the basis of lost services.[69] In cases of seduction, the protection extended women was articulated not in the form of their embodied rights, but in terms of the master's entitlement to his servant's services and the right to compensation for the injury or impairing of his servant. These laws sheltered white women from harm, or, more aptly, placed a premium on virginity as they intensified the regulation and control of white female sexuality, since the security of family and property depended upon chaste and virtuous behavior and an allegiance to racist regulatory norms. The selective protection of the law only encompassed "respectable" women, and this respect ultimately depended upon the legitimate proprietary rights of men over female sexuality. (As neither enslaved black fathers nor husbands bore any sanctioned or lawful relation to their daughters and wives, enslaved women existed outside the circle of protection in this regard, too.)

Proper and legitimate relations determined a white woman's respectability. In cases of rape involving white women and black men, the charges were sometimes dismissed if these women were known to associate with blacks. White women's liaisons with black men denied them the protection of the law. As well, the fact that the rape of black women was not a crime had important consequences for white women. The minimal conditions of existence deemed suitable for slave women made it necessary to secure whiteness in order to guarantee that only white women received certain protections. Because slave women were not subject to the protection of common law (or slave law) regarding rape, the whiteness of white women who were raped by slave men or by free black men had first to be established in order to prosecute the assailant. Cases were dismissed in which the race of white women was not explicitly declared.

In *Commonwealth v. Jerry Mann*, Mann had been indicted, tried, and convicted for "feloniously making an assault upon a woman, with intent to ravish her. The law declares that if a slave shall attempt to ravish a white woman, he shall be adjudged a felon."[70] However, the judgment was arrested because "it was nowhere in the indictment stated, that Mary M'Causland was a white woman." In *Grandison (a Slave) v. State*, Grandison was convicted of assault and battery with intent to ravish Mary Douglass.[71] He was sentenced to death. But the judgment was reversed and arrested, and the prisoner was remanded to jail because "such an act committed on a black woman, would not be punished with death.... This fact [that the woman assaulted was white] gives to the offence its enormity.... [It] must be charged in the indictment and proved on trial." Yet the "enormity of offence" and "offences not affecting existence" are neither endowments nor privations of gender but instead demonstrate the manner in which deployments of sexuality act concertedly with processes of racialization, accumulation, and domination.

It is necessary to belabor the issue because too often it has been argued that the enslaved female existed outside the gendered universe because she was not privy to the entitlements of bourgeois women within the white patriarchal family. As a consequence, gender becomes a descriptive category for the social and sexual arrangements of the dominant order rather than an analytic one. As well, it naturalizes the discourse of protection and mystifies its instrumental role in the control and regulation of the body, sexuality, and kinship. Most important, it affirms the normative whiteness of the category "woman." What I am attempting to explore here is the divergent production of gender rather than a comparison of black and white women that implicitly or inadvertently assumes that gender is relevant only to the degree that generalizable and universal criteria define a common identity. Can we employ the term "woman" and yet remain vigilant that "all women do not have the same gender?"[72] Or "name as 'woman' that disenfranchised woman whom we strictly, historically, geopolitically *cannot imagine* as a literal referent" rather than reproduce the very normativity that has occluded an understanding of the differential production of gender?[73] By assuming that "woman" designates a known referent, an a priori unity, a precise bundle of easily recognizable characteristics, traits, and dispositions, we fail to attend to the contingent and disjunctive production of the category. In other words, "woman" must be disassociated from the white middle-class female subject who norms the category. The disregard for the sexual violation of enslaved women, the reproduction of slave status across generations, and the negation of kinship cannot simply be explained or explained away as the absence of normative conditions of womanhood, for the work of feminist criticism is precisely the interrogation and deconstruction of this normativity, rather than the determination of who is or is not woman in accordance with this measure. How can we conceive the racialized gendered difference (or the gendering of racial difference) of the black female captive in terms other than deficiency or lack in relation to normative conditions, and instead understand this production of gender in the context of very different economies of power, property, kinship, personhood, and sexuality?

If we approach this disavowal of violence and disregard of injury as specific to female engenderment and as largely defining the category "woman" rather than "captive," do we reproduce the presumed masculinity of the categories "person" and "slave"? What happens if we assume that the female slave serves as a general case for explicating social death, property relations, and the pained and punitive construction of blackness? What would be made possible if, rather than assuming the subject, we began our inquiry with a description of subjectification that did not attempt to name or interpret anything but to simply describe its surfaces? How would woman (or female or femme or mater) be cast in this process? Could we, in fact, release the category of woman from its fixity and white normativity and likewise examine racial subjection in articulation with gender differentiation? What possibilities of resignification would then be possible?[74]

The disregard of sexual injury does not divest slave women of gender but reveals the role of property relations—the possession of the enslaved, the making and exchange of human commodities, the harnessing of reproductive capacity, the inheritance and transmission of slave status through the maternal line, and the enjoyment of the thing—in the making of gender and sexuality. In this case, possession occurs not via the protections of the patriarchal family and its control of female sexuality but via absolute rights of property. Terms like *protection*, *domesticity*, and *honor* need to be recognized as specific articulations of racial and class location. The captive female does not possess gender as much as she is possessed by gender—that is, by way of a particular investment in and use of the body. What "woman" designates in the context of captivity is not to be explicated in terms of domesticity or protection, but in terms of the disavowed violence of slave law, the sanctity of property and the necessity of absolute submission, the alienability of intimate capacity, the sale of offspring, the pathologizing of the body, the restriction of sentience, the multifarious use of property, and the precarious status of the slave within the public sphere and the plantation household. The instrumental deployment of sexuality operated in disregard of white regulatory norms like chastity and marriage. The constituent features of slavery as a mode of accumulation and production—the extreme violence, the possession of life and capacity, coerced reproduction, kinlessness, fungibility, and the value of the slave as both a direct producer and a commodity—marked and determined the character of sexuality and gender. Within this economy, legitimate and proper relations were foreclosed. The particular investment in and exploitation of the captive body dissolved all networks of alliance and affiliation not defined by property ownership. This was evidenced by the courts' description of slave children neither as illegitimate nor bastards but as simply "not legitimate."[75]

At stake here is the construction of "woman" not as a foundational category with given characteristics, attributes, or circumstances, but as a marked and particular figure within a racial economy of property that intensified its control over the object of property through the deployment of sexuality. Despite the proclaimed ties of affinity between those "born and bred together," the enslaved female was subjected to violence within the plantation household and within the public arena. Within the private realm of the plantation household, she was subject to the absolute dominion of the owner and also experienced abuse within the slave enclave, and in the public sphere, absolute submission defined the relation of the "public" to blacks, whether captive or free. The law's failure to recognize rape as either crime or injury can be related to the prerogatives and entitlements of the private sphere, the full enjoyment of property that defined the rights of slave owners, and, in the public sphere, the necessity of black submission and the license granted all whites to exercise the violence requisite to preserving the public good.

In many respects, the domination of the captive body makes the experience of men and women more similar than different and enslaved men, too, were subjected to forms of sexual violation. Yet the law also created gendered subjects, if only in regard to the distribution and severity of punishment and the disavowal of injury.[76] What does the female designate within Cobb's restricted scope of subjective value? Does it merely mark the disavowed violence and pained condition of enslavement or make palpable the negligible injury? Does the condition of the enslaved female suggest an obtuseness to pain and injury? By interrogating gender within the purview of "offenses to existence" and examining female subject-formation at the site of sexual violence, I am not positing that forced sex constitutes *the* meaning of gender but that the erasure or disavowal of sexual violence engendered black femaleness as a condition of unredressed injury, which only intensified the bonds of captivity and the deadening objectification of chattel status.[77] Unlike the admittedly indispensable and requisite violence of *State v. Mann*, or the protections extended to other forms of injury, or the criminalization of particular acts of violence, homicide, mayhem, and battery (despite the procedural restrictions that made prosecution extremely difficult, if not impossible), rape was given tacit sanction by its erasure. Sexual violence proliferated without limit because unknown to the law. Ironically, the intervention of affection and the calculation of black sentience magnified the violence permissible within the scope of the law. Rape made apparent the many categories of injury, the many ways of being harmed that could not and would not ever be redressed. The effort to regulate violence simply underscored the great violence necessary to sustain slavery. In the very attempt to recognize the slave as person, blackness was reinscribed as pained embodiment and as indifference to suffering. Black humanity was constituted as a state of injury and punishment.

The Shadow of the Law

The failure to recognize the harm of sexual violence had devastating consequences for the female captive. The category of negligible injury further reduced the already circumscribed scope of black humanity. The body could be seized, broken, assaulted, taken on a whim, yet slave statute deemed these crimes against the flesh inconsequential. Offenses *not* affecting existence epitomized the brutal calculation of subjectivity in its various nominations—black, slave, female—and defied a singular or sovereign axis of dispossession. An injury of no account determines the differential production of woman and the engendering of blackness. In the confines of chattel slavery, gender is discernible primarily in terms of the uses, reproduction, and conveyances of property, measures of sentience, magnitudes of injury, and determinations of punishment. These structural elements determine the life of the slave girl; and they inaugurate the crisis of consent or consensual sexual relations under domination.

In *Incidents in the Life of a Slave Girl, as Written by Herself*, Harriet A. Jacobs explores the intimate dimensions of the captive's dispossession: the inability to choose a lover, the shame produced by sexual violence, the negation of motherhood, and the loss and sale of children. Jacobs requires that we consider not only the restricted scope of black humanity, but also the effort to act as a desiring subject in a context in which consent inadequately designates the enactment of possibility and the constraints of agency.[78] By exploring these issues within the frame of seduction, the narrative precludes facile distinctions that would enable us to disentangle desire and domination or purportedly willed exchange from coercion. By underlining the unwieldiness of sexuality—the entanglements of instrumentality and pleasure—and the crisis induced by this contradictory state of affairs, *Incidents* challenges conventional interpretations that deem issues of desire and consent irrelevant in the context of enslavement or that celebrate desire as the triumph of the captive will. To the contrary, the narrative illuminates the equivocations that surround agency, the unavoidable linkages of desire and domination, and the dangers of seduction. The nexus of desire, consent, violence, and coercion that situates the discussion of the slave girl's sexuality perhaps entails a reconsideration of seduction and one that attends to the agency of the dominated in terms other than those we have previously considered, for if not a conspiracy of power, seduction in this instance enables opportunities for disruption and offers a glimpse of possibility in the context of peril.

The dangers of seduction concern the insinuation and simulation of the subordinate's will and agency to legitimate the arrangements of power and dominance. This framing of consent enacts the captive will through the displacement of coercion and the designation of the enslaved as the originary locus of transgression and shame. The question that we have yet to decide is whether there is more at stake in seduction than the legitimation of despotic power and absolute dominion and the displacement of brute force via the projection of the slave's guilty agency. By utilizing seduction and inquiring into its dangers, *Incidents* suggests the possible gains to be had by "making do" with the given or "using" seduction. Such an effort is fraught with dangers precisely because there is no secure or autonomous exteriority from which the enslaved can operate or to which they can retreat. The double-edged nature of this gaming with power threatens to intensify constraints, rend the body, or result in inevitable losses, since within this domain the chances of safeguarding gains are already foreclosed. So how does one act without exacerbating the constraints of captivity or the violation of surrender?

The question arises as to whether seduction can provide a way of acquiring power or remains the exclusive purchase of the dominant—a strategic disavowal of power that masks the violence of property relations and the despotism of domestic institutions behind the guise of the subaltern's willed surrender and consent to subjection. Can seduction also serve as a weapon of the weak or a vehicle for the articulation of needs and desires? Is it possible to consider the contested interaction of the captive female and white man/slave owner within this frame? Do points of resistance inhabit the enactment of willed surrender, or is it a surrender of another order? If the latter is the case, then the delineations of power are murky and uncertain. This does not mitigate the brutality or instrumentality of seduction, but signals a use of tactics or possibilities previously unconsidered. As deployed in Jacobs's narrative, seduction also suggests agency and subjection, a detour around an expected violence, a move toward something hard to name, an expansion of refractory, if not impossible, desire. The exploration of seduction in *Incidents* strives to differentiate between the constraints of acting in circumstances that render consent inadequate, the tactics employed by the enslaved to negotiate and manipulate relations of power, and the absolute dominion exercised by the slaveholder. Given the extreme coercion and absolute submission characteristic of slavery, how might the enslaved female elude the unrestricted uses and whims of the master and his surrogates? The relation of injury and subjectivity is revisited at crucial sites of the law's repression and omission—the sexual violation of the captive female, the negation of kinship, and the (dis)possession of the body and its issue. These elements or "incidents" determine the condition of enslavement and its gendered differentiation. In the legal discourse of seduction, the equivocations of will and submission are taken as the guarantees of reciprocity and possible reversals of power; in *Incidents* the equivocations of seduction involve matters of calculation, coercion, and the rendering of fact (and its failure) in the law's domain. More important, the textual staging of the scenario of seduction provides an opportunity to explore the meaning of consent from the perspective of the dispossessed and noncontractual subject. This inquiry specifically addresses the possibilities for action, recognition, and relationality that exist in the default of consent. The "deliberate calculation" of the slave girl reckons with the possibilities for acting under conditions of duress, coercion, dispossession, manipulation, and constraint and seeks possibilities where none exist. Seduction, as the vehicle of this exploration, raises the question of whether a noncontractual subject can give consent and, if so, under what terms?

The Narrative of Seduction: Slave and Paramour

Incidents makes use of seduction and recasts it by emphasizing the degradations of enslavement, the perverse domesticity of the plantation household, the severing of kinship, and the violence enacted on the captive body within an arena purportedly defined by ties of sentiment, mutual affection, and interest. The narrative recounts endless episodes of violence as a way of exposing the tacit entitlements of property relations and the "living death" of slavery as it attends to the unredressed injury of the enslaved. In this deployment of seduction, the inadequacy of consent and the vexed enactment of desire in the context of domination are foregrounded. The text offers a more complex vision of power and the uncertain and circumscribed terms of agency by refusing to pose the question of desire in terms of compulsion versus unhindered choice. By doing so, *Incidents* represents the complicated terrain of sexuality and the limited possibilities for action under constraint and duress. This is accomplished by demystifying virtue and disclosing the legal mechanisms that secure and safeguard it. Virtue and consent are resituated through an analysis of the sexual contract—marriage, paternity, and the protection of the daughter's purity.[79] The textual performance of seduction historicizes virtue by revealing the role of the law in sustaining and defiling virtue. The work of narrative entails making visible the mechanisms that deny and intensify injury and that produce and sustain chastity as a racial and status entitlement. It also strives to grapple with the risky enterprise of desire and the pleasures of inviolate and nonpunitive embodiment.

"A Perilous Passage in the Slave Girl's Life" enacts the dilemma of seduction in the navigation of surrender and compulsion. As the following passage makes clear, the "deliberate calculation" of interest and the hope to avoid degrading and coerced submission rather than the freedom to choose the objects of one's affection determine what might be described as an "exchange" for freedom: "It seems less degrading to give one's self, than to submit to compulsion. There is something akin to freedom in having a lover who has no control over you, except what he gains by kindness and attachment. A master may treat you as rudely as he pleases, and you dare not speak. . . . Revenge and articulations of interest were added to flattered vanity and sincere gratitude for kindness. I knew nothing would enrage Dr. Flint so much as to know that I favored another; and it was something to triumph over my tyrant even in that small way."[80] Although "giv[ing] one's self" occurs without the coercion of violent threats, ownership, and direct control and is described as "akin to freedom," it is within the scope of power and domination that invariably structure the relations between white men and enslaved women. It is important to note that it is not equality or the absence of constraint that is celebrated in this inscription of "calculation," but the possible gains to be made within the confines of domination. Jacobs emphasizes this by describing Linda Brent's (Jacobs's pseudonymous identity) act as "something akin to freedom," but different from the freedom to choose the object of one's affection enjoyed by white women because of the legitimate/legal domestic arrangements of the white family (54).

Linda's choice cannot be explicated within the range of options available to white women. "Akin to freedom" expresses the limited possibilities, constraint, despair, and duress that condition the giving of the self, and not boundless options or unencumbered choice. Even if we understand protection as an idealization of the control and regulation of white female sexuality, the point is that the "fall from virtue" is only intelligible in a context in which there is customary and legal protection of women, whether realized through the sanction of marriage, the recognition of paternal right, or the criminalization of sexual violence. The status of this act, whether a "headlong plunge" or a revengeful and interested bid for freedom, matters less than the exercise of quite restricted agency over and against coercion and compulsion. This "giving of oneself" is an option that is the "less degrading," and it is intelligible only within the scope of "laws [that] reduce you to the condition of chattel" and that make slaves "entirely subject to the will of another" (55).

The issue of consent is framed by the law's negation of the captive will and the violent domination of slave relations.[81] Yet if this restricted or truncated state of consent is determined by the law's failures and omissions, it also critically refracts the nonconsent that ever and always stipulates the willingness of the captive female. Certainly, the belabored comparison between the domestic arrangements of free white Northern women and those of the enslaved is intended to expose the role of the law in the construction and negation of consent in the patriarchal family and in the plantation household. In this regard, it is appropriate that Dr. Flint can only make sense of Linda's calculated defiance, this "acting out" or acting on behalf of hoped-for freedom as revenge and as a crime, reinscribing any limited exertion of will, outside the scope of the master's dominion and not for his use, as interdicted: "Linda . . . you have been criminal towards me." The sovereignty endowed to the slave owner extends itself in this inversion of crime and law in which the law acts to inflict injury and then deny it, and crime, in its elasticity, encompasses all efforts to escape, expose, and redress injury. The repeated use of the term "crime" throughout the narrative documents the onus of guilt projected onto the enslaved and criminality as a predominant mode of black subjection.[82]

The feat of *Incidents* is not simply its representation of the habitual and routine character of sexual violence, but the endeavor to actualize something "akin to freedom," even if it affords little more than having a lover whom one is thankful not to despise. The narrative's attention to injury serves to expose the violence of law and the entitlements requisite to exercise consent; namely, virtue and chastity, since it is impossible for an unchaste woman to be raped. These entitlements and the negation of choice or hollowing out of consent come to depend not only on one's civil status, but also on the presumption of virtue. Virtue designates a racial entitlement not accorded to the enslaved; consent is nullified on the grounds of one's civil status and also on the basis of presumed sexual predilections and excess, which in the case of slave women come to be defined by default.

The Seduction of the Reader

"A Perilous Passage" recounts the slave girl's "fall from virtue" in order to recontextualize modesty and innocence within the sexual economy of slavery and trouble distinctions between the chaste and the fallen. The enactment of seduction encompasses Linda's deliberate calculations and Sands's (Linda's white lover and the father of her two children) temptations and flattery, as well as the tactics employed to overcome the resistances of the reader, specifically an orchestrated display of weakness. The shamefaced appeals to the reader and the narrative's confessional tone reveal the contingency of virtue, and they effect a reversal in which the standards of virtue are deemed inappropriate in measuring the lives of enslaved women.[83] The language of guilty prostration lures the reader by manipulating her investments and desires. The seemingly naive and apologetic declarations work their designs upon the reader. This enactment of seduction exemplifies the necessary cunning required to survive slavery.[84] As Jacobs writes elsewhere, "Who can blame slaves for being cunning? They are constantly compelled to resort to it. It is the only weapon of the weak and oppressed against the strength of their tyrants" (100–101). The exercise of cunning ensnares the reader at precisely the point in the narrative where the contemporaneous readership was most likely to sever identification with the slave girl because of her "recklessness." With the aid of the "weapon[s] of the weak," the narrator masterfully exercises her authority and sustains the reader's empathic identification.

The narrator guides us through the perilous passage in the slave girl's life by documenting the constant obstacles that confront the enslaved female and the inevitably of her violation. It is the cumulative effects of these "adverse circumstances" that are responsible for her "degraded condition." The narrator's appeal situates the reader in the position of the slave girl and implores the implied reader not to judge from the perspective of those whose homes are protected by law.[85] After all, it is desperation and "living death" that drive Linda into the arms of Sands. Her recklessness registers the inexorability of her undoing, as well as her despair. The naïveté of a fifteen-year-old girl and the slave's longing for freedom facilitate Linda's seduction by Sands's eloquent words. By detailing the defilements that characterize the slave girl's life, the narrator instructs the reader that the "degraded condition" of the slave woman must be situated

within the tyranny of the master-slave relationship and not naturalized as a racial predilection or propensity for sexual excess. The
inescapability of this violated condition provides the narrator with
the license to speak the indelicate, albeit within defined limits, and,
at the same time, forestalls the condemnation of white Northern
women. The narrative creates a dramatic vortex that engulfs the
reader and vividly displays the relentless forces of sexual undoing;
even the most obdurate reader cannot resist such entreaties.

"A Perilous Passage" is narrated in the mode of recollection. However, the measured tone of recollection is disrupted here by the narrator's urgency. "And *now*, reader, I come to a period in my unhappy
life, which I would gladly forget if I could" [emphasis mine].[86] The
use of "now" in Linda's recollection seems to indicate that the entire
narrative had been leading to this point. "Now" reflects the urgency
of the effort to keep the reader's empathy and refers to the relationship between narrative and reader, at a place where narrative
control is in jeopardy. It signals an endangered moment of negotiation between reader and narrator. It indicates not only the narrative
location, but the self-reflexivity of the narrative about the crisis of
its authority as it attempts to navigate the contemporaneous readership through the perilous passage.[87] The revisited event of crisis
flashes before the reader by way of this temporal eruption, which
figures the fall (from virtue) as the imperiled present, placing the
reader in the moment of danger and enabling her to apprehend the
enormity of the crisis and the fatedness of the slave girl's undoing.
This instant of peril flashes before the reader, beckoning her to fully
experience this moment of danger, this "hour of extremity" (57).
The reader, overwhelmed by the pain, shame, sorrow, pleas, and
guilt, falls prey to the narrator's eloquent words just as Linda fell
prey to Sands.

"There may be sophistry in all this," acknowledges the narrator; however, sophistry is essential to the seduction of the reader.

Though concealed by the confessional tenor and proclaimed naïveté of the narrative, the duplicity of the narrative lies in its appeal to the reader for sympathy and understanding, while actually deposing the reader as judge. By seemingly conceding the higher moral ground to the good women of the North, the narrator introduces them to the situational ethics of the enslaved and the necessary practices of cunning, duplicity, and sophistry: "Slaves, being surrounded by mysteries, deceptions, and dangers, early learn to be suspicious and watchful, and prematurely cautious and cunning" (155). As a narrative strategy, this duplicity involves conforming to the reader's desire to advance contrary arguments and transform the reader's incredulity and resistance into identification and empathy.[88]

The crisis of seduction is ameliorated by the seductiveness of the narrative.[89] In conforming to and indulging the reader's desires, the narrative proceeds by stealth, affirming what it will negate—the moral superiority of the dear white woman reader. The narration topples the pedestal on which they stand, unmooring them in the storm of events and stating explicitly that white Northern women cannot judge the slave girl by the same standards with which they judge themselves. The narrator's humbling appeal to the reader covertly forwards her own desires and secures a recognition of those desires. The identification of the slave girl as "victim" does not negate her role as agent.

However, the narrative's negotiating of desire and violation does not entirely escape the displacement of violence and omission of injury that characterize the discourse of seduction in slave law. The displacement of violence is inscribed as what the narrator "dares not speak." The urgent and desperate effort to keep the reader within the narrator's authority creates disruptions in the narrative and provides a line of exit that enables brutal facts to be avoided. On the one hand, we are to believe that Linda eludes her master, despite the extremity of violence exercised by Flint to force her "to change this line of policy."[90] On the other hand, the narrator's recurring maxim that she dare not tell the worst, the author's constant reminders that "no pen can give adequate description of the all-pervading corruption produced by slavery," and the slave girl's belief that "resistance is hopeless" would seem to preclude any escape from sexual violence.[91]

The impossibility of adequately representing the life of the slave girl is due not only to the severity of the degradation of the captive body and the unwillingness of the reader to fathom or believe the extremity or magnitude of this violence, but by speaking of these crimes the narrator carries the burden of the indecent and the obscene. On those occasions in the narrative when Linda tries to disclose her abuse to her mistress, confide in her grandmother, or act to escape Flint's assault, she becomes the object of reproach and is encumbered with guilt, crime, shame, and disgrace. The double bind is that she must offer testimony about these degradations to help her sisters in bondage, but speaking of these crimes places the burden of guilt upon her. To speak of the foul wrongs committed against her is to enact the indecent and give voice to the unspeakable. As a consequence of this double bind, rape is represented only in terms of its effects—mute, pregnant women and near-white offspring. This is also the case in Elizabeth Keckley's narrative, *Behind the Scene; or, Thirty Years a Slave and Four Years in the White House*, in which children stand as the embodiment of undisclosed and unspoken sexual violence: "Suffice it to say, that he prosecuted me for four years, and I—I—became a mother." The elisions articulate both the literal absence of rape in the law, "the edicts of that society which deemed it no crime to undermine the virtue of [slave] girls," and the textual crisis engendered by the effort to represent it.[92]

The unspoken and the censored haunt the narrative: "The degradations, the wrongs, the vices, that grow out of slavery are more than I can describe. They are greater than you would willingly believe."[93] The constraints on what can be said, the impossibility of representing the magnitude of slavery's violence, and the pain of recollection account for the selective character of the narrative: "I know that some are too much brutalized by slavery to feel the humiliation of their position; but many slaves feel it most acutely, and shrink from the memory of it."[94] Is the evasion of rape in the narrative an evasion of memory? Does anticipated disbelief on the part of the reader and the pain of recollection prohibit a full disclosure? Or can Jacobs's evasion be attributed to a concern for the reader's sensibility and delicacy? The avowedly fragmentary character of the narrative and the inhibitions to full disclosure prevent us from easily championing Linda's purported escape from Dr. Flint's sexual assault(s).

Anxiety and withholding characterize the accounts of sexual violence in the narrative. A general unwillingness to disclose "the humiliations of their position" can be attributed to a complex of factors: the law's disavowal of violence, the strictures of decency, the reluctance to offer one's intimate life to public scrutiny, the pain of recollection, the resistance of the reader, and the conventions of sentimental literature.[95] In a letter to Amy Post, Jacobs described the difficulty involved in presenting a full account of her past because of the degradations she experienced and the pain of remembrance: "I have striven faithfully to give a true and just account of my own life in slavery. There are some things that I might have made plainer—Woman can whisper her cruel wrongs into the ear of a dear friend much easier than she could record them."

The dashes in Jacobs's letter to Post, like the admittedly selective incidents of the narrative, obscure the materiality of violence in order to avoid the pain and humiliation necessarily a part of its retelling. If one thinks of these dashes and elisions as literal and figurative cuts in the narrative, then they display and displace the wounds of the violated captive body, a body that acts out its remembrances without the symbolic endowments to articulate its history of injury. The dashes, ellipses, and circumlocutions hint at the excluded term by way of the bodies of slave women, which are textual enigmas to be interpreted by the reader since they are literally pregnant with the secrets of slavery. These figures dramatize the predicament of embodiment. This is not uncommon in sentimental fiction, where "bodily signs are adamantly and repeatedly presented as the preferred and most potent mechanisms both for communicating meaning and marking the fact of its transmission."[96] The sheer magnitude of violence exceeds the scope of the representable and prevents a full disclosure of slavery's crimes. Even descriptions that "fall far short of the facts" risk prurience and entail a Sisyphean effort to unveil that which is said not to exist in the law's domain of fact.

The anxiety that attends Jacobs's understated and avowedly selective narration of sexual violence must also be attributed to the character of this particular charge, which sullies the one who speaks it; to be a victim is to invite suspicion and carry the stigma of wrongdoing. To utter the "foul words" or point to the crime, even by way of indirection, is to be claimed by it, to be made blameworthy, to bear all responsibility for the violence that rends the body and lays it open. The conflation of blackness and criminality tightens the stranglehold. To avow the deed is to be engulfed by it. All the terrible things that have happened are lodged in silence, sealed in shame.

The defilements and violations of slavery are incorporated as shame. Not only do the enslaved bear the burden of crime—the onus of guilt indissociable from speaking the obscenity of slavery—and withstand the violence that defines the status of the captive or object as will-less, as affectable, as vulnerable to the demands and wants of all whites as masters. The inability to marry renders all desire illegitimate, since it is unlicensed and without a sanctioned domain. Intimate arrangements of love and kinship are invaded and annexed by the market. Racial slavery imprints and disfigures how one might love, binding it to anticipated loss and unavoidable violence. In the absence of a licit space for the captive female's desire, it, too, becomes identified as crime. The slave girl is guilty because she has chosen a love object not decided by the slaveholder's "management of [her] intercourse" or plans for future increase driven by unwanted coupling or forced procreation. Just as sophistry articulates the constraints of agency, shame reveals the legal predicament of the subject, defined by the negation of will and illicit and criminal willfulness. Shame symptomatically articulates the inevitable construction of desire, willfulness, and agency in terms of the dishonorable and the unlawful. Within the economy of slavery, neither love nor affiliation is legitimated through the formal recognition of marriage or parenting. These relations are simply not legitimate, they are without standing because they are not recognized or endowed with legal right. In order to create a space for desire, fully cognizant of this absence of right, the narrative emphasizes the role of law in determining the (il)legitimacy of desire and the inevitability of wrongdoing. As a structure of feeling, shame expresses the devaluation of chattel status, the dissolution experienced in being absolutely subject to another, and the recognition of one's abjection. It denotes the affective dimension of the general condition of dishonor constitutive of enslavement.[97] In this regard, being "shamefaced at the telling" cannot be explained solely by contrasting it with virtue or true womanhood; it registers the particular mechanisms of subjection.

Deliberate Calculation

For the slave girl, disgrace is conditioned by the very act that grants a limited and provisional freedom. If deliberate calculation is unable to provoke or incite an "event," a reversal of forces in the relations of domination, it is clearly double-edged, for the bid for freedom culminates in another "tie" or "link" to bondage, a child threatened by sale or violence. The same act both holds out the possibility of freedom and intensifies the burdens and constraints of enslavement. If this negotiation of desire is eclipsed by shame, it is also important to recognize the transience of this desire and its resolutely ambivalent character. It is renounced and justified. It is fueled by the need for recognition, protection, and reciprocity and by revenge, yet it can be neither sustained nor actualized because of the absence of a proper domain. Desire presupposes guilt. For these reasons, Jacobs foregrounds the role of the law in the construction of the "not legitimate": guilt must be seen as the social production of wrongdoing due to the absence of marital relations with any legal standing, the negation of maternity, and kinlessness; the inability to form contracts; and the attenuation of sociality by the chattel principle. Bereft of these legal entitlements, calculation rather than courtship, purchase rather than proposal, manumission rather than marriage delimit the circuits of desire in the economy of slavery.

These circuits or perilous passages occur in the default of legal or suitable arrangements. Outside the shadow of law, compulsion eclipses choice, as neither right nor protection secures the line between consent and nonconsent. The effort to distinguish between being compelled to submit and "giving oneself" relies on Flint's vile proposals and assaults to define choice by contradistinction. Yet, the line between something akin to choice and nonconsent is permeable and uncertain because no absolute distinction between them can be sustained in the context of racial slavery. This uncertainty expresses the dilemma of consent for the noncontractual subject. The very term "deliberate calculation," in contrast to "free choice," illuminates the incommensurability of consent and its indebtedness to a contractual model of social relations. Choice is a legal entitlement beyond the scope of the enslaved, who are reduced to chattel, unprotected by law, and "entirely subject to the will of another" (55). At the same time, the narrative endeavors to represent Linda's choice, precisely to make claims for freedom, claims that are only intelligible within the terms of willed exchange, self-possession, and the alienability of the self as property definitive of liberty.

The effort to differentiate between compulsion and "giving oneself" proves difficult. Coercion and calculation become interwoven in the narrative as in the law. Largely because the assertion of consent requires an impossible approximation, it assumes a space of desire defined neither by white dominance ("a lover who has no control over you") nor by coercion, but by kindness and willed exchange ("it seems less degrading to give one's self"). This "giving of the self" presupposes a degree of autonomy over the self. This "deliberate calculation" acts as a transmutation of property in which chattel, absolutely subject to the will of another, gives way to property in the self. As in the case of "stealing away," the slave's property in the self is defined not by possession or legal title, customarily understood as inalienable rights, but by appropriation and theft. The relation of the enslaved to the self is possible only by way of wrongful possession or possession without right or permission. The act of the deliberate calculation reinscribes the status of the self as property in order to undo it. This is true on a formal and substantive level in that Linda hopes this exchange will result in freedom for herself and her children. This state "akin to freedom," like freedom itself, reveals the indebtedness of liberty to property and to an alienable and exchangeable self.

The effort to represent desire and momentarily grant it a space requires that a degree of choice, however constrained, be exercised, or else there is no basis on which to differentiate Linda's relation with Sands from her relation with Flint, or choice from nonconsent. In the effort to distinguish between "giving one's self" and "submit[ting] to compulsion," the narrative reinscribes the paradox of seduction. Force, will, and submission become entangled in ways that obscure violence and disavow injury. This is most apparent in regard to the slave girl's resistance and Linda's refusal to "yield" to Flint. Jacobs repeatedly asserts that the slave girl's resistance to her master's violation is hopeless and her degradation inevitable. However, unlike other slave girls whipped and starved into submission, Linda eludes this fate. This is attributed to her determined will.

This assertion seems to contradict the main thrust of Jacobs's argument, which maintains that being forced to submit to the will of the master in all things defines the predicament of enslavement, yet this condition of subjection, resignation, and enforced will-lessness imposed by domination should not be mistaken for compliance or assent. It simply registers the fact that resistance is hopeless. This inevitable rout, coupled with the demystification of virtue, dislodges the burden of guilt that had been foisted onto the slave girl in the course of her violation. In depicting Linda's seemingly successful evasions of Flint's intended rape, Jacobs contravenes this argument and inadvertently reinforces the idea that if determined enough, one can escape violation, implicitly suggesting that submission is to some degree an act of compliance and that utmost resistance establishes the meaning of nonconsent. Clearly, she does not intend to imply that the absence of physical resistance instantiates consent or that the struggle to the death defines nonconsent. Nonetheless, when moving from the general case to the specific, from the slave girl to Linda, Jacobs attempts to establish her innocence by strict adherence to this formula. The inability to resist one's master does not imply consent, but determined and frontal resistance is required to establish nonconsent. These assertions are at cross-purposes and act to displace and extend the discourse of seduction, while fully illuminating the double bind of agency. This is compounded by the representation of Flint's assaults, which are directed at securing Linda's submission precisely as an admission or declaration of her consent and willful participation in coerced sexual arrangements. Rather than illustrating the utter negation of consent and the triumph of violence, the event of rape would be taken as the very emblem of willful submission.

In the effort to reveal the violence requisite to acquiring submission and to document resistance, Jacobs must resort to extreme measures to hypothesize an exercise of will not yoked to submission. Utmost resistance becomes the means by which she establishes the difference between will-lessness and willfulness or perfect submission and consent. If the possibility of refusing or evading Flint is precluded, then Linda's choice of Sands cannot be differentiated from sexual assault (the indiscriminate use of the object of property) by Flint. As well, the presumption is that only a chaste woman can exercise nonconsent.[98]

The opportunity for nonconsent is required to establish consent, for consent is meaningless if refusal is not an option. Nonetheless, the very effort to demonstrate consent reveals its impossibility if consent is understood as a voluntary agreement free from constraint or compulsion or as unimpeded by relations of power and dominance. After all, if desperation, recklessness, and hopelessness determine "choosing one's lover," absolute distinctions between compulsion and assent cannot be sustained. Yielding to another or giving one's self is no less subject to constraint, though it is certainly different from and preferable to being forced to submit. Consent is unseemly in a context in which the very notion of subjectivity is predicated upon the negation of will. The impossibility of an absolute disassociation of choice and compulsion and the inability to escape the entanglements of will-lessness and willfulness condition the ambiguous representation of sexual violence in the narrative and culminate in the displacement of rape as seduction.

In light of this, how can one account for the force of determined will without reproducing the dilemmas of seduction—facile declarations of reciprocity and reversal that serve to obscure the violence of law, the extremity of domination, and the regularity of injury—in the very effort to elude sexual assault? It appears that seduction inevitably entails a calculated misreading or misrecognition of the state of domination, one that presumes a degree of latitude in directing the conduct of others and predicated on reciprocity and the ties of mutual affection or, conversely, on withholding and calculated action. Whether for the instrumental ends of securing subordination or in order to seize opportunities to protect oneself and further one's aims under conditions that one does not control, seduction assumes that the enslaved possess the power to withhold and/or exercise influence by giving or yielding. Do the provisional forms of action available to the enslaved necessarily entail utopian premises that assume a greater degree of power and possibility than usually exists? Are these misreadings necessary and purposeful? Can these impossible approximations of the desired and the longed for be refused, or are they simply an aspect of the arduous and imaginative labor required in advancing claims for freedom? If these tactics are unable to effect reversals of power and instead evidence the provisionality of resistance and the dead weight of domination, at the very least, they are guided by the yearning to refuse and transform the given.[99]

Contrary to the instrumental will that produces the docile body or the simulated will of the enslaved that underwrites the brutality and beneficence of the master-slave relation in cases like *State v. Mann*, the determined will or willfulness that enables Linda to elude Flint is not a form of action or can-do-ness guaranteed by volition or self-possession, but a rudimentary form of action harnessed by constraint. It is an exercise of willfulness and cunning estranged from the assured and univocal expressive capacity of the intending subject. Rather, the weapons of the weak are contingent and riddled with contradictions. Jacobs's deliberate calculation is an effort to enact and imagine the will in terms contrary to the reproduction of subordination or the incitement to punishment. The willfulness of the slave girl is an occasion for action and change.

To act, Linda must do the impossible and "assume the self" as her own, not only in order to "give herself," but also to experience something akin to freedom. To be a subject, she must feign self-possession, rather than elaborate or disclose the extended dispossession entailed in choosing a lover. This deliberate calculation enables the experience of a limited freedom; however, it requires that she take possession and offer herself to another. This act also intensifies the constraints of slavery and reinscribes her status as property, even if figuratively property of another order, at the very moment in which she tries to undo and transform her status. If she must enter this exchange in a bid for freedom, then it serves to reveal the indebtedness of freedom to notions of property, possession, sovereignty, and exchange.[100] This order of property, although markedly different from that of chattel slavery, essentially constructs the self as alienable and exchangeable, and notably sexuality is at the heart of this transaction. In "giving herself to another," Linda hoped to achieve her freedom and that of her children. Ultimately, what is revealed in the course of Linda's "deliberate calculation" is that the very effort to "liberate" the slave girl positions her in a network of exchange, constraint, and property from which she had hoped to be extricated.

At the conclusion of the narrative, Jacobs writes: "Reader, my story ends with freedom; not in the usual way, with marriage. I and my children are now free! We are as free from the power of slaveholders as are the white people of the north; and though that, according to my ideas, is not saying a great deal, it is a vast improvement in *my* condition." This implicit critique of the limits of freedom, prefigured by the "loophole of retreat," anticipated the burdened individuality that awaited the emancipated masses whose only resource was newly acquired property in the self.

Part II

THE SUBJECT OF
FREEDOM

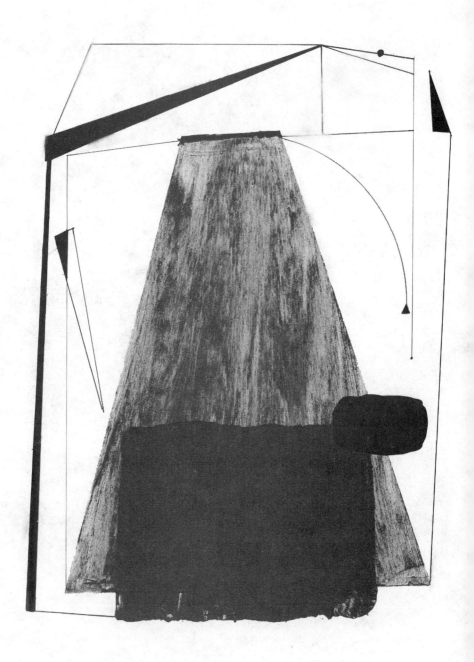

set/interval/enclosure

4

The Burdened Individuality of Freedom

> The limits of political emancipation appear at once in the fact that the state can liberate itself from constraint without man himself being really liberated; that a state may be a free state without man himself being a free man.
>
> —Karl Marx, *On the Jewish Question*

> The emancipation of the slaves is submitted to only in so far as chattel slavery in the old form could not be kept up. But although the freedman is no longer considered the property of the individual master, he is considered the slave of society.
>
> —Carl Schurz, *Report on the Condition of the South*

> Are we to esteem slavery for what it has wrought, or must we challenge our conception of freedom and the value we place upon it?
>
> —Orlando Patterson, *Slavery and Social Death*

The entanglements of bondage and liberty shaped the liberal imagination of freedom, fueled the emergence and expansion of capitalism, and spawned proprietorial conceptions of the self. This vexed genealogy of freedom plagued the great event of Emancipation, or as it was described in messianic and populist terms, Jubilee. The complicity of slavery and freedom or, at the very least, the ways in which they assumed, presupposed, and mirrored one another—freedom finding its dignity and authority in this "prime symbol of corruption" and slavery transforming and extending itself in the limits and subjection of freedom—troubled, if not elided, any absolute and definitive marker between slavery and its aftermath.[1] The longstanding and intimate affiliation of liberty and bondage made it impossible to envision freedom independent of constraint or personhood and autonomy separate from the sanctity of property and proprietorial notions of the self. Moreover, since the dominion and domination of slavery were fundamentally defined by black subjection, race appositely framed questions of sovereignty, right, and power.[2]

The traversals of freedom and subordination, sovereignty and subjection, and autonomy and compulsion are significant markers of the dilemma or double bind of freedom. Marx, describing a dimension of this paradox, referred to it with dark humor as a double freedom—being free to exchange one's labor and free of material resources. Within the liberal "Eden of the innate rights of man," owning easily gave way to being owned, sovereignty to fungibility, and abstract equality to subordination and exploitation.[3] If sovereignty served "to efface the domination intrinsic to power" and rights "enabled and facilitated relations of domination," as Michel Foucault argues, then what we are left to consider is the subjugation that rights instigate and the domination they efface.[4]

It is not simply that rights are inseparable from the entitlements of whiteness or that blacks should be recognized as legitimate rights bearers; rather, the issue at hand is the way in which the stipulation of abstract equality produces white entitlement and black subjection in its promulgation of formal equality. The fragile "as if equal" of liberal discourse inadequately contends with the history of racial subjection and enslavement, since the texture of freedom is laden with the vestiges of slavery, and abstract equality is utterly enmeshed in the narrative of black subjection. Slavery undergirded the rhetoric of the republic and so too equality was defined to sanction subordination and segregation. Ultimately, I am trying to grapple with the changes wrought in the social fabric after the abolition of slavery and with the nonevent of emancipation insinuated by the perpetuation of the plantation system and the refiguration of subjection.

By examining the metamorphosis of "chattel into man" and the strategies of individuation constitutive of the liberal individual and the rights-bearing subject, I hope to underscore the ways in which freedom and slavery presuppose one another, not only as modes of production and discipline, but through contiguous forms of subjection. The founding narrative of the liberal subject was revised in the context of Reconstruction, allowing belated entry to the formerly enslaved; yet the sweeping changes wrought by Emancipation failed to disestablish or eradicate slavery. At issue are the contending articulations of freedom and the forms of subjection they beget. It is not my intention to argue that the differences between slavery and freedom were negligible; certainly such an assertion would be ridiculous. Rather, it is to examine the shifting and transformed relations of power that brought about the resubordination of the emancipated, the control and domination of the free black population, and the persistent production of blackness as abject, threatening, servile, dangerous, dependent, irrational, and polluting. In short, the advent of freedom marked the transition from the pained and minimally sensate existence of the slave to the burdened individuality of the responsible and encumbered freedperson.

The nascent individualism of the freed designates a precarious autonomy, since exploitation, domination, and subjection inhabit the vehicle of rights. The divisive and individuating power of discipline, operating in conjunction with the sequestering and segregating control of black bodies as a species body, permitted under the guise of social rights and facilitated by the regulatory power of the state, resulted in the paradoxical construction of the freed both as self-determining and enormously burdened individuals and as members of a population whose labor, capacity, forms of movement and association, and sexual practices were fiercely regulated and policed in the interests of an expanding capitalist economy and the preservation of a racial order on which the white republic was founded. Lest "the white republic" seem like an inflated or unwarranted rhetorical flourish, we must remember that the transformation of the national government and the citizenship wrought by the Reconstruction Amendments were commonly lamented as representing the loss of the "white man's government."[5]

In light of the constraints that riddled conceptions of liberty, sovereignty, and equality, the contradictory experience of emancipation cannot be adequately conveyed by handsome phrases like "the rights of the man," "equal protection of the law," or "the sanctity of life, liberty, and property." Just as the peculiar and ambivalent articulation of the chattel status of the enslaved black and the assertion of his rights under the law, however limited, had created a notion of black personhood or subjectivity in which all the burdens and few of the entitlements of personhood came to characterize this humanity, so, too, the advent of freedom and the equality of rights conferred to blacks a status no less ambivalent. The advent of freedom held forth the possibility of a world antithetical to slavery and portended transformations of power and status that were captured in carnivalesque descriptions like "bottom rail on top this time." In the same moment, extant and emergent forms of domination intensified and exacerbated the responsibilities and the afflictions of the newly emancipated. I characterize the nascent individualism of emancipation as "burdened individuality" in order to underline the double bind of freedom: being freed from slavery and free of resources, emancipated and subordinated, self-possessed and indebted, equal and inferior, liberated and encumbered, sovereign and dominated, citizen and subject. (The transformation of black subjectivity effected by emancipation is described as nascent individualism because blacks were considered less than human and a hybrid of property and person prior to emancipation and because the abolition of slavery conferred belatedly the inalienable rights of man and brought them into the fold of liberal individualism. Prior to this, legal precedents like *State v. Mann* and *Dred Scott v. Sanford* made the notions of blacks' rights and black citizenship untenable, if not impossible.)

The antagonistic production of abstract equality and black subjugation rested upon contending and incompatible predications of the freed—as sovereign, indivisible, and self-possessed, and as fungible and individuated subjects whose capacities could be extracted, quantified, exchanged, and alienated. The civil and political rights bestowed upon the freed cloaked the encroaching and invasive forms of social control exercised over black bodies through the veneration of custom; the regulation, production, and protection of racial and gender inequality in the guise of social rights; the repressive instrumentality of the law; and the forms of extraeconomic coercion that enabled the control of the black population and the effective harnessing of that population as a labor force. The ascribed responsibility of the liberal individual served to displace the nation's responsibility for providing and ensuring the rights and privileges conferred by the Reconstruction Amendments and shifted the burden of duty onto the freed. It was their duty to prove their worthiness for freedom rather than the nation's duty to guarantee, at minimum, the exercise of liberty and equality, if not opportunities for livelihood other than debt peonage. Emancipation had been the catalyst for a transformed definition of citizenship and a strengthened national state. However, the national identity that emerged in its aftermath consolidated itself by casting out the emancipated from the revitalized body of the nation-state that their transient incorporation had created.[6] In the aftermath of the Civil War, national citizenship assumed greater importance as a result of the Fourteenth Amendment, which guaranteed civil rights at the national level against state violation and thus made the federal government ultimately responsible for ensuring the rights of citizens.[7] Yet the illusory universality of citizenship once again was consolidated by the mechanisms of racial subjection that it formally abjured.

This double bind was the determining condition of black freedom. The belated entry of the newly freed into the realm of freedom, equality, and property, as perhaps expected, revealed the boundaries of emancipation and duly complicated the meaning of freedom. Certainly, manhood and whiteness were the undisclosed, but always assumed, norms of liberal equality, although the Civil Rights Act of 1866 made this explicit in defining equality as being equal to white men. The challenge of adequately conveying the dilemmas generated by this delayed entry exceeds the use of descriptions like "limited," "truncated," or "circumscribed" freedom; certainly, these designations are accurate, but they are far from exhaustive. This first order of descriptives begs the question of how race, in general, and blackness, in particular, are produced through mechanisms of domination and subjection that have yoked, harnessed, and infiltrated the apparatus of rights. How are new forms of bonded labor engendered by the vocabulary of freedom? Is an emancipatory figuration of blackness possible? Or are we to hope that the entitlements of whiteness will be democratized? Is the entrenchment of black subordination best understood in the context of the relations of production and class conflict? Is race best considered an effect of the operation of power on bodies and populations exercised through relations of exploitation, domination, accumulation, and subjection? Is blackness the product of this combined and uneven articulation of various modalities of power? If slave status was the primary determinant of racial identity in the antebellum period, with "free" being equivalent to "white" and slave status defining blackness, how does the production and valuation of race change in the context of freedom and equality?[8]

The task of describing the status of the emancipated involves attending to the articulation of various modes of power, without simply resorting to additive models of domination or interlocking oppressions that analytically maintain the distinctiveness and separateness of these modes and their effects, as if they were isolated elements that could be easily enumerated—race, class, gender, and sexuality—or as if they were the ingredients of a recipe for the social whereby the mere listing of elements enables an adequate rendering. Certainly venturing to answer these questions is an enormously difficult task because of the chameleon capacities of racism, the various registers of domination, exploitation and subjection traversed by it, the plasticity of race as an instrument of power, and the divergent and sundry complex of meanings condensed through the vehicle of race, as well as the risks entailed in generating a description of racism that does not reinforce its fixity or neglect the variations constitutive of its force and violence. It is important to remember that there is not a monolithic or invariable production of race/racism. Mindful of these concerns, I do not attempt to theorize blackness as such, but instead examine varied and contested articulations of (anti) blackness in regard to issues of responsibility, will, liberty, contract, and sentiment.

If race formerly determined who was "man" and who was chattel, whose property rights were protected and recognized and who was property, which consequently had the effect of making race itself a kind of property, with blackness as the mark of object status and whiteness licensing the proprietorship of self, then how did emancipation affect the status of race? The proximity of black *and* free necessarily incited fundamental changes in the national fabric. The question persists as to whether it is possible to unleash freedom from the history of property that secured it, for the security of property that undergirded the abstract equality of rights-bearers was achieved, in large measure, through black bondage. As a consequence of emancipation, blacks were incorporated into the narrative of the rights of man and citizen; by virtue of the gift of freedom and wage labor, the formerly enslaved were granted entry into the hallowed halls of humanity, and, at the same time, the unyielding and implacable fabrication of blackness as subordination continued under the aegis of formal equality. This is not to deny the achievements made possible by the formal stipulation of equality but simply to highlight the fractures and limits of emancipation and the necessity of thinking about these limits in terms that do not simply traffic in the obviousness of common sense—the denial of basic rights, privileges, and entitlements to the formerly enslaved—and yet leave the framework of liberalism unexamined. In short, the matter to be considered is how the formerly enslaved navigated between a travestied emancipation and an illusory freedom.[9]

When we examine the history of racial formation in the United States, it is evident that liberty, property, and whiteness were inextricably enmeshed. Racism was foundational to the development and expansion of capitalist relations of accumulation and production, the organization, division, and management of the laboring classes, the regulation of the population through licensed forms of sexual association and conjugal union and the allocation and distribution of death, and to the creation of an internal danger to the purity of the body politic. Whiteness was a valuable and exclusive property essential to the integrity of the citizen-subject and the exemplary self-possession of the liberal individual. Although emancipation resulted in a decisive shift in the relation of race and status, black subordination continued under the aegis of contract; life remained precarious and disposable. In this regard, the efforts of Southern states to codify blackness in constitutions written in the wake of abolition and install new measures in the law that would secure the subordination of freed black people demonstrate the prevailing disparities of emancipation. The discrepant production of blackness, the articulation of race across diverse registers of subjection, and the protean capacities of racism illuminate the tenuousness of equality in a social order founded on chattel slavery. Certainly, the freed came into "possession" of themselves and basic civil rights consequent to the abolition of slavery. However, despite the symbolic bestowal of humanity that accompanied the acquisition of rights, the legacy of freedom was an ambivalent one. If the nascent mantle of sovereign individuality conferred rights and entitlements, it also served to obscure the coercion of "free labor," the transmutation of bonded labor or involuntary servitude, the invasive forms of discipline that shaped individuality, and the regulatory production of blackness.

Notwithstanding the dissolution of the seemingly inviolable body of property resulting from the abolition of slavery and the uncoupling of the master-and-slave dyad, the breadth of freedom and the shape of the emergent order were the sites of intense struggle in everyday life. The absolute dominion of the master, predicated on the annexation of the captive body and its standing as the "sign and surrogate" of the master's body, yielded to an economy of bodies, yoked and harnessed, through the exercise of autonomy, self-interest, and consent. The use, regulation, and management of the body no longer necessitated its literal ownership since self-possession effectively yielded modern forms of bonded labor. As Marx observed with notable irony, the pageantry of liberty, equality, and consent enacted within this veritable Eden of rights underwent a radical transformation after the exchange was made, the bargain was struck, and the contract was signed. The transactional agent appeared less as the self-possessed and willful agent than as "someone who has brought his own hide to market and now has nothing to expect—but a tanning."[10] Although no longer the extension and instrument of the master's absolute right or dominion, the laboring black body remained a medium of others' power and representation.[11] If control was formerly effected by absolute rights of property in the captive body, dishonor, and the quotidian routine of violence, these techniques were supplanted by the liberty of contract that spawned debt peonage, the bestowal of rights that engendered indebtedness and obligation and licensed naked forms of domination and coercion, and the cultivation of a work ethic that promoted self-discipline and induced internal forms of policing. Spectacular displays of white terror and violence supplemented these techniques.[12]

At the same time, the glimpse of freedom enabled by the transformation from chattel to man fueled the resistance to domination, discipline, exploitation, and subjugation and created new conditions for the reproduction of life. The equality and personal liberty conferred by the dispensation of rights occasioned a sense of group entitlement intent on collective redress. These newly acquired rights also obfuscated and licensed forms of social domination, racial subjection, accumulation, and exploitation. Despite the inability of the newly emancipated to actualize or enjoy the full equality or freedom stipulated by the law and the ways in which these newly acquired rights masked the modes of domination attendant to the transition from slavery to freedom, the possession of rights was nonetheless significant.

The failures of Reconstruction are perhaps best understood by examining the cross-hatchings of slavery and freedom as modes of domination, subjection, and accumulation.[13] Just as "the veiled slavery of wage labourers in Europe needed the unqualified slavery of the New World as its pedestal," so, too, did slavery provide the pedestal upon which the equality of rights appeared resplendent and veiled the relations of domination and exploitation harbored within the language of rights. If the violation of liberty and rights exacted by slavery's presence disfigured the revolutionary legacy of 1776—life, liberty, and the pursuit of happiness—then no less portentous was the legitimation and sanctioning of race as a natural ordering principle of the social during the transformation of national identity and citizenship. The legacy of slavery was evidenced by the intransigence of racism, specifically the persistent commitment to discriminatory racial classifications despite the prohibition of explicit declarations of inequality or violations of life, liberty, and property based on prior condition of servitude or race. On one hand, the constraints of race were formally negated by the stipulation of sovereign individuality and abstract equality, and on the other, racial discriminations and predilections were cherished and protected as beyond the scope of law. Even more unsettling was the instrumental role of equality in constructing a measure of man or descending scale of humanity that legitimated and naturalized subordination. The role of equality in the consolidation and expansion of whiteness as the norm of humanity and the scale and measure of man was not unlike the surprisingly adverse effects wrought by the judicial assessment of the Thirteenth Amendment, which resulted in progressively restricted notions of enslavement and its incidents that, in turn, severely narrowed the purview of freedom.

The advent of freedom was characterized by forms of constraint, which resembling those experienced under slavery, relied primarily on force, compulsion, terror, and which, signaling the new day, restricted and coerced through the language of sovereignty, contract, and self-possession. The revolution of sentiment consequent to emancipation supplanted paternalist affections with racial antipathy and reciprocity with revulsion. This discrepant or discordant bestowal of emancipation can be gleaned in the law and in a variety of everyday sites and practices, and it entailed new forms of subjection. "Burdened individuality," as a critical term, attempts to convey the antagonistic production of the liberal individual, rights-bearer, and black(ened) subject as equal yet inferior, independent yet servile, freed yet bound by duty, responsible yet reckless, carefree yet brokenhearted. "Burdened individuality" designates the double bind of emancipation—the onerous responsibilities of freedom with the enjoyment of few of its entitlements, the collusion of the disembodied equality of liberal individuality with the dominated and disciplined embodiment of blackness, the entanglements of sovereignty and subjection, and the transformation of involuntary servitude effected under the aegis of free labor. This is not to suggest simply that blacks were unable to achieve the democratic individuality of white citizens but rather something darker—the discourse on black freedom emphasized hardship, travails, and a burdened and encumbered existence. Burdened individuality is both a descriptive and a conceptual device utilized to explicate the particular modes and techniques of power in which the individual serves as the object and instrument. The power generative of this condition of burdened individuality encompassed repression, domination, techniques of discipline, strategies of self-improvement, and the regulatory interventions of the state.

The mantle of individuality effectively conscripted the freed as indebted and dutiful worker and incited forms of coercion, discipline, punishment, and regulation that profoundly complicated the meaning of freedom. If it appears paradoxical that the nomination "free individual" illuminates the fractures of freedom and begets methods of bondage quite suited to a free labor economy, it is only because the mechanisms through which right, exchange, and equality bolster and advance domination, subjection, and exploitation have not been interrogated. Liberal discourses of freedom enable forms of subjection seemingly quite at odds with its declared principles, since they readily accommodate autonomy and domination, sovereignty and submission, and subordination and abstract equality. This can be attributed to the Lockean heritage of U.S. constitutionalism, which propounded an ideal of liberty founded in the sanctity of property, and the vision of liberty forwarded in the originary narrative of the Constitution, which wed slavery and freedom in the founding of the nation and the making of "we the people."[14] The question remains as to how the effort to sever the coupling of liberty and bondage, which, albeit disavowed, inaugurated the republic and continued to produce new forms of domination.[15] How did emancipatory figurations of a rights-bearing individual aimed at abolishing the badges of slavery result in burdened individuality?

Restrictive and narrow conceptions of liberty derived from bourgeois constructions of the market, the atomizing and individualizing character of rights, and an equality grounded in sameness facilitated the domination and exploitation of the postbellum order. Prized designations like "independence," "autonomy," and "free will" are the lures of liberalism, yet the rendering of the individual as proprietor (of the self) and sovereign is drastically undermined by the forms of repression and terror that accompanied the advent of freedom, the techniques of discipline that bind the individual through conscience, self-knowledge, responsibility, and duty, and the management of blackened bodies and populations effected through the racism of the state and civil society.[16] Liberalism, in general, and rights discourse, in particular, assure entitlements and privileges as they enable and efface elemental forms of domination primarily because of the atomistic portrayal of social relations, the inability to address collective interests and needs, and the sanctioning of subordination and free rein of prejudice in the construction of the social or the private. The universality or unencumbered individuality of liberalism relies on tacit exclusions and norms that preclude substantive equality; all do not equally partake of the resplendent and steely singularity that it proffers. Abstract universality presumes particular forms of embodiment and excludes or marginalizes others.[17] For the subjected and dispossessed, those castigated and saddled by varied corporeal maledictions, are the fleshy substance that enable the universal to achieve its ethereal splendor.

The abstract universality of the rights of man and citizen potentially enable these rights to be enjoyed by all, at least theoretically. Universality could conceivably exceed its stipulated and constitutive constraints to the degree that these claims can be taken up and articulated by those subjects not traditionally entitled to the privileges of disembodied and unencumbered universality. At least, that is the promise. The abstractness and instability of rights make possible their resignification. When those formerly excluded are belatedly conferred with rights and guarantees of equal protection, they traditionally have had difficulty exercising these rights, as long as they are seen as lesser, derivative, or subordinate embodiments of the norm. Plainly speaking, this is the gap between the formal stipulation of rights and the legitimate exercise of them.[18] In light of this, it is necessary to consider whether the effort of the dominated to "take up" the universal does not remedy one set of injuries only to inflict injuries of another order. It is worth examining whether universalism merely dissimulates the stigmatic injuries constitutive of blackness with abstract assertions of equality, sovereignty, and individuality. Indeed, if this is the case, can the dominated be liberated by universalist assertions?[19]

As citizens and rights-bearers, were the newly emancipated merely enacting a role they could never legitimately or authentically occupy? Were they fated to be hapless aspirants who, in their effort to exercise newly conferred rights, only revealed the distance between the norm and themselves? As Mrs. Freeman, a character from Helen E. Brown's *John Freeman and His Family*, a fictional account of emancipation, declared: "I want we should be just as near like white folks as ever we can ketch it."[20] Certainly this remark highlights the chasm between the mimetic and the legitimate. It is not simply fortuitous that Mrs. Freeman expresses this sentiment, for she, even more than her husband, is ill-suited for the privileges and responsibilities attendant to citizenship. The discourse of citizenship presupposed a masculinist subject on which to drape the attendant rights and privileges of liberty and equality, explaining why the transition from slavery to freedom was usually and quite aptly narrated as the journey from chattel to man. Alas, the joke is on Mrs. Freeman, as expressed by the convoluted phrasing and orthographic nonsense that articulate her insuperable distance from the norm and intimate the unspoken exclusions of the universal rights of man and citizen.

Chattel becomes man through the ascension to the hallowed realm of the self-possessed. The individual fabricated is "free from dependence on the will of others, enters relations with others voluntarily with a view of his own interest, is the proprietor of his own person and capacities, and free to alienate his labor."[21] Assertions of free will, singularity, autonomy, and consent necessarily obscure relations of power and domination; but the genealogy of freedom discloses the intimacy of liberty, violence, theft, and subjection. This intimacy is discerned in the inequality enshrined in property rights, the conquest and captivity that established "we the people," and the identity of race as property, whether evidenced in the corporeal inscriptions of slavery and its badges or in the bounded bodily integrity of whiteness secured by the abjection of others.[22] The individual, denuded in the harsh light of scrutiny, reveals a subject tethered by various orders of constraint and obscured by the figure of the self-possessed, for lurking behind the disembodied and self-possessed individual is the fleshy substance of the disposable and the encumbered, the castigated particularity that shores up the universal.[23] With this in mind, the transubstantiation of the captive into volitional subject, chattel into proprietor, and the circumscribed body of blackness into the disembodied and abstract universal seems improbable, if not impossible.

The transition from slavery to freedom cannot adequately be represented as the triumph of liberty over domination, free will over coercion, or consent over compulsion. The valued precepts of liberalism provide an insufficient guide to understanding the event of emancipation. The ease with which sovereignty and submission and self-possession and servility are yoked is quite noteworthy. In fact, it leads us to wonder whether the insistent and disavowed production of subordination, the inequality enshrined by the sanctity of property, and the empty universality of liberalism are all that emancipation proffers. Is not the free will of the individual measured precisely through the exercise of constraint and autonomy determined by the capacity to participate in relations of exchange that only fetter and bind the subject? Does the esteemed will replace the barbaric whip or only act as its supplement? In light of these questions, the identity of the emancipated as rights-bearer and free laborer must be considered in regard to processes of domination, exploitation, accumulation, and subjection rather than in the benighted terms that desperately strive to establish slavery as the "prehistory" of man.

CYCLES OF ACCUMULATION

PR(

Evasion as a rudimentary form of
action harnessed by constraint

REDRESS

Moving about occurred
below the threshold of formal
equality and rights and
articulated the limits of
emancipation

Stealing / Expropriat

Redress as context
for collective action
and social transformation

Fugitive zones without
the traces of human
habitation

The transformation
of the broken body
into a site of
pleasure, a vessel of
communication, a
bridge between the
living and the dead

Absolutist distinctions
between slavery and
freedom are untenable

Politics with
a proper locu

Pieza
Framework

The care of the
captive body as
human flesh

PRACTICE

Flesh

V
A

The articulation of the
desire for a different
economy of enjoyment

The appropriation of
dominant space in
itinerant acts of defiance
contests the spatial
confinement and
surveillance of slave life
and, ironically, reconsiders
the meaning of property,
theft, and agency

Stealing away

Opacity

Other modes of existence

The plurality of resistance
details the relations of power

Practice as a collective
articulation of freedom, as
a process without a subject

Us is human flesh

The constancy of
minor transgressions

REFUSAL

Forms of action by the
enslaved are an index of the
unrealizable; a politics of
transfiguration exceeds
the given

BLA(

AND DISPOSSESSION

TY

he extent of protection to life and limb
as decided by diminutions in the value
f capital

The *longue durée* of our dispossession

PERSON

ney are harvested
ke any other crop.
he maternal marks
e condition of
ervitude.
atal alienation,
omb abyss.

Personhood of the
enslaved only appears
as criminal

Partus sequitur ventrem

onhistory

The object of
property eludes the
grid of legibility

The slave is the object
or the ground that makes
possible the existence
of the bourgeois subject
and by negation defines
liberty, citizenship, and
the enclosures of the
social body

Fungible life

The recognition of the
self as property is
definitive of liberty

3
5

Owners /
Owned

The figurative capacities
of blackness subtend
the enjoyment of
property

An eternal alien

RIGHTS

nomalous
ormations

A social nonperson
bereft of kin

The entanglement of
slavery and freedom
trouble facile notions of
progress. Rights didn't
negate the vestiges of
slavery

Will = criminality

lackness marks a social
lationship of dominance and
bjection and potentially one
redress and freedom; it is
contested figure at the very
enter of social struggle

Rape of the enslaved as
"negligible injury," which
did not violate law or
threaten the existence
of property

She becomes
expert at the
art of cunning

SUBJECTION

Her refusal takes the form of a
revolution at the level of
reproduction

hey break the tools

SS

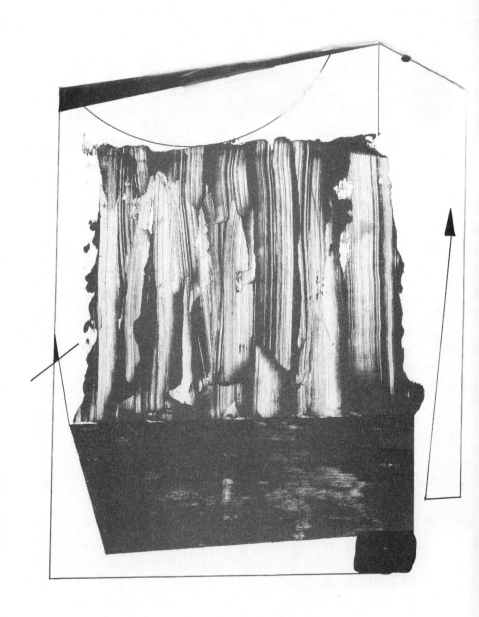

trace elements of human habitation

5

Fashioning Obligation

INDEBTED SERVITUDE AND THE LEGACY OF SLAVERY

> With the enjoyment of a freedman's privileges, comes also a freedman's duties and responsibilities. These are weighty. You cannot get rid of them; they must be met; and unless you are prepared to meet them with a proper spirit, and patiently and cheerfully to fulfil these obligations, you are not worthy of being a freedman. You may tremble in view of these duties and responsibilities; but you need not fear. Put your trust in God, and bend your back joyfully and hopefully to the burden.
>
> —Isaac W. Brinckerhoff, *Advice to Freedmen*

> It is not enough to tell us that we will be respected according as we show ourselves worthy of it. When we have rights that others respect, self-respect, pride and industry will greatly increase. I do not think that to have these rights would exalt us above measure or rob the white man of his glory.
>
> —*National Freedman*

Emancipation announced the end of chattel slavery; however, it by no means marked the end of bondage. The free(d) individual was nothing if not burdened, responsible, and obligated. Responsibility entailed accounting for one's actions, dutiful suppliance, contractual obligation, and calculated reciprocity. Fundamentally, to be responsible was to be blameworthy. The exercise of free will, quite literally, was inextricable from guilty infractions, criminal misdeeds, punishable transgressions, and an elaborate micropenality of everyday life. Responsibility made man an end in himself, and as such, the autonomous and intending agent was above all else culpable. As Nietzsche observed: "The proud realization of the extraordinary privilege of responsibility, the awareness of this rare freedom and power over himself and his destiny, has penetrated him to the depths and become an instinct, his dominant instinct: what will he call his dominant instinct, assuming that he needs a word for it? No doubt about the answer: this sovereign man calls it his conscience."[1] The burden of conscience attendant to the formation of the sovereign individual was decisive not only in the ways it facilitated self-disciplining but also in its ability to create resentment toward and justify the punishment of those who fell below "the threshold of responsibility" or failed to achieve the requisite degree of self-control.[2] The onus of accountability that rested upon the shoulders of the self-responsible individual—the task of proving oneself worthy of freedom—combined with the undue hardships of emancipation, produced an anomalous condition betwixt and between slavery and freedom. The individual was not only tethered by the bonds of conscience and duty and obliged by the ascetic imperatives of restraint and self-reliance, but literally constrained within a mixed-labor system in which contract was the vehicle of servitude and accountability was inseparable from peonage. Moreover, the guilty volition enjoyed by the free agent bore an uncanny resemblance to the only form of agency legally exercised by the enslaved: criminal liability.

Responsibility and restraint all too easily yielded to a condition of involuntary servitude, and culpability inevitably gave way to indebtedness. I use the term "indebted servitude" to amplify the constraints of conscience (discipline internalized and lauded as a virtue), the coercion and compulsion of the free labor system, and the "grafting of morality onto economics" in the making of the dutiful free laborer and, as well, to illuminate the elasticity of debt in effecting peonage and other forms of involuntary servitude.[3] The feelings of guilt, obligation, and responsibility, according to Nietzsche, originated in the relationship of creditor and debtor. Debt as the measure of morality sanctions the imposition of punishment; debt serves to reinscribe both servitude and the punitive constitution of blackness.[4] A telling example of this calculation of conscience or the entanglement of debt and duty can be found in Jared Bell Waterbury's *Advice to a Young Christian*. Here the duty of self-examination is compared to bookkeeping: "Let the duty [of self-examination] be duly and thoroughly performed, and we rise to the standard of the skilful [*sic*] and prudent merchant, who duly records every item of business; who never closes his counting-house until his balance sheet is made up; and who, by a single reference, can tell the true state of his accounts, and form a correct estimate of his commercial standing."[5] In the case of the freed, the cultivation of conscience operated in the whip's stead as an overseer of the soul, although the use of compulsion was routinely employed against those seemingly remiss in their duties. As it turned out, the encumbrance of freedom made one not only blameworthy and vulnerable to hardship and affliction in the name of material interests, but also no less susceptible to the correctives of coercion and constraint.

Idle Concerns

Irony riddled the event of emancipation. How does one narrate a story of freedom when confronted with the discrepant legacy of emancipation and the decidedly circumscribed avenues available to the freed? What does autonomy mean in the context of coercion, hunger, violence, and uncertainty? Is the unavoidable double bind of emancipation an illusory freedom and a travestied liberation? At the very least, one must contend with the enormity of emancipation as both a breach with slavery and as a reproduction or reorganization of the plantation system. What follows is an examination of eclipsed possibility and another lament of failed revolution.[6]

The paradox of emancipation involved the coupling of coercion and contract, liberty and necessity, equality and subjection. At the most basic level, this paradox was articulated in planter opposition to a free labor system and the subjugation of free labor through contractual and extralegal means, the most notable examples of these efforts being compulsory labor schemes, often supported by the Freedmen's Bureau, the predominance of nonwage and conscript labor, vagrancy statutes that criminalized those not holding labor contracts, and the prevalence of white violence. To understate the case, the South proved unwilling to embrace a free labor system or to tolerate assertions of black liberty. Blacks were blamed for this opposition to free labor, presumably because they entertained fanciful and dangerous notions of freedom and refused to work, except under duress. As we shall see, these "fanciful notions" articulated an alternate imagination of freedom and resistance to the imposition of a new order of constraint.

The pressing issue was not simply whether ex-slaves would work, but rather whether they could be transformed into a rational, docile, and productive working class; could they be assimilated to standards of productivity, sobriety, rationality, prudence, cleanliness, and responsibility? Intemperate notions were to be eradicated, and a rational work ethic inculcated through education, religious instruction, and, when necessary, compulsion. Under slavery, the whip rather than incentive, coercion rather than consent, and fear rather than reasoned self-interest had motivated their labor; now it was considered imperative to cultivate the behavior and moral outlook necessary to remake the formerly enslaved into free laborers.[7] However incongruous and inconceivable, nearly three centuries of black servitude could not relieve the nation's anxiety about the productivity of black labor or assuage the fear that the freed would be idle if not compelled to work.[8] The advent of freedom was plagued with anxieties about black indolence that hinted at the need to manage free black workers by more compelling means.[9] From the vantage point of abolitionists, policy makers, Freedmen's Bureau officials, and Northern entrepreneurs, the formerly enslaved needed to be trained as free laborers since they had never worked under conditions of consent and contract and were ignorant of the principles of self-discipline and restraint. The goal of this training, spearheaded by missionaries, teachers, and Freedmen's Bureau officials, was to replace the love of leisure with the love of gain and to supplant bawdy pleasures with dispassionate acquisitiveness.[10]

The discourse on idleness focused on the forms of conduct and behavior at odds with the requirement of a free labor system, given all its anomalies in the postbellum context. Named as offenses were a range of itinerant and intemperate practices considered subversive and dangerous to the social order. The panic or alarm about indolence registered the contested and disparate understandings of freedom held by plantation owners and the freed. The dangers targeted by this emergent discourse of dependency and idleness were: the movement of the freed, the refusal to enter contractual relations with former slaveholders, and the ability to subsist outside wage labor because of their limited wants. Not only is the elusiveness of emancipation indicated by the continued reliance on force and compulsion in managing black laborers, but, similarly, the flight from the plantation, the roving and searching, the restless movement of the freed exposed the chasm between the grand narrative of emancipation and the circumscribed arena of possibility. As a practice, moving about accumulated nothing and did not effect any reversals of power, but indefatigably held on to the unrealizable—being free—by temporarily eluding the restraints of order. Like stealing

away, it was more symbolically redolent than materially transformative. These itinerant practices were elaborations of fugitivity and
extensions of the general strike against slavery. As Absalom Jenkins
remembered, "Folks roved around for five or six years trying to do
as well as they done in slavery. It was years before they got back to
it." If moving about existed on the border of the unrealized and the
imagined, it nonetheless was at odds with the project of socializing
black laborers for market relations.[11] In effect, by refusing to stay in
their place, the emancipated insisted that freedom was a departure,
literally and figuratively, from their former condition.[12]

In the effort to implant a rational work ethic, eradicate pedestrian practices of freedom, assuage fears about the free labor system, and ensure the triumph of market relations and wage labor,
self-proclaimed "friends of the Negro" took to the South. Through
pedagogical manuals, freedmen's schools, and religious instruction, teachers, missionaries, and plantation managers strove to
inculcate an acquisitive and self-interested ethic that would motivate the formerly enslaved to be dutiful and productive laborers.
The indecorous, proud, wayward, and seemingly reckless behavior through which the newly emancipated asserted their freedom
was to be corrected with proper doses of humility, responsibility,
and restraint. These virtues chiefly defined the appropriate conduct
of free men. Practical manuals like Isaac Brinckerhoff's *Advice to
Freedmen*, Jared Bell Waterbury's *Friendly Counsels for Freedmen*,
Helen E. Brown's *John Freeman and His Family*, and Clinton Bowen
Fisk's *Plain Counsels for Freedmen* attempted to remedy the predicament of emancipation through the fashioning of an ascetic and
acquisitive subject, prompted to consume by virtue of his wants
and driven to exchange his labor because of his needs.[13] Issues of
productivity and discipline were of direct concern to the authors
of these texts, not only in their role as "old and dear friends of
the Negro" or as sympathizers who "labored incessantly for their

well-being," but also as plantation managers and Freedmen's Bureau agents directly involved in the transition to a free-labor economy. Isaac Brinckerhoff had served as a plantation superintendent in the Sea Islands. Clinton Bowen Fisk was an assistant commissioner for the Tennessee and Kentucky Freedmen's Bureaus and the eponym of Fisk University.

Advice to Freedmen, *Friendly Counsels for Freedmen*, *John Freeman and His Family*, and *Plain Counsels for Freedmen* were handbooks written for the emancipated to assist them in the transition from slavery to freedom. They were published by the American Tract Society, an evangelical organization established in 1825 "to diffuse a knowledge of our Lord Jesus Christ as the Redeemer of sinners, and to promote the interests of vital godliness and sound morality, by the circulation of Religious Tracts, calculated to receive the approbation of all evangelical Christians."[14] The texts, designed to impart practical advice to adults as well as children, focused primarily on rules of conduct that would enable the freed to overcome the degradation of slavery and meet the challenges of freedom. The lessons imparted were about labor, conduct, consumption, hygiene, marriage, home decorating, chastity, and prayer. Most important in the panorama of virtues imparted was the willingness to endure hardships, which alone guaranteed success, upward mobility, and the privileges of citizenship. Not surprisingly, certain tensions arose in the teaching of these lessons because the antagonism between slave holders and those who had once been property was sharp and undisguised. The effort to reconcile asceticism and acquisitiveness, material interests and low wages (or none at all), and autonomy and obeisance was not without notable difficulties attributable to the postbellum mixed economy. The disparities between liberal democratic ideology and the postbellum marketplace were glaring. The varied forms of compulsion utilized to force free workers to sign labor contracts by far exceeded the coercion immanent in the relations of labor and capital and instead relied on direct forms of extra-economic coercion. In short, violence remained a significant device in cultivating labor discipline.[15] Domination as much as exploitation defined the state of Negro toilers. Undeniably, inequality was the basis of the forms of economic and social relations that developed in the aftermath of emancipation.[16] And it was this naked coercion and reliance on force that provided labor relations with their distinctive Southern character.[17]

Advice to Freedmen, like the other primers, aimed to instill rational ideals of material acquisition and social restraint and correct "absolute" notions of freedom and the excesses and indulgences that resulted from entertaining such "far flung" conceptions. As their titles indicate, these handbooks were geared to practical ends: how-to advice, instructions for living, and rules of conduct being their primary concerns. The instrumental objectives of these books were explicitly declared in lessons of discipline, duty, and responsibility. The lessons contained in these primers were basically a series of imperatives—be industrious, economical, useful, productive, chaste, kind, respectful to former masters, good Christians, and dutiful citizens. The full privileges of citizenship awaited those who realized the importance of proper conduct and applied the principles of good management to all aspects of their lives, from personal hygiene to household expenditures. Not surprisingly, freedom was defined in contradictory terms in these textbooks. They encouraged both a republican free-labor vision, in which wage labor was the stepping-stone to small proprietorship, and a liberal vision, in which freedom was solely defined by the liberty of contract.

These disparate notions of freedom were complicated further by the servility freed laborers were encouraged to assume in negotiating the racial antipathy of the postwar period. The urging of servility begrudgingly acknowledged the less-than-ideal labor conditions of the South and the aversive racial sentiments to be negotiated and defused by the obeisance of the freed. Above all else, it was imperative not to rob the white man of his glory. As apparent was the constrained agency conferred by the will of contract; although it was the cherished vehicle of self-ownership, the contract documented the dispossession inseparable from becoming a propertied person. This ascendant liberal discourse disclosed the constrained agency of freedom because volition and compulsion were regularly conflated and the legal exercise of will most often resulted in servitude and indebtedness. As it turned out, the liberty of contract and bondage were reconciled in the social economy of postbellum relations. Only the cultivation of rationality and responsibility could eradicate the badges of slavery, yet sometimes harsh measures were required to re-form the Negro in accordance with the new requirements. In this respect, the success of emancipation depended on the remaking or self-making of the formerly enslaved as rational individuals and dutiful subordinates.

It is difficult to read these texts without lapsing into a predictive pessimism grounded in the certitude of hindsight. After all, we are painfully aware of what followed—debt peonage, a reign of terror, nearly one hundred years of remaining separate and resolutely unequal, second-class citizenship, and an as-yet unrealized freedom. My approach to these texts emphasizes the disciplinary, punitive, and normalizing individuation conducted under the rubric of self-improvement. It is an interested reading that does not pretend to exhaust the meaning of these texts but instead considers the fashioning of individuality, the circulation of debt, the forms of subjugation that prevailed in this proclaimed sphere of equality and liberty, and, most important, the impossibility of instituting a definitive break between slavery and freedom, compulsion and consent, terror and discipline. In explicating the terms of this new dispossession, this interpretation focuses on the forms of subjection yielded by the narrative of emancipation and the constitution of the burdened individuality of freedom.

The Debt of Emancipation

"My friend, you was [sic] once a slave. You are now a freedman."
Advice to Freedmen opens with this bestowal, as if by the force of its
declaration it were manumitting the enslaved; or as if freedom were
a gift dispensed by a kind benefactor to the less fortunate or unde-
serving. Beneficent gestures launch the stories of black freedom
narrated within these texts and also establish the obligation and
indebtedness of the freed to their friends and benefactors. The burden of debt, duty, and gratitude foisted onto the newly emancipated
in exchange or repayment for their freedom is established in the stories of origin that open these textbooks. In the section "How You
Became Free" of *Advice to Freedmen*, the emancipated are informed
that their freedom was purchased by treasure, millions of government dollars, and countless lives: "With treasure and precious blood
your freedom has been purchased. Let these sufferings and sacri-
fices never be forgotten when you remember that you are not now
a slave but a freedman" (7). Similarly, *Plain Counsels* advised the
freed not to take lightly the gift of freedom but rather to "prize your
freedom above gold, for it has cost rivers of blood" (9). The blood
of warring brothers and mothers' sons that stained the battle-torn
landscape of the United States granted the enslaved freedom, but
the blood regularly spilt at the whipping post or drawn by the cat-
o'-nine tails in the field, the 200,000 black soldiers who fought
for the Union, or the general strike, the hundreds of thousands of
slaves who contributed to the defeat of the Confederacy by fleeing
the plantation and flocking behind Union lines failed to be included
in these accounts of slavery's demise. Blood, the symbol of Christian redemption, national reunion, and immutable and ineradicable
differences of race, was routinely juxtaposed with gold and other
treasure expended on behalf of black freedom, and which presumably indebted the freed to the nation. The language of blood not only

figured the cherished expenditures of war but also described the difficulties of freedom. As Jared Bell Waterbury remarked in *Southern Planters and Freedmen*, "Social difficulties of long standing cannot be suddenly or violently overcome. They are like wounds that must bleed a while before they will heal, and the process of cure, though slow and requiring much patience, is nevertheless certain."[18] The wounded body stood as figure of the nation and the injuries of war were to be redressed not only by the passage of time but also by the compulsory exchange and moral remittances of the emancipated.

Emancipation instituted indebtedness. Blame and duty and blood and dollars marked the birth of the free(d) subject. The very bestowal of freedom established the indebtedness of the freed through a calculus of blame and responsibility that mandated that the formerly enslaved both repay this investment of faith and prove their worthiness. The temporal attributes of indebtedness bind one to the past, since what is owed draws the past into the present, and suspends the subject between what has been and what is. Indebtedness confers durability, for the individual is answerable to and liable for past actions and must be abstinent in the present in the hopes of securing the future. Indebtedness was central to the creation of a memory of the past in which white benefactors, courageous soldiers, and virtuous mothers sacrificed themselves for the enslaved. This memory was to be seared into the minds of the freed. Debt was at the center of a moral economy of submission, and servitude was instrumental in the production of peonage, or slavery in all but name. Above all, debt operated to bind the subject by compounding the service owed, augmenting the deficit through interest accrued, and advancing credit that extended interminably the obligation of service. The emancipated were introduced to the circuits of exchange through the figurative deployment of debt, which obliged them to both enter coercive contractual relations and faithfully remunerate the treasure expended on their behalf. The paradox is that those from whom everything had been taken—their life and labor stolen, their children removed and sold—emerged as free subjects owing the world everything. Debt literally sanctioned bondage and propelled the freed toward indentured servitude by selling off future labor.[19] As Gerald Jaynes observes, "The southern sharecropper bore all the burdens of an entrepreneur but was dispossessed of freedom of choice in making managerial decisions. . . . No government which allows its laboring population to mortgage its labor by enforcing debt peonage can claim to have free labor."[20] Yet debt was not simply a pretext but an articulation of the enduring claims on black life and labor, the affective linchpin of reciprocity, mutuality, extraction, and inequality, the ideational hybrid of responsibility and servitude, and, most important, the agent of bondage. The transition from slavery to freedom introduced the ex-slave to the circuits of exchange through this construction of already accrued debt, an abstemious present, and a mortgaged future. In all essential ways, to be free was to be a debtor—that is, obliged and duty bound to others.[21] The inaugural gestures that opened these primers announced the advent of freedom and, at the same time, attested to the impossibility of escaping slavery.

"How you became free" stories narrated an account of the past and the transition from slavery to freedom that begat the indebted and servile freed individual. These primers surpassed the immediate goals of a how-to book and produced a chronicle of recent events, a history, as it were, that began the process of revision, repression, and reconciliation essential to the xenophobic and familial narrative of national identity that became dominant in the 1880s and 1890s.[22] However, as many former slaves asserted, they had not incurred any debt they had not repaid a thousandfold. In black counterdiscourses of freedom, remedy was sought for the injuries of slavery, not through the reconstruction of the Negro—in other words, the refashioning of the emancipated as rational and docile individuals—but through reparations. Andy McAdams complained that the government gave former slaves nothing but a hard deal: "They was plenty of land that did not belong to anyone except the government. . . . We did not get nothing but hard work, and we were worse off under freedom than we were during slavery, as we did not have a thing—could not write or read."[23] In similar terms, Anna Lee, a former slave, conveyed the weight of duty and the burden of transformation placed upon the freed. Noting that the efforts to transform the South in the aftermath of the war were focused immoderately on free blacks, she recounted, "The reconstruction of the negro was real hard on us."[24] These contending accounts of slavery and freedom quite differently represent the past and assess the burden of responsibility. In light of this, we need to question whether the stories of emancipation narrated in the freedmen's handbooks simply refigured enslavement through the imposition of debt. Discernible in these stories of origin was the struggle over the meaning of emancipation and the possibilities of redress, since these possibilities, in fact, depended upon the terms of recollection.

Despite the invocation of the natural rights of man, the emphasis on the "gift" of freedom and the accompanying duties, to the contrary, implied not only that one had to labor in exchange for what were deemed natural and inalienable rights, but that the failure to do so might result in their revocation. The liberty and equality conferred by emancipation instituted the debt and established the terms of its amortization. But what could a mortgaged freedom yield? The tabulation of duty and responsibility resulted in a burdened individuality in which one enjoyed the obligations of freedom without its prerogatives. The import of this cannot be underestimated, for the literal and figurative accrual of debt reproduced black servitude within the terms of an emancipatory narrative.

The imposition of debt was premised upon a selective and benign representation of slavery that emphasized paternalism, dependency,

reciprocity, and will-lessness. Given this rendition of slavery, responsibility was deemed the best antidote for the ravages of the past;
never mind that it effaced the enormity of those injuries, necessitated the erasure of history, and placed the onus of all that had happened onto the shoulders of the individual. The journey from chattel
to man entailed a movement from subjection to self-possession,
dependency to responsibility, and coercion to contract. Without
responsibility, autonomy, will, and self-possession would be meaningless.[25] If the slave was dependent, will-less, and bound by the dictates of the master, the freed individual was liberated from the past
and capable of remaking themself through the sheer exercise of will.
Responsibility was an inestimable component of the bestowal of
freedom, and, it produced individual culpability and national innocence, temporal durability and historical amnesia.

As explicated in the language of liberal individualism, the vestiges of chattel slavery and the degradations still clinging to the
freed after centuries of subjection to the white race were obstacles
to be overcome through self-discipline, the renunciation of dependency and intemperate habits, and personal restraint. By identifying
slavery rather than race as responsible for this degraded condition, these texts did reflect a commitment, albeit circumscribed, to
equality. The primers on freedom also revealed the limits of liberal
discourse: an atomized vision of master-slave relations prevented
a structural understanding of the social order created by the plantation and apportioned individual responsibility, if not blame, for
what were clearly the consequences of extreme systemic domination. Seemingly, blacks gained entry to the body of the nation-state
as expiators of the past, as if slavery and its legacy were solely their
cross to bear. This ahistorical and amnesic vision of racial slavery
instituted the burden of obligation placed upon the freed. It leads
us to consider whether the gift of emancipation was the onus of
individual responsibility, or whether guilt was inseparable from the

conferral of rights. Or whether the newly acknowledged/acquired rights safeguarded the individual or merely obscured the social relations of slavery and the predicament of the emancipated. Were recrimination and punishment the rewards of self-possession? Did emancipation confer sovereignty and autonomy only to abandon the individual in a self-blaming and penalizing free society?[26] The bound and sovereign self of rights was an island unto himself, accountable for his own making and answerable to his failures; the world built on stolen labor and commodified life receded before the singular exercise of the will and the blameworthy and isolated individual.

The repression of slavery's unspeakable features and the shockingly benign portrait of the peculiar institution produced national innocence, yet enhanced the degradation of the past for those still hindered by its vestiges because they became the locus of blame and the site of aberrance. While the enduring legacy of slavery was discernible in the disfigurements of freedom, its vestiges and degradations were addressed almost exclusively as problems of conduct and character. It is clear that the injuries of the past could not be remedied through simple acts of forgetting or selective acts of erasure, nor could they be conjured away by the simple declaration of abolition, nor could the onus of responsibility placed upon the newly emancipated institute a definitive break between slavery and freedom.

While these stories of origin cast the freed as an indebted and servile class, they nonetheless demanded that the freed also be responsible and sovereign actors. Yet if the emancipated were beholden to friends, benefactors, and even former masters in their new condition, how could rational self-interest rather than obsequiousness be cultivated? How could those marked by the "degradations of the past" overcome the history of slavery through their own individual efforts, especially given the remnants of slavery shaping the present? How could the designated bearers of slavery be liberated from that past? Were not the vestiges of the former condition enduring beyond the triumph or failure of their own efforts in the pervasiveness of white violence, emergent forms of involuntary servitude, and the intransigence of racism? In anticipation of such questions and cognizant of the hardships of freedom, the self-appointed counselors of the freed tirelessly repeated the directive that the attainment of freedom depended upon the efforts of the freed themselves. By following wise counsel and through their own exertions, they would, as *Advice to Freedmen* assured them, one day become "worthy and respected citizens of this great nation" (4).

One risks stating the obvious in observing that the circumstances of the freed—the utter absence of resources, the threat of starvation, the lack of education, and the want of land and property considered essential to independence—were treated as private matters best left to their own bloody hands, bent backs, and broken hearts, rather than as the culmination of three centuries of servitude. If a sea of blood and gold had enabled the violent remaking of the nation and eventually effected a reunion of warring "families," purchased at the expense and exclusion of the emancipated, it delivered blacks to the shore of freedom and deposited the detritus of the war at their feet. Like the ghosts of the Confederate dead paraded by the Ku Klux Klan in their nighttime raids to intimidate blacks, reminding them that the war continued and that the price was yet to be exacted for those white men lost in the war, debt too frighteningly refigured the past. Debt ensured submission; it insinuated that servitude was not yet over and that the travails of freedom were the price to be paid for emancipation.

The Encumbrance of Freedom

The discrepant bestowal of emancipation conferred sovereignty as it produced subjection. The lessons of independence and servility contradictorily espoused in these texts epitomized the double bind of freedom—the tension between the universalist premises of liberalism, which included the freed within the scope of rights and entitlements definitive of liberty and citizenship, and the exclusionary strategies premised upon the presumed inferiority of blacks. These manuals advocated mastery and control over one's condition and destiny—autonomy, self-possession, resolve, and discipline—and conflated self-making and submission. Overwhelmingly, self-mastery was given expression through the laboring body. In *John Freeman and His Family*, laboring hands are the synecdoche for the self-possessed individual: "Look here, do you see these hands? They were made to work, I'm persuaded, for haven't they always worked hitherto? I've used 'em, and given all I made to Master Lenox; now I'll use 'em, and give all I make to *Master John*" (14). To be a subject was to master the body, possess it as object, alienate and exchange its capacities for wages. If the gains of self-possession are illuminated by the profits to be earned and enjoyed by John's laboring hands, by his perilous inclusion in the category "master," then the emphasis on laboring hands and a back designed for hard work also insinuate that this new role might not be so different after all. Whether slave or free, manual labor defined his horizon.

Self-mastery was invariably defined as willing submission to the dictates of former masters, the market, and the inquisitor within. If, as *Advice to Freedmen* declared, "your future, under God, must be wrought by yourselves," then clearly the future to be wrought was one of interminable toil, obligation, and humility. In line with these values, the emancipated were encouraged to remain on the plantation, be patient, to toil interminably, and make do with the readily available, including low wages. This decided emphasis on submission, self-denial, and servile compliance was not considered at odds with autonomy or self-interest. Rather, mastery became defined by self-regulation, indebtedness, subordination and responsibility, careful regard for the predilections of former masters, and agility at sidestepping the "sore toes" of prejudice and resentment. The robust and mutable capacities of mastery are to be marveled at. If mastery was an antidote for the dependency of slavery—the lack of autonomy, will-lessness, inability to direct one's labor or enjoy its rewards, and psychological disposition for servitude—it bore a striking resemblance to the prostration of slavery. Indeed, the propertied person (proprietor of the self) remained vulnerable to the dispossession exacted by violence, domination, predation, and exploitation.

The images of the laboring body represented in these texts made clear that the freedman's duties coupled the requirements of servitude with the responsibilities of independence. Let us reconsider the following passage from *Advice to Freedmen*: "With the enjoyment of a freedman's privileges, come also a freedman's duties. These are weighty. You can not get rid of them. They must be met. And unless you are prepared to meet them with a proper spirit, and patiently and cheerfully fulfill these obligations, you are not worthy of being a freedman. You may well tremble in view of these duties and responsibilities. But you need not fear. Put your trust in God, and *bend your back joyfully and hopefully to the burden*." The joyful bending of the back refigured the "backbreaking" regimen of slave labor and genuflected before the blessings and privileges of freedom. The back bent joyfully to the burdens foisted upon it transformed the burdened individuality and encumbrances of freedom into an auspicious exercise of free will and self-making. This unsettling description avows servility and submission as prerequisites to enjoying the privileges of freedom. Bending one's back joyfully to extant and anticipated burdens unites the sentimental ethic of submission with the rational and ascetic ideals of the marketplace. Freedom, although a release from slavery, undoubtedly imposed burdens of another order. The body no longer harnessed by chains or governed by the whip was instead tethered by the weight of conscience, duty, and obligation.

In this scenario, the indebtedness instituted by the gift of freedom was unmistakable. It obliged a worthy return—a bent back, agile hands, averted eyes, and lowered expectations. The failure to meet this obligation risked the loss of honor, status, and manhood, if not the loss of freedom or life.[27] Only industry, diligence, and a willingness to labor, even at a negligible wage, proved one's worthiness for freedom.

The joyfully bent back of the laborer conjures up a repertoire of familiar images that traverse the divide between slavery and freedom. If this figure encodes freedom, then it does so by making it difficult, if not impossible, to distinguish the subjection of slavery from the satisfied self-interest of the free laborer. The bent back offers an image of freedom that leaves us unable to discern whether the laborer in the field is driven by the lash or by the inward drive of duty and obligation. The toiling figure, the bent back, and the beast of burden, summoned by this chain of association, elide the belabored distinction between will and will-lessness. As it turns out, the anatomy of freedom laid out in these texts attends to the body as object and instrument, effacing the distinctions between slave and laborer, for as *John Freeman and His Family* tells us, the body "meant to work" hints at the racial division of labor in which "some must work with the hands, while others work with the head. . . . Everyone must be willing to do his part, just where he is needed most" (42).[28] Yet the bent back readily invokes deference, obedience, prostration, and humility and bespeaks the utilization of the body as a laboring machine. Just as the lowered eyes, stooped shoulders, and shuffling feet were the gestural language of enslavement, the bent back similarly articulated the servility and exploitation of the postbellum economy.

Duty imposed burdens of the soul, too. For the free laborer doubled over by the sheer weight of his responsibilities, hopeful and obedient, work was to be its own reward, since the exertions of manual labor were also demonstrations of faith.[29] The bent back was testament to one's trust in God. As John Freeman informed his brethren, "If you don't work, you can't pray; for don't the Lord Jehovah say if we regard sin in our hearts, he won't hear us?" (35). Idleness was the "devil's playground." The broken heart replicated the subjugated and suppliant body and transformed rules of conduct into articles of faith. As Waterbury declared, "You must have 'the broken heart,' sorrow for sin—sorrow before God, because you have broken his laws" (17). Just as the broken heart was the recognition of one's guilt and sin before God, so, too, the bent back assumed the posture of repentance, as if the sins of slavery were to be repaid by the travails of the freed.

If freedom appeared only as a hardship because of the alliance of liberty, servility, and obligation, this was explained by recourse to the dependency of slavery, the want of ease and idleness, and the adversity inseparable from independence. *Friendly Counsels for Freedmen* conceded the hardships of emancipation but promised that rewards would flow from perseverance: "Your condition is in some respects much better, and in others somewhat worse, than when you were slaves. Your master, if he was kind, took good care of you. Now that you are free, you have got to take care of yourselves. At first this may be a hardship; but by and by you will see that it is a good thing. In slavery you had little or no care, except to see that your task was done. Now that you are your own men, you have got to think and work both" (4). While the pedagogical manuals attributed the hardships of freedom to idleness, dependency, and intemperance, or contrasted the burden of independence with the ease of slavery, the emancipated identified the sources of adversity as their lack of resources, the government's unwillingness to provide reparations, the pervasiveness of white violence, and the failure of the law to protect black lives. The emancipated also shared a different perspective on who comprised the dependent class of slavery. They argued irrefutably that they were the producing class and that the riches of their owners and the nation came from their labor. Andy McAdams acknowledged that although he was uncertain about what freedom meant, he certainly expected something different than what he had experienced: "I think they ought to have given us old slaves some mules and land too, because everything our white people had we made for them."[30]

The emancipated complained about the hardships of freedom, but their grievances were an indictment of the absence of the material support that would have made substantial freedom ultimately realizable. Being emancipated without resources was no freedom at all. As Felix Haywood recalled, "We knowed freedom was on us, but we didn't know what was to come with it. We thought we was goin' to get rich like the white folks. We thought we was going to be richer than the white folks, 'cause we were stronger and knowed how to work, and the white didn't and they didn't have us to work for them anymore. But it didn't turn out that way. We soon found out that freedom could make folks proud but it didn't make them rich."[31] Dire necessity, rather than opportunity or gratitude for the gift of wage labor, resulted in their return to the plantation. As many pointed out, the ravages of hunger and rampant white violence were the embittered gifts of emancipation. "Dependency" and "responsibility" were pliable and contested terms that ambiguously named the predicament of freedom. On one hand, responsibility restored the self-respect that slavery had taken, and on the other, responsibility meant that blacks were more encumbered after emancipation than before. According to Parker Pool, the freed were better slaves than they had been when they were owned because they still had nothing, and yet they had to bear their own expenses.[32] Countering these protestations, Plain Counsels enjoined the freed to remember: "You cannot be too glad that you are free; that your hands, your head, your heart are your own" (9). However, it was not a shortage of joy that afflicted the freed; rather, it was an awareness that although one's hands and heart and head were now one's own, without resources it was impossible to live, and the body that labored for another's profit was perhaps only seemingly one's own. Self-possession secured little, particularly when this nascent sense of autonomous embodiment was identified with hunger, degradation, and violent assaults on one's person and quickly eclipsed by the encumbered existence of emancipation.

Possession by Contract

One wonders how readers of these primers responded as they encountered representations of slavery as dependency rather than captivity and the depiction of the ravages of the institution as careless habits.[33] If literacy was the avenue to humanity, the lesson to be gleaned from these texts was that the price of entry entailed silencing the very factors that determined the condition of degradation and impoverishment. Not only was the violence of slavery expunged, but also the productivity of slave labor was denied. Yet how could the joy of emancipation be understood without recourse to the enormity of loss, the senseless and innumerable acts of violence, the severed kinship, or the constancy of dishonor and humiliation that typified slavery? Did it seem a paradox that the language of mastery was the vehicle of self-realization? Could possession and property ever seem inalienable? How could the ambivalence of freedom be voiced without being woefully misunderstood as a longing for the good old days of slavery? How could the awful feeling induced by being released like "stray cattle," never having had anything and having no place to go, be expressed without seeming like nostalgia for life on the plantation?[34]

While these texts were written by self-proclaimed friends of the Negro who had "marched with them through the Red Sea of strife, sympathized with them in all their sufferings, labored incessantly for their well-being, and rejoiced in their prosperity," the coercive and servile character of the freedom espoused must be considered in regard to an ascendant liberal discourse of liberty of contract and self-regulating markets. Freedom seemed elusive when slavery was no longer its antagonist. Abolitionist discourse, expurgated of the terrifying details that scandalized and titillated Northern audiences, was little more than a colloquy on the degraded character of the enslaved and the unproductivity of slave labor. The anemic vision of freedom expounded by Northern industrialists and white abolitionists most often failed to exceed the minimal requirements for a disciplined and productive workforce. This rhetoric deployed in the context of Reconstruction insinuated the need for compulsion when inclination failed and condoned the use of coercion, if and when it aided in the transition to free labor. This was reflected in the policy of the Freedmen's Bureau and in the advice dispensed by the authors of these handbooks, some of whom were the policy makers and managers of Reconstruction. The liberal proclivities of abolitionist discourse in the antebellum period had provided a powerful natural rights argument against the institution of slavery, but in the postbellum period, it yielded ambivalent effects—elitist and racist arguments about the privileges of citizenship, an inordinate concern with discipline and the cultivation of manhood, and contractual notions of free labor.[35]

It is important to note the role played by abolitionist and antislavery reformers in the conceptualization and dissemination of repressive free labor ideals. In examining the relation between slavery and the discourse of labor management in early industrial England, David Brion Davis argues that Jeremy Bentham's vision of the model prison was a parodic intensification of the ideals of plantation management.[36] If Bentham's panopticon is the model of discipline, the exemplary exercise of a modern power that is mild-lenient-productive, then how does our understanding of the carceral society change if, in fact, the carceral is a derivative or offshoot of the plantation and presumes continuities between the management of slave and free labor? If this totalizing vision of managing labor had one eye directed toward slavery and the other toward freedom, it then becomes necessary to consider the way discipline itself bears the trace of what Foucault would describe as premodern forms of power, but which perhaps are more aptly described as "discipline with its clothes off." None of this is surprising when slavery is contextualized within a transatlantic capitalist system that traded information and strategies of labor management between the plantation and the factory.[37] Not only did the crisis of industrialization—problems of pauperism, underemployment, and labor management—occur in the context of an extensive debate about the fate of slavery, but also slavery informed the premises and principles of labor discipline. As Davis notes, the focus on the coercion and barbarism of slavery and the whip as the only incentive to work "lent sanction to less barbarous modes of social discipline. For reformers, the plantation offered the prospect of combining virtues of the old agrarian order with new ideals of uplift and engineered incentive." The terror and violence of the plantation, too, would shape the contours of the new racial order.

The forms of compulsion used against the unemployed, vagrants, beggars, and others in the postbellum North, as Amy Dru Stanley notes, mirrored the transition from slavery to freedom. The contradictory aspects of liberty of contract and the reliance on coercion in stimulating free labor modeled in the aftermath of the Civil War were the lessons of emancipation employed against the poor. Many of the architects of scientific charity (a bureaucratic campaign to assist the poor by transforming their behavior, whereby idleness and dependence on charity, rather than poverty, were identified as the enemy of the poor), vagrancy statutes, and compulsory contracts were leading abolitionists—Edward Pierce, Josephine Shaw Lowell, and Samuel Gridley Howe, to name a few.[38] Stanley writes: "The experience of war and emancipation not only honed efficient techniques of philanthropy but also schooled Yankees in schemes for forcing beggars to work. The endeavor of reconstructing the southern labor system and installing contract practices recast conceptions of dependency, obligation, and labor compulsion. Just as the ideal of free labor was transported south, so its coercive aspects—articulated in rules governing the freed people—were carried back north."[39] The compulsion and intimidation necessary to dominate the ex-slave licensed the additional force wielded against the poor. Duress would steer them into the world of exchange.

The specter of slavery's barbarism, symbolized by the whip and the auction block, legitimated milder but more intensive forms of discipline. Slavery serves as the model and provides the conditions for the exploitation of the white working class. The circulation of techniques of discipline across the Atlantic, between the plantation and the factory, and from the plantation to Northern cities trouble arguments based upon epochal shifts of power or definitive notions of premodern and modern forms of power. Rather, this movement reveals the ways in which the violence of originary accumulation and multiple modes of domination and coercion conditioned bourgeois relations of production and exploitation.[40] Certainly, the techniques of free-labor management employed during Reconstruction were informed by styles of management used under slavery, and often these techniques were abandoned only as a result of labor resistance to continued work routines of slavery.[41] The compulsory contract that was the signature of free labor relations also traveled beyond the South. What concerns me here are the forms of discipline unleashed by the abandonment of the whip. Although the slave system had become "a discredited form of authority that seemed to require the personal imposition of constant pain," in contrast to the rational incentives of free labor, these new forms of discipline were also invasive and coercive.[42] The ascendant forms of constraint and compulsion did not depend upon the exhibition of whipping but nonetheless produced compliant and productive bodies. For black toilers, the spectacle of violence, whether the lynching post or the convict labor system or police brutality or extrajudicial killing (massacre), never disappeared. The spectacle of violence and the sovereign right to kill proved enduring.

A comparative examination of slavery and freedom reveals less about the barbarism of slavery than it does about the contradictions and antagonisms of freedom. By focusing on the ways in which antislavery and reform discourse paved the way for brutal forms of "modern" power, it becomes clear that slavery is less the antithesis of free labor than an intemperate consort, a moral foil, a barbarism overcome, and the pedestal on which the virtues of free labor are declaimed. Here, the point is not to efface the differences between slavery and freedom, albeit precarious, or deny the dishonor, degradation, and extreme violence of slavery, but rather to stress the difficulty of installing an absolute distinction between slavery and freedom and to reveal the perverse entanglements of the "grand narrative of emancipation."[43] Slavery established free labor as a rational ideal and determined the scope of freedom and equality conferred by the Reconstruction Amendments and scrutinized in the *Civil Rights Cases* and *Plessy v. Ferguson*. Whether it was understood as the negation of fundamental liberties or as "mere chattelism," slavery fundamentally shaped the experience and interpretation of freedom. Was freedom simply the absence of constraint, or was it full and equal protection of the laws?[44] Was freedom more than the ability to alienate one's labor, or to embrace dispossession as autonomy? As liberal notions of freedom superseded republican ideals, freedom increasingly became defined in terms of the release from constraint and liberty of contract rather than positive entitlements.

Freedom remained elusive, despite the heralding of consent, contract, liberty, and equality. Violence and coercion underlay the discourse of reason and reform. It must be emphasized that for black laborers, the liberty of contract primarily served to entrap them in a system of debt bondage.[45] Perhaps it was enough of a difference to make it clear that you were no longer a slave, or perhaps not, no doubt it was far short of the autonomy yearned for.[46] As Anna Lee and countless others testified, "We done just about what we could after the war, as we were worse off then than we were in slavery time."[47] Only a determined misreading could interpret the disappointments of freedom constantly reiterated in slave testimony as a longing for slavery. To the contrary, what haunts such laments is the longing for an as-yet unrealized freedom, the nonevent of emancipation, and the entwining of slavery and freedom.

If one dares to "abandon the absurd catalogue of official history" and the historical partitions to which the dominated are subject, as Édouard Glissant suggests, then the violence and domination perpetuated in the name of slavery's reversal come to the fore.[48] Emancipation becomes double-edged and even obfuscating, since involuntary servitude and freedom were synonymous for many of the formerly enslaved. Although those faithful to narratives of historical progress greet such an assertion with disapprobation and disbelief, consider remarks like those of former slaves Anna Lee and Absalom Jenkins. By focusing on the ambiguity and elusiveness of emancipation, I hope to glean this subterranean history of emancipation, one not fully recoverable and only glimpsed through the grid of dominant organizing narratives—the repressive pastoral of the WPA testimony, the grand narrative of emancipation, and liberal discourses of free will and self-possession.

The Will and the Whip

Freedom did not abolish the lash. The regular use of coercion, the share system, debt bondage, the convict-lease system, the prevalence of white violence, and the threat of death hardly signal the sovereignty of the will, the ascendancy of the contract, or the triumph of "rational" methods of management over the barbarism of slavery. Rather, what occurred was the displacement of the whip by the cultivation of conscience, the repressive instrumentality of the law, coercive forms of labor management, and orchestrated and spontaneous violence aimed at restoring the relations of mastery and servitude and quelling assertions of liberty and equality. Maria Sutton Clements recalled the habitual exercise of violence—the Klan attacks on black homes forced people to "mostly hide out in the woods." If blacks assembled, they were accused of sedition, that is, talk about equality: "If dey hear you talkin they say you talkin bout equalization. They whoop up."[49] Tom Holland said that people were afraid to go out and assert their freedom because "they'd ride up by a Negro and shoot him jus' like a wild hog and never a word said or done 'bout it."[50]

In freedmen's handbooks, the displacement of the whip can be discerned in the emphasis on self-discipline and policing. The whip was not to be abandoned; rather, it was to be internalized. The emphasis on correct training, proper spirit, and bent backs illuminated the invasive forms of discipline idealized as the self-fashioning of the moral and rational subject. The whip was routinely invoked, less to convey the actual violence of the institution than the willlessness of those compelled to labor. In summoning the whip, the contrast was made between a legitimate order founded on the contract and the compulsion of slavery, and between rational agents and those motivated by force or fear. *Plain Counsels* provides just such an example: "When you were a slave, it may have been your habit to do just as little as you could to avoid the lash. But now that you are free, you should be actuated by a more noble principle than fear" (45). The inflated assessment of the will, the exalting of liberty, and the idealization of choice masked the violence of exchange.

The disparity between free will and the coercion that fundamentally defined the postbellum economic order might be laughable if its consequences were not so tragic. If the will ultimately distinguished liberty from bondage, with the attendant assumptions of the power to control and define one's circumstances or actions, then the event of emancipation instituted a crisis regarding the meaning of freedom and the free individual. In the nineteenth century, the will theory of contract was dominant. "The idea that contractual obligation has its source in the individual will," observes Clare Dalton, "persisted into the latter part of the nineteenth century, consistent with the pervasive individualism of that time and the general incorporation into law of notions of liberal political theory."[51] Yet despite the lauding of the will, the feature of the contracts most emphasized was the binding character of agreements and the legal force to compel the signatory's conduct. The point here is not simply to expose what is disavowed by this construction of free will or to engage in the oft-repeated critique of possessive individualism, but to explore the tension between the cultivation of liberal individualism, with its emphasis on will, mastery, autonomy, and volition, and the requirement of submission, docility, fear, and trembling. The easy coexistence of the coerced free laborer and the volitional subject moving unrestrainedly along the path of self-interest and prosperity hints at the distance between the emancipatory ideal and the conditions of its actualization. The uncertainty elicited by the figure of the burdened and weary laborer toiling in the field, the looming doubt as to whether he is slave or free, exposes the breach between the hallowed ideal of self-possession and the encumbrances of freedom.

Was the only difference between freedom and slavery to be ascertained in the choice to labor dutifully, bend one's back joyfully, or act willingly as one's own inquisitor? If so, didn't this only disclose the elusiveness and intangibility of freedom? The black laborer enjoyed neither the illusions of free exchange nor volition because of the imposition of the contract labor system by the Freedmen's Bureau, the coercion and repression that shaped the market, the establishment of wage ceilings, and the effort to prevent the free movement of laborers through vagrancy, breach-of-contract, anti-enticement laws, and the prevalence of violence.[52] The threat of arrest or starvation, rather than voluntary action or inner compulsion, resulted in the return to the plantation. In light of this, what was to be gained by the cultivation of the noble rather than the base? After all, was not the only choice to work or starve?

Obligation and responsibility rather than necessity clothed the exhortation to labor dutifully. Necessity was at odds with the proclaimed liberty of the volitional subject/liberal individual, since it was distinguished by encumbrance, compulsion, and the utter lack of options. Necessity uneasily contended with the sovereignty and autonomy that purportedly delineated freedom; it exemplified all that was presumably negated by the abolition of slavery—the primacy of compulsion, the weightedness of embodiment, and the sway of needs. Certainly the pangs of hunger were no less compelling than the whip, but motives nobler than the drive of need and the avoidance of discomfort were to motivate the free laborer. The rational faculty was emphasized over the bodily, and liberty was premised on an unencumbered will and the capacity to choose. Necessity presumed a lack of choice. It signaled the return of the repressed—the primacy of base motives and bodily needs.[53] The manuals clothed necessity primarily as rational choice in order to fashion a liberal individual driven by free will and to shore up the eroding partition between compulsion and consent.

In *Friendly Counsels*, necessity was minimized in favor of stories of duty and self-making, and the acknowledged obstacles were easily overcome by directed effort. For example, Waterbury writes that freedom "acts on the mind. It obliges you to make a livelihood—to look up work such as you can do, that you may support yourself and your families." By emphasizing the willingness to work and the mental disposition and outlook of freedom, these texts privileged the rational faculty rather than bodily need as the primary motivation or determinant of the choice to labor. Rational decision and moral and ethical obligations motivate the decision to labor. Although *Friendly Counsels* more readily admits the material hardships of freedom than the other texts, it focuses exclusively on the character of the freed, inasmuch as the difficulty of circumstance was still to be overcome by the strength of character: "Free people have to work, and some of them have to work very hard even to get their bread. Some of the free colored people have by their own labor gained the means of a comfortable livelihood and made themselves respectable. You can do the same, if you will use the same diligence." The onus of necessity can be managed, if not overcome, by the exercise of the will.

In *Southern Planters and Freedmen*, a text written for former slave owners, Waterbury frankly admitted that the burden of freedom fell upon the freed because emancipation shifted the burden from the proprietor to the laborer: "Considering the poverty and dependent condition of the negro, it is evident that he will be the first to suffer and will experience the most inconvenience until the arrangement [of free labor] is established" (8). The emphasis on moral cultivation so pronounced in *Friendly Counsels* plays a secondary role to necessity and the threat of starvation in this dialogue with planters. They are assured that the freed will work simply because they have no choice: "Whatever fanciful notions he may have entertained of freedom as conferring happiness, he will soon be obliged, through *stern necessity*, to look at his actual condition, which is that of work or starve" (27). In the context of emancipation, necessity rather than the whip compels the black laborer: "Necessity may at first compel a reluctant service, which afterwards may be rendered under the influence of higher motives" (29).

Despite the fixation on the will, issues of agency and volition, albeit different, were no less vexed for the freed than for the
enslaved. It is equally clear that the emphasis on volition was strategic and intended to cultivate motivation and self-interest. Hence,
the first step on the road to independence was sedulous and con-
scientious labor. In *Advice to Freedmen*, Brinckerhoff explained that
freedom did not mean that one was no longer required to work, but
that one chose to work. He imparted this lesson through an anec-
dote about Isaac, a freedman he met while a superintendent of several plantations on the Sea Islands. Isaac mistakenly thought that as
a freedman, he need not work unless he so desired. But as Brinckerhoff explained, "One of the greatest privileges of a freeman is to
choose for himself. Slaves must do as they are commanded, but free-
men *choose* for themselves. 'And now, Isaac,' I said, 'you can make
your *choice*. You may stay on this plantation with your family and
work, and thus earn your bread, or you must leave the plantation
and find a home elsewhere. Which will you *do*?' He, like a freeman,
made his *choice*, and like a wise man remained with his family and
worked with them in the field" (15–16). As the repeated use of the
word "choose" indicates, self-directed and deliberate action was
of the utmost importance, since volition distinguished free labor
from slavery. At the same time, the obligation to work cannot be
eluded, for the privilege of choosing does not include the choice to
work or not, but rather the orientation and disposition toward this
requirement. Isaac's capacity to choose is possible only because
of the liberty he enjoys. This example is revealing because work is
defined exclusively by laboring on the same plantation where he was
enslaved. A refusal to do so is met with the threat of expulsion to an
unnamed elsewhere, identified as the space of idleness. Free labor is
identified solely as contracted labor on the plantation; the personal
autonomy exercised in the decision to resist wage work and strike
out for oneself never entered this conception of choice.

The emphasis on volition also has as its consequence the effacement of the work of slavery, since slave labor was coerced, unlike the
willful and self-directed labor of the freed. Labor as a social activity
becomes visible only in the context of freedom. As a result of this,
a plantation pastoral with nonproductive slave laborers dependent
upon the kindness of their master and irregularly prompted by the
whip is the prevailing scenario of slavery. The whip was discussed
only in contrast to rational ideals of discipline; it figured not in the
violence of slavery but in the dependence of slave laborers, not in
the theft and destruction of life, but in the lack of drive and motivation. By effacing the actual work of slavery and belaboring the
issue of idleness, these texts endorsed paternalistic arguments about
the incapacities of black laborers and the need for extensive control
over laborers to ensure productivity.[54] In this regard, Northern and
Southern visions of slavery coincided, as did their respective visions
of labor management. As Amy Stanley observes, the "victors and
vanquished [the triumphant North and the defeated South], ostensibly still struggling to implement opposing visions of emancipation . . . adopt[ed] similar methods of labor compulsion."[55] The
interests of Northern capitalists and Southern plantocrats con-
verged in instituting new forms of servitude. The consequences of
this were profound. The emergent discourse on idleness targeted
irresponsible characters and unbecoming conduct as a social danger
and justified labor coercion and the repressive measures of the state
enacted in the name of the prosperity of the population. (The masterless, like the fugitive, had stolen away and needed to be returned
to their place.)

The fixation on idlers and shirkers in these handbooks attests to
the widespread panic about the refusal to work. In *John Freeman
and His Family*, the love of leisure and dutiful labor are contrasted
in a predictable exchange of platitudes between characters discussing the challenges of freedom. The exchange between George and

Prince, two freedmen, resembles the back-and-forth of Jim Crow and Zip Coon on the minstrel stage and should not go unnoticed. George, a hardworking field laborer, accuses Prince of laziness: "S'pose you'd go back to slavery, if ye could. You a'n't worth the name of contraband; you're nothing but the old nigger still." Prince is appropriately named, for he possesses all the pretensions of the prototypical Zip Coon, a love of fancy goods, and a refusal to exert himself. The love of leisure, sumptuary excess, and addiction to pleasure mark Prince as "nigger."

Miss Horton, a good white teacher from the North, overhears their conversation as she returns from one of her weekly visits to the freedwomen, to whom she imparts the lessons of domestic economy. Aghast, she asks the men: "Did I hear rightly? . . . Would either of you, young men, be willing to go back to slavery?" (37). Miss Horton is incredulous and disappointed that they would willingly return to slavery. Her misreading of the exchange reproduces the repressive problematic of consent and the simulated willfulness typical of the rhetorical gestures of proslavery discourse. In short, the happy slave consents to bondage. In Miss Horton's expression of horror, one discerns the contrary sentiments of these texts—abolitionist discourse sedimented with racist and paternalist views of black character and restrictive notions of free labor, which shamelessly encourage black laborers to accept low wages and comply with unfair contracts. Basically, the freed are advised to work at all costs, since "work at low wages is better than idleness" (6).

George responds eagerly to Miss Horton's disheartened inquiry, defending himself and other freedpeople, "Not this child, but that darkey," pointing accusingly at Prince. Miss Horton repeats her question, directing it at Prince: "But what would you wish to go back to slavery for?" Prince replies, "I never been used to work, miss, and fact is, I don't like it." His remarks, inflected with the romanticism and nostalgia of minstrelsy, attest to the good old days on the plantation. Under slavery, he had lived the leisurely life of a coachman, with minimal work and fancy clothes; under freedom, he would be taught to work. The lesson of freedom was first and foremost the obligation to labor dutifully.

The other primers endorsed these views. *Friendly Counsels* notably contrasted the challenges of freedom with the ease of slavery: "In slavery you had little or no care, except to see that your task was done." But it warned the freed not to "fall into the mistake of some, that freedom means idleness" (4–5). The lessons expounded in these schoolbooks encouraged the freed to work for their former owners, remain on the plantation, accept poor wages, and comply strictly with a contract, even a bad one. *Plain Counsels* stressed the sanctity of the contract and its prescriptions, not the liberty conferred by its exercise. Regard for one's word, respect for the rights of others, and self-interest required strict compliance with its terms. Abiding the terms of a hard contract was in one's interest because the good reputation acquired by remaining true to one's promises would lead to further employment. The obligations or duties of the other member of the contracting party were not mentioned, nor were the violations that commonly led to the breaking of contracts. The most common reason for breach of contract was poor treatment by the employer, including physical violence and other forms of abuse. Other reasons included invasive measures that implemented forms of control practiced under slavery—pass laws, restrictions on leaving the plantation during the week, the prohibition of visitors, and interference in the domestic lives of laborers. Planters failed to live up to the terms of the contract regarding shares and wages, and routine altercations expressed the racial antagonism and class conflict of the postbellum period. It is remarkable that neither self-interest, will, nor liberty is mentioned in *Plain Counsels*' explication of contract; instead, it is simply explained as "something which binds two or more parties" (47). This is particularly egregious given that its author was a commissioner for the Freedmen's Bureau, but not surprising because the Freedmen's Bureau negotiated yearlong labor contracts between planters and freedmen. The control of the formerly enslaved through the contract labor system and the punitive measures instituted by the Black Codes and vagrancy laws made it a criminal offense to be without a contract, or to break contracts, or to refuse work, or to act improperly; or to enjoy freedom in a manner offensive to whites. The consequences of this social and economic imperative to return black workers to the plantation negated bourgeois constructions of the free market and conscripted and retained free workers by force and all available means. The right of contract and the espousal of volition secured involuntary servitude.

Unbecoming Conduct

The freedmen's handbooks disclosed the linkages between domination and the training of the freed population. These conduct books aimed at cultivating a dutiful and productive laboring class and a submissive and orderly black population. The inordinate concern with idleness and other forms of unbecoming conduct exposes a convergence of interests between the pedagogical mission of the Freedmen's Bureau and the mandates of plantation owners and Northern manufacturers. The cultivation of docile and dutiful laborers, whether through the molding of a moral and rational subject, securing the control of the laboring body, or policing the population, was their shared aim. For example, the Black Codes of Mississippi stated that if "the laborer shall quit the service of his employer before the expiration of his term of service without good cause, he shall forfeit his wages for that year up to the time of his quitting." Any white person or civil officer was entitled to arrest a black laborer who quit the service of his employer without good cause. Anti-enticement laws made it a crime for a laborer to quit one plantation and sign a contract on another. (These laws kept wages low and severely limited the laborer's options for employment. Anti-enticement laws were common and continued to control the mobility and options of black agricultural laborers until the 1940s.)

Vagrancy laws facilitated the convict and bonded labor system in that any person not in possession of a contract was declared a vagrant. This person was fined and, if unable to pay the fine, hired out to planters or put to work on public roads for a period as long as a year.[56] Although vagrancy laws that applied specifically to blacks were overturned, race-neutral vagrancy laws continued to have the same effect.[57] Vagrancy statutes provided a means of enforcing the contract system, for basically these laws subjected the unpropertied classes to arrest if they were without a labor contract. With the exception of Tennessee and Arkansas, all of the former Confederate states passed vagrancy laws in 1865 and 1866.[58] The effect of these measures, according to Major General Alfred Howe Terry, was "*a condition of servitude worse than that from which they have been emancipated*—a condition which will be *slavery in all but its name*" [emphasis mine].[59] Louisiana's Black Code required all freed laborers to contract for a year within the first ten days of January. The contracts to be signed by the head of the household embraced the labor of all members of that household, including minors. The breach of contract resulted in the loss of all wages earned to the "time of abandonment."

In this context, the liberty of contract can rightly be called a fiction; for it was employed to enforce black subordination and legitimize a range of coercive measures, from the contract system to the regulation of domestic affairs. It made seamless the transition from slavery to involuntary servitude. What kind of freedom was granted by these compulsory exchanges of property in the self? The lessons of duty and self-discipline disseminated in the manuals colluded in

the making of a new racialized enclosure and extending the life of
the plantation for another century with the practices of domination conducted under the sanction of law. Notable is the complicity between the fashioning of the individuality promulgated in the
handbooks and the repressive individuation and governance of the
Black Codes, which regulated the freed as a population by installing
racial classifications within state constitutions, by prohibiting interracial sexual liaisons and social association, and by dictating the
terms of contract and the rules of appropriate conduct. The emergent forms of domination and control launched by the Black Codes
focused on individual behavior and the management of free blacks
as a threatening internal element.

The Black Codes and contract system mandated forms of dutiful
and proper conduct. Unmistakably, the proper spirit was one of submission. Georgia's Penal Code stated that "all persons wandering or
strolling about in idleness, who are able to work, and who have no
property to support them; all persons leading an idle, immoral, or
profligate life, who have no property to support them" are to be considered vagrants and could be fined, imprisoned, sentenced to public
work, or bound out to a private employer for a period of a year. Those
without property or contract were subject to arrest. According to the
Florida Black Code, any able-bodied person without visible means of
support was leading an idle, immoral, or profligate course of life and
subject to arrest. However, the state's concerns about proper conduct
were not limited to those without visible means of support; its intervention extended to labor contracts and relations. A laborer could be
convicted in a criminal court for the willful disobedience of orders,
impudence, or disrespect to his employers.[60] In Louisiana, the failure
to comply with orders, leaving the plantation without permission,
impudence, use of indecent language, and quarreling were acts of
disobedience that subjected the offender to fines ranging from $1 to

$2 a day.[61] Decidedly, this micropenality of everyday life reinforced the virtue of submission lauded in these manuals.

The charge of idleness and profligacy gave license to the repressive governance of the black population; these accusations illuminate the forms of social struggle regarding the conditions of work and contestation about the scope of freedom. The problem of idleness and the compulsion necessary to command the labor of the ex-slave underscore the convergence between policing the poor and policing the freed black population.[62] If blacks refused the condition of work, then they would be forced to work by the threat of arrest and imprisonment, or death. A variety of everyday activities that enabled a measure of subsistence or autonomy were considered "troublesome" assertions of freedom and were criminalized. These activities ranged from moving about or errancy, to living off the land, which made it possible to subsist without a wage, to styles of comportment that challenged the racial hierarchy of life and value. In addition to vagrancy laws, new laws mandated the fencing of animals, hunting and fishing required licenses, public lands were enclosed and privatized, all of which made subsistence living increasingly difficult and largely illegal.[63] Punishment was increased for crimes that blacks were "likely" to commit, for example, stealing pigs. These offenses received harsh sentences and were responsible for at least half of the prisoners in the convict-lease system.[64] The liberty of contract was eclipsed by a compulsory contract system, self-interest overtaken by the threat of criminal sanction, and quotidian practices of freedom and styles of self-elaboration thwarted and interdicted. The crosscurrents of slavery and freedom produced a new mode of involuntary servitude. The "I" of the proprietorial self yielded easily to the burdened individuality of freedom.

The contracts administered by the Freedmen's Bureau dictated the terms of proper conduct. The magnitude of employers' interference in the lives and private affairs of workers is illuminated by the terms of contract. An example of the extent of employer invasion in the private lives of workers was a contract in which the laborer, in the attempt to protect his domestic life and family, stipulated that he had just cause to leave his employer's service if the employer violated his conjugal rights.[65] In a study of labor contracts administered by the Freedmen's Bureau, Lewis Chartock found that the contracts arranged by the bureau were used primarily to regulate behavior rather than to establish the tasks to be performed.[66] The key words used to describe the desired form of personal behavior were "quiet," "orderly," "respectable," "prudent," "well-behaved," and "sober." Contracts also established the terms for personal and private governance. One contract stipulated that a husband was allowed to visit his wife as long as he remained orderly and respectful; others entitled employees to visit their spouses on Saturday night as long as they returned home by Monday morning.[67] Chartock concludes that "southern planters were able to use the contract system to define a social role for freedmen which was not far removed from the status they had occupied when they were slaves."[68] The liberty of contract forged the link between slavery and freedom not only because it provided the fiction of free exchange that enabled debt bondage, but it also prescribed terms of social interaction, reproducing the dynamic of master-slave relations and regulating the personal and private lives of free laborers.

The liberty of contract could not be disassociated from the imposition of forms of involuntary servitude facilitated by Black Codes, vagrancy laws, the convict-lease system, the criminal surety system, breach-of-contract laws, and the share system. Of course, even those wage laborers operating under the presumably ideal conditions of the "free market" were unable to enjoy the fruits of their labor. The liberty of contract veiled the inequality at the heart of this exchange. In the absence of a free market, even as understood in the mystified terms of bourgeois economics, what did it mean to define freedom or free labor primarily in terms of the liberty of contract? Given the coercive measures regularly employed by agrarian capitalists to regain control of black laborers, the liberty of contract merely acted as the vehicle of involuntary servitude. Consent cloaked coercion, and relations of domination and exploitation were masked by the designation "free will." The contract enshrined involuntary servitude as freedom and reduced the free worker to a debtor, peon, and bonded laborer.

The fashioning of rational and moral individuals undertaken in the manuals was attuned to the dictates of capitalism and the new racial order of the postbellum South. The self-discipline and humility advocated in these pedagogical texts must also be considered in the context of postbellum violence, where inappropriate and improper conduct—in other words, behavior out of line with one's status—were penalized in the law and sanctioned extralegal forms of white violence.[69] The ever-present threat of punishment and death, legal and otherwise, awaited acts of transgression or the failure to adequately comply with the rules. The majority of the violence committed against the freed in the aftermath of slavery was incited by charges of unbecoming conduct, which included one's dress, demeanor, movement through public space, tone of voice, and companions. "Unbecoming conduct" encompassed any and all possible affronts to racist mores and imposed great penalties for everyday expressions of freedom.[70] While the handbooks encouraged autonomy fostered in the spirit of servitude, charges of unbecoming conduct brutally undermined any notion of "mastery of the self," even that conducted in the spirit of self-disciplining, precisely because any comportment other than servility risked affronting the ruling race and the dictates of racial decorum that structured the social.[71]

The striking similarities between antebellum regulations regarding black conduct and postbellum codes of conduct leave us hard-pressed to discern even those intangible or inchoate expressions of black freedom. Antebellum cases like *State v. Tackett* held that the "impudence and insolence of a slave" were to be considered extenuating circumstances in the homicide of a slave, though the same would not prove adequate in the homicide of a white person because the relation of white man and slave made such impudence the equivalent of a "grave indignity upon one's person." Likewise, *State v. Jowers*, a case that involved a white man indicted for battery against a free black man, reached similar conclusions in arguing that remedies for black insolence, whether slave or free, necessitated violence: "If a slave is insolent he may be whipped by his master, or by order of a justice of the peace; but a free negro has no master to correct him, a justice of the peace cannot have him punished for insolence, it is not an indictable offense, and unless a white man, to whom insolence is given, has a right to put a stop to it in an extra-judicial way, there is no remedy for it. This would be insufferable." The enormity of the offense resided in the status of the offender. Insolence challenged the very foundation of the social order—black subordination and white dominance. In the context of emancipation, the need to reimpose black subordination was no less pressing, and it was actualized not only through forms of legal repression and punishment, but also through the inculcation of rules of conduct. As Carl Schurz remarked: "A negro is called insolent whenever his conduct varies in any manner from what a southern man was accustomed to when slavery existed."[72]

The lessons of conduct imparted in freedmen's primers refigured the deference and servility of the social relations of slavery. Property in slaves was annulled in law, but the structural relations of slavery endured. The restoration of the plantation proceeded through the regulation of conduct, the imposition of debt, the making of individuality, and the naturalization of race. Clearly, these lessons instilled patterns of behavior that minimized white discomfort with black freedom. The regulation of conduct lessened the dislocations of the war by restoring black subordination on the level of everyday life: "White people have old, strong prejudices, and you should avoid everything you can which will inflame those prejudices. You know how easy it is to hurt a sore toe. Prejudices are like tender toes. Do not step on them when it is possible to avoid it." The insults that regularly confronted the freed were to be countenanced by turning the other cheek and meeting harsh words with kind ones, as if the obstacles to freedom could be easily avoided or the goodwill of white folks nurtured with the aid of simple promptings that declared black unworthiness—"I am not as good as I plan to be." The lessons on proper conduct exceeded admonishments about duty and defiance; indeed, they demanded the self-immolation of the free individual; only this would ensure the reconciliation of former masters and slaves. Not only were the freed encouraged to be subservient, obedient, respectful and humble and to remain with their former owners until death, but also, they were asked to refrain from asserting their liberty in every meaningful and imaginable way. One was obliged to endure these encroachments on freedom not because one was still a slave without choice, but, ironically, to exemplify the dutiful and rational behavior of a free person; this remains puzzling only if we fail to understand the idealization of self-abasement as a virtue. Implictly, the emphasis on proper conduct acceded the excessive and indiscriminate violence of the postbellum period.

The lessons of *Plain Counsels* promoted the nobility of work and excoriated idleness as they sought to reconcile former masters and slaves. Sections pointedly titled "About Your Old Master" and "About White Folks" enumerated the predilections and prejudices of white folks so that insolence and other potentially troublesome assertions of equality might be avoided. The freed were instructed in rules of racial etiquette that would enable them to effectively navigate white resentment and racism and adjust to their new status without creating unnecessary turbulence. Since the task of reconciliation fell primarily upon blacks, humility and patience in their interactions with whites were encouraged. As "About Your Old Master" explained, the difficulties experienced by former slave owners as a result of the abolition of slavery—the loss of wealth, sons on the battlefield, and slave property, in addition to the "new state of things"—naturally induced anger and resentment. Moreover, it would take years before former slave owners "put off the airs and manners of a master, just as you find it hard to shake off the habits of slaves" (11). Not only were the vestiges of the past to be endured, but also the strictures of the present had to be embraced in good faith. This sympathetic explication of white resentment was allegedly for the benefit of the freed, which is not surprising; or at least it is quite consistent with the general spirit of schooling them for a "new slavery," since the lessons of freedom invariably involved the adaptation of the freed to a new order of labor and social relations that transformed and refigured those of slavery. Instructing the freed in the "ways of white folks" was intended to improve the interactions between black folks and their former owners and other whites. If the formerly enslaved remembered the losses suffered by their owners, the action and attitudes of whites would be more understandable and kind feelings more quickly reestablished. Blacks were admonished to "think kindly about your old master. . . . Do not fall out now, but join your interests if you can, and live and die together." Although slavery had been abolished, the ties between former masters and slaves were expected to endure until death, binding the free laborer to his employer in perpetuity. This interminable servitude no longer required the mark of the mother for its justification. Duty and coercion achieved this end. In the new state of things, the ties of affection and mutual interests enabled this eternal proprietorship.

The extant familial affection between former masters and slaves eventually would overcome resentment if blacks discreetly navigated the sore spots of emancipation. This rapprochement, auguring the terms of national reconciliation, was to be actualized at their expense.[73] By means of this resurrection of the customs of slavery, along with the sentimental rhetoric of reciprocity, the past continued to endure in the "new state of things." By providing a rationale for white resentment, *Plain Counsels* minimized the injuries imposed by "severe feeling," particularly the abiding stigmatic injury of racism and the reign of terror launched by this antipathy. Unfortunately, good conduct could not mitigate the sway of coercion, resentment, violence, and terror. Clinton Fisk declared slavery a crime against humanity because of its abrogation of natural rights, and described the relations of slavery as beneficent. *Plain Counsels* insisted the kind feelings that formerly existed between masters and slaves had not been terminated by the Civil War, as if the absolute dispossession of slavery was akin to loyalty and had been achieved through mutual affection rather than inordinate violence and brutal domination. The aspects of slavery most readily criticized in these schoolbooks were black dependence and the lingering failures of character exhibited in dishonesty, profligacy, idleness, irrationality, and sumptuary excess.

Plain Counsels claimed that despite the old master's anger about the new state of things, he still retained "a kind of family affection, and in spite of his bad feelings, I have noticed, he desires to see you do well in life" (12). Not surprisingly, this preamble about familial affection culminated in the directive to stay put: "Do not think that, in order to be free, you must fall out with your old master, gather up your bundles and trudge off to a strange city. This is a great mistake." The plantation was the designated sphere in which blacks would overcome the "disheartening influence of belonging to a subjugated race" and achieve a modicum of equality. It was clear, given the recommendations about unassuming and modest conduct, that blacks were not to move as equals in civil society, nor were they endowed with rights that others were bound to respect or permitted to entertain ideas of equality without risking accusations of "putting on airs." The tragic limits of emancipation were bared in the designation of the plantation as the imagined space of freedom and happiness; this restricted landscape was deemed a place presumably as good as anywhere else in the world to explore the nascent experience of liberation. The freed could be as "free and happy" in their old home "as anywhere else in the world" (12). This was true to the degree that freedom was no less elusive on one plantation than on another, no easier in Georgia than in Alabama.

For many, the only palpable evidence of freedom was the sheer capacity to move, as demonstrated by the mass movement off the plantation, despite the disappointment or the loss experienced at the long-awaited destination.[74] As Felix Haywood recalled, when former slaves received news of their freedom, "everybody went wild. We all felt like heroes and nobody had made us that way but ourselves. Just like that we was free. . . . Nobody took our homes away, but right off colored folks started on the move. They seemed to want to get closer to freedom, so they'd know what it was—like it was a place or city." This desire set thousands on the road in search of a distinct and tangible freedom. The ambulant expressions of freedom are detailed again and again in slave testimony. The search for a parent, child, or lover, or the longing to return to the place of one's birth or simply instantiate being free through the exercise of this nascent mobility. Locomotion was definitive of personal liberty. Blackstone's *Commentaries* defines personal liberty in terms of the power of locomotion: "Personal liberty consists in the power of locomotion, of changing one's situation, or removing one's person to whatever place one's inclination may direct, without restraint, unless by due course of law."[75] Itinerancy, fugitivity, nomadism, migration, roving, traveling aimlessly, or moving about occurred below the threshold of formal equality and rights and articulated the limits of emancipation. It is clear that the freedom experienced was in the search and not the destination.

Admonitions to remain on the plantation, stay in place, abstain from assertions of equality, turn the other cheek when faced with insult, and step gingerly around white hatred attest to the reorganization of the plantation and the enduring character of servility, which was deemed necessary in navigating the upheavals of Reconstruction. *Plain Counsels* opened with a lecture on freedom that forcefully proclaimed the natural rights of all men to life, liberty, and property, and denounced the high crime of slavery in abrogating these rights; yet the body of the work is devoted to instruction in obsequiousness and humility in interracial social interactions. Accordingly, regular confessions of unworthiness would best serve blacks in their transition to freedom rather than distasteful expressions of equality: "Some white men will put on airs, and look down on you. Now, instead of putting on airs, too, and saying, 'I am as good as you are,' it is better to say nothing, or if you do answer, to say, 'I am not as good as I ought to be, as I want to be, and as I hope to be.'" The coupling of radical pronouncements about the evils of slavery with conciliatory and conservative admonishments to avoid inciting social turbulence by "not putting on airs" and remaining in one's place, quite like the increasingly conservative judicial assessment of the Thirteenth Amendment and the measure of equality, preserved the incidents and vestiges of slavery while exalting its abolition.

The good conduct encouraged by such counsels eased the transition from slavery to freedom by imploring the freed to continue in old forms of subservience, which primarily entailed remaining on the plantation as faithful and obedient laborers, but also included manners, styles of comportment in work relations, objects of consumption, leisure, and domestic relations.[76] In their emphasis on proper conduct, these how-to-be-free manuals resuscitated the social roles of slavery, not unlike the regulation of behavior in labor contracts or the criminalization of insolence in the Black Codes. The pedagogical injunctions to obedience and servility cast the freed in a role starkly similar to the one in which they had suffered under slavery. These texts heralded the natural rights of all men, and they advised blacks to refrain from enjoying this newly conferred equality. Despite proclamations about the whip's demise and the gift of emancipation, emergent forms of involuntary servitude and routine and spectacular forms of violence were employed to regulate all conduct out of step with being a slave. Everyday life revealed the entanglements of slavery and freedom.

Every Man Is a Master

If pronouncements of equality were to be eschewed lest one risked offending white folks, this is not to suggest that all opportunities for self-improvement were hindered by these oft-repeated behests to resume the social demeanor of slavery. Notwithstanding the compromises of freedom endlessly being negotiated in the manuals, it was still believed that every man possessed the capacity to (re)make himself in accordance with his ideals.[77] The discourse on self-improvement asserted that neither race nor the badge of slavery need impede possibilities for success or advancement. The emphasis on self-making represented an attempt to counter racist arguments about blacks' limited capacities and the prevalent notion that "the negro exists for the special object of raising cotton, rice and sugar for the whites, and that it is illegitimate for him to indulge, like other people, in the pursuit of happiness in his own way," yet it also placed the burden of self-advancement solely upon the individual.[78] History receded before the individual, anointed as the master of his fate. The only impediment to advancement was the self. Other obstacles to social betterment and independence were conveniently neglected, and failure was attributed to deficiencies of character and habit. The individual abandoned to his own efforts savored assurances that the market provided a level playing field and the distribution of awards was based upon one's efforts and merits. Every man, according to *Plain Counsels*, was "under God, just what he makes himself; it matters not whether he be white or colored. Frederick Douglass was born a slave and had no friend to help him. . . . Now you have yourself in charge, and I want you to make a man of yourself. Will you do it?" (18).[79]

If the emphasis on individual responsibility and self-making inevitably attributed the wretched condition of blacks to their shortcomings, the remedy invariably suggested was "showing thyself a man," and the favored demonstration of this nascent manhood was dutiful labor. As John Freeman declares, "We are men now, and we're free men, too; and we've got to do just what free men do. You look round and you see every freeman, black or white, works for a living; works I say, not grubs and roots" (11). The equation of man and laborer conflates self-cultivation with the extensive capacities of the laboring body; it establishes the isomorphism of making the self and making objects by likening distinct forms of production and, notably, by effacing the presence of women within the discourse of freedom, and restricting the act of making to masculinity. This emphasis on the creative capacity of making and self-making identified freedom as work. However, in lauding the body's extensive capacities and the individual's innate facility for self-making, various techniques of making and using were ranked, "working for a living" and "grubbing and rooting" differentiated the constancy of application from mere subsistence and, ultimately, responsibility from idleness.

The individual prepared to meet the challenges of freedom and ready to make a man of himself was deemed capable of throwing

off the vestiges of slavery by his own efforts. The frequent references
to white people who had started out with less than the emancipated
and achieved great success endorsed this capacity for self-making.
Such comparisons were only plausible if a blind eye was turned to
the instrumentality of race as a vehicle of subjugation and white
opposition to a new social order: "Many white persons who com-
menced married life twenty-five years ago with as little as you
have now, and who worked with their hands for less than is given
to you . . . are [now] in very easy circumstance" (58). White people
were to be regarded as living proof of the rewards realized by hard
labor rather than as examples of the privileges afforded by whiteness. Of course, race mattered little if rewards were actualized on
the basis of hard labor and everyone enjoyed the fruits of their labor.
The willed innocence of abstract equality depicted a democratic distribution of opportunities in the context of racist domination, pervasive violence, and extreme exploitation, and anticipated outcomes
that obfuscated the condition of the South. Moreover, whiteness
remained the standard-bearer of value, so the possibility and opportunity proffered were inherently racialized.

John Freeman and His Family represented the prospects of citizenship and manhood as inseparable from whiteness. If blacks
advanced and modeled themselves after whites, they, too, might
receive the rewards that the latter enjoyed. John Freeman, taking
this promise seriously, becomes the definitive mimic man: "Every
good custom of the white people, which came to his knowledge,
inspired within him the ambition to go and do likewise; while he
was humble and respectful as a *subordinate*, he was eager to be and
do all that would make him a *true man*. He certainly had the right
idea of *manhood* and liberty" (45) [emphasis mine]. Unfortunately,
John was destined to remain a mimic man because of the palpable distance between the true manhood to which he aspired, and
his actual condition as a humble and respectful subordinate. The

distinct temporalities of John's actual condition ("he was a humble and respectful subordinate") and his as yet unrealized aspiration ("he was eager to be ... a true man") insinuate that although he aspired to reach the measure of true manhood, he might be unable to achieve it. *John Freeman* intimated that the chasm between the universal tenets of equality and the conditions of their actualization might never be bridged. We are left to wonder if the promised equitable enjoyment of material rewards, like manhood itself, was an aspiration not to be realized, or if the liberty proffered with one hand was withdrawn by the other.

Was it possible for John Freeman to be a humble subordinate and a true man? The articulations of race, gender, and citizenship require us to answer both yes and no. Certainly, in formal terms, black men and women were citizens as rights-bearing individuals protected by the state. However, realizing these rights and entitlements was another matter. Not only was political equality greatly contested and social equality opposed, but even the enjoyment of basic civil rights was unrealizable given the relations of power and property that mocked and negated these rudimentary rights. The implied citizen of the Constitution and subject of "we the people" was the propertied white male. Citizenship presupposed the equality of abstract and disembodied persons, and this abstraction disguised the privileges of white men and the ruling elite. The presumed whiteness and maleness of the citizen transposed the particular into the universal, enabling white men to enjoy the privileges of abstraction and a noncorporeal universality.[80]

To the degree that blacks were challenged to assume the duties of freedom and prove their worthiness by showing themselves as men, the implicit masculinism of citizenship was reinforced. Yet the task of demonstrating the "manhood of the race" was not simply imposed from without, but also taken up as the blazon of an emergent black citizenry.[81] The considerable weight attached to the manhood of the race in large measure determined the abolition of slavery, the conferral of citizenship, and the eventual granting of manhood suffrage.[82] The military service of black men in the Civil War was an important determinant in the passage of the Thirteenth Amendment and the Civil Rights Act of 1866. (The women's war against slavery did not figure in public debates about the contours of freedom.) The participation of over 200,000 black men in military service made it necessary for the nation to recognize blacks as citizens.[83] The importance attributed to soldiering exemplifies the masculinism of citizenship and, moreover, shows citizenship itself to be a kind of soldiering. This conception of the citizen-soldier, according to Nancy Fraser, imagines the citizen as "the defender of the polity and protector of those—women, children, and elderly—who allegedly cannot protect themselves." The citizen as soldier introduces a gendered division between those who protect and those who are protected and suggests that one achieved true manhood through the ritual theater of fratricide and established one's humanity by the capacity to kill and the willingness to die.[84] *Advice to Freedmen* espoused this sentiment in noting that the presence of black combatants confirmed that "colored men prize[d] liberty sufficiently to fight for it." (This willingness to die negated slave status, since, in theory, the slave had forfeited his personal liberty for his life.) The soldier fulfilled the citizen's obligation to "stand by the government and aid in saving our country and its institutions" (49).

As men and citizens, blacks were implicitly involved in the mimetic enactment of identity and entitlements. Certainly, John Freeman's fashioning of manhood was modeled accordingly: "A purpose to do right as far as he knew how animated him daily, and the eager desire to rise above the degraded sphere in which he had always existed, to live and think, learn and do like white folks, was never for a moment abated" (45). Mimicry, according to Homi Bhabha, is a production of the subject as the same and other. The mimic man is a partial representation of the dominant subject; however, he is not reassured by this displacement but menaced. The familiar transported to the distant becomes estranging and grotesque.[85] However, the threat or menace that possibly attends this displacement and reproduction of the dominant was minimized by the reassuring distance that separated the true man and John Freeman. Despite the unabated desire "to do right," rise above his "degraded sphere," and "do like white folks" that animated John Freeman's every day, he remained trapped in this degraded sphere. His efforts at self-advancement were mocked by the subtle insinuation of an insurmountable barricade in the passage between the debased sphere in which he had always existed and the celestial sphere of right, equality, and whiteness. This insurmountable barrier was blackness. The danger of mimicry was eclipsed by the comfort of minstrelsy. The requisite subordination of blacks foreclosed the threat of "true manliness."

The anxiety and discomfort surrounding black masculinity were registered in the ambivalent demand to "show thyself a man." This command brings to mind the compulsory display of black value on the auction block. Dread and desire inflected the directive, as the freedman was required to prove his manhood and remain a humble subordinate. This delicate balancing act demanded that he display and cloak true manliness with the facility of an illusionist—now you see it; now you don't. The obligation to display the self in this fashion was at odds with the declared intent of the directive. How did the subject splayed before the scrutinizing gaze enact masculinity? Would the flaunting of black manhood before white inquisitors, skeptics, and enemies establish the vitality and worthiness of the race? Could such exhibitions establish anything other than the distance between the ex-slave and the true man?

The relation between Lieutenant Hall, a Union army officer assisting in the transition from slavery to freedom, and John Freeman underlines the distance between the authentic and the mimetic, or between the true man and the freedman. The white lieutenant, fulfilling his missionary duties with the "benighted Africans" of the United States, is savior, father, and disciplinarian. Lieutenant Hall bestows John with the name Freeman: "A new name it was, distinct, clean of slavery, savoring of the life of liberty and equal rights upon which he was entering. He was determined that he would never disgrace it by idleness or want of integrity, or by any act unworthy of freedom; and he was earnestly desirous that those who bore it with him would esteem and cherish it as he did" (22). The surname is assigned rather than adopted, so the independence and dignity that it is intended to connote are undermined. Figuratively, it extends the lieutenant's patriarchal reach as he confers the patronymic. The surname, in this light, not only expresses John's new condition, and the ambivalence of that condition, but also designates Lieutenant Hall as white father.

Henry Banner, a former slave, ironically noted that a surname was the sole inheritance of freedom: "The slaves weren't expecting nothing. It got out somehow that they were going to give us forty acres and a mule. We all went to town. They asked me who I belonged to and I told them my master was Banner. One man said, 'Young man, I would go by my mama's name if I were you.' I told him my mother's name was Banner too. Then he opened a book and told me all the laws. He told me never to go by any name except Banner. That was all the mule they ever give me."[86] In Banner's account, the surname does not confer true manhood, only the paradox of emancipation and the dispossession that is the slave's only legacy. The surname here denotes "the captor father's mocking presence," to borrow Spillers's term, and the inheritance of dispossession that engenders the African American. It is a poor substitute for what is owed and an inadequate form of redress, it being "all the mule" that Banner received.

In *John Freeman*, the patronymic announces the law of the father and his rightful claim to his wife, Clarissa, and their offspring, marking the decisive shift in the reproductive economy of freedom. John's wife and children are placed under his control and dominion by virtue of his surname: "You must give your wife the same name, then, mind, and all your children. Then we shall know you all belong together. You'll be the Freeman family" (21). When Clarissa is first addressed as Mrs. Freeman, she marvels at her new acquisition: "She has never been called Mrs. Freeman before. That sounds a heap like white folks, she thought to herself, and now I must honor the name, as John says" (26). However, this acquisition, valued for its simulation of whiteness rather than for the new order of conjugal and contractual relations it announces, betokens both her freedom and her death as civil subject. In the doctrine of coverture, the wife existed under the cover of her husband's status and identity; therefore, married women were subsumed under the civil personality of men.[87] Yet freedwomen existed within and without the privatized enclosure of domesticity, since Mrs. Freeman straddled the demands of laborer, caretaker, and legal dependent. It is important to note that these primers treated freedwomen the same as men in one respect—they were expected to work and support their families.[88]

Just as anxieties about national prosperity and social order required that the freed prove their worth, exhibit their capacities, confirm their loyalty to former masters, and practice temperance, restraint, and humility, so, too, the responsibility of each citizen to bear his part of the common burden and increase the strength and wealth of the nation created a curious domesticity at the interface of the public and private, regulated by the state.[89] The emphasis on ordered domesticity is best understood in regard to issues of prosperity and hygiene, the making of worker-citizens, the policing of the private, and the strategies of state racism. Cleanliness and domestic order are confluent with social stability, economic health, safety and security, and the eradication of idleness. In this case, the family does not provide a barrier to the values of the marketplace; to the contrary, the domestic is valued because it is essential to managing laboring families, inculcating suitable ideas of settlement and stability, regulating populations, and nurturing responsible and rational individuals. The complementarity of home and work can be discerned in the general inattention to feminine virtues and the imperative that all members of the family work. If the gender of the female slave becomes intelligible through a calculus of injury and inheritance, then gender must be reconsidered here within a different economy of kinship and reproduction, dispossession and servitude. At issue are the ambiguous role of Mrs. Freeman and the work of normalization conducted within the domestic sphere.

Much fine scholarship has been written on women's agency within the private sphere, on domesticity as an allegory of political desire, and on marriage as the symbol of "liberation and entitlement to democracy and desire."[90] The line of argument undertaken here is not intended to underestimate the joy experienced in creating and maintaining families for those long denied this benefit, or to minimize women's agency within the household, or to cast the family as a monolithic and uniformly oppressive institution, but rather to consider the question of the family in regard to issues of racial and class formation and the governing of the social.[91] The advent of freedom placed black women and children within a locus of patriarchal control and protection that signified the gains of freedom. Yet the privatization of marital and familial relations assured neither women's protection from the violence of outsiders nor protection from their spouses.[92] Conflicts and tensions within the freed family sometimes resulted in the physical abuse of women. Moreover, the illusive security and comfort of the private require that we forget the kinds of violence that women are subjected to within the home, or the private household as an enclosure. Classically, the private sphere designates men's liberty from the state and the encroachments of others and ensures their custody of women and children rather than women's safety. This is to argue neither that freedwomen were controlled by their husbands nor that they didn't enjoy a measure of autonomy in their personal lives, but rather to highlight the masculinist constitution of the private and the forms of encumbrance that enabled men to secure their liberty. As well, the sanctity of the private did not shield black women or men from racist attacks in their homes.

It has been argued forcefully that domesticity and the consequent reprivatization of female sexuality within kinship versus captivity networks were marked advances over slavery and great leaps on the road of black progress, given the destruction of natal and conjugal relations under slavery. Yet here I advance a different reading, one less intent on celebrating the achievement of heterosexual domesticity than illustrating the perviousness of kinship to the incursions of capital and the state. While the ability to forge and maintain familial relations must not be minimized, neither should the family be naturalized as the measure of racial progress. To the contrary, the utility of the family as a mechanism of state racism and social reproduction tempers claims of progress. In fact, what is articulated at the site of the family is a shared concern about matters of racial hygiene, morality, and prosperity. The articulation of black politics at the site of the family is often consistent with the regulatory efforts of the state. The domestic articulation of a politics of racial uplift risks displacing the political, endorsing a repressive moral economy, and privileging the family as a site for the reproduction of racial values. The shifting configuration of familial relations cannot be seen as inherently progressive or oppressive but rather as a changing institution, or, as Jacques Donzelot describes it, "an uncertain form whose intelligibility can only come from studying the system of relations it maintains with the sociopolitical level."[93]

A Curious Domesticity, an Uncertain Form

The transition to a free-labor system required the household to function as a laboring unit and site of social reproduction; it imposed a new set of obligations and expectations on this wounded and emergent kinship. Just as the difference between "grubbing and rooting" and "working for a living" provided a measure of the ex-slave's suitedness for freedom and a scale of development, domesticity was contrasted with the itinerancy and subsistence of those intent on eluding the contract system. An orderly and settled household ruled by a patriarch was the sign of civilization and rational desire. In the primers, matters of family and domesticity emerge obliquely and in relation to issues of labor, hygiene, progress, and discipline. In these representations of domestic economy, the social comes into the view—that is, the hybrid space that shifts the lines of the public and private for the purposes of securing the public good—the health, safety, and morality of the people. The advice dispensed in these primers regarding household and intimate arrangements was a critical component of a broader discourse on managing the working poor, eradicating pauperism, annexing the home to the workplace, and domesticating asocial, dangerous, and itinerant classes. The importance of domesticity and implanting the proper idea of home life was elaborated in texts like *Public Relief and Private Charity* by Josephine Shaw Lowell and *A Handbook of Charity Organization* by Rev. S. Humphreys Gurteen.[94] These theoretical and practical treatises on eradicating pauperism and implementing effective forms of charity relief that didn't produce dependence share a common language with the freedmen's texts. A convergence of issues regarding proper association, hygiene, hard work, and frugality extends beyond the immediate sphere of the family and poverty to fears about national prosperity and the health of the social body. These anxieties and fears would be critical to the endorsement of racial segregation in *Plessy v. Ferguson.*

The second edition of *Advice to Freedmen* added a new chapter on "Household Life," which placed great emphasis on association and hygiene in its representation of a properly regulated domestic life: "Heretofore, although father, mother and children have resided in the same cabin, yet to a great extent you have not lived as families. We hope that before long there will be a change for the better in this respect. And how pleasant, when returning from the day's toil in the field, to sit down in a neat room where all is in good order, the furniture free from dust, the floor and hearth well swept, and the ceiling and wall nicely white-washed." Living together defines the hearth, but these arrangements are threatened by dirt and disorder, which not only present physical dangers in the form of illness and pestilence but are also signs of immorality. Hygiene—such as the cleanliness of persons, the need of fresh air, the importance of bed linen, not sleeping in one's day clothes—is as important as taking meals together in "beget[ting] system and regularity in the management of household affairs" and "cultivating those graces of manners and habits which distinguish cultivated and refined society" (33). Brinckerhoff induces the freed to strictly follow such guidelines not only for purposes of moral cultivation and refinement but also to battle the sickness that afflicts their children because of their lack of personal cleanliness.

The emphasis on hygiene expresses larger concerns about national well-being, since hygiene legitimated, if not invited, the policing of dwellings and the setting of guidelines for marriage and other forms of social association, particularly those considered dangerous or destabilizing of social order. Regulating hygiene or ensuring public health was a fundamental aspect of the police power of the state.[95] In the governing of poverty, as Giovanna Procacci remarks, hygiene provides a "grid for reading social relations, a system which serves at once to canalize them and to invent new paths of circulation that are more 'orderly' and more decipherable."[96] Managing immorality, indolence, criminality, and disease was the target of these lessons of hygiene, and they were fundamentally allied with Reconstruction, the return of national prosperity and reunification, the purity and elevation of the white race, and the establishment of a responsible and domesticated black laboring class. The coincidence of good housekeeping and national prosperity is keenly articulated in *John Freeman*, which utilizes the devices of sentimental literature, specifically the kitchen as the microcosm of the nation and the ethic of submission. As Gillian Brown observes, in the domestic politics of sentimentalism, "Uniformity and neatness in the kitchen matter profoundly, since these habits create a standard of harmony for America."[97] However, domestic economy is not separated from or opposed to the market but continuous with it. Because of this, the household, for the most part, is not treated as the special province of women. *Advice to Freedmen*, *Friendly Counsels*, and *Plain Counsels* associate the well-managed and ordered home with the transition from slavery to freedom and the birth of the proprietorial self. The entanglements of the state and the family and capitalism and the household illuminate the nonautonomy of the private.

The visions of domesticity promoted within these texts represent the family as a laboring unit. Accordingly, the home is in service of the plantation and the market, and its proper management stabilizes and induces good habits in the laboring classes. The discourse on domesticity is geared primarily to battling moral degradation and idleness. It is a discourse aimed at managing the laboring classes and the poor rather than creating a protected sphere outside market relations. Even the guardian of the hearth, Mrs. Freeman, participates in the world of the market as a laborer by taking in washing, once again eliding distinctions between the home and the world outside. It is important to note that all of these manuals encouraged freedwomen to labor, despite the contrary desires of the freed exhibited in the mass exodus of women and children from the field.

Domestic disorder was held responsible for criminality and a range of other sins, from vanity and consumption of tobacco and liquor to stealing. In *John Freeman*, Miss Horton tries to eradicate the "old, lazy, filthy habits of the slave quarters" which were still clinging to the freed by imparting lessons on hygiene during her regular visits to their homes. Of course, the disorder she observes within these dwellings indicates that the freed do not possess "the true idea of home" (31–32). Miss Horton is not only a teacher and friend of the race but a home visitor with a mission.

Miss Horton, upon her visit to the ladies, immediately scanned the room, detailed the problems, and identified the changes to be made. As her eyes surveyed the room, she was surprised "that a woman who was so tidy in her dress, as Clarissa certainly was, could live in a room so completely littered and filthy; and she made up her mind to give her new acquaintance a few useful hints." Clarissa is determined to follow these hints less because of the importance of neatness than because of her inclination to mimicry. Neatness is not only a virtue, but an expression of whiteness as well, at least as far as Clarissa can discern. The virtues of domesticity and the perfect picture of heteronormative arrangements were indistinguishable from whiteness and the bourgeois family. The linking of whiteness with purity, neatness, morality and health accedes to a politics of contagion that eventually serves to justify segregation and license the racist strategies of the state in securing the health of the social body. In this respect, Clarissa's desire to be "just as near like white folks as ever we can ketch it" bespeaks the association of race and hygiene, or more specifically, purity and whiteness, which gives shape to the biopolitical imperatives of the nineteenth-century state.

The lack of cleanliness and household disorder is associated with moral depravity, animal habits, and criminality. The connection between hygiene and social danger is demonstrated by the case of Sam Prentiss. Sam was proud, wore fine clothes and bright buttons and other things he couldn't afford, smoked and chewed tobacco, and drank whiskey. To maintain these habits, he stole money from his employer, for which he was imprisoned. Clarissa, feeling sorry for his mother, Prudence, and the suffering and shame his imprisonment has caused her, pays her a visit. Now learned in the principles of home management, Clarissa literally replicates the former scene; she stands in Miss Horton's stead, and Prudence plays the role of a more wretched version of Clarissa's former self. The omniscient narrator describes the dark, dirty, and miserable hut of Prudence, and as Clarissa enters the hut, she casts her eyes about and confirms this assessment. Prudence's lack of domestic skills and her dirty and disorganized home, cluttered with dirty dishes, are as responsible for Sam's criminality as his own bad habits. Prudence's own habits of consumption are continuous with his. She doesn't know how to use her rations properly and consumes them all at once (81–83). This excess of consumption is associated with dirt and disorder, the imbibing of intoxicants, and criminal behavior. However, as a result of Clarissa's instruction, Prudence comes to embody the virtue denoted by her name. When Sam is released from jail, he returns to a cheery and pleasant home, which makes him feel better and induces him to try to do better: "Since his mother was taking pains to be smart, he would try to do better" (87).

The domestic sphere elaborated in these texts was a threshold between the public and private rather than a fortified private sphere. In these portraits, the fragility of the private was exemplified by the intrusion of strangers and "friends of the race" who policed the management of household affairs, regularly trespassing the border between the home and the world. Nineteenth-century social reformers considered the home visit essential to eradicating slothful habits and enhancing the moral dignity of the poor. Gurteen's

Handbook of Charity Organization asserted that the chief need of the poor—we can easily substitute the freed—was "the moral support of true friendship—the possession of a real friend, whose education, experience and influence, whose general knowledge of life, or special knowledge of domestic economy are placed at the service of those who have neither the intelligence, the tact nor the opportunity to extract the maximum of good from their slender resources."[98] The home visitor was the predecessor of the social worker; she dispensed household advice and assessed the character and development of the freed.[99] Miss Horton's visits conform to the genre of the philanthropic visit; the evaluation of progress, the inspection of order, an examination of proper domestic hygiene, and the dispensation of advice were the purposes of the visit.

The domestic was the ultimate scene of surveillance; a fence in need of white washing, a dusty house, or a non-obedient child thus invited punitive judgments. The description of the good life, although purportedly about the pleasures afforded by a well-managed domestic sphere, actually authorized the normalizing gaze, which by detailed observation of all areas of life, judged the suitedness of the formerly enslaved to freedom and their conformity to the rules of household management. As *Friendly Counsels* advised:

> Make things as pleasant as you can in and around your house. What a difference there is! ... Now, when a stranger approaches your house, let him notice a pretty gardenspot, with flowers and vegetables, all well kept. When he enters, let his eye be cheered by seeing how nice every thing looks, how well swept the floor is, how the tin things shine. Let him notice a few books, with marks of study or reading upon them. ... As he glances around, it would be pleasing if he could see a little picture here and there hanging on the wall, or a flower-pot with a pretty pink or rose blooming in it, showing that you

have a liking for such things. He would say, "Well, this looks
like freedom. I think you must be quite a happy family." It will
be a very pretty picture to show some who maintain that it is
useless to attempt to elevate or to improve the condition of the
colored race. (27)

Under the inspecting eye and the scrutiny of the stranger's gaze,
every item in the home was portentous with meaning and arrested in
a moral drama in which disorder and inefficiency decided one's fate.
Sanctions awaited those outside the purview of acceptable behavior.
The inculcation of good habits was achieved by creating a sense of
hypervisibility. The stark intervention of power takes the form of
the stranger, or "friend of the race." The visitor figuratively embodied the police power of the state to inspect and oversee matters of
family, sexuality, and hygiene, which were necessary in maintaining the health and security of society. The public good sustained the
invasion of the private and, like the entry of the friend/inspector,
this surveillance determined whether all objects and persons were
in their proper place.

Although ideologically designated as the putative sphere of liberty, the private failed to safeguard against the intrusions of individuals or the state.[100] Rather, home was an extension of the workplace,
more specifically the plantation, and subject to the impositions of
charitable inspectors like Miss Horton and the regulations of the
state. Those without a "proper home" could be arrested for vagrancy
and hired out, their children could be taken away, and they risked
imprisonment, if not death, for violating rules of racial hygiene
regarding sexual and conjugal relations. The mutable boundaries of
the private were also employed to restrict black mobility and freedom of association by designating much of public space as the private and exclusive realm of whites. The sanctuary of the private was
violated regularly, quite unlike the portrait of domesticity heralded

by the culture of sentiment and the exponents of domestic economy. Clearly, intimate matters were subordinate to the economic interests and social imperatives of the postbellum order. The privacy of the private was rather tenuous. The domesticity propounded in these texts revealed the utility of the household to the marketplace and the regulation of the private through techniques of discipline and normalization.[101]

Proximate Dangers, Habitual Intercourse

In *Southern Planters and the Freedmen,* a guide for the embittered ruling class of the plantocracy, Jared Waterbury observes that the health and well-being of the nation depended upon the ability to control and contain the dangers posed by the presence of emancipated blacks within the body politic. The manual makes explicit the instrumental ends of rational and moral cultivation: the production of servile and dutiful laborers and the management of a potentially threatening population within the body politic. The work of molding the freed into rational and moral subjects is explicated primarily in terms of social and bodily dangers, the threat of disorder, and the dangers posed by the physical proximity of sensual and childish men ruled by passions. *Southern Planters* discloses the work of cultivation to be fundamentally that of discipline and regulation. Waterbury, employing the language of sentiment, first appeals to the reciprocity of the master-slave relation when delineating the obligations of planters to the freed: "The long years of toil by these patient and in most instances faithful slaves, now that they are free, impose an obligation on their former masters of sympathy and obligation." It is a paternal obligation that enjoins planters to aid in the moral uplift and education of the freed. However, if noble motives fail to inspire, Waterbury adopts a surefire strategy; he exploits base instincts and hints at the lurking dangers that await the commingling of an unschooled and passionate element with the civilized: "The planters have a direct interest in educating and elevating this large working class with whom they must hereafter, and for a long time, be in intimate contact.... To be surrounded by such hordes of men and women, so different from the whites in their antecedents; so marked and contrasted in their physical traits; possessing the strength of manhood and the passion of children; to be in constant contact with them as household and field servants and laborers, must make it evident to reasonable and reflective men that some culture is absolutely necessary to insure both safety and comfort" (39). The domestic is assigned a pivotal role in the management of this threatening black population. The cultivation of reason and morality is required to maintain safety and comfort. The threat lurking in the specter of powerful and childish men and in the habitual intercourse between two very different races borders on the indecent, and without the restraints imposed by education and development, such close association poses great dangers. The body—its physical traits and great strength, the vast difference between the races, the primacy of the sensual element—incites fears about proximity and intimacy. In other words, how might this free laboring class be incorporated in the body politic as citizens while maintaining the integrity of whiteness? For the races to dwell comfortably side by side, the cultivation of the black hordes was essential, lest the dangers of such proximity rend the fabric of the social order: "It is for his interest and safety to place the negro in a career of improvement, so that the sensual shall not swallow up the intellectual life. His manhood must be developed by education, or he will remain in his darkness and depression; and who could endure to dwell amid congregated masses of men and women whose fiery impulses are restricted by no knowledge of their relations to society and to God?" (42).

Only the work of self-cultivation would enable the freed to properly exercise and enjoy the privileges of which they were as of yet

unworthy: "Step by step he must gain that social and moral standing which will vindicate his claim to the privilege of citizenship, and
exempt him from the privileges which hitherto have denied him its
exercise" (31). The need to vindicate one's claim to the privileges
of citizenship undoubtedly indicates a lingering suspicion about
black worthiness and exposes the chasm between the endowment
of rights and the capacity to exercise them. The freed are required
"to defend, maintain and insist on the recognition of" their inalienable and natural rights.[102]

The emphasis placed on the molding of a reasonable and moral
subject, one restricted by recognition of God and social relations,
hinted at the shifting register of blackness from status-race—
blackness ascribing slave status—to formal race—a "neutral" conception of race undergirded by notions of biological and cultural
difference.[103] The abolition of slavery presumably announced the end
of subjugation based on race or servitude, but the ascendancy of formal race—that is, immutable and naturalized racial differences—
perpetuated the "stigma of inferiority based on race" or "stigmatic
injury," to employ the language of *Brown v. Board of Education*, in the
guise of neutrality and objectivity.[104] While the freed would no longer
"feel the disheartening influences of belonging to a subjugated race,"
it was expected that they would "have to struggle under difficulties and embarrassments arising out of recent slavery, or connected
with a social repugnance founded principally on physical traits" (31).
The conflict between equality in the body politic and the threatening physical presence of blackness was also at issue in the debates
concerning the Fourteenth Amendment and the Civil Rights Acts of
1866 and 1875. The "repugnance of the physical" denotes the abjection of blackness and accounts for the ambivalent and uncertain
incorporation of black citizens into the national body and the containment or enclosure of blackness required to maintain the integrity
of whiteness.[105] This visceral aversion reinscribed the degradations

of slavery, although augmented by the antipathy incited by the perceived dangers of freedom—the proximity of the races dwelling side
by side and the fiery impulses and untamed passions of the untutored.

The peril associated with the proximity of black and white bodies fueled the anxiety unleashed by the legal equality of citizens—
in particular, the menacing masculinity of the freedman endowed
with rights and privileges. It was this anxiety that invariably associated equality with miscegenation and the hazard of promiscuous
sociality, which jeopardized the providential line drawn between the
races. The peaceful coexistence of the races, according to Waterbury, depended not only on the education of blacks, but on maintaining the unwavering line that separated the races and established
the superiority of whites: "The two races are, it seems probable, to
dwell side by side for years to come. Amalgamation is not desirable.
A broad, distinctive, separating line has been fixed by an all-wise
Providence" (41). The law, too, would eventually accede to an "all-
wise Providence" and act to constrict liberty and apportion equality
in conformity with the color line; as a result, the citizenship conferred upon blacks reproduced the enduring marks of inferiority. As
Waterbury himself admitted, despite the efforts of self-improvement
undertaken by the freed, "the African must still acknowledge the
superiority of the Saxon race" (42).

the black morning

6

Instinct and Injury

THE JUST AND PERFECT INEQUALITY OF THE COLOR LINE

> But when a deed is done for slavery, caste and oppression, and a blow is struck at human progress, whether so intended or not, the heart of humanity sickens in sorrow and writhes in pain.
>
> —Frederick Douglass,
> *Life and Times of Frederick Douglass*

> There are certain words which are so universally considered injurious to a person in his social or business relations if spoken of him that the courts have held that the speaker of such words is liable to an action for slander, and damages are recoverable even though the one of whom the words were spoken does not prove that he suffered any special damage from the words having been spoken of him. . . . From early times, it has been held to be slander, actionable *per se*, to say of a white man that he is a Negro or akin to a Negro.
>
> —Gilbert Thomas Stephenson,
> *Race Distinctions in American Law*

In "The Freedman's Case in Equity," George Washington Cable, reflecting on the aversive racial feelings that had acquired the status of God-given instinct in the aftermath of the war, noted that foremost among the sentiments responsible for the curtailment of the liberties of the freed was the idea that the African was inherently and unalterably "an alien." Also identified as prompting this qualification of liberties was the conviction that the African, by nature's decree, was a "perpetual menial" and an incorrigible male-factor. Summoned as evidence of this innate servility was the sunny disposition of the slave, and darkly shadowing this amiability were the vice and depravity presumed to reside in each and every drop of black blood.[1] Having traced the source of the sentiments that fueled the "odious distinction" of race and the "public indignities" suffered by blacks to the institution of slavery, Cable observed that although the war destroyed the foundation of the ruling race and the serving race, it did so "without removing a single one of the sentiments in which they stood rooted."[2] To the contrary, the war solidified these sentiments: "When the slave became a freedman, the sentiment of alienism became for the first time complete."[3] Without the illusion of "patriarchal ties" or the "benevolent sentiments of dependence or protection," the African seemed only an outsider and a danger to the social order.

If, as Cable contended, the greatest social problem before the American people in the 1880s was, as it had been for a hundred years, "the presence among us of the negro," then this problem lay precisely in the placement and proximity of blacks among and within the greater body of Americans. The perception of a discernible "us" encroached upon by black intruders identified the "Negro problem" with the question of the social, a nebulous and interstitial realm which involved matters of intimacy, association, and need. The position occupied by "those of African tincture," as Cable was wont to describe blacks, was largely as an alien, inferior, and threatening element within the social body. In his words, "grafted into the citizenship of one of the most intelligent nations in the world [were] six millions of people from one of the most debased races on the globe." This description of black citizenship as a foreign appendage grafted onto the national body bespeaks the anxieties about amalgamation attendant to the enfranchisement of blacks. The transformation of the nation-state and citizenship instituted by the Civil War and Reconstruction was manifested in fears of bodily defilement instigated by the civil equality of blacks. These alien appendages symbolized the transmogrification of "the white man's republic" and expressed the discomfort and hostilities that greeted such changes.

In the essay published in *The Century Magazine* in 1885, Cable challenged the segregation of the races in public society upheld by the Supreme Court's decision in the *Civil Rights Cases* of 1883, insisting that the color line only served to perpetuate relations of mastery and subservience. The *Civil Rights Cases* centered on the enforcement of the Civil Rights Act of 1875. The first section provided all persons the full and equal enjoyment of the accommodations in inns, public conveyances, and places of public amusement regardless of race or previous condition of servitude, and the second section indicated the fines levied for the violation of the act. However, as John Hope Franklin writes: "The determination of blacks to enjoy their civil rights was at least matched by the spiritual and vigorous resistance offered by whites in all parts of the country." This resistance, combined with indifferent federal reinforcement, signaled the Act's defeat before formally being struck down by the Court.[4] The *Civil Rights Cases* involved the denial of accommodation to blacks at inns in Kansas and Missouri, the ladies' car of a train in Memphis, a theater in San Francisco, and the Grand Opera House in New York City. The Supreme Court found the first and second sections of the Civil Rights Act of 1875 unconstitutional. It held that *racial discrimination did not constitute a badge of slavery* and that the Fourteenth Amendment was prohibitive only upon the state; it did not extend equal protection to public railways and hotels. In addition, the Court distinguished between the legal and the social, a distinction that laid the groundwork for segregation and racial subordination while upholding legal equality. The "ignominious separation exacted by the race line," observed Cable, branded whites and

blacks as the ruling race and the serving race, respectively, and ushered in "the hush of peace" after the maelstrom of war and Reconstruction. The race line enabled the perpetuation of slavery in all but
its official guises and denied the basic principles of human equity.[5]

Opposed to the humiliating distinctions of race that were indifferent to external appearance and decency, Cable argued that the
separation of the races presumably necessitated by the danger of the
black presence in fact resulted in a far greater danger—the mixing
and association of the upper ranks and the lower orders imposed by
the color line. The color line brought the white upper classes into
regular contact with uncouth whites and black menials in the public
space of privilege reserved for the ruling race. Instead, Cable advocated the "just assortment" of refined and uncouth elements indifferent to color, thereby displacing issues of race with those of decency
and refinement. While maintaining the necessity of a line of distinction dividing the decent from the ill-bred, Cable championed the
uplifting of the "lower masses," or in less charitable terms, he advocated the policing and training of the abhorrent and degraded lower
orders, primarily because of the danger they posed—"the fear that
the stupid, the destitute, and the vicious [would] combine against
them [the upper ranks] and rule by sheer weight of numbers."[6] Yet
the standards of virtue and decorum upheld in place of odious distinctions of race were no less influenced by the aversions of white
propertied men. Decency encoded the antipathies harbored against
blacks and the lower classes in the enlightened terms of bourgeois
civility and fortified the alienism Cable condemned; but the advantage of the language of decency was that it seemingly provided a
standard or measure that could be aspired to by all and, as well, it
enabled the "wise, upright, and wealthy" to embrace the common
man in the fight against ignorance and vice without disturbing the
lines of rank or distinction.[7]

Cable strenuously objected to the color line because it equalized all whites and permitted the presence of servile blacks among the white upper ranks. The presence of the lower orders, the tatterdemalions, uncouth whites, and menial blacks allowed to cross the threshold of privilege, incited Cable's disapprobation as much as the humiliating treatment of refined blacks. He desired a different measure for discrimination rather than the abolition of rank and distinction. To this end, he argued that without the intrusion of offensive racial distinctions, just assortments would occur agreeably, naturally, and heedful of decency and refinement: "Nothing is easier to show than that these distinctions on the line of color are really made not from any necessity, but simply for their own sake—to preserve the old arbitrary supremacy of the master class over the menial without regard to the decency or indecency of appearance or manners in either the white individual or the colored.... Any colored man gains unquestioned admission into innumerable places the moment he appears as the menial attendant of some white person, where he could not cross the threshold in his own rights as a well-dressed and well-behaved master of himself."

What is interesting here is the displacement of race as the central question of the social and the recommendation of a more encompassing and, dare we say, nefariously "egalitarian" mode of social incarceration targeted at the lower classes. In other words, Cable hoped that the abolition of invidious racial distinctions would lead to a social order structured by preferences and affinity and, of course, class differentiations. (In *The Souls of Black Folk*, W. E. B. Du Bois would advance a similar position, arguing that the color line prevented a union of intelligence and sympathy among the best men of each racial group, those who would be natural friends, and complaining that prejudice classed the educated and refined with the lowest of their people.) It may be asked, what is to be gained from this? First, the muddled feat accomplished by Cable in this focus on the lower orders was, at the very least, an exposure of the

unexhumed roots of slavery and, more important, the disentangle-
ment of the skeins of race and property. Two and a half centuries of
chattel slavery had successfully conflated race and status; the fal-
tered attempt to unloose this snarl revealed the degree to which race
operated to obscure the very presence of the Euro-American lower
orders by promoting them to the other side of the color line. Second, by stressing the heterogeneity of those who enjoyed an illusory
equality only by virtue of the color line, Cable made clear that the
primary purpose of the race line was to preserve mastery, which
made propertyless whites invisible by way of their inclusion in the
master race and sustained the subjection of blacks. Third, the fleeting but conspicuous presence of the propertyless whites intimated a
rather different configuration of need, security, and happiness than
that which unfolded in the aftermath of Reconstruction. All of this
greatly determined the contours and character of the social.

Public discriminations made solely on the basis of race were inju-
dicious and dangerous because they "blunt[ed] the sensibilities of
the ruling class" and "waive[d] all strict demand for painstaking
in either manners or dress of either master or menial, and, for one
result, [made] the average Southern railway more uncomfortable
than the average of railway coaches elsewhere." Basically, the menace of segregation was that it enforced the very social equality that it
was intended to prevent by making all whites equal to one another,
regardless of whether they were decent or offensive, and, likewise,
all blacks were equal to one another in their inferior status. Cable
skillfully used the fear of social equality, the rhetorical mainstay of
both white supremacist and state sovereignty arguments, against
itself and, in the course of this disputation, expressed his antipathy to social equality, defined here by the compulsory association of
white ladies and gentlemen with the white lower classes and black
menials (who served the upper classes) imposed by the color line. The
"just assortment" of persons advocated by Cable undeniably rested

upon the identification and sequestering of the degraded and threatening lower orders—the unschooled hordes who existed on either side of the race line and induced the discomfort of their betters by virtue of their shocking proximity. Cable argued that the imposition of social equality interfered with "society's natural self-distribution" and that just distinctions were essential to an enlightened society (35). What separated Cable from Justice Henry Billings Brown, who delivered the majority opinion in *Plessy v. Ferguson*, was a different perspective on what constituted an artificial and arbitrary distinction as opposed to a natural one. To restate this in the form of a question, how were "just assortments" to be determined, and were they any more reasonable or any less invidious than racial distinctions?

Despite his opposition to segregation and condemnation of the aversion that led to the violation of the rights and liberties of Black people, racial feelings, social preferences, reasoned discriminations, and natural affinities figured prominently in Cable's vision of a liberal democratic order. Ultimately, his contention with the Court's decision in the *Civil Rights Cases* involved the mapping of the private—specifically, determining where the boundary between public and private society should be drawn. For Cable, the equivocations of the public and private and the conflation of civil and social equality were attributable to the "social confusion" of slavery. The close contact of master and slave and the character of slavery as a civil and public institution had necessitated an annihilation of public right and private choice to escape the "utter confusion of race and corruption" that typified the West Indies. Consequently, all blacks not visibly servants were considered "an assault upon the purity of private society."[8]

The convergence between Cable's construction of the social domain and the Court's rests in the privileging of feeling and sentiment in the determination of social boundaries and the "just inequality of private society." We should not minimize the consequences of setting the exact location of these boundaries or the benefits of a more "enlightened" elaboration of racial feeling and social preference as opposed to aversive "racial instinct." The designations of the public and the private ultimately involved the sanctioning or prohibition of inequality. In the majority of cases involving matters of racial equality or the rights and liberties to be enjoyed by the formerly enslaved, the concept of the private and the privileging of sentiment and natural affinity authorized and supported black subordination as well as the violation of rights and liberties. What is noteworthy in Cable's essays is the effort to disentangle the Negro question and the social question, even if by way of a bourgeois ethos of cultivation, manners, and decency and the chastening embrace of the lower orders. The issue is not whether "natural self-distribution" was any less insidious or injurious than racial distinctions but whether, as I contend, the very effort to pry apart the Negro question and the social question exposes their enduring entanglements. Owing to Cable's labor, the imbroglio of affect, instinct, and aversion assumes an importance that cannot be dismissed as expedience. What better proof of this than his own inability to escape this messy knot of issues, whether by the dismissal of racial instincts as twaddle, the substitution of natural self-distribution for racial distinctions, or the subtle shading of difference between his preferences and the Court's natural affinities? Indeed, the well-intentioned but nonetheless failed effort of this friend of the Negro and avowed foe of segregation makes apparent the undue importance of the "biological," whether in the guise of racial instinct, natural affinities, or the disinclination to mix, in the (con)scripting of blackness. The "biological" stands in for needs and desires, judgments about the health, morality, and prosperity of the population, and the designated duties of the state—protection, withholding, and interference. No less paramount in this conscription of blackness is the work of affect in muting violence and concealing injury.

An Obscurity Blacker Than Poverty

The "Negro question" eclipsed the question of the social in the United States. Racism thwarted the development of social rights; perhaps the amazing indifference to physical and material needs resulted from the ascription of blacks as the ultimate bearers of the bodily and/or to the quieted needs of the white working class effected through an imagined racial integrity—membership in a grand and incorruptible ruling group that enabled an escape from the immediacy of needs or the willingness to forfeit them. Blacks have largely occluded and represented the social, and by dint of this, the issue of social rights was neglected until the New Deal. Worse yet, when social rights were belatedly addressed, they were configured to maintain racial inequality and segregation.[9] When one is examining the social question from this historical vantage point, it is clear that the history of enslavement and racism shaped the emergence of the social in the United States. This is not to minimize the clash of capital and labor that stirred the regulatory efforts of the state in the attempt to alleviate crisis or the role of private organizations in relief of the poor and scientific charity.[10] However, it is equally apparent that the parameters of the social were shaped by racial slavery and its vestiges and an indifference to black misery.

Hannah Arendt noted the "absence of the social question from the American scene" and correlated this neglect of the social question with an indifference to the abject and degrading misery present everywhere in the form of slavery and black labor. The hungry, the suffering, and the wretched did not mar the American scene because the specter of black misery failed to arouse "the passion of compassion," as the misery of the populace had during the French Revolution. Compassion for the impoverished and the hungry ushered the question of social rights onto the stage of the

French Revolution. However, in the United States black suffering did not provoke similar results. Arendt writes: "From this, we can only conclude that *the institution of slavery carries an obscurity even blacker than the obscurity of poverty; the slave, not the poor man, was wholly overlooked.*"[11] The obscurity of blackness had everything to do with the seeming absence of poverty on the American scene in ways unsuspected by Arendt.[12] All the same, Arendt celebrates this indifference to the voices of poverty and the disregard of the social as essential to the success of the American Revolution, since "the fearful specter of human misery" and the "haunting voices of abject poverty" never penetrated the ivory tower of the American Revolution.[13] She decried the social as the intrusion of bodily needs and biological life processes into the domain of politics.[14] It designated the triumph of necessity over reason. This obsession with the bodily and biological life processes also characterized the occluded emergence of the social question in the United States, but its concerns were blood, cohabitation, intimacy, and comfort rather than the hunger and security of the clamorous lower orders.[15] The managing of life was of foremost concern to the purity and health of the nation.

The obscurity of blackness observed by Arendt and the decency lauded by Cable are at the very nexus of the social as it was elaborated in the nineteenth century, for the connections forged between morality and opacity came to justify the normalizing efforts of the state. Opacity or the obscurity of blackness was held responsible for the vice and degradation that warranted the surveillance and regulatory intervention of the state.[16] It necessitated both the state's management of life and ostensible withdrawal, the power to let live or make die.[17] The "Negro question" as *the* social question arose primarily as it concerned the dangers posed by association and intimacy, since the fledgling efforts of the state to address the material needs of the freed were quickly abandoned.

(In addition, the short-lived Freedmen's Bureau exemplifies the double-edged nature of the government's intervention and relief, as relief was entwined with coercion and discipline. Reform efforts were undertaken primarily by private organizations, generally missionary societies and philanthropical associations, and were singularly devoted to the creation of a rational and submissive black working class.) As it surfaced in the nineteenth century, the social fortified the barrier between the races and named it providential, for the aborted efforts of the federal government to provide economic security largely contributed to the evolution of involuntary servitude. Moreover, the division of federal and state power and the sovereignty of the state sanctioned white supremacy by granting the states police power—to regulate and prohibit forms of social relation and enforce segregation—and by the "noninterference" of the federal government. The emergence of the social can be traced in relation to the police power exercised by the state and its severity, and what occurred in its wake was the banishing of blacks from public or civil society.[18] The state defined its duty to protect the health and morality of the population, and this duty entailed the isolation or exclusion of blacks. The separate but equal doctrine achieved the cordoning of public space for the health and happiness of the greater body of Americans, and it produced a series of racialized enclosures for the rest of us.

This expulsion or separation acted to consolidate national identity, just as the incorporation of blacks had earlier effected its transformation. Although blacks enjoyed short-lived participation and qualified membership in the body politic, they also were envisioned as internal dangers, if not enemies. The transformation of national identity, the remaking of the Constitution, and the redefinition of the United States as a nation-state had been catalyzed by the abolition of slavery and the enfranchisement of blacks. However, as this process unfolded, defining the relation of the states and citizen to the national government assumed primacy rather than the condition of the freed, especially since the nation's interest in the condition of black people and the securing of their freedom and equality had waned.[19] Similarly, the remaking of national identity and the construction of public memory that facilitated the reconciliation of North and South failed to include blacks.[20] The indifference to black misery that averted the question of the social during the American Revolution in fact marked its subsequent emergence, for as the social unfolded, it reinforced the subordinate status of blacks. At the end of the nineteenth century, the health and prosperity of society presumably necessitated segregation and the reimposition of slavery in all but its official guises.

The racial distinctions deemed tolerable within the framework of "equal before the law" and the seeming ease with which reasonable classifications yielded to injurious ones reveal a central conflict about the meaning of slavery, its formal constituents as well as its badges and indices. These matters determined the scope of rights and liberties enjoyed by the freed and the state's willingness and refusal to protect these rights and liberties. The surrender of distinction to discrimination can be gleaned in the crafting and interpretation of Reconstruction legislation. The question to be considered is how the legislative enactment and judicial assessment of universal principles like liberty and equality facilitated the subjection of the recently freed.

By focusing on the congressional debate surrounding the Reconstruction Amendments, it is not my intent to recover "original intention" or to enter the debate on constitutional interpretation per se, but rather to glimpse the tensions and contradictions that plagued the discourse of equality.[21] These debates outline the discursive contours of the post-emancipation social order and shed light on the hopes and antagonisms that defined this moment of transition. It is not my goal to impose historicist limits on the interpretation of Reconstruction legislation, but rather to examine the disputed and antagonistic terms of freedom. While I acknowledge the indeterminacy of the law, it is as important to consider the impact of the prevailing lines of interpretation and their dire outcome for black freedom. The reading advanced here explores the limits and contradictions of equality and the lineaments of state racism.[22] Above all, I do not contend that the debates establish *the* meaning, application, or interpretation of the amendments, and, for the most part, I try to resist the certitude of historicist conceit. The aim is to illuminate the limits of equality and the subterranean affiliations that bridge the divide between congressional legislation and judicial assessment. This is not to ignore the disparities between the Court's assessment of Reconstruction legislation and the intent and imagined scope of these amendments by the Congress, for without question the goal of the Civil Rights Act of 1875 and the Fourteenth Amendment was to provide equal protection of the law. Nonetheless, neither the Congress nor the Court considered equal protection at odds with certain modes of discrimination. Rather, the question was the character and context of this discrimination.

Much of this admittedly heterodox examination concentrates on that which is officially outside the scope of the law or before which the law is presumably powerless. My reading focuses on the border of the law and its excess in unearthing the disparities of equal protection. So I am not interested in the "aberrance" of *Plessy v. Ferguson* or whether the Court was right in its assessment of the Thirteenth and Fourteenth Amendments, but rather in the withdrawal of law before aversion and instinct, desire and natural affinities, because this withdrawal is at the same time a declaration of value. Of signal importance in *Plessy* is the law's production of and involvement in matters of the social and the primacy granted to affect in determining the enjoyment of rights and the duties of the

state.[23] To this end, let us turn to the congressional debates on the
Reconstruction Amendments.[24]

The Ambivalence of Freedom

The abolition of slavery incited a debate on the meaning of equality,
the constituents of rights, and the sovereignty of the states and their
institutions. The debate on the Thirteenth Amendment primarily concerned the consequences of slavery's abolition and whether
such action was constitutionally sanctioned. The fears unleashed
by the specter of black freedom concerned the menacing proximity
of the races, the impending demise of the white man's government
by the inclusion of blacks in the body politic, and the relation of the
federal government to the states. In addition, misgivings abounded
that the changes wrought by the Thirteenth Amendment would
violate the sanctity of "domestic institutions" other than slavery,
if not the integrity of the white race, since equality and miscegenation were inextricably linked.[25] A raging debate about the character of slavery raised questions about the meaning and scope of
its abolition. What is entailed in the disestablishment of slavery?
What were slavery's constituent elements and how best to eradicate them? Such questions would decide the boundaries of abolition and shape the contours of freedom. In this way, the roots of
freedom were located in slavery and the meaning of freedom was
ascertained by its negation; not surprisingly, contending narratives
of slavery inaugurated the debate on freedom.

The imbrications of slavery and freedom determined the character of the postbellum social order. Not only had slavery and freedom been mutually constitutive as modes of production, as Marx
noted, with free labor standing on the pedestal of slavery, but this
history, in turn, conditioned the forms of liberty and servitude that
emerged in the aftermath of the Civil War. This observation is not

intended to efface the discontinuities and transformations inaugurated by the abolition of slavery, but to underline how this mutual
dependence and collusion affected the character of the postbellum social formation. The entanglements of slavery and freedom
trouble facile notions of progress that endeavor to erect unequiv-
ocal distinctions between bondage and liberty.[26] Although the
Thirteenth Amendment abolished the institution of slavery, the
vestiges of slavery still acted to constrict the scope of black freedom. It proved virtually impossible to break with the past because
of the endurance of involuntary servitude and the reinscription of
racial subjection. What becomes starkly apparent are the continuities of slavery and freedom as modes of domination, exploitation,
and subjection.

The Thirteenth Amendment endowed the national state with the
power to eradicate the lingering "badges of slavery." Certainly, this
was imperative if emancipation was to be more than the exten-
uation of the institution of slavery in a new guise. Yet the fierce
disagreements about the character of slavery and its legacy shed
light on the ambivalent and belated incorporation of blacks into
the body politic and the fact that this dilatory enfranchisement was
attributable to military expediency. After the amendment's passage, the status and condition of the freed remained in question.
For example, did equality and suffrage follow upon the abolition of
slavery? Were blacks citizens? Did the abolition of slavery annul
all distinctions of race?[27] Did the abolition of slavery entail more
than nominal freedom, the freedom from constraint and the right
to own one's person, or did it "secure to the oppressed slave his
natural and God-given rights" and annul invidious distinctions of
color?[28] Was slavery merely a *status*, condition, or private situation
in which one man belonged to another and was subject to his absolute control, and thus could it be abolished without conferring on
former slaves the civil or political rights that whites enjoyed?[29] Did

the abolition of slavery entail an equality of rights and privileges? Were those formerly enslaved free if they did not possess an equality of civil rights and immunities?[30]

If the constituent elements of slavery as broadly understood were the lack of rights and liberty, coercion, chattel status, absolute submission to the will of an owner and other white persons, and nonexistence in the national community, at the very least, the eradication of slavery entailed the dispensation of fundamental rights, the liberty of contract, the mantle of sovereign individuality, and, eventually, political rights, as well as the cultivation of personhood or, more exactly, manhood, self-reliance, and responsibility in the newly emancipated, for these were the norms of liberal individuality. The right of each man to enjoy the rewards of his labor and the comfort of his family, according to Ebon Ingersoll, mandated the Thirteenth Amendment. "I believe the black man has certain inalienable rights, which are sacred in the sight of heaven and those of any other race. . . . He has a right to till the soil, to earn his bread by the sweat of his brow, and to enjoy the rewards of his own labor. He has a right to the endearment and enjoyment of family ties; and no white man has any right to rob him of or infringe upon any of these blessings."[31]

Some, like Thaddeus Stevens and Charles Sumner, contended that the central feature of chattel slavery was the inferiority and subordination of blacks; therefore, the abolition of this legacy, at the very least, required a commitment to formal equality, if not the prohibition of all discrimination on account of race or color.[32] Although slavery and its incidents were to be abolished, race was considered a neutral category and reasonable classification. The inability to pass earlier drafts of the Civil Rights Bill of 1866 and the Fourteenth Amendment that contained explicit nondiscrimination provisions documents an abiding commitment to discrimination. Despite assertions that blacks were no longer a subjugated race because of the triumph of liberty, equality, and contract, the shifting register of race from a *status* ascription to a formal and purportedly neutral category ineluctably refigured blackness as an abject category, as a marker of disposable life.[33]

Ex post facto, the breadth of the Thirteenth Amendment was clarified, chiefly due to the escalating violations of black freedom and the reimposition of slavery via the Black Codes. As discussed earlier, these codes reduced blacks to a condition described by Freedmen's Bureau officials as worse than slavery. While the vagrancy laws, pass laws, and unequal sentences for criminal offenses committed by blacks enacted by the Black Codes were eventually overturned, albeit only to reappear in race-neutral trappings, the codification of race undertaken in these state constitutions was not considered at odds with liberty or equality, nor were antimiscegenation statutes found to be a violation of civil rights. Ubiquitous assaults on freed blacks mandated legislation to secure personal liberty and required additional clarification of the fundamental civil rights conferred by the Thirteenth Amendment. In the aftermath of emancipation the place of blacks within the body politic was still uncertain. Had the Thirteenth Amendment conferred rights of citizenship? Did abolition portend black equality? And if so, what were the components of this disputed equality?

Those who contended that the Thirteenth Amendment did not confer basic civil rights to the formerly enslaved argued that slavery was not a public relation between the slave and the state but a private relation between two persons—the master and the slave—and therefore its abolition required nothing more than the abrogation of this relation: "What is slavery? It is not a relation between the slave and the State; it is not a public relation; it is a relation between two persons whereby the conduct of the one is placed under the will of the other. It is purely and entirely a domestic relation.... The constitutional amendment broke asunder this private relation between the master and his slave, and the slave then, so far as the right of the master was concerned, became free; but did the slave under the amendment acquire any other right than to be free from the control of his master? ... No new rights [were] conferred on the freedman."[34] This line of argument rendered slavery a domestic matter, thereby obscuring the state's sanctioning and support of the institution and denying the racial order founded upon mastery and servitude. This restricted interpretation of slavery cast the freed as liminal agents, neither slaves nor citizens, by repudiating the need for national remedy in eradicating the vestiges of slavery and annulling the existence of dominant and subjugated races. As well, such arguments, in their refusal to acknowledge slavery as a public institution authorized by the Constitution and federal and state law, endeavored to erase the plight of the emancipated from the national agenda.

This unabashed denial of slavery as a public institution fabricated the nation's innocence by masking the foundational character of slavery to the state and civil society, and by focusing on private relations between individuals. Certainly *Prigg v. Pennsylvania*, the Fugitive Slave Law, the power of police exercised by any and every white person over slaves and free blacks, the interference of the state in disposals of slave property, laws forbidding interracial assembly, and the modeling of racial relations in the image of master-slave relations attest to the public character of the institution. In short, if the Thirteenth Amendment conferred no new rights and only abolished "mere chattelism," then blacks in effect were denied the privileges of citizenship. As might be expected, advocates of this position contended that the republic was a white man's government and that, as *Dred Scott* held, blacks were neither embraced nor included in the "person" of the Constitution. If the Thirteenth Amendment only liberated the slave from his master, then blacks occupied the precarious position of being free but without the basic rights of citizenship.[35]

These arguments were countered by contending interpretations of slavery that foregrounded the negation of fundamental civil rights, the national disregard of the rights of the individual, and the protection of slavery by the armament of the Constitution, as well as federal and state law.[36] What better illustrated the degradation of bondage than the sexual practices it condoned? Republicans decried miscegenation as a Democratic institution and envisioned one of the principal rewards of freedom as the preservation of family ties sundered by slavery. Radical Republicans insisted that the abolition of slavery encompassed all laws, relations, and customs that acted to deny blacks their rights. Therefore, the servitude abolished by the amendment included the state as well as the individual. As Lyman Trumbull argued, unless "we have merely taken from the master the power to control the slave and left him at the mercy of the State to be deprived of his civil rights, the trumpet of freedom that we have been blowing throughout the land has given an 'uncertain sound,' and the promised freedom is a delusion. . . . With the destruction of slavery necessarily follows the destruction of the incidents of slavery."[37] Any statute that deprived black citizens of civil rights that were secured to others was a "badge of servitude," especially since blacks were being systematically reenslaved through vagrancy laws and the criminal surety system.[38] If slavery annulled fundamental rights, the corrective required the restoration of these rights. According to Trumbull, these rights included "the right to make and enforce contracts, to sue and be sued, and to give evidence, to inherit, purchase, sell, lease, hold and convey real and personal property, and to full and equal benefit to all laws and proceedings for the security of person and property."[39] However, if the formerly enslaved were entitled to the rights enjoyed by the white men, irrespective of distinctions of race

or former condition of servitude, did this suggest that all discriminations of race were to be negated or only those involving basic
civil rights?[40] As it turned out, black equality did not imply "equality in all things . . . simply before the laws, nothing else."[41] Yet the
question begged by this matter-of-fact assertion was the reach of
the law and, in particular, the acquiescence of the law to natural
affinity and natural distinction.[42]

The Most Representative Person,
or a Man Like Any Other

> Everywhere mature manhood is the representative type of the
> human race.
>
> —Senator Jacob Howard, *Congressional
> Globe*, 39th Congress, 1st Session

The congressional debates on the Civil Rights Act of 1866 and
the Fourteenth Amendment document the union of exclusion and
equality within the liberal order. The Act was intended to clarify
the status of the freed and protect the forms of personal liberty
regularly violated by the Black Codes and social custom. The Act
declared that all persons "shall have the same right in every State
and Territory of the United States to make and enforce contracts,
to sue, to be parties and give evidence, to inherit, purchase, lease,
sell, hold, and convey real and personal property, and to full and
equal benefit of all laws and proceedings for the security of person
and property, as is enjoyed by white citizens." Of particular importance in the congressional debate on the Civil Rights Act and Fourteenth Amendment is the extent to which this new equality of rights
depended upon the transformation of former slaves into responsible
and reasonable men. The norms at issue were masculinity, rationality, industry and restraint, and they determined one's ability to han-
dle the duties and privileges of the citizen-subject and participate

in the body politic. Ostensibly at stake in the question of manhood were the criteria for citizenship, yet it was apparent that espousals of responsible manhood and equality invariably aroused anxieties about the commingling of the races. In light of such fears, responsible manhood accrued undue gravity.

Mature manhood, reason, will, and responsibility were variously invoked in promulgating legislation on behalf of the freed and in the concerted efforts to derail "special" legislation like the Civil Rights Act, the Freedmen's Bureau Bill and the Fourteenth Amendment. The invocation of manhood must be understood as an invitation to freedmen to enter the brotherhood of man. The cultivation of responsible manhood compelled the protection of basic civil rights that would enable the freed to become self-sustaining independent laborers, homeowners, and providers for their family and, at the same time, underscored the distance between the freed and the white propertied men who presumably were their counterparts. The opponents of Reconstruction were intent upon exploiting this discrepancy. After all, the logic proceeded, if the Negro was a man like any other, why did blacks need special legislation to secure rights and privileges guaranteed by the Constitution? As Senator James McDougall challenged in the debate on the Freedmen's Bureau Bill, "If the negro, being made free, cannot take care of himself, how long shall we be his guardian, and take more care of him than we do the poor boys of our own race and people?"[43] Similarly, in his veto of the Freedmen's Bureau Bill, President Andrew Johnson argued that Congress "has never deemed itself authorized to expend the public money for the thousands not to say millions of the white race who are honestly toiling from day to day for their subsistence."[44] Such legislation implied that the freed were incapable of self-sustenance, it was "injurious to their character and their prospects." From this vantage, efforts to remedy the extant legacy of slavery such as the Freedmen's Bureau Bill or the Civil Rights Act of 1875 could only appear as special legislation "favoring" blacks or efforts to impose unwanted association.

Responsibility essentially denoted the duty of self-making and the virtue of individual accountability. Invoked in this manner, it effaced the salient features of racial slavery and the vestiges that prevented even the illusion of autonomy or independence.[45] For the democratic advocates of responsibility, the legislative remedies proposed in assisting the freed were believed unnecessary because of this conspicuous faith in the freed's capacity to overcome the obstacles before them. While this line of argument was cynical and disingenuous, it nonetheless revealed self-making as a central tenet of democratic individuality and evidenced an unwavering belief in the fairness of the marketplace in providing each man his due. The emphasis on self-making in the conferral of formal equality illumined the tension between equality and redress within a liberal framework. It was easier to recognize and correct the exclusion and inferiority written into slave law through formal measures like the Thirteenth Amendment than it was to remedy the disparities and inequalities that were the consequence of this former condition. Basically, subjugation was to be undone by the conferral of formal equality; this was believed to be sufficient to abolish slavery and sever the present from the preceding centuries of enslavement. As a result of this dispensation, the freed now possessed the same advantages and opportunities available to others and enjoyed the natural liberty previously denied them. While the conferral of basic civil rights and equal protection in the Civil Rights Act of 1866 and the Fourteenth Amendment overturned the precedent established in *Dred Scott v. Sanford*—blacks were neither citizens nor possessed any rights that whites were bound to respect—these newly acquired rights were much less effective in obliterating the everyday vestiges of slavery.[46]

By insisting that blacks avail themselves of the remedies already procurable within the law, equality was defined by an identity of treatment rather than by legislative intervention designed to actualize this equality. Ironically, those who advocated identical treatment—which in this case meant offering no assistance to the emancipated in matters of relief—insisted upon equivalent treatment regarding delicate matters that might potentially unsettle the extant arrangements of the racial order. The equation of equal treatment with like treatment, as in the comparison of the toiling white and black races, denied the gulf produced by centuries of enslavement and the privileges made available to all whites because of chattel slavery. The recognition of difference posed dangers no less great. The acknowledgment of difference in the law sanctioned and legitimated the denial of civil and political rights, and eventually the separate but equal doctrine more readily than it provided remedy to the enduring legacy of slavery.

The "man" fabricated in documents like the Thirteenth Amendment, the Civil Rights Act of 1866, and the Fourteenth Amendment was liberated from the past by the abolition of slavery and by virtue of his own endowments, the capacity for self-making and the reasonable exercise of free will. The arguments on behalf of Reconstruction measures also attached great weight to the development of "true manhood" in realizing freedom and equality. As Congressman Ignatius Donnelly advocated on behalf of the Freedmen's Bureau Bill:

> If degradation and oppression have, as it is alleged, unfitted him for freedom, surely continued degradation and oppression will not prepare him for it. If he is not to remain a brute you must give him that which will make him a man—opportunity. If he is, as it is claimed, an inferior being and unable to compete with the white man on terms of equality, surely you will not add to the injustice of nature by casting him beneath the

feet of the white man. With what face can you reproach him
with his degradation at the very moment you are striving to
still further degrade him? If he is, as you say, not fit to vote,
give him a chance; let him make himself an independent
laborer like yourself; let him own his homestead; and let his
intelligence, darkened by centuries of neglect, be illuminated
by all the glorious lights of education. If after all of this he
proves himself an unworthy savage and brutal wretch, condemn him, but not til then.[47]

It is clear that the generic "man" is not being used here; rather,
the masculinity of the citizen-subject is being pronounced. The
attention to manliness, self-making, maturation, and assimilation
displayed Republican dedication to transforming brutes into men
and actualizing the admirable ends of autonomy, political inclusion, self-sufficiency, and enlightenment. Upon the success or failure of this project depended the future of the Negro—true man or
unworthy savage? The sexual reverberations of this project, though
muted, are conveyed by fraught terms like "savage" and "brute,"
and the lurking sexual rapaciousness exceeds their cover. As Jared
Waterbury argued in *Southern Planters and Freedmen*, the failure to
educate the freedmen and effect this transformation from brute to
man endangered the very terms of social order, for unschooled and
passionate men dwelling within and moving amid society hinted
at unspeakable dangers, but dangers regularly exploited by those
opposed to black equality. In his veto of the Civil Rights Bill of
1866, President Johnson equated the "perfect equality of the white
and black races" proposed in the bill with "the contract of marriage
between the two races."

For Johnson, the attested need for legislation like the Freedmen's Bureau Bill and the Civil Rights Acts fueled arguments
that the Negro was a child, not a man, because these provisions

made him a ward of the state.[48] As Senator Edgar Cowan argued, "If they are put upon the same footing as white people, then they have the same remedies as white people; they have the same remedies that the honorable Senator has; and there is no new necessity for this jurisdiction, this new power that is to be invoked for their protection."[49] Those opposed to "special" legislation demanded that blacks stand on their own or forever prostrate themselves before the superiority of the Saxon race. This perhaps cynical insistence on an equality of treatment, indifferent to the history of servitude and abiding vestiges of slavery, denied the extant legacy of racial subordination while maintaining white dominance. However, when equality is defined by sameness, blacks either prove themselves the same, and therefore not in need of state intervention to aid their condition, or they bear the stigma of difference. Others argued that after having been reduced to the "lowest grade of being," how were the freed instantaneously capable of resuming the duties of citizenship? As a representative from Missouri argued: "For thirty years it has been steadily proclaimed that African slavery has reduced the enslaved to the very lowest grade of being. The enslavement of his body had, by consequence, almost obliterated his intellect. He could scarcely be called a man. That he might be rescued, he must be freed. He is freed. Presto, change! As soon as the chains fall he is no longer the brutalized being over whom, for thirty years, we have made the land to mourn; he is an American citizen, fully qualified and prepared to take upon himself the responsibilities of an elector, and qualified for all these important duties. Wonderful!"[50]

Friends and foes of the Negro alike assumed that the degradation of enslavement made blacks less than men; so this emergent manhood was anticipated, groomed, doubted, and feared. The infantile condition of the race both necessitated legislation on their behalf and justified black subordination. Noteworthy is the

discursive tenor of these statements—the masculinist and paternalist lens through which the condition of the freed was refracted,
with terms like "infantile race" and "mature manhood" framing issues of equality and citizenship. Degradation accurately
described the wretched material and social conditions of the freed,
but as it was deployed in Congressional debate, it was transposed
into an ontology of black difference, which reproduced, inadvertently or intentionally, the sophistry of Justice Roger Taney in *Dred
Scott*. The decision established the innate inferiority of blacks by
reference to the laws and social conditions that situated blacks
as inferior. It was a brutal tautology. (The liberal conception of
the individual as an isolated entity divorced from social and material conditions made it difficult, if not impossible, to acknowledge
difference without ontologizing it as abnormality or inferiority.)
A slippage between race and status can be detected in the uncertain identification of the source of black degradation—was nature
responsible, or the wretched conditions of slavery, or both? Could
degradation be cured or was it innate? And if nature was responsible for both this degradation and the antagonism between the
races, then what did the abolition of slavery portend? And how was
equality to be understood? Would blacks be incorporated into the
body politic or cast out and condemned?

    The only sure way to quell these doubts and prove black wor-
thiness was to license this question of equality and sameness by
aspiring to meet and exceed the norm—by adapting or aspiring to
a normative masculinity, by striving to be self-possessed and sovereign, ideals which ultimately were inseparable from the entitlements of whiteness. No wonder the "manhood of the race" was the
prized figure of the discourse of racial uplift. However, this proved
an impossible strategy; while freedmen were able to gain entrance
to the discourse of citizenship, unlike freedwomen, the nexus of
race, sexuality, and capital operated to discipline and regulate this

nascent manhood.[51] The ineluctable production of taxonomies of purity and contagion, supremacy and degradation, decency and lasciviousness, and order and danger constituted an impassable and insurmountable barrier to "perfect equality." The construction of nature upon which these debates proceeded ultimately frustrated equality. While the discourse of civil and (eventually) political rights assumed that a modicum of normalization could be achieved and the erstwhile brute could be inculcated with the virtues of mature manhood, the indelible markers of difference ensconced within the social marked the limits of equality. The law retreated in the face of instinct and affinity.

The universalist embrace of man was not as expansive as it purported to be. Leaving aside for the moment the exclusion of women from the purview of equal rights and protection, since gender was considered a reasonable basis for discrimination, race or former condition of servitude was no longer considered a reasonable basis for discrimination. The masculinist universalism of equality was belied by racism. As many theorists and critics of liberalism have duly noted, the identitarian formula upon which equality is predicated encloses difference within an arena marked as inferior, pathological, immoral, or perverse.[52] The universalist embrace and exclusions constitutive of liberalism reveal the gap between formal and substantive equality. The universalist reach of liberalism, according to Uday Mehta, despite its declarations of natural equality, conceals "the thicker set of social credentials that constitute the real bases of political inclusion."[53] "Liberalism's commitment to principles of universality is practically sustained only by the reinvented and rationalized exclusions of racial particularity."[54] The demand to display one's worth instantiated only the want of equal rights rather than their enjoyment and likewise revealed the menacing double bind of mimicry—almost the same, but not quite.[55] Human, but not quite.

The content of equality was uncertain.⁵⁶ As the debates on the Reconstruction Amendments confirm, equality was ensnared with proliferating classifications and categories, discernments of reasonable and unlawful discriminations, and doubts concerning the classes of individuals within the reach of the amendments. A disagreement between Robert Hale and Thaddeus Stevens is illuminating in this regard. What is remarkable is the confused response of Stevens to Hale's interrogation of the coverage of the Fourteenth Amendment, in particular, his questioning of whether it provided "all persons equal protection." Would it override the discrimination that he rightly argued was practiced in virtually every state of the Union? Stevens argued the amendment simply provided that "where any State makes a distinction in the same law between *different classes of individuals*, Congress shall have the power to correct such discriminations and inequality," and that inequality only pertained to the discriminations made between *individuals of the same class*. "When a distinction is made between two married people or two femmes sole, then it is unequal legislation; but where all of *the same class* are dealt with in the same way there is no pretense of inequality" [emphasis mine].

Hale contended that "by parity of [this] reasoning it will be sufficient if you extend to the one negro the same rights you do to another, but not those you extend to a white man."⁵⁷ According to Stevens's logic, the selective recognition of sameness guarantees the identity of rights and privileges, while difference determines rights in accordance with one's place in society. One is left to wonder what exactly equality does entail and, by the same token, what constitutes a violation of equal protection. Did blacks constitute a different class of individuals or were all men of one class? The vacillation between the disavowal and recognition of difference encapsulates the predicament of equality. Stevens's reasoning exemplifies the indefinite and nebulous character of equality and the uncertainty of its object—individuals or classes of individuals. We are left to wonder what comprises a class of individuals. Are men of one class, but married women and single women distinct classes? Are blacks and Chinese both equally included in the concept of persons?[58] Certainly these questions were at the heart of the debate on who and what were included within the embrace of equality.[59] As Andrew Kull observes, "Men like Stevens thought it was so obvious which 'inequalities' they were aiming at they momentarily lost sight of the fact that the entire legal system is necessarily a fabric of inequalities and discriminations, of categories and classifications."[60]

The equality propounded in the Civil Rights Acts of 1866 and the Fourteenth Amendment relied upon classifications of like classes and like individuals in comparable situations. Equal protection permitted discernments between equivalent privileges and identical privileges and allowed for the differential treatment of individuals technically within the scope of the law.[61] In this regard, equality was ensnared with discriminatory evaluations of classes of persons, for to be treated differently was inevitably to be treated as an inferior or subordinate. Certainly, this is indisputable when considering the status of blacks and women. The transparency of nature—natural difference and natural affinities—was everywhere assumed in the law, and the contentions over reasonable and invidious classifications nonetheless presupposed the anteriority of such categories; the matter to be decided was whether rights should be dispensed in recognition of these differences or "blind" to them. As these issues were settled in the wake of the Thirteenth and Fourteenth Amendments, reasonable classifications were permitted, while injurious ones were prohibited. Obviously, what constituted "reasonableness" or injury was the subject of debate. In the end, the selective recognition and dismissal of difference in the conferral of rights presumed the neutrality of the law and the exteriority of these differences, as if these differences didn't inhabit the text of law or the law was uninvolved in their production, the sterling example of this being the idea of the color-blind Constitution. So we need ask: How was it possible for the racialized text of the Constitution to declare its neutrality and enact its blindness? The success of the Reconstruction legislation revolved around this issue. How these issues were decided in practice often meant ignoring distinctions of race and former conditions of servitude regarding certain rights, while permitting these distinctions as reasonable regarding others. In question is the connection between racial distinctions and the legitimate exercise of rights, and the forms of inequality that rights sustain. Rights were unstable and in flux, and their reach or exercise was decided by this recognition of difference or sameness.

The rejection of an explicit antidiscrimination clause in the Civil Rights Act of 1866 and the Fourteenth Amendment in favor of the language of equal protection attests to the nebulous character of the equality conferred. The Civil Rights Act both permitted discrimination in certain arenas and narrowly defined the scope of civil rights.[62] An earlier draft of the Civil Rights Act contained the following declaration, which eventually was stricken by the Senate's judiciary committee: "There shall be no discrimination in civil rights or immunities among the inhabitants of any State or territory on account of race, color, or previous condition of servitude." This clause was stricken to assure the passage of the act and amid uncertainty as to whether the rights and entitlements extended by "the full and equal benefit of laws" reached beyond the scope of those rights explicitly mentioned in the act.[63] Worse yet, the very term "civil rights" was stricken because "some gentlemen were apprehensive that the words we propose to strike out might give warrant for a latitudinarian construction not intended." The construction obviously not intended was that all forms of discrimination based upon race, color, or previous condition would be prohibited by the Act.

The vision of equality advanced in documents like the Civil Rights Act of 1866 and the Fourteenth Amendment was malleable enough to permit certain classes of discrimination while prohibiting others. Discernments of identity and equivalence yielded a protean concept of equality. For example, the language of the Civil Rights Act of 1866 permitted the restriction of freedwomen's rights by granting the freed the same basic civil rights enjoyed by white citizens. The vision of equality forged in the law permitted the subordination of women while attempting to prevent discrimination based on race or a former condition of servitude. Without question, equality was entangled in a network of classifications, categories, and measures that ultimately rested on a tautology: those who are equal shall be treated equally.[64]

The amorphous content of equal protection rhetoric in large measure resulted from the effort to prohibit certain classes of discrimination while permitting others. This latitude was warranted by the fact that virtually every state in the Union discriminated on the basis of race in respect to civil rights. Although Stevens, Trumbull, and Sumner argued on behalf of an explicit nondiscrimination clause in the Civil Rights Act of 1866 and the Fourteenth Amendment, these proposals were defeated.[65] The compatibility of equal protection with extant forms of gender discrimination is indisputable; less obvious are the extant forms of racial discrimination permitted within its scope. Nor did equality before the law suppose the equality of men in their social and material conditions, but simply that men deserved equal treatment as humans endowed with natural rights and liberties. Treatment as an equal, writes Judith Baer, "depended on the individual's status as a human being. It was this right that prevented inferior treatment, not some notion that the freed slaves were equal to whites in ability and thus deserved equal status."[66] This restricted notion explains why radicals like Trumbull stated that equal protection of the laws did not presume the equality of the Negro, for the natural equality of men neither negated nor minimized the unequal capacities, abilities, or standing of social men.[67] As Wendy Brown writes, liberal equality "guarantees only that all individuals will be treated as if they were sovereign and isolated individuals . . . and that the state will regard us all as equally abstracted from the social powers constituting our existence, equally decontextualized from the unequal conditions of our lives."[68]

The gap between abstract equality and extant social arrangements exposed the want, or the folly, of substantive equality, as Cowan contended. By exploiting the discrepancy between the stipulated equality of all men and actual social arrangements, the intoxicating rhetoric of natural equality and sovereign individuality was deflated. This celebratory disrobing of universal man not only bared the distinctive properties of the citizen-subject, but also insinuated that the "plane of manhood" might be a private social club after all. The repercussions of this would be fleshed out in *Plessy*. In this spirit, Cowan asked if equality dictated that

> all men in this country are to be six feet tall, and they shall all weigh two hundred pounds, and that they shall all have fair hair and red cheeks? Is that the meaning of equality? Is it that they shall all be equally rich and equally jovial, equally humorous and equally happy? What is meant by equality, as I understand it, in the language of the Declaration of Independence, is that each man shall have the right to pursue in his own way life, liberty, and happiness. That is the whole of it. . . . If all men were to be as learned as my honorable friend from Massachusetts [Sumner], who would black boots and curry the horses, who would do the menial offices of the world? . . . This world . . . is pretty well arranged. . . . The imaginary evils that people see in the distribution of honors and all that kind

of thing are not so nearly oppressive as they are made out to
be in the warm and glowing imaginations of those who see fit
to champion their victims.[69]

It is only appropriate that the impossibility of equality was represented by way of an inventory of immutable physical features.
Cowan's cheery acknowledgment of a well-arranged world not
only underlined the easy coexistence of equality with the unequal
distribution of wealth and honor, but also implicitly distinguished
the normative embodiment of the citizen-subject from the inferior
lower ranks. This vision of equality exalted the extant racial order of
senators and bootblacks. Unmistakable in Cowan's gleeful observations was that natural liberty, the right of each man to pursue
his own way of life, and happiness without the interference of others, in fact took for granted the inequitable distribution of wealth,
honor, and power and embraced black servility. While declarations
of equality announced the end of slavery, the well-arranged world
sustained itself.

Blood and Sentiment

In 1865, the Constitution of the nation was in flux. The entry of
four million blacks into the body politic transfigured the narrative of national identity. The pedestrian signs of this upheaval were
apparent in the movement of the freed. They roamed the country-
side, took to the roads, and rushed to the cities; at the very least,
this peregrination documented the collapse of the former order. Yet
the changes wrought by this massive upheaval and revisioning of
citizenship also instituted a collective crisis, since black exclusion
and subordination formerly had defined membership in the civic
and political community and the scope of rights and entitlement.
The integrity and self-certainty founded upon the division between

master and slave races was now without foundation. As Theodore W. Allen remarks, "By making freedom a human right, negro emancipation has destroyed it as a racial privilege, and thereby threatened to dissolve on the instant the mortar holding together the system of bourgeois social control and the system of white labor privilege based on the prescription of African American chattel bond-servitude."[70] The vision of former masters and former slaves as equal members of the national community incited a wave of reaction registered in the opposition to the Thirteenth Amendment, the imposition of the Black Codes, the resurgence of white violence, a series of massacres, and the reign of terror.[71] Emancipation, beheld through the nostalgic longing for the old order and a determined resistance to the new, was regularly and insistently decried as the "miscegenation proclamation" and "Negro government." Anxieties about the newfound power and centrality of federal government in the aftermath of the Civil War and the subordinate position of the individual states in regard to the rights of citizens, complaints about the states having been made into handmaidens of the government and positioned as truculent underlings subject to various modes of correction and enforcement, were articulated as fears about black insolence, sexual mixing, amalgamated bodies, and interracial families. The encroachments of the federal government were feared and described as the intrusion of the Negro. To the opponents of Reconstruction it appeared that the augmentation of federal power in the context of the Civil War acted to conflate black interests and the supremacy of the national government.

In the congressional debates, the issue of miscegenation arose virtually every time a new amendment, bill, or act was on the floor, from the Thirteenth Amendment to the Civil Rights Act of 1866, the Fourteenth Amendment, and the Civil Rights Act of 1875—Democratic anxiety was met by Republican laughter. The Republicans derided these fears with jokes that revealed a classic

abolitionist anxiety, dread, and fascination with black bodies.[72] The
Republican vision of liberty, rather like that of Miss Ophelia or Harriet Beecher Stowe herself, endorsed a requisite distance between
the races, if not the banishment of blackness.[73] After explaining
repeatedly that an equality of civil rights neither embraced interracial marriage nor discriminated between the races since the Negro
was denied the right to marry a white person and a white person
a Negro, Trumbull pointedly argued that laws against miscegenation were not needed where there was no disposition for amalgamation: "The Senator says the laws of Kentucky forbid a white man or
woman marrying a negro, and that these laws of Kentucky are to
exist forever; that severe penalties are imposed in the State of Kentucky against amalgamation, between the white and black races.
Well, sir, I am sorry that in noble Kentucky there is such a disposition for amalgamation that nothing but penalties and punishments
can prevent it."[74]

These remarks served to disavow the abolitionist fascination with
miscegenated bodies and, as well, to assert the Republican commitment to liberty and the color line. This divided commitment to equality and inferiority best explains the anomalous position of blacks
within the body politic. Trumbull's remarks were of the same spirit
as the favored and oft-repeated campaign joke of Lincoln: "I protest, now and forever, against that counterfeit logic which presumes
that because I do not want a negro woman for a slave, I do necessarily want her for a wife."[75] This joke was regularly met by laughter
and cheers on the campaign trail. Of course, the joke turned upon
the absurd notion of the black woman as wife, but like Trumbull's
remarks hinted at other forms of possession. Given that the weight
of prohibition against interracial marriage and amalgamation fell
largely upon black men and white women, the joke about the Negro
wife united political opponents in ribald laughter and left open the
back door of other arrangements.

The Republican commitment to the equal privileges of citizenship and black inferiority was evidenced throughout the debates. As
one representative quipped, "If I believed that there was a man in
this country with so little sense as to believe that he would become
the equal of the negro, notwithstanding the protection he can obtain
from Congress, then I would be willing to vote for a resolution to
give him two medals, one to be worn before and the other behind,
with the inscription upon them, 'I am afraid of the negro, and here
is my sign, stuck out prominently, that I am not to be considered
the equal of the negro.'"[76] As supporters of these amendments regularly reminded their opponents, equality did not mean "equality in
all things—simply before the laws, nothing else."[77] If the Reconstruction Amendments brought the formerly enslaved within "the
pale of the Constitution," they certainly did not imply that distinctions of race were annulled or that all were equal.

If abolition, as the opponents of emancipation and black equality contended, predestined the amalgamation of the races, then
only the return of the freed to their proper role as subordinates
would preclude such an occurrence. Equality was blamed for the
increased likelihood of miscegenation. It was "impossible that two
distinct races should exist harmoniously in the same country, on the
same footing of equality by the law. The result must be a disgusting and deteriorating admixture of the races."[78] President Johnson,
too, exploited this racial reasoning in his veto of the Civil Rights
Act of 1866. Although the equal protection of the laws advanced in
that act and in the Fourteenth Amendment neither encompassed
nor sanctioned interracial marriage, this did not prevent him from
raising the banner of miscegenation in his opposition to the extension of civil rights to the freed: "If Congress can abrogate all State
laws of discrimination between the two races in the matter of real
estate, of suits, and of contracts generally, Congress may not also
repeal the State laws as to contract of marriage between the two

races?"[79] The phantom of Negro equality, as some were wont to call it, portended black men with white wives because the civil rights to be conferred were fundamentally understood as the rights and prerogatives of white men and by extension this included the right to marry white women. As one representative argued during the discussion of the Fourteenth Amendment: "If this amendment be passed Congress can pass under it a law compelling South Carolina to grant to negroes every right accorded to white people there; and as white men there have the right to marry white women, negroes, under this amendment would be entitled to the same right; and thus miscegenation and mixture of the races could be authorized in any State, as all citizens under this amendment are entitled to the same privileges and immunities, and the same protection in life, liberty, and property."[80]

As the pivotal figure of counterinsurgent popular sentiment, miscegenation gave expression to the outrage that the bottom rail seemed to be on top, anger at the assault on white ownership of property in black persons, fear that whiteness as it had once existed was endangered or doomed, and indignation at the prominence of the federal government and subordinate status of the states in relation to questions of citizenship and equality. The specter of the miscegenous body acquired this great visibility, according to Eva Saks, because it was a site for working out political issues of federalism and race.[81] In short, the body "allegorized the battlefield of federalism" (66). The amalgamated body materialized the dreaded loss of racial/bodily integrity associated with the abolition of slavery and the violation of state sovereignty by federal jurisdiction. As well, lingering doubts as to whether the equality of civil rights included the marriage contract placed miscegenation at the center of the discussion of equal protection.

Antimiscegenation statutes emerged during the colonial period; however, by the nineteenth century thirty-eight states had incorporated such statutes.[82] In the aftermath of emancipation, miscegenation acquired a political currency that was perhaps unprecedented. During Reconstruction, states passed stricter anti-miscegenation statutes. Although the political currency of miscegenation can be credited in part to Democratic scare tactics deployed to undermine black freedom, as had been the case in the miscegenation controversy of 1864, this hardly exhausts the subject.[83] Chiefly, miscegenation discloses the obsessions of the state with pure blood, procreation, life, and legitimate union. It was a symptom of the emergent antipathy and anxiety attendant to the new terms of interracial association, now that slavery no longer provided the guidelines or rules for such interactions. This fixation on imagined sexual trespasses revealed the degree to which the integrity and security of whiteness depended upon black subordination. The coexistence of the races as putative equals within the body politic threatened the integrity of both races—the mongrelization of the white race and/or the engulfment of freed blacks by the white race due to Saxon superiority.[84] The proximity and intimacy of black and white bodies deemed proper or appropriate under the social relations of slavery became menacing in the aftermath of emancipation. Under slavery, such intimacy extended the power and dominion of the master, since captive bodies were the literal and figurative appendages of the master's body and "the sign and surrogate" of his power. This proximity did not imperil the racial order, for this intercourse was in the service of black subordination and white enjoyment.

Miscegenation figuratively articulated the dislocations of power, property, and status caused by the abolition of slavery and Reconstruction, and the anxieties and apprehensions incited by this tumult; antimiscegenation statutes were a concrete expression of racism as state policy.[85] The materiality of racism as a mode or technique of power encompasses a range of social processes: it is a way of managing life and death, of extracting value and accumulating capital, of translating humans into objects and raw materials, of dividing valued lives from the disposable; it is not simply "ideology." An extended web of state and civil institutions acted concertedly to maintain the purity of family and nation, to regulate race and reproduction. After all, miscegenation was an aberrant and unlawful behavior targeted by the regulatory efforts of the state. As it constituted a threat to the health and morality of the population, the resources of the state were dedicated to its prevention and punishment. This entailed the codification of race, the securing of property, sexual and gender proscriptions, and the managing of individuals and populations. The production of a miscegenation crisis facilitated the classification and control of blacks as a subjugated population. The threat of contagion and defilement associated with blackness necessitated these statutes, which aimed to protect and police whiteness.[86] The first step in this effort was the codification of race—who was black and who was not, and who was white and who was not—which involved a metaphysics of blood that transformed race into a sanguinous substance detectable not only by discernible traces but also by genealogy. Miscegenation belied the purported neutrality of racial codification and exhibited the aversion and antipathy that demanded the policing of such distinctions. The work of classification, surveillance, and regulation that was part and parcel of this monitoring of legitimate and sound unions focuses our attention upon the state's role in producing racial subjects and managing populations, while ostensibly working to eradicate forms of discrimination based upon race and servitude.

The taxonomies of race that found their way into the law of freedom made apparent the contradictions that shaped the emergent vision of black equality. The "equal protection of the law," albeit intended to correct the violation of black liberty by the Black Codes and social customs embraced legal classifications of racial difference—white, negro, mestizo, and person of color. Certainly, these taxonomies produced race rather than simply accounting for it, and they were instrumental in effecting new forms of servitude. (Let me state clearly that this is not an argument on behalf of color-blindness. The insincerity or naïveté of the color-blind position cannot redress the injuries of racism by wishing race away in the desire for an imagined neutrality. The invidious effects of racism also operate in race-neutral forms, which we see in the successful implementation of "impartial" laws that disproportionately fined, sentenced, and imprisoned the freed and mushroomed into the convict-lease system. Color-blindness naturalizes race by assuming its anteriority to discourse. Through this failure or "blindness," it is unable to account for racism's social production or material consequences.) The state's production and recognition of racial distinctions was not considered at odds with its guarantees of an equality of rights and protection (although difference invariably produced a hierarchy of human life and value).

The conception of race produced by centuries of slavery made "black" virtually synonymous with "slave" and "white" with "free" and had created a master race and a subject race. In Cable's words, slavery "made our master caste a solid mass, and fixed a common mastery and subserviency between the ruling and serving race. Every one of us [whites] grew up in the idea that he had by birth and race, certain broad powers of police over any and every person of color."[87] Now that race no longer defined status, classificatory schemes were required to maintain these lines of division. The effort to maintain the color line or, properly speaking, black subordination involved securing the division between the races and controlling the free black population. Central to this effort was the codification of race, which focused primarily on defining and containing blackness.

The classification of Negroes or persons of color was most often discussed in the context of the law's designation of lawful and prohibited unions, firmly establishing the connection between sexuality and sanguinity. As Mississippi's Act to Confer Civil Rights on Freedmen stated: "It shall not be lawful for any freedman, free negro or mulatto to intermarry with any white person; nor for any white person to intermarry with any freedman, free negro or mulatto; and any person who shall so intermarry shall be deemed guilty of a felony, and on conviction thereof, shall be confined in the State penitentiary for life; and those shall be deemed freedmen, free negroes and mulattoes who are of pure negro blood, and those descended from a negro to the third generation, inclusive though one ancestor of each generation may have been a white person."[88] The Act also recognized the relations of those cohabiting as legal unions and recognized the right of the freed to marry, while prohibiting interracial unions. North Carolina declared that "negroes and their issue, even where one ancestor in each succeeding generation to the fourth inclusive, is white, shall be deemed persons of color."

Post–Civil War state statutes included provisions for legalizing black marriage, meting punishment for illicit cohabitation, and prohibiting marriages between white persons and persons of color. In most states, persons having one-eighth Negro or African blood were designated persons of color (but in South Carolina, seven-eighths Caucasian blood deemed one a white person). Although Alabama's code of 1866 claimed to make no distinction on account of color, marriages between whites and blacks were prohibited. Section 4189 of Alabama's code of 1876 imposed harsh punishment for interracial fornication. Florida's 1866 Act Concerning Marriage Licenses recognized interracial marriages that had been previously contracted, but provided "that if any white female resident shall hereafter attempt to intermarry, shall live in a state of adultery or fornication with any negro, mulatto, or other person of color, she shall be

deemed to be guilty of a misdemeanor, and upon conviction shall be
fined a sum not exceeding one thousand dollars, or be confined in
the public jail not exceeding three months, or both, at the discretion
of the jury; and shall, moreover, be disqualified to testify against
any white person." According to the Florida law, to cohabit with a
Negro was to become a Negro and, ultimately, to lose the privilege
of testifying against other whites.

This order of codification and prohibition was not considered discriminatory or a violation of equal protection under the law because
it was believed to be in the service of providential law, nature's
boundaries, and immutable facts of human existence. Marriage was
more than a civil contract; it was a sacred domestic institution controlled by the state's sovereign power. It was within the exercise of
the state's police power, and so the states controlled the institution
of marriage.[89] According to *State v. Gibson* (1871), marriage was a
"public institution established by God himself . . . and is essential
to the peace, happiness, and well-being of society. . . . The right of
all the states to regulate and control, to guard, protect and preserve
this God-given, civilizing and Christianizing institution is of inestimable importance, and cannot be surrendered, nor can the States
suffer or permit any interference therewith."[90] (This case was cited
as a precedent in *Plessy* to confirm the police power of the state and
the constitutionality of prohibiting certain forms of social intercourse between the races.) Similarly, *Green v. State*, which upheld
the constitutionality of Alabama's code against interracial fornication, held: "Marriage is not a mere contract, but a social and domestic institution upon which are founded all society and order, to be
regulated and controlled by the sovereign power for the good of
the State."[91] In asserting the importance of marriage to the well-
being of society, the court described the "*homes* of a people" as the
"true *officinai gentium*—the nurseries of States" (194). *Green v. State*
makes apparent the slippage between the public and the private and

that the state's incursions into the domestic arena are sanctioned as the legitimate exercise of police power.

Antimiscegenation statutes were not considered a violation of the Fourteenth Amendment because these laws presumably were applicable to whites and blacks in an identical manner. It was argued repeatedly that these laws served the "peace and happiness" of the black race as well as the white: "And surely there can not be any tyranny or injustice in requiring both alike to form this union with those of their own race only, whom God hath joined by indelible peculiarities, which declare that he has made the races distinct." Clearly, racial distinctions easily gave way to discrimination, albeit disavowed by the law or ordained by God. In *Pace v. Alabama*, the Supreme Court upheld section 4189 of the Alabama code against interracial fornication because it presumably treated black and white transgressors equally.[92] The linking of racial codification, legitimate union, and state power acted to segregate blacks from the rest of the population and reproduce domination. Life, sexuality, reproduction, blood, and alliance were in the hands of the state. Antimiscegenation cases expose the linkage of race, hygiene, and degeneracy, since the logic that prohibited interracial marriages also prohibited those with hereditary diseases from marrying; in both cases, the restrictions of liberty had in view "the physical well-being of future generations." Such matters were within the police power of the state because the "health of unborn generations [was] a matter of profound concern to the community which may justly assume the guardianship of their interests."[93] The prohibition of interracial marriage, mixed associations, and intimacy across the color line was a prized element of a broader effort intent upon preserving racial order—that is, the vertical hierarchy of life and the relation of mastery and subjection. Maintaining this hierarchy and fragmentation (of the human into racialized groups) was synonymous with the health and prosperity of the population. In *Jones v. Commonwealth*, being a Negro determined the existence of the crime: "To be a negro is not a crime; to marry a white woman is not a crime; but to be a negro, and *being a negro* to marry a white woman is a felony; therefore it is essential to the crime that the accused shall be a negro—unless he is a negro he is guilty of no offense." An earlier indictment had been reversed in part because the whiteness of Jones's wife had not been established by the commonwealth.[94] The slippage between being black and a felon is quite remarkable in this punitive ontology of race. By now it is clear that classification and condition cannot be separated, even in the aftermath of the Thirteenth Amendment. Classification, discrimination, and delimited rights and entitlements were inextricably linked.

Miscegenation statutes protected and preserved the exclusiveness of whiteness as property. As Stephenson in *Racial Distinctions in American Law* tellingly observes: "Miscegenation has never been a bridge upon which one might cross from the Negro race to the Caucasian, though it has been a thoroughfare from the Caucasian to the Negro."[95] The absoluteness of this assertion belies its confidence; to the contrary, it betrays the anxiety of the antimiscegenation mandate and the trepidation that perhaps the thoroughfare permitted black crossings, too. The irony of such reasoning is that while it claims to protect nature's boundaries with the force of positive law, it exposes the laws of nature as rather enfeebled. Despite assertions of omnipotence and divine sanctioning, the laws of nature require state protection and intervention to prevent unnatural and expressly repugnant practices from proliferating. Unmistakably, it is the fear of blacks infiltrating the perhaps permeable border between the races that fosters these statutes; in fact, they are instituted to police these awaited infractions. As we shall see in *Plessy*, these taxonomies produce racial value, such that the reputation of whiteness itself becomes a form of property.

The inordinate fear incited by the threat of miscegenation also must be considered in relation to the revolution in property relations enacted by the Thirteenth Amendment. As a result of the war, Eva Saks notes, Confederate money was worthless; land values dropped; slave property was liberated; there was the threat of land redistribution; and last and most important, "the value of white skin dropped when black skin ceased to signify slave status. However, this racial devaluation would be reversed if white blood could internalize the prewar status of whites over blacks" (47). While miscegenation had increased property under slavery, now it threatened to democratize or expropriate the exclusive property of whiteness, as had emancipation itself by making freedom a right enjoyed by all rather than a racial privilege.[96] The concept of property-in-whiteness is of primary import when examining antimiscegenation statutes, and the gender prescriptions of the state's racial mandate placed white women under intense scrutiny and regulation, meeting sexual transgression with the full force of the law. As the Florida code illustrates, one could, in fact, lose white privilege as a result of associating with blacks.[97] Interracial marriage received stricter punishment than concubinage, which was the usual form of sexual relations between white men and black women; to the contrary, efforts were made to decriminalize concubinage.[98] (All of the aforementioned cases involved black men married to white women.)

The discourse of amalgamation disclosed the rights of property that men exercised over women. If miscegenation jurisprudence was instrumental in stabilizing white property, then women and children, legitimate heirs, were its particular objects of concern. Incontrovertibly, civil rights entailed property in women and children. The challenge was to retain the masculinist prerogatives of the citizen-subject while prohibiting an unqualified extension of these conjugal rights of property across racial lines. Governing the transmission of property-in-whiteness tempered the masculine prerogatives to be enjoyed by black men. Men's sovereignty entailed authority over women and children (and slaves); they were the vessels of his mastery and possession. Extrapolating from the racialized premises of this logic, the possession of white women was made the ultimate figure of manliness. The apprehension about amalgamation exposed the forms of encumbrance constitutive of liberty.[99] Patriarchal uncertainties about legitimate heirs and the rightful transmission of property were exacerbated by the belated arrival of blacks as citizen-subjects. The scandal of black men with white wives verifies the pivotal role of marriage in the reproduction and transmission of property and in the preservation of the social body. The emphasis on the marriage contract tellingly exposes the degree to which men's liberty and equality were premised upon the power exercised over women in the private sphere. The contractual subjugation and possession of women were inseparable from the elaboration of civil rights.

The tenacity of miscegenation as an incitement to reaction exceeded the upheavals of Reconstruction and its aftermath. It was not until 1967 that the Supreme Court found antimiscegenation laws unconstitutional.[100] The maintenance of white supremacy was effected not only through the linkage of sanguinity and sexuality but also through the prevention of all forms of association that formally presumed the equality of races. By prescribing the terms of civil conduct and contact between the races, the relations of mastery and subjection were resurrected. The protection of basic civil rights continued to be perceived as an assault on whiteness and a violation of the natural boundaries between the races. If association inevitably yielded to amalgamation or increased antipathy between the races, what place was there for blacks within the national body? If equal access to public facilities, inns, theaters, railroad cars, bus depots, schools, churches, and cemeteries was an unwanted imposition of social equality rather than the mere guarantee of civil rights, what did the equal protection of the law entail? If equality was premised upon limited forms of association in the public arena and even this restricted association was an incitement to amalgamation, then disenfranchisement and the purification of the social body went hand in hand.[101] Here the body politic acquires an unprecedented literalness, for it was the body, in its obdurate materiality, that was at the nexus of social and civil rights.

The Place of Race

Despite the assurances of individual freedom and equality conveyed by phrases like "neither slavery nor involuntary servitude shall exist within the United States" and "no state shall abridge the privileges and immunities of citizens," racial classifications produced subjection, albeit disguised by nature, sentiment, health, or prosperity. The actual conditions of things as honed by centuries of chattel slavery exposed the chasm separating the ideals of equality from their consummation. As *Roberts v. City of Boston*, a pre–Civil War school desegregation case cited as a precedent in *Plessy*, held:

> [Equal before the law] as a broad general principle, such as ought to appear in a declaration of rights, is perfectly sound; it is not only expressed in terms, but pervades and animates the whole spirit of our constitution of free government. But, when this great principle comes to be applied to the actual and various conditions of persons in society, it will not warrant the assertion, that men and women are legally clothed with the same civil and political powers, and that children and adults are legally to have the same functions and subject to the same treatment; but only that the rights of all, as they are settled and regulated by law, are equally entitled to the paternal consideration and protection of the law, for their maintenance and security. What those rights are, to which individuals, in

the infinite variety of circumstances by which they are surrounded in society, are entitled, must depend on laws adapted
to their respective relations and conditions.[102]

If the actual condition of things did not warrant men and women
and blacks and whites enjoy equality before the law, then what did
equal protection confer? Equivalent rights fixed these "respective
conditions" by sanctioning distinctions of race, by avowing the
chasm between the great principle of "equal before the law" and the
actual and various conditions of persons in society.[103]

This vexed conception of equality augured the Court's assessment
in Plessy, which was not inevitable. The Constitution had abolished
the status-race of slavery, but black subordination was sustained
by naturalizing the major incident of slavery—the burden of race.
The cogency of blackness as a legal classification was inseparable
from the captivity putatively annulled by the Thirteenth Amendment. The law's recognition of purportedly natural categories like
race, blood, and affinity denied the constitutive role of the law in
the making and consolidation of these categories. In fact, it was
the declared neutrality of race as a legal category that effectively
perpetuated this legacy for another century. The racial taxonomies
inhabiting the law, whether in the terms of property, criminality, or
contagion, maintained white dominance and belied declarations of
formal equality.[104] As the attorneys for Homer A. Plessy insisted,
classification per se was offensive and "an injury to any citizen of
the United States as such."[105]

While anticipated by Roberts v. City of Boston, the ease with which
invidious and regulatory racial classifications were embraced by
equal protection discourse is noteworthy in the post-emancipation
context. If the citation of Roberts and other pre–Civil War cases
in the majority opinion of Plessy v. Ferguson attests to the longevity of antebellum attitudes toward blacks and neglects the changes

instituted by emancipation, it similarly confirms the hesitancy or fragility of the law as compared with the durability of sentiment. The law, seemingly powerless, retreats in the face of sentiment. In acquiescing to the sway of sentiment, *Plessy* echoed *Roberts*: "Prejudice, if it exists, is not created by the law and cannot be changed by the law." Yet if the law cannot change prejudice, is its role to affirm it, to succumb to its authority? Following this logic to its end, it appeared that "simple chattelism" was only to be supplanted by legal subjection to (the antipathy of) the dominant race. For the progeny of the *Civil Rights Cases* and *Plessy* was a governed population that exercised tentative claims to citizenship and was denied the equal protection of the law. The slippery logic that gave rise to this gutted conception of freedom contended that racial discrimination was not a badge of slavery; in short, the enduring condition of black subjection had nothing to do with slavery. It was claimed that these racial taxonomies were neutral and noninjurious, and thus they bore no relation to the degradation of slavery. The reasonableness of racial classifications reached its grotesque apogee in *Plessy v. Ferguson*, and the spatial segregation sanctioned in this case must be situated within the negrophobic (or antiblack) obsession with health and security that infused antimiscegenation statutes. Sentiment, instinct, aversion, and affinity were called upon to justify the wedding of perfect equality and racial distinctions. In the post-emancipation context, antipathy, rather than mutuality and reciprocity as had been the case in slave law, determined the terms of relations allowed and prohibited by law. Ironically, the separate but equal doctrine could only be annulled by the development of mutuality and reciprocity. The interpretation of rights and the separation of public and private domains enabled equivalent rights to substitute for equal protection.

The social looms above all else in the melding of equality and exclusion. The social is an amorphous and mutable domain that overlaps the divisions of family, civil society, and the state; it is a crisis category that designates the slippage of the public and the private and the "intrusion" of the bodily—health, hunger, cohabitation, and reproduction—into the public space of politics. The law's constitutive recognition of the social—in particular the dominion of racial differences, corporeal impulses, natural instincts, and aversive feelings—authorized the violation of rights inaugurated by the separate but equal doctrine. At the outer reaches of the law, "just and perfect inequality held forth in the social."

The relations of mastery and servitude formally annulled by the Thirteenth Amendment were remade through presumably neutral ascriptions of race. The "perpetual and impassable barrier" between "the white race and the one which they had reduced to slavery" that Taney insisted upon in *Dred Scott*, resuscitated in the post-emancipation context, instituted modern relations of servility and subjugation. However, unlike *Dred Scott*, which held that blacks were "beings of an inferior order, and altogether unfit to associate with the white race either in social or political relations," *Plessy* did not insist that blacks be excluded from the body politic, but upheld the idea of proper associations between the races, instead of an enforced equality that imposed unwanted proximity; it endorsed the spatial arrangements of the separate but equal doctrine and the partition erected by immutable difference. This decidedly post-emancipation solution entailed both the casting out and the incorporation of blacks.[106] *Plessy* recognized limited rights enjoyed by blacks and abjured the language of inferiority and subjugation, and yet sustained the relations of mastery and servitude by declaring them equal. The affirmation of the separate but equal doctrine was intended to avoid and minimize the repulsion and antagonism between the races, which was fostered by compulsory association. This homeopathic approach prevented the escalation of racial antipathy through the stigmatization of blackness. In the following reading of *Plessy v. Ferguson*, it is not my intention to establish the inevitability of the separate but equal doctrine, nor to gloss over the discontinuities between Reconstruction and its aftermath, but rather to interrogate the continuities between antebellum and postbellum figurations of blackness as a degraded and abject category and the sentimental solutions of the "Negro problem."[107]

Plessy v. Ferguson

On June 7, 1892, Homer A. Plessy boarded an intrastate passenger train in Louisiana and took a seat in a coach designated for white passengers. When questioned by the conductor as to his race, Plessy responded that he was colored. The conductor demanded that he move to the coach assigned to the colored race or be removed from the train and imprisoned.[108] Plessy refused to comply with the conductor's order and was expelled from the train and arrested. At issue in *Plessy v. Ferguson* was the Louisiana statute that required railway companies to provide separate but equal accommodations for white and colored passengers. The statute also provided that "no person shall be permitted to occupy seats in coaches other than the ones assigned to them, on account of the race they belong to." Plessy boarded the coach with the intention of defying the statute. The plaintiff challenged the constitutionality of the act because it was in violation of the Thirteenth and Fourteenth Amendments and argued that racial distinctions were social placeholders that reproduced the legal subjection of blacks. As reflected in the Louisiana statute, this place-keeping measure reduced blacks to the condition of a subject race and reinforced the stigmatic construction of blackness.

In the words of the brief filed for Plessy by Albion Tourgée, "This act is intended to keep the negro in his place.... Instead of being intended to promote the general comfort and moral well-being, this

act is plainly and evidently intended to promote the happiness of
one class by asserting its supremacy and the inferiority of another
class."[109] Although the majority denied that this assignment of place
"stamp[ed] the colored race with the badge of inferiority," blacks
were remanded to their proper place and forced to remain there.
This insidious ascription of place under the guise of equality resurrected the subjugation of slavery. As Tourgée argued, the definitive
characteristic of American slavery was the slave's bondage to the
entire white race as well as his owner. It was this subjection to the
dominant race individually and collectively that had been abolished
by the Thirteenth Amendment. It was meant to "undo all that slavery had done in establishing race discrimination and collective as
well as personal control of the enslaved race."[110]

The Court insisted that such an interpretation was fallacious and
not supported "by reason of anything found in the act, but solely
because the colored race chooses to put their construction upon it."
Likewise, the Court dismissed the argument that racial discrimination constituted a badge of slavery by reiterating the majority opinion
in the *Civil Rights Cases*: "The Thirteenth Amendment has respect,
not to distinctions of race, class, or color, but to slavery," and "it
would be running the badges of slavery argument into the ground
to make it apply to every act of discrimination."[111] The Court narrowly argued that "slavery implies involuntary servitude—a state
of bondage; the ownership of mankind as chattel, or at least the
control of labor and services of one man for the benefit of another,
and the absence of legal right to the disposal of his own person,
property and services" (542). By defining slavery primarily as chattelism, plain and simple, the subjection of blacks fundamental to
slavery and the antebellum social order, as well as the public nature
of the institution, was denied, enabling the Court to conclude that
legal distinctions between the white and colored races had "no tendency to destroy the legal equality of the two races, or reestablish a

state of involuntary servitude" (543). This interpretation of slavery sanctioned segregation precisely by minimizing the scope of slavery, denying its extant legacy and its racial character, and intensifying its badges and incidents.

The majority contended that the badges-of-slavery argument was fallacious because it assumed that social equality could be imposed by the unwelcome proximity of the races. The choice of the term "social equality" transposed the contested issue of civil equality into one of unfit association and settled the matter through this sleight of hand. As evidenced in everyday practice, the social rights of the white race depended upon segregation.[112] Health, happiness, prosperity, and comfort could only be secured by preventing "offensive contact" with Negroes. Yet the Court insisted upon the fairness of the statute because it provided for the equivalent treatment of the races, as though the symmetry of the statute itself prevented injurious and degrading effects. The Court speculated that if the situation were reversed and the colored race were dominant in the state legislature and enacted a law in precisely similar terms, the white race would not acquiesce to this assumption of inferiority. One can only surmise that this imagined reversal was intended to establish the neutrality of racial distinctions and the reversibility of racist reason, thereby denying the deleterious construction of blackness and the remaking of a servile class effected through this neutrality or equivalent treatment.

The codification of race in the law secured the subjection of blacks and prescribed the terms of interracial conduct and association, despite protestations to the contrary. Blackness became the primary badge of slavery because of the burdens, disabilities, and assumptions of servitude abidingly associated with this racial scripting of the body; inversely, whiteness became "the most valuable sort of property" and the "master-key that unlock[ed] the golden door of opportunity."[113] The Louisiana statute imposed the badges of slavery; it interfered with the personal liberty and full enjoyment of the entitlements of freedom and regulated the civil rights common to all citizens on the basis of race. Undoubtedly, it placed blacks in a condition of legal inferiority (563). The badges of slavery argument advanced by the attorneys for Plessy and in the dissenting opinion of Justice John Marshall Harlan refuted the purported neutrality of racial distinctions and held that racial classifications produced "caste-distinctions" or a superior and inferior race among citizens.

The Louisiana statute placed blacks in a condition of inferiority. It accomplished this not merely by the designation of a physical location, a seat in a particular railroad car. In directing individuals to separate cars, the conductor, in effect, assigned racial identity, a peril that did not go unmentioned by the Court and which was at the heart of Plessy's challenge. On what basis and with what authority could a conductor assign race? Was not such assignment and assortment based on race a perpetuation of the essential features of slavery? Moreover, what did it mean to assign race when race exceeded the realm of the visually verifiable? Tourgée's brief emphasized the instability of race and asserted the codification of race was purely in service of white dominance. In questioning why Homer Plessy should not be allowed to enjoy the reputation of whiteness, Tourgée asked: "By what rule then shall any tribunal be guided in determining racial character? It may be said that all those should be classed as colored in whom appears a visible admixture of colored blood. By what law? With what justice? Why not count everyone as white in whom is visible any trace of white blood? There is but one reason to wit, the domination of the white race." Blood functioned as the metaphysical title to racial property.[114] Yet as there was no actual way to measure blood, the tangled lines of genealogy and association, more accurately, the prohibition of association, determined racial identity. If inheritance determined identity (and what could be more appropriate than inheritance in naming the law's production of racial subjects given the transmutation of blood into property?), then it opened the golden door of opportunity for those able to enjoy the reputation of whiteness and disenfranchised those unable to legally claim title to whiteness.

While it has been claimed that the plaintiff's line of reason was intent on little more than granting those visibly of mixed race the full benefits of whiteness, the argument was much more ambitious in its reach. In arguing that the reputation of being white was property, that whiteness possessed actual pecuniary value, and that the current rules for its distribution were simply in service of maintaining black subordination, Tourgée overreached the simple demand for a more flexible and encompassing category of whiteness (as was the case in the Caribbean and Latin America) and instead demonstrated the degree to which race, class, and caste continued to be shaped by slavery. The exclusivity of whiteness was identified as the essential ingredient in reproducing black degradation. The uncertainty of reading race, the arbitrariness of its assignment, the withholding of whiteness and its privileges, and the damage inflicted by this fixing of race were issues raised by Plessy's challenge.

The preservation of racial integrity and the attendant enforcement of racial legibility required the constant examination of bodies for visible inscriptions of blackness. However, as in the case of Plessy himself, these racial signs sometimes were misread or failed to be detected, since "the mixture of colored blood was not discernible in him" (538). If blackness was no longer visually discernible, then how was racial integrity to be preserved? While the Court ignored Plessy's claim to whiteness, it did concede that whiteness was a property that commanded distinct entitlements. The majority opinion in *Plessy* strove to secure racial meanings through a realignment of status, property, and rights, specifically by limiting who may be considered white, affirming that the reputation of whiteness was property and protecting its exclusivity through the sanctions of law. The Court affirmed the value of whiteness while admitting the uncertainty that attended the reading and fixing of race.

Those who attempted to defy conscription into this system of racial assignment risked a more permanent placement, since would-be trespassers faced fines, expulsion, and/or incarceration. The Louisiana statute decided who would enjoy the entitlements of whiteness and, by extension, the universal rights of citizens. Although the language of the statute addressed the assignment of black and white passengers, it was the passageway to the "other race," to whiteness, that was being patrolled. The third section of the statute indicated this: "Nothing in this act shall be construed as to apply to nurses attending children of the other race." The subject of the statute was implicitly the colored race, as opposed to the "other race." Entering the "other" coach in defiance of one's assigned place meant assuming an identity that one did not legitimately possess, the charge made against Plessy, or having one's property rights in whiteness violated, as Plessy claimed. Having been accused of forcing himself into the company of a "race to which he did not belong," despite his seven-eighths Caucasian blood, Plessy countered that he had been deprived of his property in whiteness—that is, the reputation of belonging to the white race. He contended "he was entitled to every right, privilege and immunity secured to citizens of the U.S. of the white race."[115]

While the Court agreed with Plessy's assertion that the reputation of belonging to the white race was property, it waffled on the issue of race. It conceded the risk involved in determining the race of passengers and the variant constructions of white and colored persons under particular state laws; however, it endorsed the necessity of this peril. The Court failed to adjudicate the matter of Plessy's claim to whiteness, thus settling the matter of race by assuming he was a colored man. Despite the efforts of the plaintiff to trouble the matter of race, the varied definitions of race across state statutes, and the difficulty of visually discerning or verifying race in given instances, the Court continued to consider race substantial and, ultimately, knowable. Plessy had contested the givenness of race through an enactment of the varied registers of racial ascription. (His visibly white skin enabled his entry into the white car. Yet, when asked by the conductor about his race, he admitted that he was colored and that he was unwilling to move to the Negro car. He filed a petition for writ of error in which he refused to aver his race or color in the plea, and he claimed the right to enjoy the reputation of being white.) By asserting that whiteness was a property denied him by virtue of the conductor's action and the Louisiana statute, Plessy demonstrated the degree to which the deprivation of civil rights and the truncated personal liberty of blacks were essential to white privilege. For the Court, race ultimately remained a fixed and stable attribute despite the reluctant acknowledgment of occasional indeterminacy.[115] Race was made the foundation upon which the disputed terms—"equality," "privileges of citizenship," and "liberty"—were decided. As Barbara Fields notes, race was "the ideological medium through which people posed and apprehended basic questions of power and dominance, sovereignty and citizenship, justice and right."[117]

Since race was considered foundational and immutable, the Court argued: "A statute which implies merely a legal distinction between the white and colored races—a distinction which is founded in the color of the two races, and which must always exist so long as white men are distinguished from the other race by color—has no tendency to destroy the legal equality of the two races, or reestablish a state of involuntary servitude." However, the conundrum in *Plessy* was precisely that the plaintiff's color did not distinguish him from the white race. The role of the state in the creation of a subjected race was disavowed by this "mere"

recognition of extant differences. As the Court stated, the "absolute equality of the two races before the law" established by the
Fourteenth Amendment was not intended to abolish distinctions of
race or to "enforce social, as distinguished from political, equality,
or a commingling of the two races upon terms unsatisfactory to
either" (543).

The introduction of the issue of social equality fostered the enjoyment, happiness, and comfort of members of the dominant race at
the expense of the rights and liberties allegedly guaranteed to all
citizens. If equal access to public facilities imposed social equality,
a compulsory association considered offensive by those forced into
contact with the inferior race, then, as Tourgée pointed out, why
were black nurses not carriers of contagion: "If color breeds contagion in a railway coach, why exempt nurses from the operation
of the Act?"[118] Why did their presence not pose the same danger
to moral order and public health? The provision regarding black
nurses made clear that the mingling of the races was allowed when
it replicated the stratified association of slavery and preserved the
hierarchy of dominant and superior races articulated by the statute's assortment of bodies. As underlings, nurses did not upset the
configurations of mastery and servitude, or the spatial articulation
of superiority and abjection established by this legal codification of
race. Yet even this exception was made only in the case of children,
perhaps because of the necessary proximity of the wet nurse and
the physical intimacy required for this availing of the body. The only
forms of intimacy and association sanctioned were those in service
of white comfort and mastery. As Cable observed in "The Negro
Question," fundamentally, the race line sustained relations of mastery and subordination: "The entire essence of the offense, any and
everywhere where the race line is insisted on, is the apparition of the
colored man or woman as his or her own master; that mastery is all
that this tyranny is intended to preserve, and that the moment the

relation of master and slave is visibly established between race and race there is the hush of peace."[119]

The "reasonableness" of race as a legal classification was animated by anxieties about black equality, the end of white sovereignty, social proximity, and degrading contact. Interracial association posed special dangers when blacks were no longer chattel property and were cloaked with the ephemeral endowment of civil equality. Segregation and exclusion became the strategies employed to quell the fears incited by equality and to preserve mastery. The legal barrier erected between racially marked bodies, under the aegis of social rights, endorsed this compulsory separation of individuals and populations on the grounds that the Louisiana statute was reasonable and promoted the public good. The reasonableness of the statute was determined in reference to "established usages, customs and traditions of the people, and with a view to the promotion of their comfort, and the preservation of the public peace and good order." This antiquated veneration of custom and tradition resuscitated the past in a nostalgic articulation of slavery and its incidents; indeed, it revived the spirit of *Dred Scott*. However, the post-emancipation compromise of *Plessy* emphasized "voluntary consent" and appreciation rather than degradation or repulsion. It confirmed the banishment and exclusion of black citizenry on the basis of unfit and unwanted associations. According to Harlan, the majority opinion resurrected *Dred Scott* by creating "a dominant race—a superior class of citizens, which assumes to regulate the enjoyment of civil rights, common to all citizens, upon the basis of race."[120] In an interesting inversion of slave law, here the lack of mutuality and shared appreciation necessitated the separate but equal doctrine. The centuries of reciprocity and mutual goodwill that legally sanctioned the violence of *State v. Mann*, while morally reproving it, had evaporated in two short decades of freedom. This antipathy prodded the state to intervene in the intercourse of its citizens. Both its willingness and inability to intervene coincided with the interest and desires of the "dominant race."

The Louisiana statute fell within the broad police power of the state; it protected the public good by sustaining and condoning legal subjection. As decided in *Plessy*, the general prosperity and health of the public compelled the separation of the races. From this vantage point, the state was enforcing segregation less than maintaining the happiness and health of its citizenry by subordinating the law to natural sentiment and protecting custom and comfort. The exercise of the state's police power superseded the matter of individual civil rights and licensed this violation of individual rights on behalf of a greater good. The exercise of police power by the state of Louisiana was considered reasonable since it was "enacted in good faith for the promotion of the public good, and not for the annoyance or oppression of a particular class" (550). Police power, as defined in *Black's Law Dictionary*, entailed "the power of the state to place restraints on the personal freedom and property rights of persons for the protection of public safety, health, and morals or the promotion of the public convenience and general prosperity."[121] In short, police power legitimated the restriction and regulation of liberty and property in the name of the public welfare and the health and prosperity of the population. As formulated in the *Slaughter-House Cases*, this power extended "to the protection of lives, limbs, health, comfort and quiet of all persons, and the protection of all property within the State; . . . and persons and property are subjected to all kinds of restraints and burdens in order to secure the general comfort, health, and prosperity of the State."[122] One senator even went so far as to suggest that the proper exercise of police power by the state dictated "legislating in relation to the prejudices of a people . . . not to legislate against their prejudices."[123] As Pasquale Pasquino notes, the exercise of police power constitutes the population as its object. The science of police power constitutes and fashions the social body. The extensive reach of this power, which is one of its defining characteristics, is evidenced in the "plethora of petty details and minor concerns." Key in thinking about the enactment of withholding by the state is Pasquino's observation that police powers are "sort of spontaneous creations of law or rather of a demand for order which outreaches the law."[124] In this regard, it is interesting to note the Court's divergent assessments of the legitimate uses of police power regarding matters of class and race. In the arena of labor relations, measures to protect the working class were regarded as invidious forms of social regulation that violated the liberty of contract. Yet the violation of liberty by racist state statutes was held to be reasonable and legitimate. At issue here is the inventiveness of the law, the ambiguity that shrouds what is within reach of the law, and what exceeds it.

As determined by the Louisiana statute and the majority opinion in *Plessy*, the health, safety, public good, and comfort of citizens were predicated upon the banishment and exclusion of blacks from the public domain. If the public good was inseparable from the security and self-certainty of whiteness, then segregation was the prophylactic against this feared bodily threat and intrusion. Harlan rightly warned that this fear would lead to further violations of civil rights: "May it not now be reasonably expected that astute men of the dominant race, who affect to be disturbed at the possibility that the *integrity of the white race* may be corrupted, or that its supremacy will be imperiled, by contact on public highways with black people, will endeavor to procure statutes requiring white and black jurors to be separated in the jury box by a partition" [emphasis mine]. The integrity of the white race delineated the public good. The identification of the health and comfort of the populace with white supremacy, as Harlan forewarned, did result in further violations of rights and only intensified the repulsion and aversive sentiment said to be contained by such measures. More-over, if one of the central aims of police power was establishing public happiness, then the links between white comfort and black suffering were reestablished in the context of emancipation. The police power of the state, as invoked in *Plessy*, basically created "biologized internal enemies," and the concern for the public good authorized the state's imposition of burdens and constraints. Of course, protecting "society" from defiling contact, contagion, and dissolution justified all.[125] In this instance, police power was little more than the benevolent articulation of state racism in the name of the public good. The identification of the state with its subjects was inseparable from the process of creating internal enemies against which the comfort and prosperity of the populace could be defended. The affiliation of happiness and subjection and pros-perity and exclusion gave shape to a social body characterized by isolated and stigmatized internal aliens and the illusory integrity of the dominant race.[126] Basically, the wholeness of the social body was made possible by the segregation and abjection of blacks, the isolation of dangerous elements from the rest of the population and the containment of contagion.

The invocation of the police power of the state eclipsed issues of equal protection and individual rights. Safety and sentiment over-shadowed equality and liberty in the discussion of the public good. The concern with health, association, and happiness displaced the issue of civil rights with that of social rights. The separation of civil, political, and social rights in nineteenth-century culture legitimated domination and precarious or impaired citizenship. This definition of rights generally acted to constrict and qualify liberty and equal-ity. Economic rights were limited to the liberty of contract; rights beyond this were frowned upon and considered sinister efforts at class legislation.[127] For example, although citizens enjoyed privileges and immunities, inclusive of basic civil rights and constitutional rights, citizenship did not imply or confer an equality of political rights. Women were citizens but could neither vote nor sit on juries. Married women had restricted property rights and could not establish contracts without the permission of their husbands. Social rights were exempt from all claims of equality, since they concerned matters designated as private and/or intimate. As Mark Tushnet observes, "government had nothing to do with guaranteeing social rights except to enforce those rights guaranteed by the common law."[128] Yet the state was involved with questions of social rights to the extent they were enmeshed with police power. For example, interracial marriages were prohibited on the grounds that marriage was a social right, not a civil right; therefore, the Civil Rights Act of 1866 and the Fourteenth Amendment did not protect this right of contract. The alliance of social rights with police power hinted at the role of the state within the domain of the social. The "interests of the future generations of the republic to come" were in the hands of the state.

The isolation of social rights from civil and political rights enabled the subordination and exclusion of black citizens by declaring racial distinctions and the feelings of fear and hatred that issued from these distinctions as natural and outside the scope of the law. Although basic civil rights were considered the rights one enjoyed in a state of nature—the right to personal freedom, to labor and enjoy the fruits of one's labor, to hold property, to enter into contracts, to marry and protect one's household, to own one's person, and to move about—the social, as defined by the majority in the *Civil Rights Cases* and *Plessy*, undermined civil rights and personal liberties. For example, being denied access to public facilities, institutions, or accommodations or being denied the enjoyment of basic rights was to be countenanced because these relations unbelievably fell into the purview of the strictly private, and an unbound power of discretion guarded the "just inequality" of private society.[129] The

Civil Rights Act of 1875 and other efforts to enforce equality were derailed by designations of the private, an encroaching and mutable sphere impervious to the rule of law. The Civil Rights Act of 1875 was found unconstitutional because it "imposed" rules for individual conduct: "It steps into the domain of local jurisprudence, and lays down rules for the conduct of individuals in society toward each other, and imposes sanctions for the enforcement of those rules."[130] Of course, segregation established rules for the civil conduct of individuals; however, it posed no dangers to the local order. Inherent in this conception of social rights was an understanding of individual and social relations as bifurcated by public and private domains and ruled by custom, prejudice, desire, and nature, rather than by lofty principles like equality. Consequently, the boundaries of the private were fiercely contested. As Justice Harlan insisted in opposition to the majority, the issue at hand in *Plessy* and the *Civil Rights Cases* was the civil rights, not the social rights, of citizens. Since inns, railroads, other conveyances, and places of amusement exercised a "public function and wield power and authority under the state," they were within the scope of the Fourteenth Amendment.[131]

An Asylum of Inequality

The nineteenth-century social is best described as an asylum of inequality, for the practices and relations allowed to flourish in this domain were liberated from the most nominal commitment to equality. Properly speaking, the social was beyond the reach of the state and exempt from its intervention. However, closer inspection reveals less an autonomous zone than an arena of messy, contradictory, and clandestine practices binding the state and its purported other, the private. The state of Louisiana's role in the creation of subordinated and stigmatized subjects was disguised by the power attributed to sentiment; at the national level, the federal government reinforced the white supremacist laws of the states by recourse to the separation of powers, state sovereignty, and declared noninterference. The recognition of sentiment and affinity disavowed the state's role in enabling "the just inequality" of the private to flourish and the governance of the social exercised through police power. The state refused to intervene in the private by declaring it a law-free and voluntary sphere, yet the state was already there and actively governing the conduct of individuals.[132] This retreat of the state before the private permitted and encouraged the subordination of blacks, while this putative noninvolvement upheld white supremacy. Aversive sentiment rather than state policy or the Court was held responsible for this separation and isolation of blacks from the rest of the population. The innocence of the law (it did not create prejudice and thus could not change it) and the state (it merely protected the public safety and promoted the general prosperity) was maintained by denying the public and structural character of racism and attributing prejudice to individual prerogatives.

An elastic construction of the private granted relations of exploitation and domination immunity from the state's interference, but, in fact, the state produced and sanctioned these relations by naturalizing them and declaring them outside the reach of law. Put differently, the construction of the private sustained and reproduced subjection through this division of social existence. Quite unlike the sphere of liberty it was presumed to be, the private was a sphere in which inequality, subordination, and exploitation reigned. Rather than accept the bifurcated construction of social existence drawn by liberalism, in which the private signifies individual autonomy and the public the infringement of this putative autonomy, these terms are contingent and partisan constructions of social life rather than disinterested explanatory terms. Instead, the public and the private need to be considered provisional designations within an ensemble of shifting, interconnected, and overlapping social relations and institutions, which cannot be distilled into discrete and independent components without the risk of reductionism or obfuscation; neither free will nor inconvenience adequately depicts the social organization of space, bodies, and power.

Plessy discloses the extent to which the construction of the private and the social as a "law-free and voluntary sphere of society" facilitates the unavowed regulatory politics of the state and sustains domination through the freedom of association.[133] By far, the set of interests protected by the shield of the private were ruling interests, although masked by the public good, equivalent rights, racial instincts, and the voluntary consent of individuals. As Neil Gotanda argues, the expansion of the private released providers of public service and amusement from the common-law duty of providing for the public if it required them to serve blacks. In this regard, the incorporation of the public by the private was inextricably linked to absented and banished blacks. The court created a protected sphere that secured white enjoyment from black encroachments by invoking and confounding the distinctions between the private and the public. For precisely this reason, the social cannot be reduced to the private; to the contrary, it elides and blurs the distinction between public and private. Its noncoincidence with the family, civil society, and the state delineates the particularity of this domain.[134]

By transposing the matter of civil rights into a question of social rights, the decision elevated sentiment and custom above constitutional principle, endorsed "racial instincts," and validated the inferiority of blacks, since even the Constitution was powerless to put them on the same plane as whites. In this fashion, the racial discriminations Harlan assessed as "steps towards reducing blacks to a subject race" were declared compatible with equal protection.[135]

To quote the majority opinion: "If two races are to meet upon the terms of social equality, it must be the result of natural affinities, a mutual appreciation of each other's merit, and the voluntary consent of individuals." The terms of mutuality espoused here characterize the idealized arrangements of private society. But the elaboration of this mutuality precludes interracial association and disavows the proscription of conduct lauded as freedom of association. Similarly, it presumes that preferences and affinities are unchanging. To impose equality or enforce "commingling" allegedly jeopardized the public peace and good order, if not the equilibrium of nature itself. As a consequence, aversive natural affinities were endowed with the status of law. As avouched by the Court, the law was powerless before racial instincts and immutable differences. The management of bodies and populations proceeded under the cover of nature or "natural affinities," despite feigned declarations of the state's weakness in the face of instinct. As it turned out, the invocation of nature merely cloaked the state's own obsession with blood, sound procreation, racial integrity, and social intercourse. It elevated white need and enjoyment to the status of public good.

The social, according to Nancy Fraser, is "the site where successfully politicized runaway needs get translated into claims for government provision."[136] Yet the needs provided for in the state's exercise of police power and sustained by *Plessy* are those incited by anxieties of contamination and dissolution and given shape by desires for purity and fears of amalgamation. What occurs in the context of the social is precisely the politicization of bodily processes and corporeal impulses in the service of white supremacy and black subjection. Again, it is notable that the particular entry of these private needs into public view invigorates racism as it occludes other kinds of needs from coming into view—in particular, demands for economic security and other types of sustenance, such as food, shelter, and education, essential to preserving life. The social, as configured along the lines of white sovereignty and black servility, thwarted an emancipatory articulation of needs and an effort to meet them. Need, like the health and prosperity of the population, was enmeshed with racism and the runaway longings of the master race. All of which was harbored within taxonomies of the private, the domestic, and the market.[137]

It is interesting to observe the manner in which arbitrary and sound distinctions undergo an inversion as they cross the divide between the public and the private, for racist antipathy and aversion were considered providential and just in private society. The traversals of reasonable and injurious distinctions document the extent to which the social is a malleable category that strives to "fix" the inevitable slippage of the public and the private and to confine and exclude those envisioned as infectious, aberrant, dangerous, and dependent. In effect, the social names a crisis and strives to alleviate it through categorical (re)solutions, usually by readjusting the boundaries of the public and the private that determine the state's duties and responsibilities in deciding whether the distinctions, classifications, and taxonomies at issue are reasonable, neutral, or injurious. The nature of association and the state's jurisdiction are irrevocably enmeshed. In a similar fashion, the classifying of behaviors—in this case, the *kind* of contact in question—whether it was appropriate, protected, or befouling, fell within the purview of the social.

While Harlan summarily dismissed the issue of the social by declaring it extraneous to the matter under consideration, he did address the issue of sentiment, specifically race hatred: "What can more certainly arouse race hate, what [can] more certainly create and perpetuate a feeling of distrust between the races, than state enactments, which, in fact, proceed on the ground that colored citizens are so inferior and degraded that they cannot be allowed to sit in public coaches occupied by white citizens?"[138] Cable, also fearing the sentiments aroused by these insidious distinctions, warned that the color line and segregation imposed unwanted association and that civil equality was the greatest safeguard of private society and natural affinity.[139] It was the tangle of state and society that underlay Cable's annoyance about the shared etymology of social and society. In "The Negro Question," he notes the unfortunate resemblance between the two and the difficulty of discussing society without the social entering the picture. Conscious of this muddle, he argues that the social, which inevitably stands as an abbreviation for the nefarious issue of social equality, should not be confused with society at large. It is this confusion that has led to the separation and exclusion of blacks from the public sphere and civil society. In expressing his frustration about the high cost of this ambiguity, it is clear that Cable longs for a free space, a space of desire and affinity ruled only by nature and free from all interventions and impositions, whether the enforcements of caste or equality, and tacitly acknowledges the impossibility of its actualization. The intrusions of the state signify the violation of natural laws by arbitrary power. We need to ask why the issue of society was so unsettling. The discomfort generally aroused by the issue of social equality was the fear of miscegenation and being blackened by way of unwanted association. However, this does not seem to be the case with Cable, since he is so confirmed in his belief about natural inclinations and disinclinations that he fears only the color line will encourage the aberrant in its violation of natural affinities.

The presence of the state is so unsettling because it imperils the category of the natural, not only with the obvious interference of arbitrary power, but also because the state in fact may be what secures and nurtures the natural rather than its other. After all, did not the fluid boundary between that within and without the state only expose the randomness of what were thought to be providential arrangements, but were actually without foundation? Certainly, this would threaten beloved sentimental possessions—the certitude of desire, the "impassable barrier" between the races, maybe even the existence of natural affinities. Although unwelcome, would it become apparent that these preferences were sustainable only by virtue of violence or its threats? In other words, Cable's consternation is directed at a kind of Gramscian behemoth that augments its power through the accretions of family, church, and civil institutions.[140]

Was the state separate from private society? Or, more to the heart of the matter, what autonomy did the private enjoy? This is precisely the question begged and belabored by the issue of social rights. Arguably, private society was "personal, selective, associative, [it] ignore[d] civil equality without violating it, and [was] form[ed] entirely upon mutual private preferences and affinities," and for Cable, these preferences and affinities discouraged the mixing of "dissimilar races."[141] What separated Cable from advocates of racial segregation was the certainty, at least as publicly proclaimed, that preference and affinity alone would prevent degrading mixture; thus there was no need for civil distinctions or regulations. (Again, the issue of disavowal raises its thorny head. What was responsible for this unlikely confidence that natural affinity alone prevented "foul mixture"? Or was Cable simply involved in the rhetorical enactment of rebuke?)

Quite striking in *Plessy* was the leeway granted the affinities and desires of the white citizen in the state's (local and national) simultaneous anointment of segregation and self-immolation. Put differently, the state's enactment of withholding and noninterference not only licensed the inequalities sustained in the sphere of the social but, indeed, also nurtured them. The retreat or noninterference of the state in matters of social rights cloaked the regulatory role of the state in the production and reproduction of racism, or natural affinities, to borrow the language of *Plessy*. The greedy reach of the social encompassed the state and civil society, since the rights of citizens and the personal liberty of the individual were intruded upon by the Louisiana statute and *Plessy*, which annexed the public sphere under the umbrella of social rights. Even if the sanctity of the private permitted the citizen to enjoy "just inequality" without guilt or needless worry about imposing a badge of slavery by refusing to invite a Negro into one's parlor, the free rein of inequality spilled into other territories and had as its cost the restriction of liberty, even for whites. For example, one could not choose a partner from the other race even if one so desired. Ultimately, liberty was defined at the expense of those marred and disfigured by racial distinction and segregated from the rest of society.

The social was a murky, unstable, and mutable arena of the state's disavowed activities, and it, in turn, defined the duties and concerns of the state, although primarily by negation. Within this shadowy realm, the state managed bodies and policed needs and desires. As elaborated in the *Civil Rights Cases* and *Plessy*, the social designated a particular crisis and/or transformation of the public and the private that resulted in the privatization or domestic incorporation of the public realm.[142] Generally, questions of social rights involve the duties or nonduties of the state.[143] While officially designated as an autonomous realm beyond or immune to the intervention of the state, to the contrary, the social was the site of intense state involvement. Perhaps this is best explained as the law's excess—that is, as a domain outside the state and deeply entangled with it. Production and concealment operate here in tandem. The social organized relations and practices in a fashion that ensconced inequalities and delegitimated and valorized particular interests, desires, acts, and longings. It was a transactional zone that defined the scope and limitation of state intervention in matters deemed private, intimate, and domestic.[144]

Social rights not only protected the realm of private relations from state interference and licensed a range of oppressive and exploitative relations, but also annexed and colonized the public sphere. (If we bear this in mind, challenges to the inequities sanctioned in this domain and the demand for remedies cannot simply seek solution in state intervention, since the state is already there and plays a formative role in the production of these inequities. Instead, remedy depends upon the disaggregation of the private, exposing its overdetermination by the state and making legible its ascription of the state's duties.)[145] An estrangement or defamiliarization of nature and instinct is necessary to target the normalizing strategies obscured by "natural affinities." In the case of *Plessy*, it first had to be established that these aversive relations or natural affinities defied broader constitutional principles and could not coexist within the frame of rights and privileges conferred by such principles, and that they were in violation of basic civil rights.[146] The separate but equal doctrine sanctioned an equivalent notion of rights that accorded symmetrical or commensurate treatment rather than universal equality. The matter *Plessy* challenged was precisely this separate but equal treatment, not by exposing the falsity of this presumed equivalence, but by insisting that racial classifications undermined universal principles of freedom and equality.[147] Against the state's claim of neutrality and equivalence, Plessy's attorneys insisted that these classifications were unconstitutional and that the injury inflicted by such taxonomies cast the Negro in a legal condition reminiscent of slavery.[148]

With keener eyes toward the productive character of racism, the state's work can be understood as securing (white) racial integrity and producing a subjected race, rather than simply ensconcing aversion in the law. This integrity was to be borne by the marked and encumbered bodies of black citizens, who shouldered the burden of the privileges esteemed as social rights. Just as the bent back of the freedmen's handbooks figured freedom in the image of slavery, so, too, was the fate of blackness figured in *Plessy*. If the fundamental task conducted under the cover of the state's police power was the protection of the health of the populace, then, as this duty took shape in the emergent era of Jim Crow, it required the surveillance and enclosure of blackness and the regulation of legitimate forms of intimacy and association, and, when necessary, the state readily imposed onerous but warrantable hardships.

The intent of the Louisiana statute and the majority opinion in *Plessy* was to preclude encounters between scandalously proximate bodies. The obsession with legible bodies, sound association, and physical proximity indicates the degree to which the social involved the governing and management of life. As *Plessy* evinced, sitting next to a black person on a train, sleeping in a hotel bed formerly used by a black patron, or dining with a black party seated at a nearby table not only diminished white enjoyment but also incited fears of engulfment and contamination. Clearly, the integrity of bodily boundaries and white self-certainty was at the heart of this anxiety, and the curative for this fear of waning or threatened sovereignty was the exclusion and subordination of blacks. So it appears that the subjection of blacks was the basis of both individuation and collective security. This phobia of impending dissolution and engulfment found expression in an organization of space that arranged and separated bodies to forestall this dreaded and anticipated intrusion. *Plessy* instantiated this fear and confirmed the need for precautionary measures. Marked ineradicably by a history of dispossession, held captive by a past not yet past, and cast into a legal condition of subjection—these features limn the circumstances of an anomalous subject no longer enslaved, but not yet free.

THESES ON THE NONEVENT

Everything our white people had,
we made for them. Freedom could make
folks proud, but it didn't make them rich.

The elasticity of debt produced
involuntary servitude.
There was no way to get ahead,
to get into the black.
It was like we were still slaves;
our only choice was to run.

The exercise of freedom
was inextricable from
an elaborate micropenality
of everyday life.

Indebted servitude was the future.
Compulsion, coercion, imprisonment,
and the threat
of death were the pillars of
the free-labor system.
We were still bound by the ledger.
In the same breath they said
we were free and we were debtors.
We were the ones who owed.

The slave went free; stood for a brief
moment in the sun; then moved back
again toward slavery.

How does one narrate a story
of freedom when confronted with
the discrepant legacy of emancipation
and the decidedly circumscribed avenues
available to the freed?

We entertained fanciful and dangerous
notions of what might be possible. We
refused to work. We were as good as any
white man. We were intoxicated with
freedom. We moved about, not wanting
to settle anywhere, or say "massa" or "boss"
ever again. We set off from one place to
the next, trying to do as well as we had
done under slavery.

$r = 1.1^{\theta}$

b

When we heard the news
folks just walked away from the fields.
We promised that we would never return.
It hurt bad when we were forced to.
For those of us working on the same
plantation where we had been slaves,
it was like the world was mocking us,
taunting us: What has changed? Nothing.

The Reconstruction
of the negro
was real hard on us.

OF EMANCIPATION

Bend your back joyfully to the burden.
Use your agile hands to work dutifully.
Avert your gaze so you don't
seem too proud, too insistent on being equal to
the white man. Bow your head in humility. Hold
your tongue. Lower your eyes and expectations.
On bended knee, give thanks. Some must work
with the hands, while others work with the head.
Bow down to the Lord. Genuflect before the
great Emancipator. Clasp your hands in prayer.
Open your legs for the boss. Shut your mouth.
Avoid the sore toes of prejudice.
Don't raise your fist against a white man.
Don't swagger. At hands unknown. You must
have the broken heart,
sorrow for the sin, sorrow for God,
for having broken his laws,
for your idleness, for your refusal to work.
The broken heart.

Emancipation delivered
blacks to the shore of freedom
and deposited the detritus
of the war at their feet.

Except as punishment for crime,
except as a state suited for blackness,
except as the real terms of emancipation,
except as necessary or expedient,
except as the natural condition of the negro,
except as necessary to produce the new racial
order, except as a whim,
except as a lark, except as necessary to maintain
the symbolic value of whiteness,
except as necessary for the public good,
except as necessary to prevent negro domination,
except as necessary to defeat Reconstruction,
except as necessary to disenfranchise,
except as necessary to maintain white over black,
except as necessary to distinguish the valued
from the disposable.

What could a mortgaged freedom yield?
They was plenty of land
that did not belong to anyone
except the government. . . .
We did not get nothing but hard work,
and we were worse off under freedom
than we were during slavery,
as we did not have a thing—
could not read or write.

We were free in every sense of the term,
free of a home, free of land, free of prospects.
Free of forty acres and a mule.
Free of reparations,
Free of everything except white folks.
They were more dangerous now.
They would kill us in the blink of an eye
and with no afterthought;
they had no one to answer to.
No one was keeping a count of dead negroes
and the ones who went missing.

It wasn't no riot. It was a massacre.

Rights will not exalt us or rob
the white man of his glory.

We still had nothing, but we had
to carry the weight of everything.
The little we could scrimp and
save, they stole that too.
How was we supposed to live
on nothing?

Freedom acts on the mind.
It obliges you to make a livelihood,
to cast down your bucket where you are.
Free people have to work, and some of them
have to work very hard even to get their bread.

The transubstantiation of even the
poorest whites into oligarchs and
would-be sovereigns. Every white
person was endowed with the power
of the police. The plantation endured.
No proclamation ended that.

A free negro has no master to correct him,
and unless a white man, to whom insolence is given,
has a right to put a stop to it in an extrajudicial way,
there is no remedy for it. This would be insufferable.

Whatever fanciful notions
they may have entertained
of freedom as conferring happiness,
they will soon be obliged
through stern necessity to look
at their actual condition,
which is that of work or starve.

They tried to convince us
that we could be as happy
and free on the plantation
as anywhere else in the world.

I was free to love whomsoever I
wanted, and nobody
could tell me otherwise.

My   soul wants something that's new, that's new

The lament of failed revolution.
An old woman on the outskirts
of the throng began singing this song;
all the mass joined with her swaying.
And we wept.

We are still waiting for them to return
all the value of the stolen life and land.

REGISTERS OF A MOAN

A negro is called insolent whenever
his conduct varies in any manner
from what a Southern man
was accustomed to when slavery existed.

We were expecting nothing
and that is what we got.
That was all the mule they ever
give us.

We were like stray cattle,
never having had anything
and having no place to go.

The slaves weren't expecting nothing.
It got out somehow that they were going
to give us forty acres and a mule.
We all went to town. They asked
who I belonged to and I told them
my master was Banner.
One man said, "Young man, I would go by my
mama's name if I were you." I told him my
mother's name was Banner too. Then he opened
a book and told me all the laws. He told me
never go by any name except Banner.
That was all the mule they ever give me.

If she allowed herself to dream,
maybe one day she could be a
lady's maid or have her own room.
Maybe she could escape the
kitchen and the field.

Everybody went wild.
We all felt like heroes and
nobody had made us that way
but ourselves. Just like that we was free.
Right off colored folks
started on the move,
They seemed to want to
get closer to freedom,
so they'd know what it was—
like it was a place or a city.

The most she could hope for
was marriage—to be subsumed
under the civil personality of a
man. But, reader, the story ends
with servitude, not marriage.

A recursive echo and return.
A black moan.

AFTERWORD

Marisa J. Fuentes and Sarah Haley

A reverence, a return, a gesture toward an otherwise. Reflecting on a book so transformative to our intellectual development and written by a person whose mentorship, friendship, and example have been crucially instrumental in our lives proved a significant struggle. Saidiya Hartman's intellectual trajectory, inspirations, and radical insistences about ways to see Black lives, our lives, in the past and present, categorically shifted the writing of history, what it means when we center Black feminist thought in our work, and how to think about Black lives and subjects in so much precarity with such care, grace, and rigor. We carried this book with us in the isolation of our writing, to the archive, in discussion groups that attempted to do justice—in our work and to this work—and continually reference, struggle with, teach, and think with our, by now worn, dog-eared, underlined, and coffee-stained copies of that first edition. And, now, a second.

We will attempt to distill the profound contributions of *Scenes of Subjection: Terror, Slavery, and Self-Making in Nineteenth-Century America* in the twenty-five years of its life. We ask: What are the terms and analyses Hartman inaugurates that have become so fundamental to our fields of critical Black and slavery studies? *Scenes* originated the ubiquitous questionings, methods, and modes of (historical) writing that we take for granted in our ethical inquiries into the conditions that structure Black life. Twenty-five years after its first publication, we reflect on the genesis of Hartman's conceptual formulations that grounded our scholarship and continue to gather critical analysis, thought, and mark the complicated ways that her field-defining theoretical interventions demand our serious engagement even as we acknowledge and lament how Black feminist theoretical interventions are often subject to erasure.

> Slavery was both the wet nurse and the bastard offspring of liberty.
>
> —Saidiya V. Hartman

Scenes of Subjection transformed our understanding of the historical relationship between captivity and emancipation by demonstrating that slavery makes and is made by something we might call freedom. Emancipation, so confounded, so indicted, is forever reinterpreted in the aftermath of *Scenes*. Saidiya Hartman presents a theory of history that centers the social reproduction of power, emphasizing gendered modes of economic extraction, and the role of repression in the construction of liberty. Refashioned technologies of terror and modes of enclosure, grisly in their cultural dependence upon prior incarnations, reflect the permanence of anti-Blackness in Western modernity. Such nonlinear unfolding prompts its readers to ask: What constitutes the ending of an era? In narrating slavery's reproductive capacity rather than its denouement, *Scenes* rewrites the script of Black history and reconfigures the practice of periodization. In delineating both the history of slavery's gestation and its obscurement, *Scenes* charts, indeed emphasizes, historical change while instigating historiographic crises. It notoriously rejects the event of emancipation and removes abolition as a horizon. Instead, in this work, Hartman forces a question that will occupy generations of scholars to come:

If declension is contained within emancipation, what or when is abolition?

The answer remains elusive, entangled in Hartman's delineation of the yet-unfinished project of freedom. The repudiation of empathy, the limitation of redress and resistance, the economic extraction in frivolity, the fabulation of debt, the ensnaring propensities of desire, the suffering imposed by human legibility—this narration of the inescapability of violation submerges the rare sentences from *Scenes* that detail the minimum threshold for a "revolution of the social order" (129). The pessimism of *Scenes*, then, lies in its infrastructure as well as its argumentation, and this aspect of the work would prove monumentally influential. Hartman does explain that revolution requires "at the very least . . . a revolution of the social order, an entirely new set of arrangements" (129). Lingering in *Scenes* (difficult as it is not to stray into future Hartmanian territory of the subjunctive and the wayward and the beautiful), does not foreclose the prospect of Black life beyond captivity and coercion. Instead, *Scenes'* unyielding analytical grip on the "savage encroachments of power" enacted through the presumably progressive constructs of "reform, consent, reciprocity, and protection" is itself a mode of unraveling (5). Rather than rejecting the possibility of possibility, *Scenes* issues a challenge for future work in Black radicalism by insisting that an accounting of the paradoxical forms of power that enforce Blackness as a "perpetual condition of ravishment" is critical to the production of an upheaval capacious enough to contest callous propensity toward reform. There is making in the unmaking. The discipline of history itself depends on the cornerstones of change and continuity. Yet *Scenes* queries the character of continuity and the gravity of change in Black life encumbered by liberalism, brutalized by recognition, and contained by freedom. Change is pivotal if progress is elusive. Pain, Hartman argues, must be recognized in its capaciousness and in its *historicity* (85). This engagement with the historical production of violation profoundly altered how the field of Black studies approaches the operation of power in the context of a past that continues to saturate political and intellectual life. Hartman issues a dual critique: of the excessive "dispensation" of agency in the field of African American history and of the repudiation of injury in dominant nineteenth-century discourses about Black life. *Scenes* suggests that the contemporary researcher is interpellated in the perils of liberal humanism—with its entangled bestowals and disavowals—in ways that intensify the burden carried by Black subjects of the past to remediate the very brutality that has besieged them.

Historians must also interrogate our complicity with the desire of liberal humanist progress in our projections onto the past of enslaved lives. Hartman's insistence in understanding the terms and actions unavailable in the enslaved condition forces us to rigorously confront our own political impositions and blind hopes. The circulation of Hartman's interventions shifted our attention away from traditional social histories of enslaved life to understanding the implication of law on how the enslaved were limited by commodification and the contradictions of slave owners' disavowals of enslaved humanity. Thinking outside of the frames of liberal humanism, *Scenes* articulates the limits of the figure of the "human" by showing how slave law at once recognized enslaved humanity by its criminalization of enslaved will, while denying enslaved people the very social categories of human identity ("man" in *Dred Scott v. Sandford* [1857] and "woman" in *State of Missouri v. Celia, a Slave* [1855]).

In studies of slavery, Hartman breaks new ground by examining the modes of violence that were otherwise indecipherable in their innocuous and quotidian iterations. Hartman's influence on the historiography of slavery and the terms with which we wrestle to narrate this past, remains unsurpassed. She taught us about the violent technicalities of the enslaved "civil condition" that rendered enslaved humanity as criminal (33). We learned about the entanglements of pleasure and violence in slave traders and enslavers forcing enslaved people's complicity in their subjugation through displays of enjoyment—music, singing, dancing. Violence, Hartman shows, emanates not simply from the use of the whip and the total power used against enslaved people, but equally insidiously from the "brutal calculations" of slave commodification wherein the performance of contentment surfaces increased sale value (56). With *Scenes* we can no longer leave uninterrogated the terms and actions of "agency" and resistance—the everyday practices that pushed against the condition of social death—but must consider how action and refusals against the constraints of domination remained precarious, elicited violence, made true redress fleeting, and demonstrated the "enormity of the breach . . . and the magnitude of domination (85)."

The enormity of *Scenes*'s intervention in the discipline of history is difficult to overstate. Yet the very ubiquity of its interventions— the critiques of agency and consent, the debates about social death and the enslaved condition, the language Hartman originates about the unfinished project of freedom, the disruption of disciplines— has allowed a kind of expropriation of this Black feminist work in the politics of knowledge production that plagues academic citational practices. Hartman's *Scenes* inaugurates a genealogy of Black feminist ethics and methods that sometimes too easily escapes the footnotes of prominent histories of slavery.

Still, writing and thinking about slavery, the enslaved condition, and freedom must by now contend with a destabilized historical archive and interrogate enslavement in relationship to freedom, free will, and agency. *Scenes* anticipates Hartman's long intervention into theories of the archive and critical historical methodologies necessary to carefully attend to slavery's violence. Hartman thinks with Black narrative voices that testify to a keen understanding of these contradictions. She demonstrates the archive's complicity in Black subjugation of voice, of experience, of sentience. It is in the declaration of the archive's power to obscure, violate, and serve as authoritative knowledge that Hartman's enduring influence on historical writing can be observed. Historians' work on slavery acknowledged the silences of enslaved perspectives inherent in the records that document this past. Yet for Hartman, to ask, "How does one use these sources?" insists that we not abandon the project of historical production but rather take as a starting point an interrogation of power in rendering Black life historically unimportant and Black people incapable of self-representation. Her purposeful methods at once "claim the [sources] for contrary purposes" while conceding that the project of recovering enslaved people from the archive and rendering Black life fully visible is never "free from the disfigurements of present concerns," nor is it possible to wrest Black enslaved subjects from an archive that is an epistemological violation of Black subjectivity (14). She makes plain how enslaved Black lives were never meant for history but provides us a way to elaborate the contours of their struggles. It is here that the method of *critical fabulation* germinates (15).

The project of ethical historical practice is at the heart of this work. Hartman endures with accounting for the quotidian expressions of Black lives in the archives while never taking for granted the unrelenting power of the archive to (dis)present traces of enslaved living. With a pioneering analysis of racialized gender, Hartman exposes the limits of historiographical certainty and generalization. Whether we work with the "abundance" of antebellum sources or the dearth of records in colonial archives, she points us to a method that allows us to hold and work through the impossibility of recovery in order to elaborate the constraints and possibilities of historical production. We, therefore, cannot engage in a project of slavery's narration without pausing on its impossibility—the failure of recovery of the full historical experience of the enslaved. Nor can we linger in scenes of slavery's violence without attending to the reproduction of the injury or the ethics of witnessing and the limits of empathy.

Further troubling the historian's reliance on a liberatory agency, Hartman centers the terrifying predicament of enslaved women whose refusal to concede to the sexual violence of the sale or the master exposed the construction of the dangers of will and the impossibilities of consent in the life of a human commodity and in the context of slave law. Indeed, Black feminist scholars continue to struggle with the language of consent and coercion in the histories of slavery that do not reproduce the terms of capitalist production and romance. At once charting the simultaneous imposition of humanity and the disavowal of subjectivity, Hartman presents a breathtaking account of Celia and her afterlife in racialized gender, asking, "What if presumed endowments of man—conscience, sentiment, and reason—rather than assuring liberty or negating slavery acted to yoke slavery and freedom?" (4). Gender appears as both a negation of the capacity for suffering that constitutes subjectivity and a yoke to the human that intensifies injury and secures slavery's violence. Gender, Hartman argues, possesses Black subjects, a framing that evinces both the category's deployment and disfigurement—an absent presence. Celia is tied to Sukie, whose lifting of skirts on the auction block is the territory of critical theory, a "deconstructive performance" that exposes power in the sexual arena and enacts a "category crisis" in which agency is tethered to criminality, property is tethered to sexuality, and enjoyment is tethered to violation (64). Crucial here is Hartman's complex engagement with the historical archive to source Black theories of power. Sukie's performance theory exposes the ruses of liberalism. *Scenes* reveals that Black subject positions have been constituted by

AFTERWORD

negated injury while straining against the historical archive to begin
what will be an evolving and career-defining process of collaboration with Black historical subjects as critical theorists.

Hartman finds these historical figures in "those scenes in which
terror can hardly be discerned," scenes that range from the activity
of domestic interiors to the production of Black legal personhood,
demonstrating how white supremacist ideology accrues its force
through concealment and alchemy (2). Hartman elucidates invisible, inconspicuous, and intimate modes of power through analyses of frolic, seduction, will, contentment, performance, possession,
obligation, and fashioning, among other configurations. *Scenes*
insists that these are the useful categories of cultural theory and
cultural history. The book exploded the fields of American history,
gender history, feminist and queer theory, and performance studies.
It is a classic in Black cultural studies generally and a requisite text
for scholars of Black radicalism specifically. The book is known for
its magnitude of scope, audacity of language, prodigious research,
and theoretical weight. Its publication was not unthreatening, nor
was it uncontroversial. Its prescience would become the basis for its
prominence.

To reflect on the profound and field-changing contributions of
Scenes is daunting—an understatement. This is a book that has
transformed our understanding of the persisting legacies of slavery
in our present. A piece of intellectual labor that has given us the language and methodologies to analyze the terrorizing forces of racism
and gender violence but also to shift our attention away from the
obvious to quotidian: that which is "barely discernible." Hartman's
gift to us in the last twenty-five years is to think more deeply about
the configurations, limitations, and possibilities for Black life in a
system that conspires to harm us. We must pause at the concepts we
now take for granted. It is our hope that the next twenty-five years
of the life of this monumental work will challenge scholars to resist

the disciplining and form-confining structures that obscure and disavow the dangers faced by Black people, past and present.

And while it would be almost obscene to use the language of indebtedness here, it is necessary to state that after *Scenes*, scholars of literary, cultural, and Black studies cannot evade the enclosures of humanism, liberalism, and agency. The force of the opening refusal of *Scenes* will shape the text and tone of future sentences crafted by writers in and beyond the academy. After *Scenes*, the aspect ratio of narrative to restraint is rewritten. After *Scenes*, the creative potential of withholding is far more evident. After *Scenes*, historians grapple anew with the character of continuity and the ghastliness of change. After *Scenes*, we are called to be more accountable to the terms of Black living. After *Scenes*, the paradigm of emancipation is the paradigm of punishment. After *Scenes*, the archive's role as resource and recalcitrant is altered in Black critical theory. *Scenes* operates in the break of genre and *Scenes* breaks genre. Cohorts of scholars have tried to follow its riotous path. It provided us with the intellectual tools and courage to do our work even in disquietude; we are among multitudes whose writing is historically contingent upon *Scenes*. Perhaps Hartman knew that her disarray of the record, consideration of constancy, queering of time, loitering in impossibility, and rebellion of form was a Rubicon of Black study. Part two of *Scenes* is the afterlife of slavery yet unnamed: the beginning of the experiment.

ACKNOWLEDGMENTS

This book owes a great deal to so many. The Charlotte W. Newcombe Foundation, the Rockefeller Foundation, and the University of California Humanities Research Institute provided financial support and time off, which helped in the development and completion of this project. The late George Bass provided support and enthusiasm during the early stages of the project, seeing promise when things were still quite vaguely defined. I would like to thank the members of the Feminism and Discourse of Power group for rigorous criticism and lively debate: Wendy Brown, Judith Butler, Nancy Campbell, Rey Chow, Nancy Fraser, Angela Harris, Jenny Sharpe, Jacqueline Siapno, and Irene Wei. I would especially like to thank Judith Butler, who has extended herself in innumerable ways to support my work.

I am also grateful to my teachers. Hazel Carby provided a model of scholarly integrity, encouraged my interdisciplinary pursuits, and was an exacting reader. Alan Trachtenberg shared his passion for the study of culture, provided invaluable criticism, and continued to lend his support even after my official student days were over. John Szwed supplied me with endless citations and shared many instructive anecdotes. Others read the manuscript and offered valuable comments: Barbara Christian, VèVè Clark, Michael Davidson, Julie Ellison, Mae Henderson, George Lipsitz, Eric Lott, Arnold

Rampersad, David Roediger, and Michael Rogin. My research assistant, Hershini Bhana, provided immensely valuable labor on this project; her dedication, enthusiasm, and commitment made my own task so much easier. Jan Anderson helped me to complete the bibliography. Glenda Carpio prepared the index.

The support of friends and colleagues has been invaluable: Elizabeth Abel, Elizabeth Alexander, Lindon Barrett, Rhakesh Bandari, Tobe Correal, Aya de Leon, Rosa Linda Fregoso, Herman Grey, Tera Hunter, Donna Jones, Lata Mani, Ruth Frankenberg, Sharon Holland, Lisa Lowe, David Lloyd, Michael Rogin, Caren Kaplan, Abdul JanMohamed, Harryette Mullen, Donny Webster, and Wendy White. Special thanks to Ula Taylor for being the best colleague I could hope to have and a good friend. Norma Alarcón provided a model of intellectual passion and commitment under fire. bell hooks has always reminded me that courage is a central ingredient of intellectual work. Angela Harris, Paul Rogers, and Robert St. Martin Westley read the chapters thoroughly, shared many important insights, and filled many an afternoon with stimulating conversation.

Farah Jasmine Griffin and Donna Daniels were the midwives of this book, helping me through many difficult moments, providing inspiration when I desperately needed it, and giving generously of their time. Bill and Julia Lowe have been an unending source of inspiration and love in my life. I thank them for believing that all things are possible, even when I did not. My parents, Beryle and Virgilio Hartman, gave generously of their love.

Oakland, California
S. V. H.
September 1996

POSTSCRIPT FOR THE NEW EDITION

I would like to thank my agent Jacqueline Ko at the Wylie Agency for working diligently to make this twenty-fifth anniversary edition possible. My editor John Glusman welcomed this project to Norton and tended carefully to this new edition. It has been a pleasure to work together again. Helen Thomaides made sure that I stayed on schedule and helped immensely with the production process. The contributors to this new edition: Torkwase Dyson, Marisa Fuentes, Sarah Haley, Cameron Rowland, Keeanga-Yamahtta Taylor have infused this second life of *Scenes* with much brilliance and wisdom. Marisa, Sarah, and Keeanga's remarks have provided a rich context for the book, though I fear they have credited me with too much. Even if undeserved, I have basked in their words. Thank you for seeing so much in this book and for guiding it into the world. You are its sentinels. Torkwase, much, much gratitude for making this incredible series of drawings amid several international exhibitions and a monstrous schedule. I am so grateful for your contribution. I have learned so much from your work about the Plantationocene and the architecture of enclosure and escape. The yearlong collaboration with Cameron Rowland has brought me much joy. I will miss our two- to three-hour conversations parsing the difference between refusal and antagonism, practice and countermemory, black geographies and captive spaces and our discussions of Sylvia Wynter,

Eric Williams, Frantz Fanon, W. E. B. Du Bois, NourbeSe Philip, and Cedric Robinson. Thank you for your willingness to revise and revise the notations after we both said, "This is good, we're there." It took months before we realized that these "scores for thought" will always be incomplete, and open to ongoing revision and improvisation. I appreciate your willingness to try your hand at this, transforming concepts into visual graphics, honoring Du Bois in this oblique way. I have benefitted from thinking deeply with you about slavery and its afterlife, property, and capitalism, and musing about what abolition might look like. Credit to Ellen Louis, Tina Campt, Mabel Wilson, Sarah Haley, and Arthur Jafa for offering valuable feedback on the early drafts of our concept maps. Juliana Ariel DeVaan secured permissions for the images in the book. Ellen Louis and Runnie Exuma helped prepare the index.

Sampada Aranke and Nikolas Oscar Sparks edited a special issue of *Women & Performance*, vol. 27 (Spring 2017), "Sentiment and Sentience: Black Performance since Scenes of Subjection," that engaged the contribution of the work to performance studies. I am honored by the brilliant introduction written by the editors and the essays by Olivia Young, Matthew Morrison, Jeremy Glick, Sarah Haley, Sarah Jane Cvernak, J. Kameron Carter, sidony o'neal, Autumn Womack, Andrew Brown, Jared Richardson, Sara Mameni, Frank B. Wilderson III, and Nijah Cunningham. The contributors to the special issue rigorously and generously addressed *Scenes* and encouraged me to reflect on what I had attempted to do.

Marisa Fuentes, Carter Mathes, Myisha Priest, and Lisa Ze Winters, I don't have the words to say how much the conference, *Scenes* at 20, meant for me, although sobbing at the podium as I delivered the concluding remarks might give you some sense of how deeply moved I was. You honored my labor at a very hard time in my life, and this made the gift you offered so much sweeter. I want to thank all the participants and my friends and interlocutors for the extraordinary papers and rich exchange of ideas: Herman Bennett, Yarimar Bonilla, Rizvana Bradley, Hazel Carby, Adrienne Davis, Erica Edwards, Nicole Fleetwood, Jennifer Morgan, Fred Moten, Tavia Nyong'o, Jared Sexton, Christina Sharpe, Stephanie Smallwood, Rinaldo Walcott, and Alexander Weheliye. All those who attended brought so much love to the proceedings. I'd like to thank Michelle Stephens and Deborah Gray White and the late Cheryl Wald for their support of resources and enthusiasm. The twentieth anniversary celebration and the special edition of *Women & Performance* opened the path to this new edition. To my brilliant students, thank you always for the ongoing experiment in thinking together.

Fred Moten, the late Lindon Barrett, Mark Reinhardt, Herman Bennett, Jennifer Morgan, Denise Ferreira da Silva, and David Scott were my first interlocutors after *Scenes*' publication. I will be ever grateful for their generous engagement and intellectual friendship. Huey Copeland and Jared Sexton provided the first occasion for an extended reflection on the book in a special issue of *Qui Parle*, which took the form of a conversation with Frank Wilderson, "The Position of the Unthought."

I have been very fortunate to be in such company. To the ancestors, the teachers, the interlocutors, the friends and the students who inhabit these pages and who made this book possible, I have not called each and every name, but know you are here.

NOTES

Foreword

1. Belinda Hurmence, *Before Freedom: 48 Oral Histories of Former North and South Carolina Slaves* (New York; Penguin Books, 1990), 68–69. In *Scenes*, Hartman notes the difficulty of using the WPA interviews uncritically, as singular sources to capture the experiences of the enslaved. There were different kinds of power dynamics that shaped these interviews, including the use of white interviewers and narrow questions meant to portray slavery as pastoral and the enslaved as simple, especially through the accentuation of Black speech patterns and dialect. But read in tandem with other sources and read against the grain, with the awareness of who conducted the interviews, what questions were asked and what objectives may have animated the participants, you can also glean insight and understanding.

2. Walter Johnson, "On Agency," *Journal of Social History* 37, no. 1 (2003): 113–24.

Preface: The Hold of Slavery

1. Frantz Fanon, *The Wretched of the Earth*, trans. Richard Philcox (New York: Grove Press, 2005). Sylvia Wynter, "Black Metamorphosis" (unpublished manuscript).

2. Olaudah Equiano, *The Interesting Narrative of Olaudah Equiano* (London, 1789).

3. "Venus in Two Acts," *Small Axe*, 12.2 (June 2008): 1–14.

4. Sylvia Wynter, "Beyond the Categories of the Master Conception: The

Counterdoctrine of the Jamesian Poiesis," in *C. L. R James's Caribbean*, ed. Paget Henry and Paul Buhle (Durham, NC: Duke University Press, 1992).

5. The work of Orlando Patterson, Hortense Spillers, and Patricia Williams was critical to thinking beyond this impasse. See Orlando Patterson, *Slavery and Social Death* (Cambridge: Harvard University Press, 1982); Hortense Spillers, "Mama's Baby, Papa's Maybe," *Diacritics* 17, no. 2 (Summer 1987): 64–81; and Patricia Williams, "On Being the Object of Property," *Signs* 14, no. 1 (Autumn 1988): 5–24. As important were Édouard Glissant, *Caribbean Discourse: Selected Essays*, trans. J. Michael Dash (Charlottesville: University of Virginia Press, 1989) and Toni Morrison, *Beloved* (New York: Knopf, 1987).

6. James Anderson, "Aunt Jemima in Dialectics," *Journal of Negro History* 61, no. 1 (January 1976): 99–114.

7. The work of Paule Marshall, Toni Morrison, Maryse Conde, David Bradley, Jamaica Kincaid, Caryl Phillips, Derek Walcott, Robert Hayden, Eduoard Glissant, and Kamau Brathwaite was indispensable to my thinking.

Introduction

1. Frederick Douglass, *Narrative of the Life of Frederick Douglass, an American Slave, Written by Himself* (Boston, 1845; repr., New York: New American Library, 1968), 25–26.

2. Jean Laplanche and Jean-Bertrand Pontalis, *The Language of Psychoanalysis*, trans. Donald Nicholson-Smith (New York: W. W. Norton, 1973), 332.

3. Elaine Scarry, *The Body in Pain: The Making and Unmaking of the World* (New York: Oxford University Press, 1985); Dori Laub, "An Event without a Witness: Truth, Testimony, and Survival," in *Testimony: Crises of Witnessing in Literature, Psychoanalysis, and History*, Shoshana Felman and Dori Laub (New York: Routledge, 1992).

4. George Rawick, ed., *The American Slave: A Composite Autobiography*, vol. 7, pt. 2 (Westport, CT: Greenwood Press, 1973), 117.

5. Ibid., vol. 11, pt. 7, p. 211.

6. Sylvia Wynter, "On Disenchanting Discourse: 'Minority' Literary Criticism and Beyond," in *The Nature and Context of Minority Discourse*, ed. Abdul R. JanMohamed and David Lloyd (New York: Oxford University Press, 1990), 447.

7. Toni Morrison, *Playing in the Dark: Whiteness and the Literary Imagination* (New York: Vintage, 1993), 37.

8. Ibid., 17.

9. James C. Scott, *Domination and the Arts of Resistance* (New Haven, CT: Yale University Press, 1991), 45.

10. Valerie Smith, *Self-Discovery and Authority in Afro-American Literature* (Cambridge: Harvard University Press, 1987), 28–32.

11. "Slavery in all but name," W. E. B. Du Bois, "The Hands of Ethiopia," *Darkwater: Voices from within the Veil* (New York: Harcourt, Brace and Howe, 1920).

12. Gayatri Chakravorty Spivak, "Subaltern Studies: Deconstructing Historiography," in *Selected Subaltern Studies*, ed. Ranajit Guha and Gayatri Chakravorty Spivak (New York: Oxford University Press, 1988), 11–12.

13. Lata Mani, "Cultural Theory, Colonial Texts: Reading Eyewitness Accounts of Widow Burning," in *Cultural Studies*, ed. Lawrence Grossberg, Cary Nelson, and Paula Treichler (New York: Routledge, 1992), 392–408.

14. Michel Foucault, *The Archaeology of Knowledge*, trans. Alan Sheridan (New York: Pantheon, 1972), 130–131.

15. Gyanendra Pandey, "In Defense of the Fragment: Writing about Hindu-Muslim Riots in India Today," *Representations* 37 (Winter 1992): 27–55; Gayatri Chakravorty Spivak, "The Rani of Sirmur: An Essay in Reading in the Archive," *History and Theory* 24, no. 3 (1987): 247–272; Renato Rosaldo, "From the Door of His Tent: The Fieldworker and the Inquisitor," in *Writing Culture: The Poetics and Politics of Ethnography*, ed. James Clifford and George E. Marcus (Berkeley: University of California Press, 1986).

16. Ranajit Guha, "The Prose of Counter-Insurgency," in Guha and Spivak, *Selected Subaltern Studies*, 77.

17. John W. Blassingame, ed., *Slave Testimony: Two Centuries of Letters, Speeches, and Autobiographies* (Baton Rouge: Louisiana State University Press, 1977), xvi–lxv; C. Vann Woodward, "History from Slave Sources," in *The Slave's Narrative*, ed. Charles T. Davis and Henry Louis Gates Jr. (New York: Oxford University Press, 1985), 48–58.

18. According to Paul Escott, the race of the WPA interviewers determined what was said or revealed, as well as variances in the representation of those statements. Paul Escott, *Slavery Remembered: A Record of Twentieth-Century Slave Narratives* (Chapel Hill: University of North Carolina Press, 1979).

19. Édouard Glissant, *Caribbean Discourse: Selected Essays*, trans. J. Michael Dash (Charlottesville: University of Virginia Press, 1989), 89.

20. Antonio Gramsci, *The Prison Notebooks*, ed. and trans. Quintin Hoare and Geoffrey Nowell Smith (New York: International Publishers, 1971), 419–425; *Selections from Cultural Writings*, ed. David Forgacs and Geoffrey Nowell

Smith, trans. William Boelhower (Cambridge, MA: Harvard University Press, 1895), 189.

21. Paul Gilroy, *The Black Atlantic: Modernity and Double-Consciousness* (Cambridge, MA: Harvard University Press, 1993), 37; Seyla Benhabib, *Critique, Norm, and Utopia: A Study of the Foundations of Critical Theory* (New York: Columbia University Press, 1986), 13, 41.

22. Walter Benjamin, "Theses on the Philosophy of History," in *Illuminations*, trans. Harry Zohn (New York: Schocken, 1969), 255.

1. Innocent Amusements

1. John Rankin, *Letters on American Slavery* (1837; repr., Westport, CT: Negro Universities Press, 1970), 45–47. In *An Appeal in Favor of That Class of Americans Called Africans*, Lydia Maria Child in her condemnation of the internal trade describes a similar scene: "In the summer of 1822, a coffle of slaves, driven through Kentucky, was met by Rev. James H. Dickey, just before it entered Paris. He describes it thus: 'About forty black men were chained together; each of them was handcuffed, and they were arranged rank and file. A chain, perhaps forty feet long, was stretched between the two ranks, to which short chains were joined, connected with the handcuffs. Behind them were about thirty women, tied hand to hand. Every countenance wore a solemn sadness; and the dismal silence of despair was only broken by the sound of two violins. Yes—as if to add insult to injury, the foremost couple were furnished with a violin apiece; the second couple were ornamented with cockades; while near the center our national standard was carried by hands literally in chains.'" *An Appeal in Favor of That Class of Americans Called Africans*, ed. Carolyn Karcher (1833; repr. Amherst: University of Massachusetts Press, 1996), 32. The descriptions of the coffle found in abolitionist texts, like this example from Child, were frequently secondhand accounts rather than firsthand reports of encounters with the coffle. This citational practice was a response to the crisis of slave testimony and a means of assembling "a thousand witnesses" against slavery in every text and documenting the woe and misery of slavery.

2. Rankin, *Letters on American Slavery*, 45.

3. Philip Fisher, *Hard Facts: Setting and Form in the American Novel* (New York: Oxford University Press, 1985), 100.

4. Peter A. Angeles, *Dictionary of Philosophy* (New York: Barnes and Noble Books, 1981); *Webster's New Twentieth Century Dictionary, Unabridged*, 2nd ed. (Cleveland, OH: Collins World, 1976).

5. Johnathan Boyarin writes that "the hegemony of empathy as an ethic of the

obliteration of otherness . . . occurs where humanism demands the acknowl-edgement of the Other's suffering humanity . . . [and] where the paradoxical linkage of shared humanity and cultural otherness cannot be expressed." *Storm from Paradise: The Politics of Jewish Memory* (Minneapolis: University of Minnesota Press, 1994), 86. See also Karl F. Morrison, *"I Am You": The Hermeneutics of Empathy in Western Literature, Theology, and Art* (Princeton, NJ: Princeton University Press, 1988).

6. In "The Politics of Translation," Gayatri Spivak outlines a politics of transla-tion that is useful in thinking about ethical relations and the terms of one's identification with others. She remarks that as ethical agents "it is not possible for us to imagine otherness or alterity maximally. We have to turn the other into something like the self in order to be ethical." Instead of ethical simili-tude, she suggests an erotics of surrender that is cognizant of the impossibility of translation. *Outside in the Teaching Machine* (New York: Routledge, 1993).

7. Zygmunt Bauman, *Modernity and the Holocaust* (Ithaca, NY: Cornell Univer-sity Press, 1991), 192.

8. Karen Sanchez-Eppler, *Touching Liberty: Abolition, Feminism, and the Politics of the Body* (Berkeley: University of California Press, 1993).

9. Thomas Jefferson, *Notes on the State of Virginia* (1787; repr., New York: W. W. Norton, 1982), 138.

10. The most gruesome of the tragic scenes described by Rankin involves the dismemberment and incineration of a slave boy.

11. See Stephen R. Munzer, *A Theory of Property* (Cambridge: Cambridge Uni-versity Press, 1990), 61, 63. In a discussion of incorporation and projection theories of property, Munzer notes that the incorporation theory holds that external things become property by being brought into the body. The projec-tion theory maintains that they become property by embodying the person in external things.

12. Rankin, *Letters*, 57. Slave narrators were literally and figuratively forced to display themselves in order to tell their stories. See Houston Baker, *Workings of the Spirit: The Poetics of Afro-American Women's Writing* (Chicago: University of Chicago Press, 1991); Robert B. Stepto, *From Behind the Veil: A Study of Afro-American Narrative* (Urbana: University of Illinois Press, 1979); William L. Andrews, *To Tell a Free Story: The First Century of Afro-American Autobi-ography, 1760–1865* (Urbana: University of Illinois Press, 1986); and Valerie Smith, *Self-Discovery and Authority in Afro-American Narrative* (Cambridge, MA: Harvard University Press, 1987).

13. Elaine Scarry, *The Body in Pain: The Making and Unmaking of the World* (New York: Oxford University Press, 1985).

14. It has been argued that this intimacy of work and song is typically African. See LeRoi Jones, *Blues People: Negro Music in White America* (New York: William Morrow, 1963); Sterling Stuckey, *Slave Culture: Nationalist Theory and the Foundations of Black America* (New York: Oxford University Press, 1987); Lawrence Levine, *Black Culture and Black Consciousness: Afro-American Folk Thought from Slavery to Freedom* (New York: Oxford University Press, 1977); and John Miller Chernoff, *African Rhythm and African Sensibility: Aesthetics and Social Action in African Musical Idioms* (Chicago: University of Chicago Press, 1979).

15. Enjoyment, as defined in the *Oxford English Dictionary*, encompasses taking delight or pleasure in; having sexual intercourse; as well as having the use or benefit of something. The various dimensions of having the use of or possessing, from holding the title to property to sexual intercourse, are what I want to explore here.

16. This argument will be fully explicated and substantiated by case law discussed in chapter three.

17. George M. Stroud, *A Sketch of the Laws Relating to American Slavery in the Several States of the United States of America* (1827; repr., New York: Negro Universities Press, 1968), 65.

18. Ibid., 98.

19. William Goodell, *The American Slave Code* (1853; repr., New York: Johnson Reprint Corporation, 1968), 308.

20. I submit that even laws designed to protect the lives of slaves were framed in terms of the loss of property and, moreover, could not be reinforced since neither slaves nor free blacks could act as witnesses against whites.

21. Slavoj Žižek, *Tarrying with the Negative: Kant, Hegel, and the Critique of Ideology* (Durham, NC: Duke University Press, 1993), 206.

22. See Karl Marx, "The Commodity," in *Capital*, vol. 1, trans. Ben Fowkes (New York: Vintage, 1977), 125–177.

23. The melodrama's structure is basically Manichaean, with the struggle between good and evil forming its dramatic core. Virtue, the heroine, and the threat of catastrophe provide its essential ingredients. The dramatic language it utilizes is emblematic, relying on a gestural and sometimes inarticulate tongue, which Peter Brooks describes as aesthetics of muteness, to provide a moral clarity that supersedes the word. The yearning for moral visibility culminates in the tableau. In some respects, minstrelsy is quite the opposite of melodrama, although it frequently utilized sentimental devices. However, generally minstrelsy luxuriates in dissemblance and in playing upon the unreliability of appearances, and by the same token, it violates moral and

social boundaries. Formally, minstrelsy was a hodgepodge of songs, dances, interacts, short skits, stump speeches, comic dialogues, and a narrative afterpiece; it was generally composed of short farces, Shakespearean burlesques, or theatrical lampoons. See David Grimsted, *Melodrama Unveiled: American Theater and Culture* (Berkeley: University of California Press, 1968), 171–203; Peter Brooks, *The Melodramatic Imagination: Balzac, Henry James, Melodrama, and the Mode of Excess* (New Haven, CT: Yale University Press, 1985), 27–62; Bruce A. McConachie, *Melodramatic Formations: American Theatre and Society, 1820–1870* (Des Moines: University of Iowa Press, 1992), 163–197; Carl Wittke, *Tambo and Bones: A History of the American Minstrel Stage* (Durham, NC: Duke University Press, 1930), 135–209; Hans Nathan, *Dan Emmett and the Rise of Early Negro Minstrelsy* (Norman: University of Oklahoma Press, 1962), 50–69, 123–134, 227–242; and Robert C. Toll, *Blacking Up: The Minstrel Show in Nineteenth-Century America* (New York: Oxford University Press, 1974), 25–65.

This discussion of melodrama is confined to the texts that explore issues of race, gender, and slavery: William Wells Brown, *The Escape; or, A Leap for Freedom*, in *Black Theatre USA*, ed. James V. Hatch and Ted Shine (New York: Free Press, 1974); Dion Boucicault, *The Octoroon*, in *The Meridian Anthology of 18th- and 19th-Century British Drama*, ed. Katharine M. Rogers (New York: New American Library, 1979); and George Aiken and Harriet Beecher Stowe, *Uncle Tom's Cabin*, in *American Melodrama*, ed. Daniel C. Gould (New York: Performing Arts Journal, 1983).

24. Although Karen Sanchez-Eppler in the insightful essay "Bodily Bonds: The Intersecting Rhetorics of Feminism and Abolition" rightly argues that the mulatto body undermines the surety of racial legibility, I contend that Zoe's body becomes legible as a black one by virtue of the violence that threatens it. *Representations* 24 (Fall 1988): 41. Hazel Carby notes the liminal status of the mulatto figure as a vehicle for exploring the relationship between the races. *Reconstructing Womanhood: The Emergence of the Afro-American Woman Novelist* (New York: Oxford University Press, 1987), 89–91.

25. In the dualistic world of melodrama, identification was absolute or not at all, for good and evil could not be reconciled. Unwavering convictions and absolute distinctions permitted the spectator an undivided state of being, which Robert Heilman defines as "the monopathic—the singleness of feeling that gives one a sense of wholeness." *Tragedy and Melodrama: Versions of Experience* (Seattle: University of Washington Press, 1968), 84. Similarly, Peter Brooks describes the "wholesome pleasures" of melodrama as the "joy of full emotional indulgence." *The Melodramatic Imagination*, 56–80.

26. Within the worldview of sentimentalism, the subordinated exercised their power through such acts of self-immolation and submission. See Jane Tompkins, *Sensational Designs: The Cultural Work of American Fiction, 1790–1860* (New York: Oxford University Press, 1985), 128. Ann Douglass contends, to the contrary, that sentimentalism merely naturalizes the social order by asserting the power of the most subordinate. *The Feminization of American Culture* (New York: Avon, 1977), 11–13.

27. Grimsted, *Melodrama Unveiled*, 206.

28. E. A. Andrews, *Slavery and the Domestic Slave-Trade in the United States* (1836; repr., Detroit: Negro History Press, n.d.).

29. According to Brooks, the motive of the tableau is to "give the spectator the opportunity to see meanings represented, emotions and moral states rendered in clear visible signs." The reliance on gesture, muteness, and the inarticulate cry marks the inadequacy of the conventional code "to convey a full freight of emotional meaning." *The Melodramatic Imagination*, 62.

30. Grimsted, *Melodrama Unveiled*, 191.

31. J. C. Furnas, *Goodbye to Uncle Tom* (New York: William Sloane Associates, 1956), 257–284; Toll, *Blacking Up*, 90–96; William L. Van Deburg, *Slavery and Race in American Popular Culture* (Madison: University of Wisconsin Press, 1984), 47–49; Stephen A. Hirsch, "Uncle Tomitudes: The Popular Reaction to *Uncle Tom's Cabin*," in *Studies in the American Renaissance*, ed. Joel Myerson (Boston: Twayne, 1978), 303–330; Eric Lott, *Love and Theft: Blackface Minstrelsy and the American Working Class,* (New York: Oxford University Press, 1992), 211–233.

32. Sam Lucas was the first black actor to play Tom in nonminstrel versions of *Uncle Tom's Cabin*. Ironically, Lucas was not famous for this role but for his minstrel performance of Uncle Tom's death.

33. The promiscuous circulation of these forms is especially clear in Brown's work. *My Southern Home* was chock-full of darky fare. Furnas has noted that Tom's rendition of "Old Folks at Home" had recently been made popular by the Christy Minstrels and that "Uncle Tom's Religion" resembled a minstrel air, though it was also melodramatic, with heavy bass tremolo effects to evoke whipping. Hirsch, "Uncle Tomitudes," 315.

34. "Old Folks at Home," in Stephen Foster, *Minstrel Show Songs*, ed. H. Wiley Hitchcock (New York: Da Capo Press, 1980).

35. Generally critics have described the development of minstrelsy in terms of the triumph of the common man. The attack on pretentiousness, the pastoral romance, and issues of identity and nationhood were also significant themes. See Toll, *Blacking Up*, 3–21, 160–194; and Lott, *Love and Theft*, 63–88.

36. Farce "invites laughter by the violation of social taboos" but "nevertheless avoids giving offence ... by adhering to a balanced structure in which the characters and values under attack are ultimately restored to their conventional positions." Jessica Milner Davis, *Farce* (London: Methuen, 1978), 85. See also Eric Bentley, *The Life of Drama* (New York: Atheneum, 1964).

37. As Houston Baker observes, the minstrel mask "is a space of habituation not only for repressed spirits of sexuality, ludic play, id satisfaction, castration anxiety, and a mirror stage of development, but also for that deep-seated denial of the indisputable humanity of inhabitants of and descendants from the continent of Africa." See *Modernism and the Harlem Renaissance* (Chicago: University of Chicago Press, 1987), 17.

38. David Roediger, *Wages of Whiteness* (London: Verso, 1991), 127.

39. "Two Declarations of Independence: The Contaminated Origins of American National Culture," in Michael Rogin, *Blackface, White Noise: Jewish Immigrants in the Hollywood Melting Pot* (Berkeley: University of California Press, 1996), 34.

40. See Edmund Morgan, *American Slavery, American Freedom: The Ordeal of Colonial Virginia* (New York: W. W. Norton, 1975); and Theodore W. Allen, *Invention of the White Race* (New York: Routledge, 1994).

41. Antislavery themes in minstrelsy were rare. "Ambivalence" best describes the representations of slavery that didn't glorify the plantation. By the 1850s any traces of antislavery sentiment had disappeared. For a discussion of antislavery themes in minstrelsy, see William F. Stowe and David Grimsted, "White-Black Humor," *Journal of Ethnic Studies* 3 (Summer 1975): 78–96; and Toll, *Blacking Up*, 81–88, 112–114.

42. Foster, *Minstrel Show Songs*.

43. *New York Clipper*, April 6, 1872, cited in Hans Nathan, *Dan Emmett and the Rise of Early Negro Minstrelsy* (Norman: University of Oklahoma Press, 1962), 288.

44. George M. Fredrickson, *The Arrogance of Race: Historical Perspectives on Slavery, Racism, and Social Inequity* (Middletown, CT: Wesleyan University Press, 1988), 215.

45. Sam Dennison, *Scandalize My Name: Black Imagery in American Popular Music* (New York: Garland, 1982), 102.

46. Nathan, *Dan Emmett*. The authorship of "Dixie" is contested. Thirty-seven white composers claimed authorship, as well as a black family, the Snowdens. The mother of Ben and Lou Snowden, Ellen Cooper Snowden, has been identified as the author. See Howard L. Sacks and Judith Rose Sacks, *Way Up in Dixie: A Black Family's Claim to the Confederate Anthem* (Washington, DC:

Smithsonian, 1993). The Sackses contend that "Dixie" can be read as protest by way of parody based on Ellen Snowden's authorship. In any case, the controversy over authorship doesn't affect the political uses of "Dixie."

47. "Gayly de Niggas Dance," reprinted in *The Negro Forget-Me-Not Songster* (Philadelphia, 1855), cited in ibid., 94.

48. "Dandy Jim from Caroline" (New York: Firth and Hall, 1843) and "Pompey Squash," in *The Negro Forget-Me-Not Songster*, both cited in ibid., 138–140.

49. *Oh, Hush! or, the Virginny Cupids, The Quack Doctor*, and *'Meriky; or, the Old Time Religion*, in *This Grotesque Essence: Plays from the Minstrel Stage*, ed. Gary D. Engle (Baton Rouge: Louisiana State University Press, 1978).

50. See *Oh, Hush! or, the Virginny Cupids, The Quack Doctor, Old Zip Coon*, and *'Meriky; or, the Old Time Religion*, in ibid. See also T. Allston Brown, *History of the American Stage* (1870; repr., New York: Benjamin Blom, 1969).

51. *Oxford English Dictionary*, 2nd ed. (New York: Oxford University Press, 1989), s.v. "Quashie."

52. "Jim Along Josey," reprinted in Nathan, *Dan Emmett*, 437.

53. Ibid., 399.

54. In his brilliant and masterful study, *Love and Theft*, Eric Lott forwards a reading of minstrelsy that focuses on the ambivalence of the minstrel texts and the transgressive identifications operative in donning blackface and cross-dressing. While much is to be admired in Lott's deft and comprehensive examination, I take issue with his claims about cross-racial solidarity and the subversive effects of minstrelsy.

55. Boucicault, *The Octoroon*, 427.

56. George Tucker, *Letters from Virginia*, trans. F. Lucas (Baltimore: J. Rubinson, 1816), 29–34.

57. American Anti-Slavery Society, *American Slavery, As It Is: Testimony of a Thousand Witnesses* (1839; repr., New York: Arno, 1968); Jesse Torrey, *American Slave Trade* (1822; repr., Westport, CT: Negro Universities Press, 1971); Theodore D. Weld, *Slavery and the Internal Slave Trade in the United States* (1841; repr., New York: Arno, 1969).

58. George W. Featherstonhaugh, *Excursion through the Slave States*, vol. 1 (London: J. Murray, 1844), 119–124.

59. Tyrone Power, *Impressions of America during the Years 1833, 1834 and 1835*, vol. 2 (Philadelphia, 1836), 80–83, cited in *A Documentary History of Slavery in North America*, ed. Willie Lee Rose (New York: Oxford University Press, 1976), 154.

60. Letter to Mary Speed, September 27, 1841, in Abraham Lincoln, *Abraham Lincoln: Speeches and Writings, 1832–1858* (New York: Library of America, 1989), 74–75.

61. Toni Morrison, *Playing in the Dark: Whiteness and the Literary Imagination* (New York: Vintage, 1993), 39.

62. Paul Gilroy, *The Black Atlantic: Modernity and Double-Consciousness* (Cambridge, MA: Harvard University Press, 1993), 37.

63. Édouard Glissant, *Caribbean Discourse: Selected Essays*, trans. J. Michael Dash (Charlottesville: University of Virginia Press, 1989), 2, 4, 161.

64. Gilles Deleuze discusses the operation of disavowal as "the point of departure of an operation that consists in neither negating nor even destroying, but rather in radically contesting the validity of that which is; it suspends belief in and neutralizes the given in such a way that a new horizon opens up beyond the given and in place of it." *Masochism: Coldness and Cruelty* (1989; repr. New York: Zone, 1991), 28–29.

65. Sellie Martin's narrative in *Slave Testimony*, ed. John W. Blassingame (Baton Rouge: Louisiana State University Press, 1977), 704.

66. William Wells Brown, *Narrative of William Wells Brown, a Fugitive Slave,* in *Puttin' On Ole Massa*, ed. Gilbert Osofsky (Baton Rouge: Louisiana State University Press, 1968), 194.

67. Blassingame, *Slave Testimony*, 691.

68. Torture, according to Elaine Scarry, "converts the vision of suffering into the wholly illusory but . . . wholly convincing display of agency." *The Body in Pain*, 27.

69. Ibid., 47.

70. Cato Carter, in George P. Rawick, ed., *The American Slave: A Composite Autobiography*, 41 vols. (Westport, CT: Greenwood, 1973), suppl. 2, vol. 3, pt. 2, p. 646.

71. Catherine Slim, in ibid., vol. 16, pt. 4, p. 74.

72. Mary Gaffney, in ibid., suppl. 2, vol. 5, pt. 4, p. 1445.

73. James Martin, in ibid., suppl. 2, vol. 5, pt. 3, p. 63.

74. Polly Shine, in ibid., suppl. 2, vol. 9, pt. 8, pp. 3514–3515.

75. Blassingame, *Slave Testimony*, 138.

76. *New Orleans Daily Picayune*, March 26, 1853, cited in Richard Tansey, "Bernard Kendig and the New Orleans Slave Trade," *Louisiana History* 23, no. 2 (Spring 1982): 160.

77. Blassingame, *Slave Testimony*, 503.

78. Dave Byrd, in Rawick, *The American Slave*, suppl. 2, vol. 3, pt. 2, pp. 564–565.

79. Ethel Dougherty, in ibid., suppl. 1, vol. 5, pt. 1, p. 63.

80. Edward Lycurgas, in ibid., suppl. 1, vol. 17, pt. 1, p. 206.

81. Blassingame, *Slave Testimony*, 347.

82. Millie Simpkins, in Rawick, *The American Slave*, suppl. 1, vol. 16, pt. 6, p. 66.

83. Winger Vanhook, in ibid., suppl. 2, vol. 10, pt. 9, p. 395.

84. Mattie Gilmore, in ibid., suppl. 2, vol. 5, pt. 4, p. 1492. See also Emma Taylor, in ibid., suppl. 2, vol. 9, pt. 8, p. 3762.

85. Scarry, *The Body in Pain*, 152.

86. *Slave Life in Georgia: A Narrative of the Life, Sufferings, and Escape of John Brown*, ed. Louis. A. Chamerovzow (London: W. M. Watts, 1855), 112–118.

87. Charles L. Perdue Jr., Thomas E. Barden, and Robert K. Philips, eds., *Weevils in the Wheat: Interviews with Virginia Ex-Slaves* (1976; repr. Bloomington: Indiana University Press, 1980), 325.

88. Chamerovzow, *Slave Life in Georgia*, 117.

89. Mrs. Fannie Berry, in Perdue, Barden, and Philips, *Weevils in the Wheat*, 49.

90. Ibid., 166.

91. Michael Tadman remarks that "the real evils of the trade lay, not with physical experiences, but with the deeply racist white assumptions on which the traffic was built, and with the emotional sufferings of slaves callously separated from parents, offsprings, siblings, and other members of their community." Between 1830 and 1850, over a quarter of a million slaves were moved due to sales and planter migration. According to Tadman, teenagers and young adults constituted the staple of trade. For slaves in the upper South, the chance of being sold in the first forty years of their life was as high as 30 percent, and forcible separations of slaves for sale destroyed about one in three of all first marriages. *Speculators and Slaves: Masters, Traders, and Slaves in the Old South* (Madison: University of Wisconsin Press, 1989), 82, 113, 133–178. See also Herbert Gutman, *The Black Family in Slavery and Freedom, 1750–1925* (New York: Vintage, 1976).

92. Pierre Bourdieu, *Outline of a Theory of Practice*, trans. Richard Nice (London: Cambridge University Press, 1977), 191.

93. Peter Sloterdjik, "Pain and Justice," in *Thinker on Stage: Nietzsche's Materialism*, trans. Jamie Owen Daniel (Minneapolis: University of Minnesota Press, 1989), 77. Sloterdjik skillfully argues that the construction of the socially endurable enables the spectacle of terror.

94. Solomon Northup, *Twelve Years a Slave*, in Osofsky, *Puttin' On Ole Massa*, 323–324.

95. Being forced to dance before the master was a common occurrence, according to the testimony of the enslaved.

96. Jacob Stroyer, *My Life in the South*, in *Five Slave Narratives: A Compendium*, ed. William Loren Katz (New York: Arno and New York Times, 1968), 45.

97. Ibid., 45.

98. Discipline, as Foucault has defined it, "is a technique of power which operates

primarily on the body." It creates a docile body that can be "subjected, used, transformed and improved." Michel Foucault, *Discipline and Punish*, trans. Alan Sheridan (New York: Vintage, 1979), 136.

99. Frederick Douglass, *Life and Times of Frederick Douglass* (New York: Collier, 1962), 147.

100. J. Hamilton Couper, Theo B. Bartow, and George Adams, "Premium Essay on the Treatment of Slaves," *Soil of the South* 3 (March 1853): 458–459, cited in *Advice Among the Masters: The Ideal in Slave Management in the Old South*, ed. James O. Breeden (Westport, CT: Greenwood, 1980).

101. Tattler, "Management of Negroes," *Southern Cultivator* 8 (November 1850): 162–164. See also Breeden, *Advice Among the Masters*, 65.

102. Guion Griffis Johnson, *A Social History of the Sea Islands, with Special Reference to St. Helena Island* (Chapel Hill: University of North Carolina Press, 1930), 143.

103. According to George Fredrickson, romantic racialism "projected an image of the Negro that could be construed as flattering or laudatory in the context of some currently accepted ideals of human behavior and sensibility. . . . The romantic racialist view endorsed the 'child' stereotype of the most sentimental school of proslavery paternalists." The notable traits of the African from this vantage point were lightheartedness, a natural talent for music, and a willingness to serve. *The Black Image in the White Mind: The Debate on Afro-American Character and Destiny, 1817–1914* (Middletown, CT: Wesleyan University Press, 1971), 103–105.

104. "The Peculiarities and Diseases of Negroes," *American Cotton Planter and Soil of the South* (1860), in Breeden, *Advice Among the Masters*, 280.

105. Unnamed Mississippi planter, "Management of Negroes upon Southern Estates," *De Bow's Review* 10 (June 1851), cited in Paul F. Paskoff and Daniel J. Wilson, eds., *The Cause of the South: Selections from* De Bow's Review, *1846–1867* (Baton Rouge: Louisiana State University Press, 1982), 24.

106. Small farmer, "Management of Negroes," *De Bow's Review* 11 (October 1851), in ibid.

107. Adeline Jackson, in Rawick, *The American Slave*, South Carolina Narratives, vol. 3, pt. 3, p. 3.

108. Gary Stewart, in ibid., Texas Narratives, vol. 5, pt. 4, p. 62.

109. Henry Bland, in ibid., Georgia Narratives, vol. 12, pt. 1, p. 90.

110. Norman R. Yetman, *Life Under the "Peculiar Institution": Selections from the Slave Narrative Collection* (New York: Holt, Rinehart and Winston, 1970), 78.

111. Ed Shirley, in Rawick, *The American Slave*, Kentucky Narratives, vol. 16, pt. 2, p. 23.

112. Ann Thomas, in ibid., Florida Narratives, vol. 17, pt. 1, p. 330.

113. Marinda Jane Singleton, in Perdue, Barden, and Philips, *Weevils in the Wheat*, 267.

114. Nicolas Herbemont, "On the Moral Discipline and Treatment of Slaves," *Southern Agriculturalist* 9 (February 1836), in Breeden, *Advice Among the Masters*, 277–278.

115. Eda Harper, in Rawick, *The American Slave*, Arkansas Narratives, vol. 9, pt. 3, p. 164.

116. Drew Gilpin Faust, *The Creation of Confederate Nationalism: Ideology and Identity in the Civil War South* (Baton Rouge: Louisiana State University Press, 1988), 69.

117. Douglass, *Life and Times*, 148.

118. The reaction to "innocent amusements" by the enslaved community is examined at length in chapter 2.

119. Henry Bibb, *Narrative of the Life and Adventures of Henry Bibb, an American Slave, Written by Himself*, in Osofsky, *Puttin' On Ole Massa*, 68.

120. Theodore Parker, "A Sermon on Slavery," in *Works*, vol. 4 (London, 1863, 1870), cited in Fredrickson, *The Black Image in the White Mind*, 119–120.

121. Douglass, *Life and Times*, 147.

122. Ibid.

123. Frederick Douglass, *Narrative of the Life of Frederick Douglass, an American Slave, Written by Himself* (1845; repr., New York: New American Library, 1968), 31.

124. Douglass's position on slave culture was an ambivalent one. He considered it both an expression of discontent, woe, and resistance and an example of the degraded condition of the slave. Waldo E. Martin argues that Douglass, like many of his contemporaries, assumed the superiority of Euro-American culture and "accept[ed] the idea of Afro-American cultural inferiority while disassociating it from his commitment to human equality." *The Mind of Frederick Douglass* (Chapel Hill: University of North Carolina Press, 1984), 243.

2. Redressing the Pained Body

1. John McAdams, in George P. Rawick, ed., *The American Slave: A Composite Autobiography* (Westport, CT: Greenwood, 1973), 41 vols., Texas Narratives, suppl. 2, vol. 7, pt. 6, p. 2461; Lu Lee, in ibid., suppl. 2, vol. 6, pt. 5, p. 2297; Mary Glover, in ibid., suppl. 2, vol. 5, p. 1518.

2. McAdams, in ibid., suppl. 2, vol. 7, pt. 6, p. 2467.

3. Frederick Douglass, *Life and Times of Frederick Douglass* (New York: Collier, 1962), 147.

4. Toby Jones, in Rawick, *The American Slave*, Texas Narratives, vol. 4, pt. 2, p. 249.

5. The hyperbolic enactment of power central to domination links performance and everyday practice.

6. Michel de Certeau, *The Practice of Everyday Life* (Berkeley: University of California Press, 1984), 21.

7. Raymond A. Bauer and Alice H. Bauer, "Day to Day Resistance to Slavery," in *American Slavery: The Question of Resistance*, ed. John H. Bracey, August Meier, and Elliott M. Rudwick (Belmont, CA: Wadsworth, 1971), 37–60.

8. Elaine Scarry, *The Body in Pain* (New York: Oxford University Press, 1985), 33.

9. Ulrich Philips, *American Negro Slavery* (New York: Vintage Books, 1972); Eugene D. Genovese, *Roll, Jordan, Roll: The World the Slaves Made* (New York: Vintage, 1972); Mark Tushnet, *The American Law of Slavery, 1810–1860: Considerations of Humanity and Interest* (Princeton, NJ: Princeton University Press, 1981); Robert William Fogel and Stanley L. Engerman, *Time on the Cross: The Economics of American Negro Slavery* (New York: W. W. Norton, 1974).

10. Raymond Williams, *The Country and the City* (New York: Oxford University Press, 1973).

11. See Clarence E. Walker, "Massa's New Clothes," in *Deromanticizing Black History: Critical Essays and Reappraisals* (Knoxville: University of Tennessee Press, 1991). In "Aunt Jemima in Dialectics," James Anderson notes the reproduction of the plantation school perspective in accounts that utilize the testimony of the enslaved. *Journal of Negro History* 61, no. 1 (January 1976): 99–114. James Oakes, *The Ruling Race: A History of American Slaveholders* (New York: Vintage, 1983).

12. As Renato Rosaldo writes, "The pastoral as a mode of ethnographic and historical inquiry suppresses and disguises the relation between power and knowledge." "From the Door of His Tent: The Fieldworker and the Inquisitor," in *Writing Culture: The Poetics and Politics of Ethnography*, ed. James Clifford and George Marcus (Berkeley: University of California Press, 1986), 97.

13. See Williams, *The Country and the City*, 36–38; and Genovese, *Roll, Jordan, Roll*, 3.

14. The pastoral is a comic romance generically about the reconciliation of opposing forces. Hayden White has argued that the mode in which a story is told reveals it to be a story of a particular kind. In White's schema of historical styles, when history is emplotted in the comic mode, its mode of explanation tends to be organicist and its ideological implications conservative. The focus on reconciliation, integrative and synthetic processes, and a conservative vision of good society, in this case the humanity of slavery, is certainly

appropriate to our understanding of the pastoral. The features of the pastoral are replicated in the very terms of the historical imagination. So what is explained comes to mirror the very terms of explication. See Hayden White, *Metahistory: The Historical Imagination in Nineteenth-Century Europe* (Baltimore: Johns Hopkins University Press, 1973), and *Tropics of Discourse: Essays in Cultural Criticism* (Baltimore: Johns Hopkins University Press, 1978). Roger D. Abrahams's work on the corn shucking as slave performance describes slavery as an "American pastoral" and the members of the plantation as "engaged in a vigorous common enterprise in which nature was placed at the service of the owners and tillers of the land. . . . Hands and masters played a role in a set piece which turned the system of power relationships of the plantation into a comedy and pastoral romance." *Singing the Master: The Emergence of African-American Culture in the Plantation South* (New York: Pantheon, 1992), 24.

15. For representations of slave culture in this mode, see Abrahams, *Singing the Master*, and Charles Joyner, *Down by the Riverside: A South Carolina Slave Community* (Urbana: University of Illinois Press, 1984), 127.

16. Nancy Fraser, *Unruly Practices: Power, Discourse, and Gender in Contemporary Social Theory* (Minneapolis: University of Minnesota Press, 1989), 17–33.

17. In "The Ethic of Care for the Self as a Practice of Freedom," Foucault describes power as the capacity of individuals to conduct or determine the behavior of others. James Bernauer and David Rasmussen, eds., *The Final Foucault* (Cambridge: MIT Press, 1994), 12, 18.

18. I am referring to the very exclusive meaning of *man* set forth in the Constitution and in eighteenth- and nineteenth-century political discourse.

19. See Judith Butler, *Bodies That Matter* (New York: Routledge, 1993), 223–242.

20. I use the terms "performance" and "performativity" interchangeably. Butler differentiates between these terms and argues that it would be a mistake to reduce performativity to performance. She defines performance as "bounded acts" characterized by hyperbole, mimicry, and denaturalizing enactments such as drag. In contrast, performativity "consists in a reiteration of norms which precede, constrain, and exceed the performer and in that sense cannot be taken as a fabrication of the performer's 'will' or 'choice'; further, what is 'performed' works to conceal, if not to disavow, what remains opaque, conscious, unperformable." Ibid., 234. Rather than reducing performativity to performance, I deploy both terms in an expanded sense that considers enactments of power, denaturalizing displays, and discursive reelaboration as a set of interrelated strategies and practices.

21. Ibid., 14. See also Judith Butler, *Gender Trouble: Feminism and the Subversion of Identity* (London: Routledge, 1990), 128–131.

22. Michael Omi and Howard Winant, in accordance with their definition of race as an "unstable and 'decentered' complex of social meanings constantly being transformed by political struggle," argue that "the meaning of race is defined and contested throughout society, in both collective action and personal practice. In the process, racial categories themselves are formed, transformed, destroyed and reformed." *Racial Formation in the United States* (New York: Routledge and Kegan Paul, 1986), 61–73.

23. Frantz Fanon, *Black Skin, White Masks*, trans. Charles Lam Markham (New York: Grove, 1967), 109–140; Butler, *Gender Trouble*, 24.

24. Paul Gilroy, "Sounds Authentic: Black Music, Ethnicity, and the Challenge of a Changing Same," *Black Music Research Journal* 11 (1991): 17. Performance "produces the imaginary effect of an internal racial core or essence by acting on the body through specific mechanisms of identification and recognition." Gilroy's definition of performance is very similar to Judith Butler's: "Acts, gestures and desire produce the effect of an internal core or substance, but produce this on the surface of the body, through the play of signifying absences that suggest, but never reveal, the organizing principle of identity as a cause. Such acts, gestures, enactments, generally construed, are performative in the sense that the essence or identity that they otherwise purport to express are [*sic*] fabrications manufactured and sustained through corporeal signs and other discursive means." *Gender Trouble*, 136.

25. Raymond Williams defines community as follows: "Community can be the warmly persuasive word to describe an existing set of relationships, or the warmly persuasive word to describe an alternative set of relationships. What is most important, perhaps, is that unlike all other terms of social organization (state, nation, society, etc.) it seems never to be used unfavourably, and never to be given any positive opposing or distinguishing term." *Keywords: A Vocabulary of Culture and Society* (New York: Oxford University Press, 1976), 76.

26. Fisk University, *Unwritten History of Slavery: Autobiographical Accounts of Negro Ex-Slaves* (Nashville, TN: Fisk University Social Science Institute, 1945).

27. Herbert Aptheker, *American Negro Slave Revolts* (1943; repr., New York: International Publishers, 1987); Gerald Mullin, *Flight and Rebellion: Slave Resistance in Eighteenth-Century Virginia* (New York: Oxford University Press, 1972); Eugene D. Genovese, *From Rebellion to Revolution: Afro-American Slave Revolts in the Making of the New World* (Baton Rouge: Louisiana State University Press, 1979).

28. See Peter Kolchin, *American Slavery, 1619–1877* (New York: Hill and Wang, 1993), 161–168; and Kenneth M. Stampp, *The Peculiar Institution: Slavery in the Ante-Bellum South* (1956; repr., New York: Vintage, 1956), 109–140.

29. John McAdams, in Rawick, *The American Slave*, Texas Narratives, suppl. 2, vol. 7, pt. 6, p. 2467.

30. Albert Raboteau defines conjuring as a "system of magic, divination, and herbalism" derived from African and European systems. *Slave Religion: The "Invisible Institution" in the Antebellum South* (Oxford: Oxford University Press, 1978), 80–86, 275–288. See also John Roberts, *From Trickster to Badman: The Black Folk Hero in Slavery and Freedom* (Philadelphia: University of Pennsylvania Press, 1986), 66–67.

31. John W. Blassingame, *The Slave Community: Plantation Life in the Antebellum South* (Oxford: Oxford University Press, 1979), 315–317. Blassingame notes that "masters frequently noticed the sense of community in the quarters; they reported that slaves usually shared their few goods, rarely stole from each other, and the strong helped the weak.... Group solidarity in the quarters enabled the slaves to unite in the struggle against the master." Ibid., 315–317.

32. Drucilla Cornell, "The Postmodern Critique of Community," in *The Philosophy of the Limit* (New York: Routledge, 1992); Iris Marion Young, *Justice and the Politics of Difference* (Princeton, NJ: Princeton University Press, 1990), 226–256.

33. This subhead is borrowed from de Certeau's discussion of tactic: "A tactic is a calculated action determined by the absence of a proper locus. No delimitation of an exteriority, then, provides it with the condition necessary for autonomy. The space of the tactic is the space of the other." Michel de Certeau, *The Practice of Everyday Life* (Berkeley: University of California Press, 1984), 38.

34. James C. Scott, *Domination and the Arts of Resistance: Hidden Transcripts* (New Haven, CT: Yale University Press, 1985); Paul Gilroy, *The Black Atlantic* (Cambridge, MA: Harvard University Press, 1993), 37.

35. David Brion Davis, *The Problem of Slavery in the Age of Revolution, 1770–1823* (Ithaca, NY: Cornell University Press, 1975), 260.

36. Morgan argues that racism made possible "the devotion to the equality that English republicans had declared to be the soul of liberty." The lumping of Native Americans, blacks, and mulattoes into the pariah class enabled whites to be united as a "master class." Edmund Morgan, *American Slavery, American Freedom* (New York: W. W. Norton, 1975), 381, 386.

37. Resistance, as Lila Abu-Lughod suggests, should be read as a diagnostics of power. To paraphrase her argument, resistance is neither an end in itself nor merely a celebration of human freedom or exercises of will but "an index to a particular figuration and transformation of power." The resistances of slave performance are "never in a position of exteriority in relation to power." "The Romance of Resistance: Tracing Transformations of Power through Bedouin Women," *American Ethnologist* 17, no. 1 (1990): 53.

38. Raymond Williams, *Marxism and Literature* (Oxford: Oxford University Press, 1977), 131.

39. Toby Jones, in Rawick, *The American Slave*, Texas Narratives, vol. 4, pt. 2, p. 249.

40. Mingo White, in Rawick, *The American Slave*, Alabama Narratives, vol. 6, pt. 1, p. 413.

41. Fisk University, *Unwritten History of Slavery*, 173.

42. John McAdams, in Rawick, *The American Slave*, Texas Narratives, suppl. 2, vol. 7, pt. 6, p. 7.

43. Susan Snow, in ibid. Mississippi Narratives, vol. 9, p. 138.

44. Neither liberal nor Marxist notions of the political subject are suited to the particular situation of the enslaved. The Marxist model is concerned with a different model of oppression-exploitation, and the free worker and does not offer an analysis of racial oppression. Ironically, "Marxist" interpretations of slavery have been quite conservative in their analysis of slavery and have focused on paternalism rather than domination or terror, and on total relations rather than racial subordination.

45. Jean Comaroff, *Body of Power, Spirit of Resistance: The Culture and History of a South African People* (Chicago: University of Chicago Press, 1985), 261.

46. Karl Marx, "On the Jewish Question," in *The Marx-Engels Reader*, ed. Robert C. Tucker (New York: W. W. Norton, 1978), 34.

47. Anne Showstack Sassoon writes that the word "political" only acquires its full sense in relation to the potential of a class to found a new integral state. Even when considering the possibilities of other political entities not defined by class, what is key is a notion of strategic action and systemic analysis. *Gramsci's Politics* (Minneapolis: University of Minnesota Press, 1987), 185.

48. Elizabeth Sparks, in Charles L. Perdue Jr., Thomas E. Barden, and Robert K. Philips, eds., *Weevils in the Wheat: Interviews with Virginia Ex-Slaves* (1976; repr. Bloomington: Indiana University Press, 1980), 276.

49. Hortense Spillers, "Mama's Baby, Papa's Maybe: An American Grammar Book," *Diacritics* 17, no. 2 (Summer 1987): 67.

50. Richard Schechner describes transportation performances as performances in which the performers are " 'taken somewhere,' but at the end, often assisted by others, they are 'cooled down' and reenter ordinary life just about where they went in." *Between Theater and Anthropology* (Philadelphia: University of Pennsylvania Press, 1985), 125–126.

51. Gustavo Gutiérrez, *A Theology of Liberation: History, Politics, and Salvation*, trans. Caridad Inda and John Eagleson (Maryknoll, NY: Orbis, 1973), 154,

cited in David B. Morris, *The Culture of Pain* (Berkeley: University of California Press, 1991), 147.

52. William Lee, in Perdue, Barden, and Philips, *Weevils in the Wheat*, 196.

53. West Turner, in ibid., 290.

54. Norman R. Yetman, *Life Under the "Peculiar Institution": Selections from the Slave Narrative Collection* (New York: Holt, Rinehart, and Winston, 1970), 263. See Raboteau, *Slave Religion*, 212–288; Sterling Stuckey, *Slave Culture: Nationalist Theory and the Foundations of Black America* (New York: Oxford University Press, 1987), 1–100; and George P. Rawick, *From Sundown to Sunup: The Making of the Black Community* (Westport, CT: Greenwood, 1973), 30–52.

55. On Christian status as a racial category, see Winthrop D. Jordan, *White over Black: American Attitudes toward the Negro, 1550–1812* (1968; repr. New York: W. W. Norton, 1977).

56. William Adams, in Rawick, *The American Slave*, Texas Narratives, vol. 4, pt. 1, p. 10.

57. Eliza Washington, in ibid., vol. 11, pt. 7, p. 53.

58. Ibid., vol. 12, pt. 2, pp. 322–323.

59. Sallie Johnson, in ibid., suppl. 2, vol. 6, pt. 5, p. 2048.

60. Spillers, "Mama's Baby," 74.

61. Rawick, *The American Slave*, suppl. 1, vol. 7, pt. 2, p. 784.

62. Ibid., suppl. 2, vol. 6, pt. 5, p. 2161.

63. Yetman, *Life Under the "Peculiar Institution,"* 229. Silas Jackson offered a similar account. See ibid., 177.

64. Jane Pyatt, in Perdue, Barden, and Philips, *Weevils in the Wheat*, 235.

65. Garland Monroe, in ibid., 215.

66. West Turner, in ibid., 290. This tactic is mentioned frequently in tales of resisting the Klan. See Gladys-Marie Frye, *Night Riders in Black Folk History* (Knoxville: University of Tennessee Press, 1977).

67. James Davis, in Rawick, *The American Slave*, Arkansas Narratives, vol. 8, pt. 1, p. 111.

68. de Certeau, *The Practice of Everyday Life*, xiv. *La perruque* is the classic example of the disruption and compliance with the system: "La perruque is the worker's own work disguised as work for his employer. . . . He cunningly takes pleasure in finding a way to create gratuitous products whose sole purpose is to signify his own capabilities through his work and to confirm his solidarity with other workers or his family through spending his time in this way." Ibid., 25–26. James Deane, in Rawick, *The American Slave*, Maryland Narratives, vol. 16, pt. 3, p. 8.

69. *Webster's New Twentieth Century Dictionary, Unabridged* (Cleveland: Collins World, 1976).

70. For a discussion of will-lessness, see Patricia J. Williams, "On Being the Object of Property," *The Alchemy of Race and Rights: Diary of a Law Professor* (Cambridge, MA: Harvard University Press, 1991), 218–220.

71. Schechner, *Between Theater and Anthropology*, 36–38.

72. Henri Lefebvre, *The Production of Space*, trans. Donald Nicholson-Smith (Cambridge, UK: Basil Blackwell, 1991), 141.

73. Jürgen Habermas, *The Structural Transformation of the Public Sphere: An Inquiry into a Category of Bourgeois Society*, trans. Thomas Burger (Cambridge, MA: MIT Press, 1991), 75–76.

74. As de Certeau states, space is "composed of intersections of mobile elements. It is in a sense actuated by the ensemble of movements deployed within it. Space occurs as the effect produced by the operations that orient it, situate it, temporalize it." *The Practice of Everyday Life*, 101, 117.

75. According to Nancy Fraser, the politics of need entail three distinct but related moments: "The first is the struggle to establish or deny the political status of a given need, the struggle to validate the need as a matter of legitimate political concern or to enclave it as a nonpolitical matter. The second is the struggle over the interpretation of the need, the struggle for the power to define it and, so, to determine what would satisfy it. The third moment is the struggle over the satisfaction of the need, the struggle to secure or withhold provision." The dominated generally lack the power to politicize need; therefore, needs are an important aspect in the self-constitution of new collective agents and political subjects. *Unruly Practices*, 164–173.

76. Williams, *The Alchemy of Race and Rights*, 152.

77. Ravish: To seize and carry away by force and violence and to carry away emotion; to fill with great joy and delight; to transport; to enrapture. *Webster's New Twentieth Century Dictionary*.

78. Juba illuminates other facets of social struggle, specifically the contestation over cultural forms. Instrumental amusements, the commodified spectacle of blackness, and resistant pleasures converge in juba. It highlights the various circuits of the black performative and the contestation and transvaluation that are part and parcel of the commodification and circulation of cultural forms. Juba was a signature piece in minstrelsy, an important example of "the nigger's good time" in proslavery ideology, and a symbolic articulation of social struggle.

79. John F. Szwed and Morton Marks, like Melville J. Herskovits, argue that it is important to consider dance as part of a dance-music ensemble because "the

steps and the music are inextricably intertwined." Music and dance have an integral relation, and the identity a dance acquires, as well as its use, depends upon music. Dance embodies the music, and the meanings of the songs themselves change as they are performed. "The Afro-American Transformation of European Set Dances and Dance Suites," *Dance Research Journal* 20, no. 1 (Summer 1988): 29; Melville J. Herskovits, *The Myth of the Negro Past* (Boston: Beacon Press, 1958), 265.

80. Stearns writes that patting juba referred to "any kind of clapping with any dance to encourage another dancer"; it became "a special routine of slapping hands, knees, thighs, and body in a rhythmic display." Marshall Stearns and Jean Stearns, *Jazz Dance: The Story of American Vernacular Dance* (New York: Schirmer, 1968), 29.

81. Northup's characterization is unmistakably condescending and satiric. Since he was a trained violinist and former freeman, inflections of contempt and superiority color his description. Nonsensical musical expression without distinct ideas is certainly a formula for primitivism. Generally, his description of the enslaved utilizes key features of racist representations (for example, "the ivory teeth, contrasting with their black complexions, exhibit two long white streaks the whole extent of the table"). He does stress the significance of pleasure and, in doing so, emphasizes the harshness of slavery. He contrasts the three days of the Christmas celebration with the "three hundred and sixty-two . . . days of weariness, and fear, and suffering, and unremitting labor." Solomon Northup, *Twelve Years a Slave*, in *Puttin' on Ole Massa: The slave narratives of Henry Bibb, William Wells Brown, and Solomon Northup* (Baton Rouge: Louisiana State University Press, 1968), 163–169. Northup described patting as a music peculiar to slaves: "The patting is performed by striking the hands on the knees, then striking the right shoulder with one hand, the left with the other—all the while keeping time with the feet, and singing."

82. William B. Smith, "The Persimmon Tree and the Beer Dance," *Farmer's Register* 6 (1838): 58–61.

83. Although Douglass emphasizes the critique of slavery embodied in the juba song, as he had stressed the tone of protest in the spirituals, and evaluated the song as "not a bad summary of the palpable injustice and fraud of slavery," he remained uncomfortable with the pleasures afforded the enslaved, for he was convinced that the pleasures enjoyed within the limits of slavery were simply means of "keeping down the spirit of insurrection." Douglass was unable to envision the pleasures afforded by dances, time off, and slave holidays as little more than "part and parcel of the gross wrongs and inhumanity of slavery"

designed to better "secure the ends of injustice and oppression." *Life and Times*, 146–147.

84. Ibid., 146. Douglass's representation of a juba song varied significantly from more common versions:

Juba dis and Juba dat;
Juba kill a yaller cat.
Juba up and Juba down;
Juba runnin' all aroun'.
Juba jump, Juba sing,
Juba cut that pigeon wing.
Juba kick off this old shoe,
Juba dance that Jubilo.
Juba whirl them feet about,
Juba blow the candle out.
Juba swing, undo the latch,
Juba do that long dog scratch.

85. Beverly J. Robinson, "Africanisms and the Study of Folklore," in *Africanisms in American Culture*, ed. Joseph E. Holloway (Bloomington: Indiana University Press, 1990), 215.

86. Ibid., 216.

87. The intensity of discipline and surveillance of the captive body, to quote Foucault, "engenders at the same time an intensification of each individual's desire, for, in and over his body." Yet "power, after investing itself in the body, finds itself exposed to a counter-attack in the same body." *Power/Knowledge: Selected Interviews and Other Writings, 1972–1977*, ed. Colin Gordon, trans. Colin Gordon, Leo Marshall, John, Mepham, and Kate Soper (New York: Pantheon, 1980), 56.

88. Lefebvre, *The Production of Space*, 41–42. Here I am playing with Lefebvre's idea that representational space has its source "in the history of the people as well as in the history of each individual belonging to that people."

89. The brilliant work of scholars like Melville J. Herskovits, Zora Neale Hurston, Mechal Sobel, Sterling Stuckey, John F. Szwed, and Robert Farris Thompson has illuminated the relation between African and African American culture. Certainly, my work is indebted to this line of scholarship and is not at odds with this work but simply adopts a different vantage point.

90. According to Benjamin, the difference between voluntary and involuntary memory turns upon the status of information. Voluntary memory is the repository of information about the past that retains no trace of it. In contrast, *mémoire involontaire* conveys no information about the past, but is a repository

of its traces. "On Some Motifs in Baudelaire," 160. As Freud noted, memory traces "have nothing to do with the fact of becoming conscious: indeed they are often most powerful and enduring when the process which left them behind was one which never entered consciousness." *Beyond the Pleasure Principle*, 19. I have borrowed the phrase "memory of difference" from VèVè Clark's "Katherine Dunham and the Memory of Difference," in *History and Memory in African-American Culture*, ed. Geneviève Fabre and Robert O'Meally (New York: Oxford University Press, 1995). However, my use of the phrase differs significantly from Clark's, which is based on Susan Foster's concept of choreography. I use it to encompass both voluntary and involuntary memory and to acknowledge the structuring presence and absence of the past. Unlike Clark's phrase, this "memory of difference" does not depend upon the cognition of the difference between a former practice and a current one. It is simply a way of insisting on the differential and discontinuous status of memory.

91. Rawick, *The American Slave*, vol. 12, pt. 2, pp. 26–27. The use of the pot is frequently mentioned throughout the slave narrative collection. See Mary Hudson, in ibid., vol. 16, pt. 6, pp. 31, 34, 45.

92. Anderson and Minerva Edwards, in Rawick, *The American Slave*, Texas Narratives, vol. 4, pt. 2, p. 6.

93. Fisk University, *Unwritten History of Slavery*, 98.

94. Patsy Hyde, in Rawick, *The American Slave*, vol. 16, pt. 6, p. 34.

95. Mechal Sobel, *Trabelin' On: The Slave Journey to an Afro-Baptist Faith* (Princeton, NJ: Princeton University Press, 1988), 171.

96. Raboteau, *Slave Religion*, 216.

97. Ibid., 360n7.

98. Robert Farris Thompson, *Flash of the Spirit* (New York: Random House, 1984), 142.

99. Drucilla Cornell defines natality as "the possibility of re-generative iterations that actually do innovate in the sense of effecting change in self-definition." Natality "emphasizes how the self is continuously 'birthed' again through time and its encounters with others." *Transformations: Recollective Imagination and Sexual Difference* (New York: Routledge, 1993), 42.

100. Paulin J. Hountondji, cited in V. Y. Mudimbe, *The Invention of Africa: Gnosis, Philosophy, and the Order of Knowledge* (Bloomington: Indiana University Press, 1988), 37: Paulin J. Hountondji, *African Philosophy: Myth and Reality*, trans. Henri Evans with Jonathan Rée (Bloomington: Indiana University Press, 1976), 177; Tsenay Serequeberhan, *The Hermeneutics of African Philosophy: Horizon and Discourse* (New York: Routledge, 1994), 31–53 (Serequeberhan deconstructs Africanity or "essentialist particularism"); Kwame Anthony

Appiah, *In My Father's House: Africa in the Philosophy of Culture* (New York: Oxford University Press, 1992); Denise-Constant Martin, "Out of Africa!: Should We Be Done with Africanism?," in *The Surreptitious Speech: Presence Africaine and the Politics of Otherness, 1947–1987*, ed. V. Y. Mudimbe (Chicago: University of Chicago Press, 1992).

101. Serequeberhan, *Hermeneutics*, 46.

102. Although traditionally, the evaluation of these practices has been conducted under the rubric of "Africa," I have tried to suspend and displace the question of Africa on the following grounds: the practice of conquest, captivity, dislocation, and "seasoning" (transculturation) makes the recovery of origins impossible; the very identification of "African" practices is mired in a reductive and racist Africanist discourse that reproduces Africa as "ahistorical" and temporally othered; investing the eyewitness accounts of these practices with the authority of historical evidence reproduces the dominion of the white gaze and lends credence to uninformed and often racist accounts; and in these accounts Africa comes to stand for the limited knowledges of whites and their failure to make a meaningful or informed assessment of these practices. As well, the very repertoire invoked to designate Africa includes a generic range of features like flat-footed dance, call and response, pelvic motion, et cetera. This is the equivalent of describing the ballet in terms of jutted chins, pointed toes, and stiff torsos. What insight does such a range of descriptions lend in terms of understanding these practices?

103. The phrase "submission to consanguinity" is borrowed from Rey Chow, *Writing Diaspora: Tactics of Intervention in Contemporary Cultural Studies* (Bloomington: Indiana University Press, 1993), 24.

104. Édouard Glissant, *Caribbean Discourse: Selected Essays*, trans. J. Michael Dash (Charlottesville: University of Virginia Press, 1989), 62.

105. Glissant discusses this noncontinuist genealogy or subterranean history in terms of "sub-marine roots: that is floating free, not fixed in one position in some primordial spot, but extending in all directions in our world through its network of branches." Ibid., 62–67.

106. See Pierre Nora, "Between Memory and History: Les Lieux de Mémoire," trans. Marc Roudebush, *Representations* 26 (Spring 1989): 7–25. Nora's distinction between memory and history depends upon an evolutionary and anthropological notion of historical progress and development. It relies on distinctions between tradition and modernity. Memory exists in a proto-peasant environment and is a prehistory or a primitive order of chronicling the past. It is an ethnohistory of sorts. For an interesting rereading of Nora, see Clark, "Katherine Dunham and the Memory of Difference."

107. The notion of "subterranean history" is informed by Foucault's notion of repressed and subjugated knowledges and Glissant's notion of the submarine roots of the African diaspora.

108. According to Cornell, "The recollection of oneself is always an act which imagines through the remembrance of its own claims of selfhood what can never be fully recollected, but only forever reimagined and re-told." *Transformations*, 42.

109. James A. Snead, "Repetition as a Figure in Black Culture," in *Out There: Marginalization and Contemporary Cultures*, ed. Russell Ferguson, Martha Gever, Trinh T. Minh-ha, and Cornel West (New York: The New Museum of Contemporary Art/MIT Press, 1990), 221. Another aspect of repetition, though not considered as redress, is the circulation and commodification of juba on the minstrel stage. It is ironically appropriate that juba was memorialized by a black performer, William "Juba" Lane, on the minstrel stage, thus absolutely confusing imitation and authenticity and highlighting the perverse lines of descent that characterize diasporic forms/transculturation. Lane was famous for his renditions of "authentic Negro dancing" and clogging. He was credited with being responsible for the minstrel show dances' integrity as a "Negro art form." What better illustration of the complicity of the authentic and the counterfeit? Certainly, the essentialist particularisms of the real Negro are wedded to unspoken normativity of whiteness, in this case marked by the classifying gaze that measures both degrees of blackness and authenticity. On the minstrel stage, the authenticity of juba is evaluated in terms of the ability to simulate the Negro. This play of authenticity and imitation transgresses racial boundaries only in order to reinscribe them.

110. Glissant, *Caribbean Discourse*, 80; Patricia Williams, "On Being the Object of Property," 217.

111. Michel Foucault, "Nietzsche, Genealogy, History," in *Language, Counter-Memory and Practice*, ed. Donald F. Bouchard, trans. Donald F. Bouchard and Sherry Simon (Ithaca, NY: Cornell University Press, 1977), 147.

112. Marshall and Jean Stearns have described juba as follows: "It is danced by the surrounding circle of men before and after each performance of the two men in the center. Both the words and the step are in call and response form, and the words must ring out as rhythmically as a drummer's solo. The two men in the center start the performance with the Juba step while the surrounding men clap, and then switch to whatever new step is named in the call, just before the response 'Juba! Juba!' sounds and the entire circle starts moving again. The result is completely choreographed, continuous group dance, combining the call-and-response pattern, dancing in a circle (generally

counter-clockwise), the shuffle, improvisation, and the rhythms of calling and clapping." *Jazz Dance*, 29.

Katherine Dunham described juba as a plantation folk dance that combined elements of the English square dance and the French quadrille. Dunham has argued that the process of enslavement and acculturation resulted in the transvaluation of African forms—their meaning and value changed even when notable similarities remained: "The disintegration of African religious ideology under the impact of European influences led to the incorporation of the forms of its dance into secular dance." Many African dances reemerged in the guise of secular forms and also incorporated European American popular forms. The transformation and emergence of African American dance forms chronicle the history of conquest, enslavement, colonization, and acculturation. The definitive transitions of African forms in the Americas are as follows: "1. The use of African ritual patterns for the expression of Christian ideology; 2. The degeneration of religious ritual patterns, by virtue of the disintegration of the ideology which sustains them, into secular use; and 3. The combination of secular African patterns with the secular patterns of whatever European nation happened to dominate the territory." The reaggregation and transformation of these patterns make the location of origins difficult and in some cases virtually impossible. Dunham argues that because of modification, the African traditions that exist in the United States "have a sound functional relationship towards a culture which is contemporary, rather than towards one which is on the decline; and therefore such traditions as have been retained are assured of survival as long as the large, strong cultural body of which they are a part survives." She traces the transformation of juba from the majumba, a plantation folk dance, to the Big Apple, a popular dance of the 1930s in New York City. "The Negro Dance," in *The Negro Caravan*, ed. Sterling A. Brown, Arthur P. Davis, and Ulysses Lee (Salem, NH: Ayer, 1991), 998.

Many critics have argued that juba had typical African patterns: the "get down" motion of feet firmly planted on the ground, squats, stomps, the polymetric combination of foot stamping, clapping, and patting juba, the vital aliveness of body parts, the use of parts of the body as independent instruments of percussive force, driving offbeat rhythmic effects, flat-footed dancing, and call-and-response. See Robert Farris Thompson, *African Art in Motion* (Berkeley: University of California Press, 1974). Songs are danced with the body, rhythmic elements are stressed, and call-and-response and repetition structure the dance and direct collective performance. Within this frame of "Africanness," juba shares much in common with African dance. What do such designations yield? Would one attempt to distill a European worldview from similarly redacted elements? I have not pursued a line of argument that focuses on issues of Africanity or African-ness because of the often-crude reduction codification of things African, rhythm, lower-body motion, arms akimbo, et cetera. More important, the conditions and terms of this knowledge of Africa and the contours of an Africanist discourse were unavoidably part of a colonizing effort and the knowledge based on missionary reports, travelers, descriptions, et cetera. Not only is the knowledge in service of racism, but more important, what it reveals are the contours of Europe in Africa and Europe's self-consolidation through the production of Africa.

113. Such facile classifications that rely on essentialist racial assumptions aban-don cultural analysis in favor of explaining culture as an expression of racial identity. It is possible to understand these attempts to fix clear lines of descent or points of origin as denial of the miscegenation of popular culture in the United States. As Brenda Dixon states, "Although Black dance remains unde-fined, Black dancers are defined and delimited by the White consensus that Black dance and Black dancers are synonymous." Second, she argues that the fact that black dance has become a general means of expression in the public domain makes classification even more difficult. American culture had been so shaped by African culture that it is merely an analytic convenience or an illusion to act as if the dominant culture were external to the dominated culture, or vice versa. Any evaluation of black dance must take into account African and New World black cultures and European forms. "Black Dance and Dancers and the White Public: A Prolegomenon to Problems of Defini-tion," *Black American Literature Forum* 24, no. 1 (Spring 1990): 119–120.

114. Robinson traces the etymology of juba to the Bantu *juba, diuba,* or *guiba,* which mean "to pat, to beat or count time, the sun, the hour," "Africanisms," 225.

115. Repetition also characterizes the musical and poetic form of this song-and-dance ensemble, call-and-response patterns, and reiteration of short phrases. Repetition is also a functional element that is an "aid to dancing without fatigue." John Storm Roberts, *Black Music of Two Worlds* (Tivoli, NY: Original Music, 1972), 184.

116. Toni Morrison, *Beloved* (New York: Plume, 1988), 35–36.

117. A conservative estimate of the number of Africans transported to the Ameri-cas is around fifteen million. However, this number fails to account for the mortality rate during the Middle Passage, which averaged between 15 and 20 percent, or the numerous deaths that resulted from capture and embarkment. Furthermore, when we consider the role of warfare as the central means of

acquiring captives, that death toll increases considerably. Thus the losses of the slave trade greatly exceed even the conservative estimate of twelve million Africans. See Philip D. Curtin, *The Atlantic Slave Trade: A Census* (Madison: University of Wisconsin Press, 1969); Joseph E. Inikori and Stanley L. Engerman, eds., *The Atlantic Slave Trade: Effects on Economies, Societies, and Peoples in Africa, the Americas, and Europe* (Durham, NC: Duke University Press, 1992); Joseph E. Inikori, "The Slave Trade and the Atlantic Economies," in UNESCO, *The African Slave Trade from the Fifteenth to the Nineteenth Century* (Paris: UNESCO, 1979); Patrick Manning, *Slavery and African Life: Occidental, Oriental, and African Slave Trades* (New York: Cambridge University Press, 1991); and Walter Rodney, *How Europe Underdeveloped Africa* (Washington, DC: Howard University Press, 1982).

118. Victor Turner, *Dramas, Fields, and Metaphors: Symbolic Action in Human Society* (Ithaca, NY: Cornell University Press, 1974), 41.

119. Ibid.

120. Ibid.

121. Anna Lee, in Rawick, *The American Slave*, suppl. 2, vol. 6, pt. 5, p. 2281.

122. Frederic Jameson writes that "pleasure is finally the consent of life in the body, the reconciliation—momentary as it may be—with the necessity of physical existence in a physical world." This is in accordance with Jameson's criteria that in order for pleasure to be political, "it must always in one way or another also be able to stand as a figure for the transformation of social relations as a whole." This argument depends upon a notion of social totality with which I do not agree. As well, it does not take into account the instrumental use of pleasure precisely to prohibit such transformations. "Pleasure: A Political Issue," in *The Ideologies of Theory*, vol. 2 (Minneapolis: University of Minnesota Press, 1989), 74.

123. Celeste Avery, in Rawick, *The American Slave*, vol. 12, pt. 1, p. 23.

124. Charles Anderson, in Rawick, *The American Slave*, Ohio Narratives, vol. 16, pt. 4, p. 3.

125. Victor Turner, *The Ritual Process: Structure and Anti-Structure* (Ithaca, NY: Cornell University Press, 1969), 95.

126. "The breakdown" was also the name of a popular plantation dance that has been variously described as an affine of juba and other challenge dances and as characterized by sharp popping motions that provided the basis for later dances. See Lynne Fauley Emery, *Black Dance from 1619 to Today*, 2nd ed., rev. (Princeton, NJ: Dance Horizons, 1988); and Katrina Hazzard-Gordon, *Jookin': The Rise of Social Dance Formations in African American Culture* (Philadelphia: Temple University Press, 1990).

3. Seduction and the Ruses of Power

1. *Cato (a Slave) v. State*, 9 Fla. 166, 182 (1860); Francis Wharton, *A Treatise on the Criminal Law of the United States* (Philadelphia, 1857), 1123–1161; John Prentiss Bishop, *Commentaries on the Law of Statutory Crimes*, 478–496.

2. *State of Missouri v. Celia, a Slave*, File 4496, Callaway County Court, October Term, 1855, Callaway County Courthouse, Fulton, Missouri. All quotes from the case are from the case record; however, Melton McClaurin's *Celia, a Slave* (New York: Avon, 1991) brought the case to my attention.

3. Slave law encompasses both the slave statutes of the South and precedents established in case law. I do not intend to suggest that this is a unified body of material or that there are not differences, inconsistencies, and contradictions across jurisdictions. However, I am concerned with the exemplary and characteristic features of slave law as they affect the construction of black subjectivity, sexual violence, and other categories of injury.

4. In accordance with the common-law definition of rape, the raped woman must, in effect, prove she was raped by giving evidence of "reasonable resistance."

5. Thomas Jefferson, *Notes on the State of Virginia* (1787; repr., New York: W. W. Norton 1982), 162.

6. The role of seduction in rape cases has previously been examined along the lines of "no means yes" in Susan Estrich, "Rape," *Yale Law Journal* 95, no. 6 (1986): 1087–1184, and Catherine A. MacKinnon, "Feminism, Marxism, Method, and the State: Toward Feminist Jurisprudence," *Signs: Journal of Women in Culture and Society* 8, no. 4 (Summer 1983): 635–658. My emphasis is different here. It is not simply a matter of a woman's "no" not being taken seriously or of unveiling the crime when "it looks like sex." What is at issue here is the denial and restricted recognition of will or submission because of the legal construction of black subjectivity and the utter negation of the crime. As well, by exploring rape and sexual domination in the frame of seduction, I risk being accused of conflating the two or effacing the violence of rape through such framing. I share the reasonable discomfort with the juxtaposition of rape and seduction because it shifts the focus from violence to women's culpability or complicity. However, this is exactly what is at stake in this exploration— the ways in which the captive is made responsible for her undoing and the black body is made the originary locus of its violation. My employment of the term "discourse of seduction" should not be confused with the crime of seduction in common law. As a crime, seduction involves "leading an unmarried woman from the 'path of virtue' by means of temptation, deception, flattery, and false promises of marriage."

7. John Forrester, *The Seductions of Psychoanalysis* (Cambridge: Cambridge University Press, 1990), 86.

8. This presumption of consent is also crucially related to the pathologizing of the black body as a site of sexual excess, torpidity, and sloth. See Winthrop D. Jordan, *White over Black: American Attitudes toward the Negro, 1550–1812* (1968; repr. New York: W. W. Norton, 1977).

9. I am working with legal definitions of rape to demonstrate that the sexual violation of enslaved women was not encompassed by the law. Not only were they not protected by the common law or slave statute, but also the extremity of socially tolerable violence throws into crisis notions of force and will. Thus the violence and domination they are commonly subjected to fall outside the legal constituents of rape as a consequence of the sheer extremity of violence that is normative in their case. See Sue Bessmer, *The Laws of Rape* (New York: Praeger Special Studies, 1976); Susan M. Edwards, *Female Sexuality and the Law* (Oxford: Oxford University Press, 1981); Zillah R. Eisenstein, *The Female Body and the Law* (Berkeley: University of California Press, 1988), 42–116; Susan Estrich, *Real Rape* (Cambridge, MA: Harvard University Press, 1987); Frances Ferguson, "Rape and the Rise of the Novel," *Representations* 20 (Fall 1987): 88–112; and Carol Smart, *Feminism and the Power of Law* (London: Routledge, 1989), 26–49.

10. On the antebellum Supreme Court of Louisiana, see Judith K. Schafer, "Sexual Cruelty to Slaves," *Chicago-Kent Law Review* 68, no. 3 (1993): 1313–1342, and *Slavery, the Civil Law, and the Supreme Court of Louisiana* (Baton Rouge: Louisiana State University Press, 1996). *Humphreys v. Utz* is one case that she has unearthed, It involved an owner's suit against an overseer for the death of a slave who was brutally beaten and suffered cruelties that included having his penis nailed to a bedstead.

11. Crime is not employed here in accordance with traditional legal usage but as a way of challenging and interrogating the logic of property, the use of chattel persons, and the contradictions of slave law. For a discussion of state crime, see Gregg Barak, ed., *Crimes by the Capitalist State: An Introduction to State Criminality* (New York: State University of New York Press, 1991); Alexander George, ed., *Western State Terrorism* (New York: Routledge, 1991); and Robert Cover, "Violence and the Word," *Yale Law Journal* 95, no. 8 (July 1986): 1601–1630.

12. Mark Tushnet notes that "opinions in slave cases strongly supported the slave-law/black-law equation, for the rhetorical opposition of slaves and white men, not slaves and freepersons, proved nearly impossible to sustain." *The American Law of Slavery, 1810–1860: Considerations of Humanity and Interest* (Princeton, NJ: Princeton University Press, 1981), 140.

13. *State v. Tackett*, 8 N.C. (1 Hawks) 218 (December 1820).

14. There were criminal sanctions against homicide and violent assaults on slaves. However, extreme and torturous violence was legitimated if exercised in order to secure submission. See *Ex parte Boylston*, 33 S.C.L. 20, 2 Strob. 41 (1845); *State v. Mann*, 13 N.C. (2 Dev.) 263 (1829); and *Oliver v. State*, 39 Miss. 526 (1860). As well, the procedural discrimination that prohibited blacks from testifying against whites made these statutes ineffective, if not meaningless. Cases in which owners were prosecuted for murder and battery involved violence that was so extreme that the "enormities" were "too disgusting to be particularly designated." See *State v. Hoover*, 20 N.C. 396, 4 Dev. & Bat. 504 (1839). On the "legitimate uses" of slave property as regards sexual abuse and domination, see William Goodell, *The American Slave Code* (1853; repr., New York: Johnson, 1968), 86; and Andrew Fede, *People without Rights: An Interpretation of the Fundamental Laws of Slavery* (New York: Garland, 1992).

15. I use the term "sexuality" cautiously in light of Hortense Spillers's admonition that it is "dubiously appropriate" as a term of "implied relationship and desire in the context of enslavement." See "Mama's Baby, Papa's Maybe: An American Grammar Book," *Diacritics* 17, no. 2 (Summer 1987): 64–81.

16. Michel Foucault, "The Deployment of Sexuality," in *The History of Sexuality*, trans. Robert Hurley (New York: Vintage, 1980), 75–132.

17. Edmund Morgan, *American Slavery, American Freedom* (New York: W. W. Norton, 1979). As Margaret Burnham notes, "In contradistinction to the common law, the slaveholding states all adopted the civil rule, partus sequitur ventrem—the issue and descendants of the slaves follow the status of the mother." "An Impossible Marriage: Slave Law and Family Law," *Law and Inequality* 5 (1987): 215. See also Karen Getman, "Sexual Control in the Slaveholding South: The Implementation and Maintenance of a Racial Caste System," *Harvard Women's Law Journal* 7 (1984): 115–152.

18. *Alfred v. State*, 37 Miss. 296 (October 1859).

19. Ibid. The case was appealed on the grounds of juror selection, the competence of a biased juror, Alfred's confession, adultery as a defense for the murder, and the exclusion of Charlotte's confession. The higher court upheld the ruling of the lower court.

20. The mechanisms of sexual control can be understood as a kind of sovereign biopolitics—an absolute power with the right to take life and control and manage the forms of life. The modality of power that was operative on the enslaved combined features of modern and premodern power. It was a combination of the "menace to life" that characterizes sovereign power as well as

the management of life in the case of the enslaved population. See Foucault, "Right of Death and Power over Life," in *The History of Sexuality*, 133–159.

21. In *State v. Samuel*, 19 N.C. (2 Dev. & Bat.) 177 (1836), Samuel was convicted of murdering his wife's lover. On appeal of this conviction, his attorney argued that Samuel's wife's testimony against him should have been barred by the marital privilege. The court held that since "the privilege is grounded on the legal requirement of marital permanence, it ought not to be held to apply where no contract exists to require such permanence.... Hence a marriage de facto will not, but only a marriage de jure will, exclude one of the parties from giving evidence for or against the other."

22. This is consistent with the law's language of protection. (White) wives and daughters are protected by way of the legal fiction of the master/servant relationship and the vessels of the father's/husband's rights and property. As well, Carby notes that in abolitionist discourse and in slave narratives "the victim [of sexual violence] appeared not just in her own right as a figure of oppression but was linked to a threat to, or denial of, the manhood of the male slave." Hazel V. Carby, *Reconstructing Womanhood: The Emergence of the Afro-American Woman Novelist* (Oxford: Oxford University Press, 1987), 35.

23. *Keith v. State*, 45 Tenn. (5 Cold.) 35 (1867).

24. Spillers, "Mama's Baby, Papa's Maybe," 67.

25. The rape of black women is registered in case law almost exclusively in contexts in which they or their husbands or lovers were being prosecuted for crimes that would otherwise be recognized as self-defense.

26. I use the terms "female" and "woman" interchangeably. However, "female" does not refer to the presumed bedrock of gender—sex—but to the dominant construction of black womanhood in which sex and sexuality were foregrounded. The use of "female" is an attempt to underline the ideology of the natural and the bestial that defined her status and her use within the sexual economy of slavery.

27. At the time of Celia's trial, she had two children who were probably Newsome's and was pregnant with a third child, which was stillborn. McLaurin, *Celia*, 121.

28. A. Leon Higginbotham "Race, Sex, Education, and Missouri Jurisprudence: *Shelley v. Kraemer* in a Historical Perspective," *Washington University Law Quarterly* 67 (1989): 694.

29. I argued that sexual violence is crucial to the construction and experience of gender for black women, unlike Elizabeth Fox-Genovese, who argues that sexual violation of slave women demonstrated that they were somehow without gender or endowed with a lesser gender, since their sexual violation defied

the "appropriate gender conventions" of the dominant class. Fox-Genovese fails to consider that gender is not a preexistent unity but is overdetermined by other social practices and discourse. *Within the Plantation Household: Black and White Women of the Old South* (Chapel Hill: University of North Carolina Press, 1988), 193: "Violations of the [gender] norm painfully reminded slaves that they did not enjoy the full status of their gender, that they could not count on the 'protection'—however constraining and sometimes hypocritical—that surrounded white women."

30. See Jordan, *White over Black*; and Jefferson, *Notes on the State of Virginia*.

31. In *Commonwealth v. Turner*, 26 Va. 560, 5 Rand. 678 (1827), the court upheld the master's right to extreme forms of punishment. The only dissenting justice argued that a slave was entitled to protection as a person "except so far as the application of it conflicted with the enjoyment of the slave as a thing." William Goodell noted: "Another use of slave property is indicated in the advertisements of beautiful young mulatto girls for sale; and by the fact that these commonly command higher prices than the ablest male labourers, or any other description of slaves. . . . Forced concubinage of slave women with their masters and overseers, constitutes another class of facts, equally undeniable. . . . Such facts in their interminable varieties corroborate the preceding, and illustrate the almost innumerable uses of slave property." Goodell, *The American Slave Code*, 86.

32. Although I am focusing on female bodies, we must not lose sight of the fact that men were also the objects of sexual violence and (ab)use. I am not arguing that female gender is essentially defined by violation, but rather I am interrogating rape within the heterosexual closures that have traditionally defined the act, the role of violence in the reproductive economy of the plantation household, and the constitution of black subjectivity, particularly the construction of female gender, in the context of the law's calculation of personhood in accordance with degrees of injury.

33. As Slavoj Žižek writes, social fantasy "is a necessary counterpart to the concept of antagonism, a scenario filling out the voids of the social structure, masking its constitutive antagonism by the fullness of enjoyment." See "Beyond Discourse Analysis," in Ernesto Laclau, *New Reflections on the Revolution in Our Time* (London: Verso, 1990), 254.

34. Mary Boykin Chesnut, *A Diary from Dixie*, ed. Ben Ames Williams (1905; repr., Boston: Houghton Mifflin, 1949), 21.

35. Fanny Kemble, *Journal of a Residence on a Georgian Plantation in 1838–1839*, ed. John A. Scott (Athens: University of Georgia Press, 1984), 270. Kemble,

noting the inappropriateness of this response, described it as foolish and, in part, a weary reaction to the "ineffable state of utter degradation."

36. Ibid., 270.

37. Pierre Bourdieu, *Outline of a Theory of Practice*, trans. R. Nice (Cambridge: Cambridge University Press, 1977).

38. Slavoj Žižek, *The Sublime Object of Ideology* (London: Verso, 1989), 126. In the North, whiteness and freedom were also defined in contradistinction to black enslavement.

39. Jean Baudrillard, *Seduction*, trans. Brian Singer (New York: St. Martin's Press, 1990), 83.

40. Ibid.

41. George Fitzhugh, *Cannibals All! Or, Slaves without Masters* (1857; repr., Cambridge, MA: Belknap Press of Harvard University Press, 1971), 204–205.

42. Ibid., 205.

43. Ibid., 204.

44. Carole Pateman, *The Sexual Contract* (Stanford, CA: Stanford University Press, 1988), 66–67.

45. Hegemony encompasses coercion and consent, as opposed to direct and simple forms of domination, which rely solely on force and coercion. See Antonio Gramsci, *The Prison Notebooks*, ed. and trans. Quintin Hoare and Geoffrey Nowell Smith (New York: International Publishers, 1971).

46. I argue that the theory of power and the ethic of submission at work in law are aspects of nineteenth-century sentimental culture. For an extensive discussion of submission as an ethic of nineteenth-century culture, see Ann Douglas, *The Feminization of American Culture* (New York: Avon, 1977); and Jane Tompkins, *Sensational Designs: The Cultural Work of American Fiction, 1790–1860* (New York: Oxford University Press, 1985).

47. *State v. Mann*, 13 N.C. (2 Dev.) 263 (December 1829).

48. Ibid., 267.

49. Ibid., 266.

50. Tompkins, *Sensational Designs*, 128.

51. *Commonwealth v. Turner*, 26 Va. 561, 5 Rand. 680 (1827).

52. The contradiction between property and person is also generated by "two distinct economic forms . . . the form of property and the labour process," since the slave was both a "form of property (with a value in circulation)" and a "direct producer (as the producer of value in some definite activity of labouring)." Barry Hindess and Paul Q. Hirst, *Pre-Capitalist Modes of Production* (London: Routledge and Kegan Paul, 1975), 129.

53. However, manumission became more difficult during this period, and codes regulating slave gatherings became more severe.

54. In his study of slave law, Mark Tushnet argues that the "dual invocation of humanity and interest," which Judge Thomas Ruffin considered essential to mollifying the harsh injunction of slavery, was responsible for the failure of slave law to develop a stable body of law. Tushnet notes that the dual invocation reproduced the contradictions of slave society: the contradiction between capitalism and slavery and the contradiction between the slave as person and the slave as property. Unfortunately, Tushnet mistakenly characterizes slave relations as total because they engage "the master and slave in exchanges which must take account of the entire range of belief, feeling and interest embodied by the other" instead of the partial views of market relations. First, whether slave relations and market relations are contradictory is the subject of extended controversy. Certainly slavery existed rather successfully as a non-dominant mode of production within a capitalist social formation until the crisis of the 1850s. Second, Tushnet fails to question the idea of personhood or the confines of the slave subject constituted in law. The suggestion that slave law was humane because it recognized certain features of slave personhood is a dangerous overstatement. Mark Tushnet, *The American Law of Slavery, 1800–1860: Considerations of Humanity and Interest* (Princeton, NJ: Princeton University Press, 1981), 57. Patricia Williams, in a rebuttal of Tushnet, characterizes slave law as provisional because it defined blacks as without will and employed "partializing standards of humanity" that "imposed general inadequacy." "If 'pure will' or total control equals the perfect white person, then impure will and total lack of control equal the perfect black person. Therefore, to define slave law as comprehending a total view of personality implicitly accepts that food, shelter, and clothing (again assuming the very best of circumstances) is the whole requirement of humanity." It also assumes either that psychic care was provided by slave owners (as if an owned psyche could ever be reconciled with mental health) or that psyche is not a significant part of a whole human. The legal conception of a slave person does not take into account the range of feelings, belief, and interest but singularly pursues "a vision of blacks as simple-minded, strong-bodied economic 'actants.'" *The Alchemy of Race and Rights* (Cambridge, MA: Harvard University Press, 1991), 219–220.

55. Mark Tushnet argues that the dual invocation of slave law demonstrates the law's concern for the slave as a "total person" and the role of sentiment in slave law: "The fundamental social relation of slave society is total, engaging the full personalities of the slaveowner and the slave." *The American Law of Slavery*, 33.

56. For an examination of the relation between nation, body, and culture, see Elaine Scarry, *The Body in Pain* (New York: Oxford University Press, 1985), 108–109.

57. The mortified flesh refers both to the "zero degree of social conceptualization" and to the condition of social death. Spillers writes: "Before the 'body' there is the 'flesh,' that zero degree of social conceptualization that does not escape concealment under the brush of discourse. . . . Though the European hegemonies stole bodies . . . out of West African communities in concert with the African 'middleman,' we regard this human and social irreparability as high crimes against the flesh, as the person of African females and African males registered the wounding." "Mama's Baby, Papa's Maybe," 67. Although I do not distinguish between the body and the flesh as liberated and captive subject positions, I contend that the negation of the subject that results from such restricted recognition reinscribes the condition of social death. See Orlando Patterson, *Slavery and Social Death: A Comparative Study* (Cambridge, MA: Harvard University Press, 1982).

58. Thomas Cobb, *Inquiry into the Law of Negro Slavery* (Philadelphia, 1858), 84.

59. Jennifer Morgan, "Partus Sequitur Ventrem," *Small Axe 55* 22, no. 1 (March 2018): 1–17. Jennifer Morgan, *Laboring Women: Law, Race, Reproduction in Colonial Slavery* (Philadelphia: University of Pennsylvania Press, 2004). Saidiya Hartman, "Belly of the World," *Souls: A Critical Journal of Black Studies* 18, no. 1 (June 2016): 166–173.

60. See Andrew Fede, *People without Rights* (New York: Garland, 1992); and A. Leon Higginbotham Jr., *In the Matter of Color: Race and the American Legal Process; The Colonial Period* (New York: Oxford University Press, 1978).

61. Cobb, *Inquiry*, 90.

62. Ibid., 83.

63. Ibid., 100.

64. On slavery and managed depletion, see Stephanie Smallwood, *Saltwater Slavery: A Middle Passage from Africa to American Diaspora* (Cambridge, MA: Harvard University Press, 2007), 51.

65. *George (a Slave) v. State*, 37 Miss. 317 (October 1859).

66. It is debated whether these protections have anything at all to do with questions of humanity, or whether they are of the same order as protections extended to domestic animals.

67. Morgan, *American Slavery*, 316–337.

68. Louisiana was the only state that forbade the separation of a mother and a child under ten years old. However, it was not a common-law state but under the jurisdiction of a civil code.

422   NOTES

69. See Mary Frances Berry, "Judging Morality: Sexual Behavior and Legal
Consequences in the Late Nineteenth-Century South," in *Black Southerners
and the Law, 1865–1900*, ed. Donald G. Nieman (New York: Garland, 1994).
According to Berry, seduction became criminalized in the 1840s, and these
statutes spread across the United States in the post–Civil War period.

70. *Commonwealth v. Jerry Mann*, 2 Va. Ca. 210 (June 1820).

71. *Grandison (a Slave) v. State*, 21 Tenn. 2 Hum. 451 (December 1841).

72. Elsa Barkley Brown, "'What Has Happened Here?': The Politics of Differ-
ence in Women's History and Politics," in *We Specialize in the Impossible: A
Reader in Black Women's History*, ed. Darlene Clark Hine, Wilma King, and
Linda Reed (Brooklyn, NY: Carlson Publishing, 1995), 39.

73. Gayatri Chakravorty Spivak, "Feminism and Deconstruction," in *Outside in
the Teaching Machine* (New York: Routledge, 1993), 139.

74. This line of argument is influenced by Judith Butler's "Contingent Foundations," in *Feminists Theorize the Political*, ed. Judith Butler and Joan Scott (New
York: Routledge, 1992), 16. Butler writes: "To deconstruct the subject of feminism is not, then, to censure its usage, but, on the contrary, to release the term
into a future of multiple significations, to emancipate it from the maternal or
racialist ontologies to which it has been restricted, and to give it play as a site
where unanticipated meanings might come to bear." Also see Evelyn Brooks
Higginbotham, "African American Women's History and the Metalanguage
of Race," in Hine, King, and Reed, *We Specialize in the Impossible*. Higginbotham examines the overdetermination of technologies of race, as well as those
of gender and sexuality.

75. *Andrews v. Page*, 50 Tenn, 3 Heisk. 653 (February 1871).

76. This encompasses the construction of rape as a capital offense when committed by black men and the castration of black men as a preventive measure against such "sexual immodesty," as well as the magnification of injury
through the omission of rape as an offense affecting the enslaved female's
existence.

77. MacKinnon, "Feminism," 650.

78. Harriet A. Jacobs, *Incidents in the Life of a Slave Girl, Written by Herself*, ed.
Jean Fagan Yellin (1861; repr., Cambridge, MA: Harvard University Press,
1987).

79. Pateman, *The Sexual Contract*, 116–188.

80. Jacobs, *Incidents*, 55.

81. For a very insightful discussion of these issues, see Frances Ferguson, "Rape
and the Rise of the Novel," *Representations* 20 (Fall 1987): 88–112.

82. See Jacobs, *Incidents*, 33, 58, 59, 77, 121, 138, 158, 160, 187, 198.

83. As Marie Maclean observes, the act of narration involves "a delicate interplay of power in which the narratee submits to the control of a narrator, while the narrator must scheme to overcome the power of the narratee." *Narrative as Performance: The Baudelairean Experiment* (London: Routledge, 1988), 17.

84. The seductiveness of narrative, according to Ross Chambers, is "the means whereby such a text succeeds in acquiring a readership and inserting itself into the new interpretive contexts that will actualize its meaningfulness." The impact of a narrative is determined by "the power of seduction. . . . The claim to seductive power is a claim of perlocutionary force. Seduction produces "authority where there is no power, [and] is a means of converting (historical) weakness into (discursive) strength." Ross Chambers, *Story and Situation: Narrative Seduction and the Power of Fiction*, Theory and History of Literature, vol. 12 (Minneapolis: University of Minnesota Press, 1984).

85. Jacobs, *Incidents*, 54.

86. Ibid., 53.

87. Chambers, *Story and Situation*.

88. As Chambers argues, this strategy is narrative in that it "conform[s] to the [projected] desires of the other in order to bring about its own desire to narrate." In this regard, the duplicity of seduction is "constitutive of the narrative situation as such." Ibid., 218.

89. "Seduction as a narrative tactic takes the form of recruiting the desires of the other in the interest of maintaining narrative authority, so it is a duplicitous act to the extent that it introduces the concept of 'point' of cleavage, conflict of motives, since the story that conforms to the hearer's desires has also the function of satisfying other desires in the storyteller." Ibid., 215.

90. Jacobs, *Incidents*, 32.

91. Ibid., 51.

92. Elizabeth Keckley, *Behind the Scenes; or, Thirty Years a Slave, and Four Years in the White House* (1868; repr., New York: Oxford University Press, 1988), 39.

93. Jacobs, *Incidents*, 28.

94. Ibid.

95. See Michel Foucault, "What Is an Author?," in *Language, Counter-Memory and Practice*, ed. Donald F. Bouchard, trans. Donald F. Bouchard and Sherry Simon (Ithaca, NY: Cornell University Press, 1977), 127; and Lynn A. Higgins and Brenda R. Silver, eds., *Rape and Representation* (New York: Columbia University Press, 1991), 3.

96. Karen Sanchez-Eppler, "Bodily Bonds: The Intersecting Rhetorics of Feminism and Abolitionism," *Representations* 24 (Fall 1988): 36.

97. See Sandra Lee Bartky, *Femininity and Domination: Studies in the Phenomenology*

424   NOTES

of *Oppression* (New York: Routledge, 1990); and Frantz Fanon, *Black Skin, White Masks*, trans. Charles Lam Markham (New York: Grove, 1967).

98. As stated earlier, the law of rape required the demonstration of "utmost resistance" in order to establish nonconsent. The need to demonstrate utmost physical resistance requires that the woman's nonconsent be proven in order to determine whether a crime has occurred. Nonconsent is ultimately what gives meaning to consent.

99. Foucault describes the state of domination as that in which "an individual or social group manages to block a field of relations of power, to render them impassive and invariable and to prevent all reversibility of movement—by means of instruments which can be economic as well as political or military." "The Ethic of Care for the Self as a Practice of Freedom," in *The Final Foucault*, ed. James Bernauer and David Rasmussen (Cambridge, MA: MIT Press, 1994), 3.

100. In the liberal genealogy of freedom, the individual possesses property in himself and is essentially "the proprietor of his own person and capacities." See C. B. Macpherson, *The Political Theory of Possessive Individualism: Hobbes to Locke* (New York: Oxford University Press, 1962), 263.

4. The Burdened Individuality of Freedom

1. David Brion Davis, *The Problem of Slavery in Western Culture* (New York: Oxford University Press, 1966), and *The Problem of Slavery in the Age of Revolution, 1770–1823* (Ithaca, NY: Cornell University Press, 1975); Orlando Patterson, *Freedom in the Making of Western Culture* (New York: Basic Books, 1991); Robert Miles, *Capitalism and Unfree Labour: Anomaly or Necessity?* (London: Tavistock, 1987); Eric Williams, *Capitalism and Slavery* (London: Andre Deutsch, 1964); Cedric J. Robinson, *Black Marxism: The Making of the Black Radical Tradition* (London: Zed, 1983); Thomas C. Holt, *The Problem of Freedom: Race, Labor and Politics in Jamaica and Britain, 1832–1938* (Baltimore: Johns Hopkins University Press, 1992); Gerald David Jaynes, *Branches without Roots: Genesis of the Black Working Class in the American South, 1862–1882* (New York: Oxford University Press, 1986).

2. Mark Tushnet notes that in the law, "lines drawn on the basis of race and those drawn on the basis of condition were almost identical, [and] slave law could have been recharacterized as black law . . . for the rhetorical opposition of slaves and white men, not slaves and free persons, proved nearly impossible to resist." *The American Law of Slavery, 1800–1860* (Princeton, NJ: Princeton University Press, 1981), 140.

3. Karl Marx ironically describes the sphere of circulation or commodity exchange as an "Eden of the innate rights of man. It is the exclusive realm of Freedom, Equality, Property and Bentham." Freedom measured by the consent of exchange or the liberty of contract reveals the chasm between substantial and formal freedom and the freed as "someone who has brought his own hide to market and now has nothing else to expect but—a tanning." Simply put, the emancipated are free to dispose of their labor and are unfettered by other possessions. *Capital*, trans. Ben Fowkes, vol. 1 (New York: Vintage, 1977), 272–280.

4. According to Foucault, "right should be viewed . . . not in terms of a legitimacy to be established, but in terms of the subjugation that it instigates." "Two Lectures," in *Power/Knowledge: Selected Knowledge and Other Writings, 1972–1977*, trans. Colin Gordon, L. Marshall, J. Mepham, and K. Soper, ed. Colin Gordon (New York: Pantheon, 1980), 95–96.

5. As well, the import of the *Dred Scott* decision cannot be minimized. The decision held that blacks possessed no rights that whites were bound to respect and that blacks were never intended to be included as citizens by the "we the people" of the Constitution. Furthermore, the Naturalization Act of 1790 had restricted citizenship to whites.

6. See W. E. B. Du Bois, *Black Reconstruction in America* (New York: Atheneum, 1935), 670–710; Barbara J. Fields, "Ideology and Race in American History," in *Region, Race, and Reconstruction: Essays in Honor of C. Vann Woodward*, ed. J. Morgan Kaisser and James McPherson (New York: Oxford University Press, 1982); and Michael Kammen, *Mystic Chords of Memory: The Transformation of Tradition in American Culture* (New York: Vintage, 1993), 101–131.

7. Herman Belz, *Emancipation and Equal Rights* (New York: W. W. Norton, 1978), 108–140; Jacobus ten Broek, *The Antislavery Origins of the Fourteenth Amendment* (Berkeley: University of California Press, 1951).

8. Legal liberalism, as well as critical race theory, has examined issues of race, racism, and equality by focusing on the exclusion and marginalization of those subjects and bodies marked as different and/or inferior. The disadvantage of this approach is that the proposed remedies and correctives to the problem—inclusion, protection, and greater access of opportunity—do not ultimately challenge the economy of racial production or its truth claims or interrogate the exclusions constitutive of the norm, but instead seek to gain equality, liberation, and redress within its confines.

9. I am indebted to Irene Wei for this question.

10. Marx, *Capital*, vol. 1, 280.

11. Ann Norton, examining the role of property in American liberalism, argues

that property became "the body's sign and surrogate, the first medium of representation. Property stands for the body. . . . Property thus served to protect men's freedom and expand their dominion, to protect their bodies and enhance their pleasure. As property became a legal and cultural surrogate for the self, it also became the medium for the self-made man: a means for the materialization of individual power, taste and authority." "Engendering Another American Identity," in *Rhetorical Republic: Governing Representations in American Politics*, ed. Frederic M. Dolan and Thomas L. Dumm (Amherst: University of Massachusetts, 1993).

12. For accounts of the kinds of violence to which the freed were subjected, see Carl Schurz, *Report on the Condition of the South* (1865; repr., New York: Arno, 1969); and U.S. Congress, *Report of the Joint Committee on Reconstruction* (Washington, DC: Government Printing Office, 1866).

13. I have opted to use the term "accumulation" because slavery is not a relation of exploitation in the classic Marxian sense, but one predicated by theft, extreme domination, and forms of extraeconomic coercion.

14. For a critique of the inequality sanctioned by property rights, see Jennifer Nedelsky, *Private Property and the Limits of American Constitutionalism* (Chicago: University of Chicago Press, 1990), and "Bounded Selves," *Law and the Order of Culture*, ed. Robert C. Post (Berkeley: University of California Press, 1991).

15. I describe this coupling as disavowed since the word "slavery" was nowhere mentioned in the Constitution.

16. See Michel Foucault, "The Subject and Power," in *Michael Foucault: Beyond Structuralism and Hermeneutics*, ed. Hubert L. Dreyfus and Paul Rabinow (Chicago: University of Chicago Press, 1982); and Paul Smith, *Discerning the Subject* (Minneapolis: University of Minnesota Press, 1988), xxiv–xxxv. For a critique of notions of autonomy, free will, and independence, see Seyla Benhabib, Judith Butler, Drucilla Cornell, and Nancy Fraser, eds., *Feminist Contentions* (New York: Routledge, 1995).

17. Etienne Balibar, "Racism as Universalism," in *Masses, Classes, Ideas*, trans. James Swenson (New York: Routledge, 1994), 191–204; David Theo Goldberg, *Racist Culture: Philosophy and the Politics of Meaning* (Cambridge: Blackwell, 1993); Raymond Williams, *Keywords: A Vocabulary of Culture and Society* (New York: Oxford University Press, 1976).

18. I am indebted to the participants of the 1995 seminar "Feminism and Discourses of Power" at the University of California Humanities Research Institute, Irvine, for this line of thought.

19. See *Brown v. Board of Education* on stigmatic injury. "For in the very same

gesture with which [rights] draw a circle around the individual, in the very same act with which they grant sovereign selfhood, they turn back upon the individual all responsibility for her failures, her condition, her poverty, her madness—they privatize her situation and mystify the powers that construct, position and buffet her." *States of Injury* (Princeton, NJ: Princeton University Press, 1995), 128.

20. Helen E. Brown, *John Freeman and His Family* (Boston: American Tract Society, 1864), 30.

21. C. B. Macpherson, *The Political Theory of Possessive Individualism: Hobbes to Locke* (New York: Oxford University Press, 1962), 263–264. In this vision, "human society consists of a series of market relations."

22. On liberty as a racial value, see Goldberg, *Racist Culture*, 36–40.

23. Discernible in the very fabric of subjectivity are the limitations of freedom. Tracing the affiliation of freedom and constraint in regard to subjectivity, Etienne Balibar asks: "Why is it that the very *name* which allows modern philosophy to think and designate the *originary freedom* of the human being—the name subject—is precisely the name which *historically* meant suppression of freedom, or at least an intrinsic limitation of freedom, i.e., *subjection*?" "Subjection and Subjectivation," in *Supposing the Subject*, ed. Joan Copjec (London: Verso, 1994), 9. See also Williams, *Keywords*.

5. Fashioning Obligation

1. See Bonnie Honig, "Nietzsche and the Recovery of Responsibility," in *Political Theory and the Displacement of Politics* (Ithaca, NY: Cornell University Press, 1993), 42–75; William Connolly, "Liberalism and Difference," in *Identity/Difference: Democratic Negotiations of Political Paradox* (Ithaca, NY: Cornell University Press, 1991), 64–94; and Friedrich Nietzsche, *On the Genealogy of Morality*, ed. Keith Ansell-Pearson, trans. Carol Diethe (Cambridge: Cambridge University Press, 1994), 40.

2. Connolly, "Liberalism and Difference," 80.

3. This phrase is Jacques Donzelot's. See Giovanna Procacci, "Social Economy and the Government of Poverty," in *The Foucault Effect*, ed. Graham Burchell, Colin Gordon, and Peter Miller (Chicago: University of Chicago Press, 1991), 157.

4. Nietzsche, *Genealogy of Morality*, 44–50.

5. Jared Bell Waterbury, *Advice to a Young Christian* (New York: American Tract Society, 1843), 84. Throughout the text, Waterbury compares the Christian to the merchant.

6. W. E. B. Du Bois described the triumph of reaction in this period as a counterrevolution. *Black Reconstruction in America* (New York: Atheneum, 1935).

7. Eric Foner, *Reconstruction: America's Unfinished Revolution, 1863–1877* (New York: Harper and Row, 1988); Willie Lee Rose, *Rehearsal for Reconstruction: The Port Royal Experiment* (Indianapolis: University of Indiana Press, 1964); Leon F. Litwack, *Been in the Storm So Long: The Aftermath of Slavery* (New York: Vintage, 1979).

8. The wartime genesis of free labor in the Sea Islands and Tennessee was the subject of great scrutiny; cotton brokers, Northern manufacturers, and industrialists visited the South in the hope of arriving at a definitive answer to this question. In 1861, Edward Atkinson, the secretary of the Educational Commission, a group devoted to the "industrial, social, intellectual, moral and religious elevation of persons released from slavery in the course of the War for the Union," wrote a pamphlet called *Cheap Cotton by Free Labor*, in which he argued that emancipation would increase the supply of cotton manufacturers, not decrease it. During this period, Atkinson was the treasurer and agent for six cotton-manufacturing firms in Boston. See Rose, *Rehearsal for Reconstruction*, 35–37.

9. Gerald David Jaynes, *Branches without Roots: Genesis of the Black Working Class in the American South, 1862–1882* (New York: Oxford University Press, 1986); Foner, *Reconstruction*; Jonathan M. Wiener, *The Social Origins of the New South: Alabama, 1860–1885* (Baton Rouge: Louisiana State University Press, 1978), 35–73; Du Bois, *Black Reconstruction*.

10. See Albert O. Hirschman, *The Passions and the Interests: Political Arguments for Capitalism before Its Triumph* (Princeton, NJ: Princeton University Press, 1977), 3–66.

11. See Thomas C. Holt, *The Problem of Freedom: Race, Labor, and Politics in Jamaica and Britain, 1832–1938* (Baltimore: Johns Hopkins University Press, 1992).

12. On the significance of flight, movement, and migration in African American culture, see Farah Jasmine Griffin's *"Who Set You Flowin'?": The African-American Migration Narrative* (New York: Oxford University Press, 1995).

13. Reverend Isaac W. Brinckerhoff, *Advice to Freedmen* (New York: American Tract Society, 1864); Jared Bell Waterbury, *Friendly Counsels for Freedmen* (New York: American Tract Society, 1864); Helen E. Brown, *John Freeman and His Family* (Boston: American Tract Society, 1864); Clinton B. Fisk. *Plain Counsels for Freedmen* (Boston: American Tract Society, 1866). Lydia Maria Child also wrote a textbook for freed people, *The Freedmen's Book* (1865; repr., New York: Arno, 1968). It was first published by Ticknor and Fields

and generally considered too incendiary for use in many Southern schools because she encouraged the freed to leave work situations where they were not respected and directly addressed the ravages of slavery.

14. Robert C. Morris, *Reading, 'Riting, and Reconstruction: The Education of Freedmen in the South, 1861–1870* (Chicago: University of Chicago Press, 1976), 188. The American Tract Society also published a series of spellers and readers, the United States series, which was widely used in freedmen's schools throughout the South.

15. Jaynes, *Branches without Roots*, 131.

16. Holt, *The Problem of Freedom*, 304.

17. Wiener, *The Social Origins of the New South*, 70.

18. Jared Bell Waterbury, *Southern Planters and the Freedmen* (New York: American Tract Society, [1865–1866]), 37.

19. Jaynes, *Branches without Roots*, 312.

20. Ibid., 313–314.

21. For a brilliant discussion of the fiction of debt and its production of slavery and death among the people of the Putumayo of Colombia, see Michael Taussig, "The Economy of Terror," in *Shamanism, Colonialism and the Wild Man* (Chicago: University of Chicago Press, 1987), 60–73.

22. See Michael Kammen, *Mystic Chords of Memory: The Transformation of Tradition in American Culture* (New York: W. W. Norton, 1978); and Walter Benn Michaels, "Anti-Imperial Americanism," in *Culture of United States Imperialism*, ed. Amy Kaplan and Donald E. Pease (Durham, NC: Duke University Press, 1993), 392–406.

23. Andy McAdams in George P. Rawick, ed., *The American Slave: A Composite Autobiography*, 41 vols. (Westport, CT: Greenwood, 1973), suppl. 2, vol. 7, pt. 6, p. 2455.

24. Ibid., Suppl. 2, vol. 3, pt. 2, p. 877.

25. As Alessandro Pizzorno writes, "The individual, in the liberal view, is assumed to be a durable unit of action, holding the same criteria of judgement, the same preferences—or at least, some general metapreferences—over time. Similarly, the individual bears the consequence of his past actions, for which he can be punished or rewarded. This makes him a responsible subject of rights and duties." "Foucault and the Liberal View of the Individual," in *Michel Foucault, Philosopher*, ed. Timothy J. Armstrong (New York: Routledge, 1992).

26. Wendy Brown, *States of Injury: Power and Freedom in Late Modernity* (Princeton, NJ: Princeton University Press, 1995), 126.

27. See Marcel Mauss, *The Gift: Forms and Functions of Exchange in Archaic Societies* (New York: W. W. Norton, 1967), 41. The discussion of the gift of freedom

is a classic example of Mauss's argument about the form and function of exchange.

28. For a discussion of labor and embodiment in nineteenth-century culture, see Elaine Scarry, *The Body in Pain* (New York: Oxford University Press, 1985), 243–277; Gillian Brown, *Domestic Individualism: Imagining Self in Nineteenth-Century America* (Berkeley: University of California Press, 1990), 63–95; and Anne McClintock, *Imperial Leather: Race, Gender, and Sexuality in the Colonial Contest* (New York: Routledge, 1995), 99–100, 108.

29. Max Weber discusses the relation of the ascetic ideal of faithful labor and capitalism. He remarks that the passionate preaching of hard labor was both a defense against temptation and an exhibition of duty in a calling. *The Protestant Ethic and the Spirit of Capitalism* (1958; repr., Unwin, 1976), 165–183.

30. McAdams, in Rawick, *The American Slave*, suppl. 2, vol. 7, pt. 6, p. 2455.

31. Felix Haywood, in ibid., vol. 4, pt. 2, p. 134.

32. See Parker Pool, in ibid., vol. 15, pt. 2, pp. 190–191; and Patsy Michener, in ibid., vol. 15, pt. 2, pp. 121–123.

33. Joe Richardson argues that blacks resented the intrusions of white missionaries into their lives and comments about forms of enjoyment. The use of these primers rather than Lydia Maria Child's, which encouraged freedpeople to leave jobs where they were not well paid, indicates the instrumental use of these texts. *Christian Reconstruction: The American Missionary Association and Southern Blacks, 1861–1890* (Athens: University of Georgia Press, 1986), 237–255.

34. Silas Smith, in Rawick, *The American Slave*, vol. 3, pt. 4, p. 119.

35. Robert M. Cover, *Justice Accused: Antislavery and the Judicial Process* (New Haven, CT: Yale University Press, 1975), 8–41; David Montgomery, *Citizen Worker: The Experience of Workers in the United States with Democracy and the Free Market During the Nineteenth Century* (New York: Cambridge University Press, 1993), 52–114; William E. Forbath, "Free Labor Ideology in the Gilded Age," *Wisconsin Law Review* (1985), 767–817.

36. David Brion Davis, *The Problem of Slavery in the Age of Revolution, 1770–1823* (Ithaca, NY: Cornell University Press, 1975), 456.

37. Peter Linebaugh, "All the Atlantic Mountains Shook," *Labour/Le Travailleur* 10 (Autumn 1982): 87–121; Peter Linebaugh and Marcus Rediker, "The Many-Headed Hydra: Sailors, Slaves, and the Atlantic Working Class in the Eighteenth Century," *Journal of Historical Sociology* 3, no. 3 (September 1990): 225–252.

38. Michael B. Katz, *In the Shadow of the Poorhouse: A Social History of Welfare in America* (New York: Basic Books, 1986), 38–84.

39. Amy Dru Stanley, "Beggars Can't Be Choosers: Compulsion and Contract in Postbellum America," *Journal of American History* 78, no. 4 (March 1992): 1288. See also "Conjugal Bonds and Wage Labor: Rights of Contract in the Age of Emancipation," *Journal of American History* 75, no. 2 (September 1988): 471–500.

40. Sylvia Wynter, "Beyond the Categories of the Master Conception: The Counterdoctrine of the Jamesian Poesis," *C. L. R. James's Caribbean* (Durham, NC: Duke University Press, 1992).

41. Jaynes, *Branches without Roots*; Foner, *Reconstruction*; Roger L. Ransom and Richard Sutch, *One Kind of Freedom: The Economic Consequences of Emancipation* (New York: Cambridge University Press, 1977).

42. Davis also asserts that "slaveholders and industrialists shared a growing interest not only in surveillance and control but in modifying the character and habits of their workers." *Slavery in the Age of Revolution*, 458, 464.

43. The term is Jean-François Lyotard's. See *The Postmodern Condition*, trans. Geoff Bennington and Brian Massumi (Minneapolis: University of Minnesota Press, 1979), xi, 31–32, 35–36, 49, 60.

44. William Forbath discusses the repercussions of this vision for labor politics in the Gilded Age in "Free Labor Ideology in the Gilded Age," 782–786.

45. Jaynes, *Branches without Roots*, 300–316. Wiener also discusses sharecropping as a form of bonded labor. *The Social Origins of the New South*, 69–71.

46. Rawick, *The American Slave*, Oklahoma Narratives, vol. 7, p. 18.

47. Anna Lee, in ibid., suppl. 2, vol. 5, pt. 4, p. 2288.

48. Édouard Glissant, *Caribbean Discourse: Selected Essays*, trans. J. Michael Dash (Charlottesville: University of Virginia Press, 1989), 88–93.

49. Rawick, *The American Slave*, vol. 8, pt. 2, p. 18.

50. Tom Holland, in ibid., vol. 4, pt. 2, p. 147.

51. As Morton Horwitz and Clare Dalton point out, in the nineteenth century the will theory of contract was dominant. In the beginning of the twentieth century, the emphasis shifted to the "proper measure of contractual obligation" as formally expressed. "An Essay in the Deconstruction of Contract Doctrine," in *Interpreting Law and Literature: A Hermeneutic Reader*, ed. Sanford Levinson and Steven Mailloux (Evanston, IL: Northwestern University Press, 1988), 292–293. According to Horwitz, "Under the will theory, the basis for enforcing a contract was a 'meeting of minds' or convergence of the wills of the contracting parties." *Transformation of American Law, 1870–1960* (New York: Oxford University Press, 1992), vol. 2, p. 35. The will theory expressed the ideology of the market economy. See *Transformation of American Law, 1780–1860*, vol. 1 (New York: Oxford University Press, 1977), 180–210.

52. See William Cohen, "Negro Involuntary Servitude in the South, 1865–1940: A Preliminary Analysis," in *Black Southerners and the Law, 1865–1900,* ed. Donald G. Nieman (New York: Garland, 1994), 35–64; Litwack, *Been in the Storm So Long,* 336–386; and Jaynes, *Branches without Roots.*

53. Brown, *States of Injury,* 156.

54. Wiener, *The Social Origins of the New South,* 68–69; Francis W. Loring and Charles F. Atkinson, *Cotton Culture and the South, Considered with Reference to Emigration* (Boston: A. Williams, 1869).

55. Stanley, "Beggars Can't Be Choosers"; Holt, *The Problem of Freedom,* 286.5

56. Section 4, 435 of the Georgia Penal Code, March 12, 1866; Edward McPherson, *The Political History of the United States of America during the Period of Reconstruction* (Washington, DC: Solomon and Chapman, 1875), 33.

57. According to Cohen, race-neutral vagrancy laws and enticement statutes were "intended to maintain white control of the labor system, and local enforcement authorities implemented them with this in mind." "Negro Involuntary Servitude in the South," 34. See also Edward Ayers, *Vengeance and Justice: Crime and Punishment in the Nineteenth-Century American South* (New York: Oxford University Press, 1984), 141–222; George Washington Cable, "The Convict Lease System in the Southern States," in *The Silent South* (New York: Charles Scribner's Sons, 1885), 113–180; Montgomery, *Citizen Worker,* 83–87; Theodore Brantner Wilson, *The Black Codes of the South* (Tuscaloosa: University of Alabama Press, 1965); and J. Thorsten Sellin, *Slavery and the Penal System* (New York: Elsevier, 1976), 133–176.

58. Only the laws of Georgia, Texas, and Virginia survived Reconstruction intact; however, race-neutral statutes achieved the same results. Cohen, "Negro Involuntary Servitude in the South," 47.

59. Order to repeal Virginia Vagrancy Act, in McPherson, *The Political History of the United States during the Period of Reconstruction,* 42.

60. Florida Black Codes, in ibid., 39.

61. This was a considerable amount given that the range of wages was between $5 and $25 a month. First-class male field hands made no more than $5–$10 a month in Virginia, North Carolina, and Tennessee; $8–$12 a month in South Carolina and Georgia; $10–$18 a month in Mississippi, Alabama, Florida, and Louisiana; and $15–$25 a month in Arkansas and Texas. Litwack, *Been in the Storm So Long,* 411. This does not take into account the cost of lodging, clothing, food, medical expenses, and so on, or the great fluctuation in wages among plantations. According to the Freedmen's Bureau, wages as low as $2 a month were offered in Georgia. The bureau generally tried to keep wages between $8 and $10 a month in the years 1865 and 1866. See Ransom and

Sutch, *One Kind of Freedom*, 60. According to Loring and Atkinson, wages generally varied from $5 to $15 a month. *Cotton Culture*, 26–27.

62. Mitchell Dean, *The Constitution of Poverty* (London: Routledge, 1991), 35–67.

63. Steve Hahn, "Hunting, Fishing, and Foraging: Common Rights and Class Relations in the Postbellum South," in Nieman, *Black Southerners and the Law, 1865–1900*. E. P. Thompson discusses the use of similar measures in effecting control of the English working class in "Custom Law and Common Right," in *Customs in Common: Studies in Traditional Popular Culture* (New York: New Press, 1993), 97–184.

64. Ayers, *Vengeance and Justice*, 203.

65. Gilbert Thomas Stephenson, *Race Distinctions in American Law* (New York: D. Appleton, 1910), 52.

66. Lewis C. Chartock, "A History and Analysis of Labor Contracts Administered by the Bureau of Refugees, Freedmen, and Abandoned Lands in Edgefield, Abbeville and Anderson Counties in South Carolina, 1865–1868" (PhD diss., Bryn Mawr College, Graduate School of Social Work and Social Research, 1973), 188.

67. Contract of Joseph Abbey with Andrew and Kitty, Edgefield, 1867, in ibid., 143.

68. Ibid., 191.

69. I use the term "extralegal" rather than "illegal" because this violence usually went unpunished and was considered a customary right.

70. Litwack, *Been in the Storm So Long*, 278.

71. It is also important to keep in mind that the convict-labor system was spawned by a combined set of interests inclusive of Northern industrialists: "The convict lease system became a sort of mutual aid society for the new breed of capitalist and politicians of the white Democratic regimes of the New South, and often the same man played the roles of both entrepreneur and office holder." The convict-labor system was crucial to forging the new industrial economy of the South. Ayers, *Vengeance and Justice*, 195, 222.

72. See Carl Schurz, *Report on the Condition of the South* (1865; repr., New York: Arno, 1969); U.S. Congress, *Report of the Joint Committee on Reconstruction* (Washington, DC: Government Printing Office, 1860); Reverend Hamilton Pierson, *A Letter to Honorable Charles Sumner with Statements of Outrages in Georgia, an Account of My Expulsion from Adams, GA by the Klu Klux Klan* (Washington: Chronicle Print, 1870); and U.S. Congress, *Testimony Taken by the Joint Select Committee to Inquire into the Condition of Affairs in the Late Insurrectionary States* (Washington, DC: Government Printing Office, 1872).

73. It is commonly accepted that the election of Rutherford B. Hayes in 1876 was

a compromise between the North and the South that granted the Republicans the presidency at the price of Reconstruction. Foner, *Reconstruction*, 575–585.

74. Most of those who left the plantation eventually returned because of the lack of jobs and opportunities elsewhere. Jacqueline Jones, *Labor of Love, Labor of Sorrow: Black Women, Work, and the Family, from Slavery to the Present* (New York: Basic Books, 1985), 73–78; Litwack, *Been in the Storm So Long*, 292–335.

75. Sir William Blackstone's *Commentaries on the Laws of England*, cited in H. N. Hirsch, *A Theory of Liberty: The Constitution and Minorities* (New York: Routledge, 1992).

76. This was also the case with Lydia Maria Child's freedmen's primer, despite its radical antislavery message, which prevented *The Freedmen's Book* from being used in freedmen's schools for fear that it encouraged enmity between the races.

77. However, self-making is defined almost exclusively as self-regulation.

78. Schurz, *Report on the Condition of the South*, 21.

79. Certainly the invocation of Douglass, the ultimate representative of the black self-made man, was quite suited to Fisk's purposes. However, for a critique of Douglass's deployment of this rhetoric and the masculinism of such rhetoric, see Hazel V. Carby, *Reconstructing Womanhood: The Emergence of the Afro-American Woman Novelist* (Oxford: Oxford University Press, 1987); and Valerie Smith, *Self-Discovery and Authority in Afro-American Narrative* (Cambridge, MA: Harvard University Press, 1987), 33–34.

80. According to Wendy Brown, "The subject is ideally emancipated through its anointing as an abstract person, a formally free and equal human being, and is practically resubordinated through this idealist disavowal of the material constituents of personhood, which constrain and contain our freedom." *States of Injury*, 106.

81. It was not until the turn of the century that this formula would be challenged by Anna Julia Cooper. She argued that the cultivation of womanhood was essential to racial uplift: "Only the black woman can say 'when and where I enter, in the quiet, undisputed dignity of my womanhood without violence and without suing or special patronage, then and there the whole Negro race enters with me.'" *A Voice from the South* (1891; repr. New York: Oxford University Press, 1988), 31.

82. Mary Frances Berry, *Military Expediency and the Thirteenth Amendment* (Washington, DC: Howard University, 1975); Herman Belz, "Origins of Negro Suffrage during the Civil War," *Southern Studies* 17 (Summer 1978): 115–130.

83. Berry, *Military Expediency*, 5.

84. Nancy Fraser, *Unruly Practices: Power, Discourse, and Gender in Contemporary Social Theory* (Minneapolis: University of Minnesota Press, 1989), 127–128.

85. Homi K. Bhabha, *The Location of Culture* (New York: Routledge, 1994), 85–92.

86. Henry Banner, in Rawick, *The American Slave*, vol. 8, pt. 1, p. 105.

87. By the end of the nineteenth century, most common-law coverture restrictions had disappeared. Most of these changes benefited middle-class women, since they concerned inheriting property, establishing separate estates, et cetera. However, married women continued to have limited control of their wages. Joan Hoff, *Law, Gender, and Injustice* (New York: New York University Press, 1991), 87–88, 127–135. According to Jacqueline Jones, black husbands controlled labor agreements, and black women received compensation based upon their gender. Men were held responsible for their wives' breach of contract; black fathers received the wages of the children hired out and expressed the grievances of their families. *Labor of Love*, 62–63.

88. As Jacqueline Jones notes, at this time 97 percent of white women of the class of agricultural laborers were full-time homemakers, while over 25 percent of black women worked. These figures underestimate the actual percentage of freedwomen who worked because of the erasure of women's work within the family; this neglect is particularly exacerbated in the care of the sharecropping household, which depended on the labor of all of its members. *Labor of Love*, 66.

89. Brinckerhoff, *Advice to Freedmen*, 46; Fisk, *Plain Counsels*, 40.

90. Denise Riley, "'The Social,' 'Woman,' and Sociological Feminism," in *Am I That Name?: Feminism and the Category of "Women" in History* (Minneapolis: University of Minnesota Press, 1988), 44–66; Claudia Tate, *Domestic Allegories of Political Desire: The Black Heroine's Text at the Turn of the Century* (New York: Oxford University Press, 1992); Ann duCille, *The Coupling Convention: Sex, Text, and Tradition in Black Women's Fiction* (New York: Oxford University Press, 1993).

91. On the importance of the black family as a site of sustenance and resistance and the importance of domesticity in a black middle-class protest politics, see Herbert Gutman, *The Black Family in Slavery and Freedom, 1750–1925* (New York: Pantheon, 1976); and Jones, *Labor of Love*, 58–68.

92. *Orders Issued by the Freedmen's Bureau, 1865–66*, 39th Cong., 1st sess., House of Representatives Executive Document 70.

93. Jacques Donzelot, *The Policing of Families*, trans. Robert Hurley (New York: Pantheon, 1979), xxv; Jeffrey Minson, *Genealogies of Morals: Nietzsche, Foucault, Donzelot and the Eccentricity of Ethics* (New York: St. Martin's Press, 1985).

94. Michael B. Katz, *In the Shadow of the Poorhouse* (New York: Basic Books, 1986), 66–84.

95. On the control of dangerous classes, see Christopher G. Tiedeman, *A Treatise on the Limitations of Police Power in the United State, Considered from Both a Civil and Criminal Standpoint* (St. Louis: F. H. Thomas Law Book Co., 1886), 102–136.

96. Procacci, "Social Economy," 165.

97. Brown, *Domestic Individualism*, 20.

98. Rev. S. Humphreys Gurteen, *Handbook of Charity Organization* (Buffalo, NY: The Courier Company, 1882), 174–186, cited in Katz, *In the Shadow*, 76.

99. Ibid.; Procacci, "Social Economy," 165. See also Joseph-Marie de Gérando, *The Visitor of the Poor: Designed to Aid in the Formation and Working of Provident and Other Kindred Societies* (London: Simpkin and Marshall, 1833).

100. Clare Dalton, "An Essay in the Deconstruction of Contract Doctrine," in Levinson and Mailloux, *Interpreting Law and Literature*, 291–294.

101. The fostering of domesticity also aided in the internalization of market values by encouraging increased and expanded consumption, thereby stimulating the desire for cash wages. See the letters of Edward Philbrick, an engineer and railroad supervisor who managed a plantation on the Sea Islands and participated in the rehearsal for Reconstruction, in Elizabeth Ware Pearson, ed., *Letters from Port Royal Written at the Time of the Civil War* (Boston: W. B. Clarke Company, 1906), 219–221, 245, 276–277.

102. *The American Heritage Dictionary* defines "vindicate" as follows: "to defend, maintain, or insist on the recognition of (one's rights, for example)."

103. Neil Gotanda uses the term "status-race" to refer to the inferior status of blacks as a legal standard. "A Critique of 'Our Constitution Is Color-Blind,'" *Stanford Law Review* 44, no. 1 (November 1991), 37–40.

104. Gotanda, "A Critique of 'Our Constitution Is Color-Blind,'" 38.

105. Julia Kristeva, *Powers of Horror: An Essay on Abjection*, trans. Leon S. Roudiez (New York: Columbia University Press, 1982), 9; Butler, *Bodies That Matter*, 223–242.

6. Instinct and Injury

1. George Washington Cable, "The Freedman's Case in Equity," in *The Silent South* (New York: Charles Scribner's Sons, 1907), 6–10.

2. Ibid., 11.

3. Ibid., 14.

4. John Hope Franklin, "The Enforcement of the Civil Rights Act of 1875," in *Race and History: Selected Essays 1938-1988* (Baton Rouge: Louisiana State University Press, 1989), 119, 131.

5. Cable, "Freedmen's Case," 5.

6. George Washington Cable, "The Negro Question," in *The Negro Question: A Selection of Writings on Civil Rights in the South* (Garden City: Doubleday Anchor, 1958), 142.

7. Ibid., 143.

8. Ibid., 145.

9. Jill Quadagno argues that racism, in fact, has primarily determined the failure to address issues of social rights in the United States. See *The Color of Welfare: How Racism Undermined the War on Poverty* (New York: Oxford Press, 1994).

10. However, a major aspect of these relief efforts was inculcating the poor with the idea that they had no rights to economic security. See Michael B. Katz, *In the Shadow of the Poorhouse: A Social History of Welfare in America* (New York: Basic Books, 1986), 58–109.

11. Hannah Arendt, "The Social Question," in *On Revolution* (London: Penguin Books, 1963), 71. My definition of the social differs from Arendt's in major respects. Arendt bemoans the introduction of the social into the sphere of the political because she considers needs pre-political and instinctual, and condemns the introduction of the bodily into the space of reason and contemplation. For her, the social denotes the violent intrusion of the bodily into the political domain. The social engulfs the political with concerns that properly belong in the sphere of the household. Ibid., 91. In *The Human Condition*, she defines the social realm as follows: "The social realm, where the life process has established its own public domain, has let loose an unnatural growth, so to speak, of the natural; and it is against this growth, not merely against society but against a constantly growing social realm, that the private and intimate, on one hand, and the political (in the narrower sense of the word), on the other, have proved incapable of defending themselves." *The Human Condition* (Chicago: University of Chicago Press, 1958), 47.

12. Theodore Allen remarks that the promotion of poor and propertyless Euro-Americans to the white race disguised and denied the existence of poverty through the privileges awarded on the basis of race. *The Invention of the White Race* (New York: Verso, 1994). David Roediger notes that the critique of capitalism and wage labor was forestalled by the racist politics of the white working class. *The Wages of Whiteness: Race and the Making of the American Working Class* (London: Verso, 1991), 87.

13. Arendt, "The Social Question," 95. Arendt's conception of the social initially led her to condemn desegregation as the effort of parvenus to gain recognition. She reduced the anti-segregation movement to an issue of social preference. See Seyla Benhabib, "Models of Public Space: Hannah Arendt, the Liberal

Tradition, and Jürgen Habermas," in *Habermas and the Public Sphere*, ed. Craig Calhoun (Cambridge, MA: MIT Press, 1993), 79. Arendt does point to the failure to build lasting republican institutions in the United States because of an obsessive concern with material comforts. The dream of the revolution was replaced by "the dream of a promised land where milk and honey flow," although Arendt implies that the massive European immigration of the twentieth century contributed to this shift. The "ideals born out of poverty" supplanted "those principles which had inspired the foundation of freedom." "The Pursuit of Happiness," in *On Revolution*, 138–139.

14. Arendt's celebration of the American Revolution and critique of the French Revolution must be considered in the context of a larger attack on society, which she accuses of conflating the public and private realms. The French Revolution opened the political domain to the poor, who were driven by necessity and biological processes. According to Arendt, these were matters of the household, not the public sphere. See Jean L. Cohen and Andrew Arato, "The Normative Critique: Hannah Arendt," in *Civil Society and Political Theory* (Cambridge, MA: MIT Press, 1994), 177–200. Nancy Fraser offers an insightful critique of Arendt's conception of the social in *Unruly Practices: Power, Discourse and Gender in Contemporary Social Theory* (Minneapolis: University of Minnesota Press, 1989), 169–170, 185n16. Fraser remarks that Arendt can only conceive of need as "wholly natural" and "forever doomed to be things of brute compulsion. Thus, she supposes that needs can have no genuinely political dimension and that their emergence from the private sphere into the social spells the death of authentic politics." Ibid., 160n32.

15. Here, I am not trying to contrast a revolutionary ideal of the social with a repressive one, for efforts to provide minimum levels of security to the working class involved repressive forms of state intervention, regulation, and discipline. Frances Fox Piven and Richard A. Cloward, *Regulating the Poor: The Functions of Public Welfare*, rev. ed. (New York: Vintage, 1993).

16. Mary Poovey, in a discussion of the making of the social body in nineteenth-century England, writes that because "morality was conceptualized within a problematic of visuality, however, and because the poor were considered to be different from, as well as part of, the national whole, surveillance and the ocular penetration of poor neighborhoods were generally considered to be as critical to the inculcation of virtue as was the cultivation of taste." *Making a Social Body: British Cultural Formation, 1830–1864* (Chicago: University of Chicago Press, 1995), 35.

17. Foucault describes this focus on the species body and the biopolitics of the population. See "Right of Death and Power over Life," *The History of Sexuality*, trans. Robert Hurley, vol. 1 (New York: Vintage Books, 1980), 138–141.

18. Cable, "Freedman's Case," 11. In *Slaughter-House Cases*, the Supreme Court held that the police power of the state was, "by its very nature, incapable of any exact definition or limitation." It is not simply fortuitous that the expansive definition of the police power of the state and the restricted reading of the Fourteenth Amendment as conferring no new rights went hand in hand. This again attests to the entanglements or race and the social. H. N. Hirsch, *A Theory of Liberty: The Constitution and Minorities* (New York: Routledge, 1992), 79–85.

19. Barbara J. Fields, "Ideology and Race in American History," in *Region, Race and Reconstruction: Essays in Honor of C. Vann Woodward*, ed. J. Morgan Kousser and James M. McPherson (New York, 1982), 163–165.

20. Michael Kammen, *Mystic Chords of Memory: The Transformation of Tradition in American Culture* (New York: Vintage, 1993), 101–131.

21. My discussion of the amendments treats them as historical documents. I am less concerned with original intent and foundational meaning than with the Reconstruction vision of equality. I am not assuming the positivity of the law or the stability or fixity of meaning of the amendments or attempting to foreclose the possibilities of resignification in practice, but rather attempting to interrogate the animating vision of equality that culminated in these amendments. See John Hart Ely, *Democracy and Distrust: A Theory of Judicial Review* (Cambridge, MA: Harvard University Press, 1980), 1–42; Stanley Fish, "The Law Wishes to Have a Formal Existence," in *The Fate of Law*, ed. Austin Sarat and Thomas R. Kearns (Ann Arbor: University of Michigan Press, 1993), 159–208; and Stanley Fish, "Fish v. Fiss," Sanford Levinson, "Law and Literature," and Philip Bobbitt "Constitutional Fate," in *Interpreting Law and Literature: A Hermeneutic Reader*, ed. Sanford Levinson and Steven Mailloux (Evanston, IL: Northwestern University Press, 1988).

22. In particular, I have in mind the dominance of capitalism and racist discourse. On articulation, see Lawrence Grossberg, "Articulation and Culture," in *We Gotta Get Out of This Place: Popular Conservatism and Postmodern Culture* (New York: Routledge, 1992), 52–62; Lawrence Grossberg, "On Postmodernism and Articulation: An Interview with Stuart Hall," *Journal of Communication Inquiry* 10, no. 2 (1986): 45–60; and Ernesto Laclau and Chantal Mouffe, *Hegemony and Socialist Strategy: Towards a Radical Democratic Politics* (London: Verso, 1985), 105–114.

23. I use the term "state" in the singular here, although I do not assume the unity of the state and its various apparatuses or that it possesses a unifying or monolithic intention, nor do I mean to elide the distinction between the states and the national state. In opting for the convenience of the singular "state," I do

not wish to obscure this or the contestations between various aspects of the
state, clearly illustrated by the antagonisms between the executive, judicial,
and legislative branches of the national state and between the national state
and the Southern states, but to underline the systemic character of the state,
the coordination and collusion of the apparatuses of the state, and the ways
in which the separation of state and federal power sanctioned black subordination.

24. Obviously, one avenue of exploration is the grounding of liberty in property,
    thereby linking it with inequality. Jennifer Nedelsky, *Private Property and the
    Limits of American Constitutionalism: The Madisonian Framework and Its Legacy*
    (Chicago: University of Chicago Press, 1990); C. B. Macpherson, *The Political
    Theory of Possessive Individualism: Hobbes to Locke* (New York: Oxford Univer-
    sity Press, 1962), 263–277.

25. For purposes of clarity about the scope of these rights, it is important to remem-
    ber that civil, political, and social rights were considered separate and distinct,
    so that the conferral of civil rights did not extend political rights (right to vote,
    hold office, and serve on juries). Voting was considered a privilege rather than
    a right of citizenship, until the passage of the Fifteenth Amendment, and social
    rights ("the sphere of personal relations and associations, either private or
    public," which the law did not enter) were, for most, beyond the scope of the
    imaginable. Herman Belz, *A New Birth of Freedom: The Republican Party and
    Freedmen's Rights, 1861–1866* (Westport, CT: Greenwood, 1976), 109. In the
    debate on the passage of the Thirteenth Amendment, many considered the abo-
    lition of slavery a violation of the state's domestic institution, as well as a viola-
    tion of property and privacy no different from marital or familial relations—the
    husband's right of property in his wife or a father's in his children.

26. Robert Miles, *Capitalism and Unfree Labour: Anomaly or Necessity?* (London:
    Tavistock, 1987).

27. Let me make it clear that the discriminations of race at issue implicitly iden-
    tified blacks as inferiors and subordinates and effectively secured their sub-
    jugation. Unlike arguments forwarded by color-blind constitutionalists that
    all recognition of race is equally pernicious, this line of argument does not
    accept the neutrality of race as an immutable substance anterior to discourse
    but instead concerns itself with the inscription and valuation of raced bodies
    and race as an indexical marker of the history of enslavement and subjuga-
    tion. Color blindness in its refusal to "see" race fails to overcome this invidi-
    ous history and merely evades the injurious and stigmatic construction of race
    through this willed innocence. Moreover, color blindness begs the question
    of racial classification in yielding to the givenness, the neutrality, and the

immutability of race. When race is conceptualized as interminable, consistent, and invariable, the subjugation historically licensed by racial classification fails to be interrogated or remedied. Race is an effect of an ensemble of social and historical relations that have determined property relations, life chances, and an economy of value, from the accruing of profit and designations of the good, the true, and the beautiful, to calculations of human worth, through the creation of subjugated, dishonored, and castigated groups. Therefore, the refusal to see race neither diminishes that originary violence nor guarantees equality but merely enables this violence to be conducted in the guise of neutrality. A radical and expansive reading of the "badges of slavery" necessarily attends to the history of captivity, enslavement, subjugation, dispossession, exploitation, violation, and abjection productive of black difference. This history of enslavement was registered in the body's racialized inscription, whether the purportedly discernible markings on the body's surface or the blood coursing through indeterminate bodies, and utilized as an index of subjective value. Nonetheless, race was codified and enshrined in the law. Thus, despite its formal abrogation, slavery infused the nascent vision of equality and determined its character. The ineluctable production of racial difference undermined the assumption that blacks were released from the history of captivity by the negatory power of the Thirteenth Amendment and free agents unencumbered by the past.

28. All citations of the *Congressional Globe* are from *The Reconstruction Amendment Debates* (Richmond: Virginia Commission on Constitutional Government, 1976). The numbers in parentheses refer to the *Reconstruction Amendment Debates*. Cong. Globe, 38th Cong., 1st Sess., June 15, 1864, 2990; and 39th Cong., 1st Sess., December 13, 1865, 42 (97).

29. Cong. Globe, 39th Cong., 1st Sess., December 21, 1865, 113 (99).

30. Cong. Globe, 38th Cong., 2nd Sess., January 9, 1865, 43; 39th Cong., 1st Sess. December 21, 1865, 111 (99).

31. Cong. Globe, 38th Cong., 1st Sess., June 15, 1864, 2990. The language of self-making was also deployed against civil rights measures for the freed. For example, President Andrew Johnson's veto of the Freedmen's Bureau Bill exploited the rhetoric of self-sufficiency: "It is no more than justice then to believe that as they have received their freedom with moderation and forbearance, so they will distinguish themselves by their modesty and thrift, and soon show the world that in a condition of freedom they are self-sustaining, capable of selecting their own enjoyment and their own places of abode, of insisting for themselves, on a proper remuneration, and of establishing and maintaining their own asylums and schools." Cong. Globe, 39th Cong., 1st Sess., February 19, 1866, 917 (148).

32. Stevens's effort to craft an amendment with an explicit antidiscrimination feature was overwhelmingly defeated. See Benjamin B. Kendrick, "Journal of the Joint Committee of Fifteen on Reconstruction: 39th Congress, 1865–1867" (PhD diss., Columbia University, 1914), 51–52; and Cong. Globe, 39th Cong., 1st Sess., January 30, 1866, 537. The first version of the Civil Rights Bill sustained this position. Cong. Globe, 39th Cong., 1st Sess., January 12, 1866, 211 (104).

33. According to Carole Pateman, status "refers more generally to ascription; human beings are born in certain social positions by virtue of their ascribed characteristics, such as sex, color, age and so on. . . . Contract refers to a laissez faire economic order, an order of 'freedom of contract,' in which substantive individual characteristics and the specific subject of an agreement are irrelevant." *The Sexual Contract* (Stanford, CA: Stanford University Press, 1988), 10. The end of status presumes that every man possesses the capacity for self-making, and thereby his condition is not limited or determined by his race. Neil Gotanda makes an analogous distinction in his discussion of the deployment of race in color-blind constitutionalism. He states that status-race "is the traditional notion of race as an indicator of social status, as elaborated by Taney in *Dred Scott*." Formal race sees racial categories as "neutral, apolitical distinctions reflecting merely 'skin color' or country of ancestral origin. Formal race is unrelated to ability, disadvantage, or moral culpability. . . . Unconnectedness (to social attributes or relations) is the defining characteristic of formal race." "A Critique of 'Our Constitution Is Color-Blind,'" *Stanford Law Review* 44, no. 1 (November 1991): 4, 36–40. Taney provides the clearest definition of the meaning of status-race in *Dred Scott v. Sanford:* "They had for more than a century been regarded as beings of an inferior order, and altogether unfit to associate with the white race, either in social or political relations; and so far inferior, that they had no rights which the white man was bound to respect; and that the negro might justly and lawfully be reduced to slavery for his benefit." *Dred Scott v. Sanford,* 60 U.S. (19 Howard) 407 (1857).

34. Cong. Globe, 39th Cong., 1st Sess., January 18, 1866, 318 (107). See also ibid., January 22, 1866, 363, January 29, 1866, 476.

35. Cong. Globe, 39th Cong., 1st Sess., January 30, 1866, 499 (126).

36. Cong. Globe, 38th Cong., 1st Sess., June 15, 1864, 2984.

37. Cong. Globe, 39th Cong., 1st Sess., January 19, 1866, 322 (108).

38. Cong. Globe, 39th Cong., 1st Sess., January 27, 29, 1866, 474 (121).

39. These were the rights detailed in the Civil Rights Act. Cong. Globe, 39th Cong., 1st Sess., January 29, 1866, 476.

40. Cong. Globe, 39th Cong., 1st Sess., January 30, 1866, 504 (127).

41. Cong. Globe, 38th Cong., 2d Sess., June 21, 1864, 125.

42. As Walter Benn Michaels observes, "The absence of any difference grounded in law became powerful testimony to the irreducibility of a difference reflected in the law; legal equality became the sign of racial separation." "The Souls of White Folks," in *Literature and the Body: Essays on Populations and Persons*, ed. Elaine Scarry (Baltimore: Johns Hopkins University Press, 1988), 189.

43. Cong. Globe, 39th Cong., 1st Sess., January 23, 24, 1866, 393, (114).

44. Edward McPherson, *The Political History of the United States of America during the Period of Reconstruction* (Washington, DC: Solomon and Chapman, 1875), 70.

45. For a discussion of the articles of the Constitution that sanctioned and accommodated slavery, see William M. Wiecek, *The Sources of Antislavery Constitutionalism: 1760–1848* (Ithaca, NY: Cornell University Press, 1977) 42; Derrick A. Bell Jr., *And We Are Not Saved: The Elusive Quest for Racial Justice* (New York: Basic Books, 1987), 26–50; *Prigg v. Pennsylvania*, 41 U.S. 539 (1842); and *Dred Scott v. Sanford*, 60 U.S. (19 How.) 393 (1857).

46. Senator John Davis argued: "My position is that this is a white man's government. It was made so at the beginning. The charters that were granted by the different sovereigns of England to the various colonies were granted to white men and included nobody but white men. They did not include Indians. They did not include negroes. . . . I say that the negro is not a citizen. He may be made a citizen by power, but it will be in disregard, I think, of principle. I deny this is a government of amalgamation." Representative John Dawson argued similarly: "It is impossible that two distinct races should exist harmoniously in the same country, on the same footing of equality by the law. The result must be a deteriorating and disgusting mixture of the races. . . . We have, then, to insist upon it that this Government was made for the white race. It is our mission to maintain it. Negro suffrage and equality are incompatible with that mission." Cong. Globe, 39th Cong., 1st Sess., January 31, 1866, 528, January 31, February 1, 1866, 542; 39th Cong. 1st, Sess., December 13, 21, 1865, 110 (98); 39th Cong., 1st Sess., January 30, 1866, 504 (127).

47. Cong. Globe, 39th Cong., 1st Sess., February 1, 1866, 589 (135).

48. Cong. Globe, 39th Cong., 1st Sess., January 30, 31, 1866, 64 (133).

49. Cong. Globe, 39th Cong., 1st Sess., January 19, 1866, 340 (109).

50. John Hogan, in Cong. Globe, 39th Cong., 1st Sess., January 30, 31, 1866, 64 (133).

51. As Robyn Wiegman observes, although the black male "entered enfranchisement through the symbolic possibilities that accrued to the masculine . . . that this entrance was marked by extreme and incontrovertible violence . . .

demonstrates how unsettling was the possibility of the male as male." *American Anatomies: Theorizing Race and Gender* (Durham, NC: Duke University Press, 1995), 68. Claudia Tate forcefully argues that women adapted the domestic as a way to allegorize their political desire and intervene indirectly in the public sphere. *Domestic Allegories of Political Desire* (New York: Oxford University Press, 1992).

52. William E. Connolly, "Liberalism and Difference," in *Identity/Difference: Democratic Negotiations of Political Paradox* (Ithaca, NY: Cornell University Press, 1991), 81. According to Iris Young, the ideal of a universal humanity turns a blind eye to difference in ways that disadvantage those marked as different, enables the privileged to ignore their own specificity, and denigrates those who deviate from the norm. *Justice and the Politics of Difference* (Princeton, NJ: Princeton University Press, 1990), 164–165.

53. Uday S, Mehta, "Liberal Strategies of Exclusion," *Politics and Society* 18, no. 4 (December 1990): 429–430.

54. David Theo Goldberg, *Racist Culture: Philosophy and the Politics of Meaning* (Cambridge: Blackwell, 1993), 39. Naoki Sakai notes that "what we normally call universalism is a particularism thinking itself as universalism, and it is worthwhile doubting whether universalism could ever exist otherwise." "Modernity and Its Critique: The Problem of Universalism and Particularism," in *Postmodernism and Japan*, ed. Masao Miyoshi and H. D. Harootunian (Durham, NC: Duke University Press, 1989), 98.

55. Homi K. Bhabha, *The Location of Culture* (New York: Routledge, 1994), 86.

56. See Andrew Kull, *The Color-Blind Constitution* (Cambridge, MA: Harvard University Press, 1992), 86–87.

57. Cong. Globe, 39th Cong., 1st Sess., February 27, 1866, 1064 (154).

58. Cong. Globe, 39th Cong., 1st Sess., May 23, 1866, 2767 (221), on manhood as the equivalent of personhood.

59. As a consequence of U.S. naturalization policy and *Dred Scott*, citizenship virtually became synonymous with whiteness. For a discussion of the racist exclusions constitutive of citizenship, see James H. Kettner, *The Development of American Citizenship, 1608–1870* (Chapel Hill: University of North Carolina, 1978); Benjamin B. Ringer, *We the People and Others: Duality and America's Treatment of Racial Minorities* (New York: Routledge, 1983); and Joan Hoff, *Law, Gender, and Injustice: A Legal History of Women* (New York: New York University Press, 1991).

60. Kull, *The Color-Blind Constitution*, 81.

61. *People ex. rel. King v. Gallagher*, 93 NY, 438, 431 (1883), cited in ibid., 108. Although feminist critics have noted the need for equivalent rights and the

recognition of difference in redressing gender discrimination, in the nineteenth century, equivalent rights invariably meant truncated and circumscribed rights. See Drucilla Cornell, *Transformations* (New York: Routledge, 1993), 112–155.

62. The argument over the legality of the Civil Rights Act of 1866 concerned the right of Congress to intervene within the states' jurisdiction over civil rights. It was argued that a constitutional amendment was required in order to do so. This was the origin of the Fourteenth Amendment. According to Herman Belz, a sweeping transformation of citizenship occurred as a result of its passage: "Congress established the existence of national citizenship beyond any question and made state citizenship derivative from it. In its national aspect American citizenship was a title to fundamental civil rights under the constitution, such as the right to own property, which the Civil Rights Act identified. From this national right flowed the right as a state citizen to enjoy equality in respect of a state's criminal and civil code." *Emancipation and Equal Rights: Politics and Constitutionalism in the Civil War Era* (New York: W. W. Norton, 1978), 120.

63. Kull, *The Color-Blind Constitution*, 78–79.

64. Ibid., 81.

65. This line of argument is not intended to suggest that antidiscrimination laws and "suspect" race classifications alone are adequate to eradicate racism. In fact, as critical legal theorists and critical race theorists have argued, the assumptions of antidiscrimination law, in fact, maintain the cogency of race as a naturalized and uninterrogated category and meritorious arguments about the distribution of resources. Alan Freeman argues that antidiscrimination law has "served more to rationalize the continued presence of racial discrimination . . . than it has to solve the problem." "Legitimizing Racial Discrimination through Antidiscrimination Law: A Critical Review of Supreme Court Doctrine," *Minnesota Law Review* 62 (1978): 1349–1369. See also "Racism, Rights and the Quest for Equality of Opportunity: A Critical Legal Essay," *Harvard Civil Rights-Civil Liberties Law Review* 23, no. 2 (Summer 1988): 295–392. Similarly, Robert St. Martin Westley argues that antidiscrimination reproduces normative conceptions of racial difference that fail to treat race as a social category. For a different perspective, see Kimberlé Williams Crenshaw, "Race, Reform, and Retrenchment: Transformation and Legitimation in Antidiscrimination Law," *Harvard Law Review* 101, no. 7 (May 1988): 1331–1387, which offers a different reading of antidiscrimination law, noting the transformative possibilities of liberalism.

66. Judith A. Baer, *Equality under the Constitution: Reclaiming the Fourteenth Amendment* (Ithaca, NY: Cornell University Press, 1983), 102.

67. As Michael J. Sandel notes, "The system of natural liberty defines as just whatever distribution results from an efficient market economy in which a formal [legal] equality of opportunity prevails. *Liberalism and the Limits of Justice* (New York: Cambridge University Press, 1982), 66–103.

68. Brown, *States of Injury*, 110.

69. Cong. Globe, 39th Cong., 1st Sess., January 22, 1866, 342 (110).

70. Theodore W. Allen, *The Invention of the White Race*, vol. 1 (London: Verso, 1994), 143.

71. Carl Schurz, *Report on the Condition of the South* (1865; repr., New York: Arno, 1969); U.S. Congress, *Report of the Joint Committee on Reconstruction* (Washington, DC: Government Printing Office, 1866).

72. Trumbull applies this logic to interracial marriage in Cong. Globe, 39th Cong. 1st Sess., 322 (108). Cowan utilized the same logic regarding integrated schools in Cong. Globe, 39th Cong., 1st Sess., 500 (127).

73. As St. Clare indicts Miss Ophelia: "You loathe them as you would a snake or a toad, yet you are indignant at their wrongs. You would not have anything to do with them yourselves. You would send them to Africa, out of your sight and smell, and then send a missionary or two to do up all the self-denial of elevating them compendiously." Harriet Beecher Stowe, *Uncle Tom's Cabin* (1852; repr., New York: New American Library, 1966), 195. See also Karen Sanchez-Eppler, *Touching Liberty: Abolition, Feminism, and the Politics of the Body* (Berkeley: University of California Press, 1993), 41–49.

74. Cong. Globe, 39th Cong., 1st Sess., January 24, 25, 1866, 420 (117), February 2, 1866, 600 (137).

75. Abraham Lincoln, *Abraham Lincoln: Speeches and Writings, 1832–1858* (New York: Library of America, 1989). See speech on *Dred Scott* at Springfield, Illinois, ibid., 398; speech at Chicago, Illinois, July 10, 1858, ibid., 454; fourth Lincoln-Douglas debate, Charleston, Illinois, September 18, 1858, ibid., 636.

76. Cong. Globe, 38th Cong., 2d Sess., January 12, 1866, 237 (84).

77. Thaddeus Stevens, in Cong. Globe, 38th Cong., 1st Sess., June 21, 1864, 125.

78. Cong. Globe, 39th Cong., 1st Sess., January 31, February 1, 1866, 542 (133).

79. Cong. Globe, 39th Cong., 1st Sess., March 27, 1866, March 27, 1866, 1680 (194); McPherson, *Political History*, 75.

80. Cong. Globe, 39th Cong., 1st Sess., February 26, 1866, 134 (151).

81. Eva Saks, "Representing Miscegenation Laws," *Raritan* 8, no. 2 (1988): 42.

82. The term "miscegenation" was coined in 1863 in a seventy-two-page booklet titled *Miscegenation: The Theory of the Blending of the Races, Applied to the American White Man and the Negro*, by David Goodman Croly and George Wakeman. The word came from the Latin *miscere*, "to mix," and *genus*, "race." The

authors created two other words to describe race mixing—"melaeukation" and "melamigleukation"—which never acquired the currency of "miscegenation." See Forrest G. Wood, *Black Scare: The Racist Response to Emancipation and Reconstruction* (Berkeley: University of California Press, 1968), 53–79; Harvey Applebaum, "Miscegenation Statutes: A Constitutional and Social Problem," 53 *Georgia Law Journal* (1964), 49, cited in Derrick A. Bell Jr., *Race, Racism and American Law* (Boston: Little, Brown), 67.

83. In 1873, a pamphlet written by two New York Democrats in order to discredit abolitionists and Republicans praised the virtues and inevitability of miscegenation. It caused much hysteria before it was exposed as a hoax. See Wood, *Black Scare*, 53–79.

84. Cong. Globe, 38th Cong., 1st Sess., April 9, 1864, 1490.

85. When considering the issue of state racism, we need to also examine the penal system, labor laws that maintained involuntary servitude well into the 1930s, and, after *Plessy*, the proliferation of Jim Crow laws.

86. According to Hubert L. Dreyfuss and Paul Rabinow, "An essential component of normalizing techniques is that they are themselves an integral part of the systemic creation, classification, and control of anomalies in the social body. Their *raison d'être* comes from their claim to have isolated such anomalies and their promises to normalize them." *Michel Foucault: Beyond Structuralism and Hermeneutics* (Chicago: University of Chicago Press, 1982), 195.

87. Cable, "Freedman's Case," 11.

88. McPherson, *Political History*, 31.

89. Gilbert Thomas Stephenson, *Race Distinctions in American Law* (New York: D. Appleton, 1910), 97.

90. *State v. Gibson*, 36 Ind. 403 (1871).

91. *Green v. State*, 58 Ala. 190 (1877).

92. *Pace v. Alabama*, 106 U.S. 583–585 (1883).

93. Ernst Freund, *The Police Power: Public Policy and Constitutional Rights* (Chicago: Callaghan, 1909), 116. In *The History of Sexuality*, Foucault uses the term "biopower" "to designate what brought life and its mechanisms into the realm of explicit calculations." Michel Foucault, *The History of Sexuality*, trans. Robert Hurley (New York: Vintage, 1980), 143. My argument differs from Foucault in significant ways, particularly concerning the issue of juridical regression and the shift from sanguinity to sexuality. When we think about state racism in the nineteenth century, it is critical to consider the repressive instrumentality of the law and the obsession with blood in the production of racial subjects and management of life. Colin Gordon observes that biopolitics is concerned with "subjects as members of a population, in which issues of individual sexual and

reproductive conduct interconnect with issues of national policy and power." Introduction to *The Foucault Effect*, ed. Graham Burchell, Colin Gordon, and Peter Miller (Chicago: University of Chicago Press, 1991), 5. For a brilliant discussion of biopower and modern racism, see Anna Laura Stoller, *Race and the Education of Desire: Foucault's* History of Sexuality *and the Colonial Order of Things* (Durham, NC: Duke University Press, 1995).

94. *Jones v. Commonwealth*, 79 Va. (4 Hans.) 218 (1884).

95. Stephenson, *Race Distinctions in American Law*, 17.

96. Derrick A. Bell Jr. "Property Rights in Whiteness: Their Legal Legacy, Their Economic Costs," *Villanova Law Review* 33, no. 5 (1988): 767; Cheryl I. Harris, "Whiteness as Property," *Harvard Law Review* 106, no. 8 (June 1993): 1709–1791.

97. Karen A. Getman, "Sexual Control in the Slaveholding South: The Implementation and Maintenance of a Racial Caste System," *Harvard Women's Law Journal* 7 (1984): 134–142; Lawrence M. Friedman, *Crime and Punishment in American History* (New York: Basic Books, 1993), 216–217. This was also true in antebellum law, for if a white woman associated with blacks, it indicated that she was of "low character" and therefore not a reliable witness.

98. Herbert Gutman, *The Black Family in Slavery and Freedom, 1750–1925* (New York: Pantheon, 1976).

99. As Brown writes, "The liberal formulation of liberty is thus not merely opposed to but premised upon encumbrance; it is achieved by displacing the embodied, encumbered, and limited nature of existence onto women, a displacement that occurs discursively and practically through a set of assigned activities, responsibilities, and emotional attributes. Insofar as this formulation of liberty requires the existence of encumbered beings, the social activity of those without liberty, it can never be fully universalizable." *States of Injury*, 56.

100. State statutes prohibiting interracial marriage were not declared unconstitutional until 1967. See *Loving v. Virginia*, 388 U.S. 1 (1967). It was also feared that the Civil Rights Act and Fourteenth Amendment would make women as equal and free as men and wives as free and equal as their husbands before the law. However, this was not the case. Cong. Globe, 38th Cong., 1st Sess., 1488.

101. The proponents of the Civil Rights Act of 1875 tried to refute this logic by separating equality from the question of society: "Nobody pretends that Equality in the highway, whether on pavement or sidewalk, is a society. And, permit me to say the Equality in all institutions created or regulated by law, is as little a question of society." Cong. Globe, 42d Cong., 2d Sess., 382 (579). Opponents like Representative John Davis argued that the bill would arouse the very prejudices that it was intended to eradicate and would "render tenfold more

intense that feeling of antipathy which, in the not distant future, must end in the conflict of races, fatal to one and brutalizing to the other in the spirit of hate it will engender." Cong. Globe, 43d Cong., 1st Sess., 481 (713).

102. *Roberts v. City of Boston*, 59 Mass. (5 Cush.) 206 (1850).

103. In contemporary politics, equivalent rights have been proposed as a means of redressing gender and racial discrimination. However, it remains to be seen if race and gender can be installed into the law without being injurious, or if difference is ultimately what is in need of recognition, rather than the injuries and exclusion constitutive of that difference. Is not the best means of negating and correcting discrimination and domination systemic transformation and redress rather than monumentalizing the effects and detritus of social and historical process?

104. Certainly this is not a novel observation. The inequalities that inhabit the discourse of rights and formal equality have been subject to critical scrutiny by everyone from Marx to Patricia Williams. Feminist critics and critical race theorists have described the tacit exclusions and partialities lauded as the universal in terms of the masculinism of the law and/or as white normativity. Here I employ the term "white norm" to designate the centrality of whiteness as the measure of humanity in the law; however, inequality can also be produced when whiteness is relegated to the position of just another race. The embodiment of whiteness and its relativization as just "another race," rather than marking an emancipatory shift or an opening, effectively reproduce domination if this purported decentering of whiteness leaves power relations intact. By focusing on the disciplinary practices that inhabit the law, I hope to be able to address the ranking of particularities produced through the homogenizing measure of equality. I am indebted to Robert St. Martin Westley, "White Normativity and the Racial Rhetoric of Equal Protection," unpublished manuscript, for these ideas.

105. Brief for Homer A. Plessy by S. F. Philips and F. D. McKinney, File Copies of Briefs 1895 (October Term, 1895), in Otto H. Olsen, *The Thin Disguise: Turning Point in Negro History; Plessy v. Ferguson, a Documentary Presentation* (New York: Humanities Press, 1967), 107.

106. *Dred Scott*, 701. This casting out and incorporation of the defiled and denigrated subjects defines abjection.

107. From 1873 to 1883, the radical scope of Reconstruction legislation was successfully dismantled by the Court. See Sidney G. Buchanan, "The Quest for Freedom: A Legal History of the Thirteenth Amendment," 357. See *United States v. Cruikshank*, 92 U.S. 542 (1876). Although segregation was not codified until the 1880s, de facto segregation was the order of the day.

108. Olsen, *The Thin Disguise*, 14; Eric J. Sundquist, "Mark Twain and Homer Plessy," in *To Wake the Nations: Race in the Making of American Literature* (Cambridge, MA: Belknap Press, 1993), 225–270.
109. Olsen, *The Thin Disguise*, 90.
110. Ibid., 101.
111. *Civil Rights Cases*, 109 U.S. 22–25 (1883). The "necessary incidents" of slavery that the majority recognized were "compulsory service, disability to hold property, to make contracts, to have a standing in court, to be a witness against a white person. . . . Such like burdens and incapacities, were the inseparable incidents of the institution."
112. Wood, *Black Scare*, 130–155.
113. Tourgée's brief for Homer A. Plessy, in Olsen, *The Thin Disguise*, 83.
114. Saks, "Representing Miscegenation Laws," 41.
115. *Plessy*, 541.
116. It was defamation to call a white person a Negro. Stephenson, *Race Distinctions in American Law*, 26–34.
117. Fields, "Ideology and Race in American History," 162. Although I agree with much of the analysis offered in this essay, I take objection to the distinction Fields makes between materiality and ideology. In noting the difference between class and race, Fields argues that "class refers to a material circumstance: the inequality of human beings from the standpoint of social power," while race is a purely ideological notion. The mistake Fields makes is in trying to dislodge the biological paradigm by minimizing the materiality of discourse or ideology, which not only embodies or reflects social relations but also produces subjects and determines a range of concrete material circumstances.
118. Olsen, *The Thin Disguise*, 89.
119. Cable, "The Negro Question," 132.
120. As an aside, it is important to note that segregation was, in fact, widespread during the Reconstruction period. Thus, *Plessy* upheld what was fairly commonplace in practice. See Howard N. Rabinowitz, "From Exclusion to Segregation: Southern Race Relations, 1865–1890," *Journal of American History* 63 (Sept. 1976): 325–350; Harold D. Woodman, "Sequel to Slavery: The New History Views the Postbellum South," *Journal of Southern History* 43 (1977): 525–555. For a different interpretation, see C. Vann Woodward, *Origins of the New South, 1877–1913* (Baton Rouge: Louisiana State University Press, 1971).
121. *Black's Law Dictionary*, 1156; Christopher G. Tiedeman, *A Treatise on the Limitations of Police Power in the United States, Considered from Both a Civil and Criminal Standpoint* (1886; repr. New York: Da Capo Press, 1971), 1–16; Alfred Russell, *The Police Power of the State and Decisions thereon as Illustrating the*

Development and Value of Case Law (Chicago: Callaghan, 1900), 23–36; Ruth Locke Roettinger, *The Supreme Court and State Police Power* (Washington, DC: Public Affairs Press, 1957), 10–22; Howard Gillman, *The Constitution Besieged: The Rise and Demise of Lochner Era Police Powers Jurisprudence* (Durham, NC: Duke University Press, 1993).

122. *Slaughter-House Cases*, 83 U.S. (16 Wall) 62 (1873).

123. Pasquale Pasquino, "Theatrum Politicum: The Genealogy of Capital-Police and the State of Prosperity," in Burchell, Gordon, and Miller, *The Foucault Effect*, 111.

124. Cong. Globe, 39th Cong., 1st Sess., January 30, 1866, 505 (128). This definition of police power was employed to defeat an earlier version of the Civil Rights Act of 1866, which contained an explicit antidiscrimination clause.

125. Stoler, *Race and the Education of Desire*, 59.

126. Poovey writes that the image of the social body was used in two distinct ways: "It referred either to the poor in isolation from the rest of the population or to British (or English) society as an organic whole . . . [and] it allowed social analysts to treat one segment of the population as a special problem at the same time that they could gesture toward the mutual interests that (theoretically) united all parts of the social whole." *Making a Social Body*, 8–9. For an insightful discussion of the police and the creation of an aggregate body or population, see Pasquino, "Theatrum Politicum," 114.

127. Efforts to provide a minimum standard of existence were largely left to private organizations. As well, by the Gilded Age, Republican free-labor ideology had been supplanted by the liberal ideal of liberty of contract.

128. Mark Tushnet distinguishes these categories along the following lines: "Civil rights attached to people simply because they were people; they were rights one had in a state of nature, such as the right to personal freedom of action, the right to life, and the right to pursue a life plan. . . . Political rights, in contrast, arose from a person's location in an organized political system. . . . Social rights were exercised in the rest of the social order and most importantly, in the market. For Reconstruction legal thought, government had nothing to do with guaranteeing social rights except to enforce those rights guaranteed by the common law." "Civil Rights and Social Rights: The Future of the Reconstruction Amendments," *Loyola of Los Angeles Review* 25 (June 1992): 1208.

129. According to Benhabib, "'Privacy' means first and foremost noninterference by the political state in the freedom of commodity relations, and in particular nonintervention in the free market of labor power." "Models of Public Space," 91; Nancy Fraser, "Rethinking the Public Sphere: A Contribution to

the Critique of Actually Existing Democracy," 109–142. in Calhoun, *Habermas and the Public Sphere*.

130. *Civil Rights Cases*, 14.

131. *Civil Rights Cases*, 36; Belz, *Emancipation and Equal Rights* and *A New Birth of Freedom*. According to Belz, "Social rights referred to the sphere of strictly personal relationships, either in the household or outside it, in which personal taste or prejudice could legitimately hold sway and into which the law did not enter. . . . Schools, voluntary associations, transportation facilities, and places of business and entertainment are perhaps the most conspicuous examples of arenas that nowadays are, but were not then (in the nineteenth century), comprehended under the rule of civil rights equality."

132. Neil Gotanda notes that the public-private distinction and the freedom of association are ways of maintaining segregation.

133. However, in the United States, unlike the situation in France, the concern about social rights is not directed by reformist impulses to attend to the material concerns of workers, women, and the poor; instead, it is an avenue of subordination and repression. Certainly, it has been argued that even in France, social rights result from the domestication and incorporation of resistance and are inseparable from the issue of governability. In the nineteenth-century United States, the social concerns were the liberties of the dominant class and the control and regulation of those variously encumbered by an array of corporeal maledictions—that is, blacks, women, and workers.

134. Fraser, *Unruly Practices*, 170.

135. Unlike the emergence of the social that typified the nineteenth-century European democratic state, in the United States, the welfare state did not emerge until the New Deal, although the 1890s were the beginning of the Age of Reform, in which issues of the needs and care of the poor, dependent, and infirm became the subject of public concern and intervention, largely through private charitable organizations. Actually, the opposite is at work in the juridical definition of the social in *Plessy*. Issues of public and political concern are privatized and relegated to the law-free sphere of desire. An erosion occurs in these interests by dismissing public matters as private. This expanse of the private has a range of reactionary and repressive effects. The social in this regard enables the privatization of public concerns rather than the encroachment of the private in an arena of public concern. Arendt, *Human Condition*, 32.

136. Fraser, *Unruly Practices*, 170.

137. Fraser argues that runaway needs are "markers of major social-structural shifts in the boundaries separating what are classified as 'political,' 'economic,' and 'domestic' or 'personal' spheres of life." Ibid., 171. The entanglements of

race and class in regard to the social can be seen in the Court's assessment of legitimate and illegitimate police power. Exercises of police power that enforced segregation and laissez-faire were upheld, while those interventions designed to protect workers were overturned as class legislation. See Hirsch, *A Theory of Liberty*, 82–85. For a different reading of the Court's assessment of police power, see Howard Gillman, *The Constitution Besieged: The Rise and Demise of Lochner Era Police Powers Jurisprudence* (Durham, NC: Duke University Press, 1993).

138. *Plessy*, 560.

139. Cable, "The Negro Question," 144–145. As Ronald Takaki notes, "Essentially Cable was calling for laissez-faire in race relations. Free from government interference and regulation, the 'instinctive antagonism' between the two races would prevail and the 'Caucasian race' would preserve its 'high purity' without the aid of 'onerous civil distinctions.'" *Iron Cages: Race and Culture in 19th-Century America* (Seattle: University of Washington Press, 1979), 209.

140. As Pasquino remarks, once we leave behind the *theatrum politicum* of the state dueling society, the state becomes the "entire body of civil society." This new vantage point thus entails "resituating the analysis of the relations of power wholly within the interior of the social body." The state then becomes one instrument among others in "the modality of government." "Theatrum Politicum," 116–117.

141. Cable, "The Negro Question," 144.

142. This is different from the emergence of the European social, which corresponds more with the Age of Reform. In the nineteenth-century United States, the social is articulated primarily through repression and the fortification of the private rather than the expansion of the state as it takes on householding duties.

143. Burchell, Gordon, and Miller, *The Foucault Effect*, 29.

144. This is not an endorsement of the state's regulation of the private or a call for more law but rather an attempt to underline the disavowed regulation conducted by way of declarations of noninterference. Nancy Fraser writes: "The private functions ideologically to delimit the boundaries in ways that disadvantage subordinate groups." "Rethinking the Public Sphere," 131.

145. For an exemplary demonstration of this critical disinterment, see Kendall Thomas, "Beyond the Privacy Principle," in *After Identity: A Reader in Law and Culture*, ed. Dan Danielson and Karen Engle (New York: Routledge, 1995), 277–293.

146. This construction of the private continues to plague feminist and antiracist politics. Patricia J. Williams, *The Alchemy of Race and Rights: Diary of a Law*

Professor (Cambridge, MA: Harvard University Press, 1991), 15–41. Nadine Taub and Elizabeth Schneider write: "Tort law, which is generally concerned with injuries inflicted on individuals, has traditionally been held inapplicable to injuries inflicted by one family member on another. Under the doctrines of inter-spousal and parent-child immunity, courts have consistently denied recoveries for injuries that would be compensable but for the fact that they occurred in the private realm." Obviously, marital rape is another instance of this order of violation. "Women's Subordination and the Role of Law," in *The Politics of Law: A Progressive Critique*, ed. David Kairys (New York: Pantheon, 1982), 155.

147. Olsen, *The Thin Disguise*, 93.
148. Ibid., 107.

SELECTED BIBLIOGRAPHY

Abrahams, Roger D. *Singing the Master: The Emergence of African-American Culture in the Plantation South.* New York: Pantheon, 1992.

Abu-Lughod, Lila. "The Romance of Resistance: Tracing Transformations of Power through Bedouin Women." *American Ethnologists* 17, no. 1 (1990): 41–55.

——. *Veiled Sentiments: Honor and Poetry in Bedouin Society.* Berkeley: University of California Press, 1986.

Adams, Edward C. L. *Tales of the Congaree.* Edited by Robert G. O'Meally. Chapel Hill: University of North Carolina Press, 1987.

Agnew, Jean-Christophe. *Worlds Apart: The Market and the Theater in Anglo-American Thought.* Cambridge: Cambridge University Press, 1986.

Aiken, George, and Harriet Beecher Stowe. *Uncle Tom's Cabin.* In *American Melodrama,* edited by Daniel C. Gould. New York: Performing Arts Journal, 1983.

Alho, Olli. *The Religion of Slaves: A Study of the Religious Tradition and Behaviour of Plantation Slaves in the United States, 1830–1965.* FF Communications, no. 217. Helsinki: Academia Scientiarum Fennica, 1976.

Allen, Theodore W. *The Invention of the White Race.* New York: Verso, 1994.

Allen, William Francis, ed. *Slave Songs of the United States.* New York: A. Simpson and Co., 1867.

Althusser, Louis. *For Marx.* Translated by Ben Brewster. New York: Random House, 1969.

——. *Lenin and Philosophy and Other Essays.* Translated by Ben Brewster. New York: Monthly Review Press, 1971.

Althusser, Louis, and Étienne Balibar. *Reading Capital.* Translated by Ben Brewster. London: Verso, 1970.

American Anti-Slavery Society. *American Slavery, as It Is: Testimony of a Thousand*

Witnesses. New York: American Anti-Slavery Society, 1839. Reprint, New York: Arno, 1968.

Ames, Mary. *A New England Woman's Diary in Dixie in 1865*. Norwood, MA: Plimpton Press, 1906.

Anderson, Benedict. *Imagined Communities: Reflections on the Origin and Spread of Nationalism*. London: Verso, 1983.

Andrews, Ethan A. *Slavery and the Domestic Slave-Trade in the United States*. Boston: Light and Stearns, 1836. Reprint, Detroit: Negro History Press, n.d.

Andrews, William L. *To Tell a Free Story: The First Century of Afro-American Autobiography, 1760-1865*. Urbana: University of Illinois Press, 1986.

Appiah, Kwame Anthony. *In My Father's House: Africa in the Philosophy of Culture*. New York: Oxford University Press, 1992.

Aptheker, Herbert. *American Negro Slave Revolts*. New York: International Publishers, 1943.

Archer, Leonie J. *Slavery: And Other Forms of Unfree Labour*. London: Routledge, 1988.

Arendt, Hannah. *The Human Condition*. Chicago: University of Chicago Press, 1958.

———. *On Revolution*. London: Penguin Books, 1963.

Armstrong, Nancy, and Leonard Tennenhouse, eds. *The Violence of Representation: Literature and the History of Violence*. London: Routledge, 1989.

Armstrong, Timothy J., ed. *Michel Foucault, Philosopher*. New York: Routledge, 1992.

Atkinson, Charles F., and Francis W. Loring. *Cotton Culture and the South, Considered with Reference to Emigration*. Boston, 1869.

Ayers, Edward L. *Vengeance and Justice: Crime and Punishment in the 19th-Century American South*. New York: Oxford University Press, 1984.

Babcock, Barbara A., ed. *The Reversible World: Symbolic Inversion in Art and Society*. Ithaca, NY: Cornell University Press, 1978.

Bacon, A. M., and E. C. Parsons, eds. "Folk-Lore from Elizabeth City County, Virginia." *Journal of American Folk-Lore* 35 (1922): 250–327.

Baer, Judith A. *Equality under the Constitution: Reclaiming the Fourteenth Amendment*. Ithaca, NY: Cornell University Press, 1983.

Baker, Houston A., Jr. *Blues, Ideology, and Afro-American Literature: A Vernacular Theory*. Chicago: University of Chicago Press, 1984.

———. *Modernism and the Harlem Renaissance*. Chicago: University of Chicago Press, 1987.

———. *Workings of the Spirit: The Poetics of Afro-American Women's Writing*. Chicago: University of Chicago Press, 1991.

Bakhtin, Mikhail. *The Dialogic Imagination: Four Essays.* Translated by Caryl Emerson and Michael Holquist. Austin: University of Texas Press, 1981.

———. *Rabelais and His World.* Translated by Hélène Iswolsky Bloomington: Indiana University Press, 1984.

Balibar, Étienne. "Racism as Universalism." In *Masses, Classes, Ideas: Studies on Politics and Philosophy before and after Marx.* Translated by James Swenson. New York: Routledge, 1994.

———. "Subjection and Subjectivation." In *Supposing the Subject*, edited by Joan Copjec. London: Verso, 1994.

Bancroft, Frederic. *Slave Trading in the Old South.* New York: Frederick Ungar, 1959.

Barak, Gregg, ed. *Crimes by the Capitalist State: An Introduction to State Criminality.* New York: State University of New York Press, 1991.

Barlow, David. *Looking Up at Down: The Emergence of Blues Culture.* Philadelphia: Temple University Press, 1989.

Barrow, David C. "A Georgia Corn-Shucking." *Century Magazine* 24 (1882): 873–878.

Bartky, Sandra. *Femininity and Domination: Studies in the Phenomenology of Oppression.* New York: Routledge, 1990.

Bastin, Bruce. *Red River Blues: The Blues Tradition in the Southeast.* Urbana: University of Illinois Press, 1986.

Baudrillard, Jean. *Seduction.* Translated by Brian Singer. New York: St. Martin's Press, 1990.

Bauer, Raymond A., and Alice H. Bauer. "Day to Day Resistance to Slavery," In *American Slavery: The Question of Resistance*, edited by John H. Bracey, August Meier, and Elliott Rudwick. Belmont, CA: Wadsworth, 1971.

Baughman, Ernest W. *Type and Motif: Index of the Folktales of England and North America.* The Hague: Mouton and Co., 1966.

Bauman, Richard. *Story, Performance, and Event: Contextual Studies of Oral Narrative.* Cambridge: Cambridge University Press, 1986.

Bauman, Zygmunt. *Modernity and the Holocaust.* Ithaca, NY: Cornell University Press, 1991.

Bell, Derrick A., Jr. *And We Are Not Saved: The Elusive Quest for Racial Justice.* New York: Basic Books, 1987.

———. "Property Rights in Whiteness—Their Legal Legacy, Their Economic Costs." *Villanova Law Review* 767 (1988).

Belz, Herman. "The Civil War Origins of Negro Suffrage." *Southern Studies* 17 (Summer 1978), 115–130.

———. *Emancipation and Equal Rights: Politics and Constitutionalism in the Civil War Era.* New York: W. W. Norton, 1978.

————. *A New Birth of Freedom: The Republican Party and Freedmen's Rights, 1861 to 1866*. Westport, CT: Greenwood, 1976.

Benhabib, Seyla, Judith Butler, Drucilla Cornell, and Nancy Fraser, eds. *Feminist Contentions: A Philosophical Exchange*. New York: Routledge, 1995.

Benjamin, Walter. *Illuminations: Essays and Reflections*. Translated by Harry Zohn. New York: Schocken, 1969.

————. *The Origin of German Tragic Drama*. Translated by John Osborne. London: Verso, 1977.

Bentley, Eric. *The Life of Drama*. New York: Atheneum, 1964.

Berger, Raoul. *The Fourteenth Amendment and the Bill of Rights*. Norman: University of Oklahoma Press, 1989.

Berlin, Ira, Barbara J. Fields, Thavolia Glymph, Joseph P. Reidy, and Leslie S. Rowland, eds. *Freedom: A Documentary History of Emancipation, 1861–1867. The Destruction of Slavery*, series 1, vol. 1, The Black Military Experience, series 2. Cambridge: Cambridge University Press, 1985.

Bernauer, James, and David Rasmussen, eds. *The Final Foucault*. Cambridge: MIT Press, 1994.

Berry, Mary Frances. *Military Necessity and Civil Rights Policy: Black Citizenship and the Constitution, 1861–1868*. Port Washington, NY: Kennikat Press, 1977.

Bessmer, Sue. *The Laws of Rape*. New York: Praeger Special Studies, 1976.

Bhabha, Homi K. *The Location of Culture*. New York: Routledge, 1994.

Bibb, Henry. *Narrative of the Life and Adventures of Henry Bibb, an American Slave, Written by Himself*. New York: published by the author, 1849.

Blake, William O. *The History of Slavery and the Slave Trade*. Columbus, OH: J. and H. Miller, 1858.

Blassingame, John W. *The Slave Community: Plantation Life in the Antebellum South*. Oxford: Oxford University Press, 1979.

————, ed. *Slave Testimony: Two Centuries of Letters, Speeches, Interviews, and Autobiographies*. Baton Rouge: Louisiana State University Press, 1977.

Blesh, Rudi, and Harriet Janis. *They All Played Ragtime*. New York: Oak Publications, 1966.

Blight, David W. *Frederick Douglass' Civil War: Keeping Faith in Jubilee*. Baton Rouge: Louisiana State University Press, 1989.

Boskin, Joseph. *Sambo: The Rise and Demise of an American Jester*. New York: Oxford University Press, 1986.

Botkin, Benjamin A., ed. *Lay My Burden Down: A Folk History of Slavery*. Athens: University of Georgia Press, 1989.

Boucicault, Dion. *The Octoroon*. In *The Meridian Anthology of 18th- and 19th-Century*

British Drama, edited by Katharine M. Rogers. New York: New American Library, 1979.

Bourdieu, Pierre. *Outline of a Theory of Practice*. Translated by Richard Nice. Cambridge: Cambridge University Press, 1977.

Boyarin, Jonathan. *Storm from Paradise: The Politics of Jewish Memory*. Minneapolis: University of Minnesota Press, 1992.

Breeden, James O., ed. *Advice Among the Masters: The Ideal in Slave Management in the Old South*. Westport, CT: Greenwood, 1980.

Brewer, J. Mason. "Juneteenth." *Publications of the Texas Folklore Society* 10 (1932): 8–54.

Brinckerhoff, Isaac W. *Advice to Freedmen*. New York: American Tract Society, 1864.

Brooks, Peter. *The Melodramatic Imagination: Balzac, Henry James, Melodrama, and the Mode of Excess*. New Haven, CT: Yale University Press, 1985.

Brown, Gillian. *Domestic Individualism: Imagining Self in Nineteenth-Century America*. Berkeley: University of California Press, 1990.

Brown, Helen E. *John Freeman and His Family*. Boston: American Tract Society, 1864.

Brown, Sterling A., Arthur P. Davis, and Ulysses Lee, eds. *The Negro Caravan*. New York: Dryden Press, 1941. Reprint, Salem, NH: Ayer, 1991.

Brown, T. Allston. *History of the American Stage*. New York: Dick and Fitzgerald, 1870. Reprint, New York: Benjamin Blom, 1969.

Brown, Wendy. *States of Injury: Power and Freedom in Late Modernity*. Princeton, NJ: Princeton University Press, 1995.

Brown, William Wells. *The Escape; or, A Leap for Freedom*. In *Black Theatre USA*, ed. James V. Hatch and Ted Shine. New York: Free Press, 1974.

———. *My Southern Home: or, the South and Its People*. Boston: A. G. Brown and Co, 1880.

———. *Narrative of William Wells Brown, a Fugitive Slave*. In *Puttin' On Ole Massa: The slave narratives of Henry Bibb, William Wells Brown, and Solomon Northup*, edited by Gilbert Osofsky. New York: Harper and Row, 1969.

Burchell, Graham, Colin Gordon, and Peter Miller, eds. *The Foucault Effect*. Chicago: University of Chicago Press, 1991.

Burke, Kenneth. *Counter-Statement*. Berkeley: University of California Press, 1968.

———. *A Grammar of Motives*. Englewood Cliffs, NJ: Prentice-Hall, 1945. Reprint, Berkeley: University of California Press, 1969.

———. *On Symbols and Society*. Edited by Joseph R. Gusfield. Chicago: University of Chicago Press, 1989.

Butler, Judith. *Bodies That Matter*. New York: Routledge, 1993.

———. *Gender Trouble: Feminism and the Subversion of Identity*. London: Routledge, 1990.

———. "Imitation and Gender Insubordination." In *Inside/Out: Lesbian Theories, Gay Theories*, edited by Diana Fuss. New York: Routledge, 1991.

———. "Performative Acts and Gender Constitution: An Essay in Phenomenology and Feminist Theory." In *Performing Feminisms*, edited by Sue-Ellen Case. Baltimore: Johns Hopkins University Press, 1990.

Butler, Judith, and Joan W. Scott, eds. *Feminists Theorize the Political*. New York: Routledge, 1992.

Cable, George Washington. "The Convict Lease System in the Southern States." In *The Silent South*. New York: Charles Scribner's Sons, 1885.

———. *The Negro Question: A Selection of Writings on Civil Rights in the South*. New York: Charles Scribner's Sons, 1898. Reprint, Garden City, NJ: Doubleday Anchor Books, 1958.

Calhoun, Craig, ed. *Habermas and the Public Sphere*. Cambridge: MIT Press, 1993.

Canclini, Néstor García. "Culture and Power: The State of Research." Translated by Philip Schlesinger. *Media, Culture and Society* 10, no. 4 (1988): 467–497.

Carby, Hazel V. *Reconstructing Womanhood: The Emergence of the Afro-American Woman Novelist*. New York: Oxford University Press, 1987.

Cartwright, Samuel. "Diseases and Peculiarities of the Negro Race." *De Bow's Review of the Southern and Western States* 11 (1851).

Catterall, Helen Tunnicliff. *Judicial Cases Concerning American Slavery and the Negro*. 5 vols. Washington, DC: Carnegie Institute of Washington, 1926–37.

Chambers, Ross. *Story and Situation: Narrative Seduction and the Power of Fiction*. Theory and History of Literature, vol. 12. Minneapolis: University of Minnesota Press, 1984.

Chamerovzow, Louis A., ed. *Slave Life in Georgia: Narrative of the Life, Sufferings, and Escape of John Brown*. London: W. M. Watts, 1855.

Chernoff, John Miller. *African Rhythm and African Sensibility: Aesthetics and Social Action in African Musical Idioms*. Chicago: University of Chicago Press, 1979.

Chesnut, Mary Boykin. *A Diary from Dixie*. New York: D. Appleton, 1905. Reprint, edited by Ben Ames Williams. Boston: Houghton Mifflin, 1949.

Child, Lydia Maria. *The Freedmen's Book*. Boston: Ticknor and Fields, 1865. Reprint, New York: Arno Press, 1968.

Chow, Rey. *Writing Diaspora: Tactics of Intervention in Contemporary Cultural Studies*. Bloomington: Indiana University Press, 1993.

Ciresi, Alberto Maria. "Gramsci's Observations on Folklore." In *Approaches to Gramsci*, edited by Anne Showstack Sassoon. London: Writers and Readers, 1982.

Cixous, Hélène, and Catherine Clément. *The Newly Born Woman*. Translated by Betsy Wing. Theory and History of Literature, vol. 24. Minneapolis: University of Minnesota Press, 1986.

Clark, VèVè. "Developing Diaspora Literacy and *Marasa* Consciousness." In *Comparative American Identities*, edited by Hortense Spillers. New York: Routledge, 1991.

Clifford, James. *The Predicament of Culture: Twentieth Century Ethnography, Literature, and Art*. Cambridge, MA: Harvard University Press, 1988.

Clifford, James, and George Marcus, eds. *Writing Culture: The Poetics and Politics of Ethnography*. Berkeley: University of California Press, 1986.

Cobb, Thomas. *Inquiry into the Law of Negro Slavery*. Philadelphia: T. S. J. W. Johnson, 1858.

Cohen, Jean L., and Andrew Arato. *Civil Society and Political Theory*. Cambridge: MIT Press, 1994.

Comaroff, Jean. *Body of Power, Spirit of Resistance*. Chicago: University of Chicago Press, 1985.

Connolly, William. *Identity/Difference: Democratic Negotiations of Political Paradox*. Ithaca, NY: Cornell University Press, 1991.

Cornell, Drucilla. *The Philosophy of the Limit*. New York: Routledge, 1992.

———. *Transformations: Recollective Imagination and Sexual Difference*. New York: Routledge, 1993.

Cortner, Richard C. *The Supreme Court and the Second Bill of Rights*. Madison: University of Wisconsin Press, 1981.

Courlander, Harold. *Negro Folk Music, U.S.A.* New York: Columbia University Press, 1963.

Cover, Robert M. *Justice Accused: Antislavery and the Judicial Process*. New Haven: Yale University Press, 1975.

———. "Violence and the Word." *Yale Law Journal* 95, no. 8 (July 1986).

Craft, William, and Ellen Craft. *Running a Thousand Miles for Freedom; or, The Escape of William and Ellen Craft from Slavery*. London: William Tweedie, 1860.

Crapanzano, Vincent. "On the Writing of Ethnography." *Dialectical Anthropology* 2, no. 1 (1977): 69–73.

Crenshaw, Kimberlé Williams. "Race Reform and Retrenchment: Transformation and Legitimation in Antidiscrimination Law." *Harvard Law Review* 101, no. 7 (May 1988).

Cummings, Katherine. *Telling Tales: The Hysteric's Seduction in Fiction and Theory*. Stanford, CA: Stanford University Press, 1991.

Curtain, Philip D. *The Atlantic Slave Trade: A Census*. Madison: University of Wisconsin Press, 1969.

Davis, Angela. *Women, Race and Class*. New York: Random House, 1981.

Davis, David Brion. *The Problem of Slavery in the Age of Revolution, 1770–1823*. Ithaca, NY: Cornell University Press, 1975.

———. *The Problem of Slavery in Western Culture*. New York: Cornell University Press, 1966.

Davis, Jessica Milner. *Farce*. London: Methuen, 1978.

de Certeau, Michel. *The Practice of Everyday Life*. Translated by Steven Rendall. Berkeley: University of California Press, 1984.

Degler, Carl N. "The Irony of American Slavery." In *Perspectives and Irony in American Slavery*, edited by Harry P. Owens. Jackson: University of Mississippi Press, 1976.

Delany, Martin R. *Blake; or, The Huts of America*. Originally published serially, 1859, 1861–62. First collected edition, edited by Floyd J. Miller. Boston: Beacon Press, 1970.

de Lauretis, Teresa. *Technologies of Gender: Essays on Theory, Film, and Fiction*. Bloomington: Indiana University Press, 1987.

Deleuze, Gilles. *Masochism: Coldness and the Cruelty*. Translated by Jean McNeil. New York: George Braziller, 1989. Reprint, New York: Zone Books, 1991.

Denning, Michael. *Mechanic Accents: Dime Novels and Working-Class Culture in America*. London: Verso, 1987.

Dennison, Sam. *Scandalize My Name: Black Imagery in American Popular Music*. New York: Garland, 1982.

Dixon, Brenda. "Black Dance and Dancers and the White Public: A Prolegomenon to Problems of Definition." *Black American Literature Forum* 24, no. 1 (Spring 1990): 117–123.

Donzelot, Jacques. *The Policing of Families*. Translated by Robert Hurley. New York: Pantheon, 1979.

Douglass, Ann. *The Feminization of American Culture*. New York: Alfred A. Knopf, 1977.

Douglass, Frederick. *Life and Times of Frederick Douglass*. Rev. ed. Boston: De Wolfe, Fiske and Co., 1892. Reprint, New York: Collier, 1962.

———. *My Bondage and My Freedom*. New York: Miller, Orton and Mulligan, 1855. Reprint, New York: Dover, 1969.

———. *Narrative of the Life of Frederick Douglass, an American Slave, Written by Himself*. Boston: Anti-Slavery Office, 1845. Reprint, New York: New American Library, 1968.

Drew, Benjamin. *The Refugee: or The Narratives of Fugitive Slaves in Canada*. Boston: John P. Jewett, 1856.

Dreyfus, Hubert L., and Paul Rabinow. *Michel Foucault: Beyond Structuralism and Hermeneutics*. Chicago: University of Chicago Press, 1982.

Du Bois, W. E. B. *Black Reconstruction in America: An Essay Toward a History of the Part Which Black Folk Played in the Attempt to Reconstruct Democracy in America, 1860–1880*. New York: Harcourt, Brace, 1935.

———. *Darkwater: Voices from within the Veil*. New York: Harcourt, Brace and Howe, 1920.

———. *The Souls of Black Folk: Essays and Sketches*. Chicago: A. C. McClurg and Co., 1903.

duCille, Ann. *The Coupling Convention: Sex, Text, and Tradition in Black Women's Fiction*. New York: Oxford University Press, 1993.

Dundes, Alan, ed. *Motherwit from the Laughing Barrel: Readings in the Interpretation of Afro-American Folklore*. Jackson: University of Mississippi Press, 1990.

Dunham, Katherine. "The Negro Dance." In *The Negro Caravan*, edited by Sterling A. Brown, Arthur P. Davis, and Ulysses Lee. New York: Dryden Press, 1941. Reprint, Salem, NH: Ayer, 1991.

Durden, Robert F. *The Gray and the Black: The Confederate Debate on Emancipation*. Baton Rouge: Louisiana State University Press, 1972.

Eaton, John. *Grant, Lincoln and the Freedmen: Reminiscences of the Civil War*. New York: Longmans, Green, 1907.

Edwards, Susan M. *Female Sexuality and the Law: A Study of Constructs of Female Sexuality as They Inform Statute and Legal Procedure*. United Kingdom: M. Robertson, 1981.

Eisenstein, Zillah R. *The Female Body and the Law*. Berkeley: University of California Press, 1988.

Elkins, Stanley M. *Slavery: A Problem in American Institutional and Intellectual Life*. Chicago: University of Chicago Press, 1976.

Ely, John Hart. *Democracy and Distrust: A Theory of Judicial Review*. Cambridge, MA: Harvard University Press, 1980.

Emery, Lynne Fauley. *Black Dance from 1619 to Today*. 2nd ed., Princeton, NJ: Dance Horizons, 1988.

Engle, Gary D., ed. *This Grotesque Essence: Plays from the Minstrel Stage*. Baton Rouge: Louisiana State University Press, 1978.

Epstein, Dena J. *Sinful Tunes and Spirituals: Black Folk Music to the Civil War*. Urbana: University of Illinois Press, 1977.

Equiano, Olaudah. *The Interesting Narrative and Other Writings*. New York: Penguin, 1995. First published by the author, London, 1789.

Estrich, Susan. *Real Rape*. Cambridge, MA: Harvard University Press, 1987.

Evans, David. "Afro-American One-Stringed Instruments." *Western Folklore* 29, no. 4 (October 1970): 229–245.

Evans, Martha Noel. "Hysteria and the Seduction of Theory." In *Seduction and*

Theory: Readings of Gender, Representation, and Rhetoric, edited by Dianne Hunter. Urbana: University of Illinois Press, 1989.

Ewing, Elbert William Robinson. *Legal and Historical Status of the Dred Scott Decision*. Washington, DC: Cobden, 1909.

Fabian, Johannes. *Time and the Other: How Anthropology Makes Its Object*. New York: Columbia University Press, 1983.

Fabre, Geneviève, and Robert O'Meally, eds. *History and Memory in African American Culture*. New York: Oxford University Press, 1994.

Fanon, Frantz. *Black Skin, White Masks*. Translated by Charles Lam Markmann. New York: Grove, 1967.

———. *The Wretched of the Earth*. Translated by Constance Farrington. New York: Grove, 1965.

Faust, Drew Gilpin. *The Creation of Confederate Nationalism: Ideology and Identity in the Civil War South*. Baton Rouge: Louisiana State University Press, 1988.

———, ed. *The Ideology of Slavery: Proslavery Thought in the Antebellum South, 1830–1860*. Baton Rouge: Louisiana State University Press, 1981.

Featherstonhaugh, George. W. *Excursion through the Slave States*. 2 vols. London: John Murray, 1844.

Fede, Andrew. *People without Rights: An Interpretation of the Fundamental Law of Slavery in the U.S. South*. New York: Garland 1992.

Felman, Shoshana, and Dori Laub. *Testimony: Crises of Witnessing in Literature, Psychoanalysis, and History*. New York: Routledge, 1992.

Ferguson, Frances. "Rape and the Rise of the Novel." *Representations* 20 (Fall 1987): 88–112.

Ferguson, Russell, Martha Gever, Trinh T. Minh-ha, and Cornel West, eds. *Out There: Marginalization and Contemporary Cultures*. New York: The New Museum of Contemporary Art; Cambridge, MA: MIT Press, 1990.

Fernandez, James W. *Persuasions and Performances: The Play of Tropes in Culture*. Bloomington: Indiana University Press, 1986.

Filene, Benjamin. "'Our Singing Country': John and Alan Lomax, Leadbelly, and the Construction of an American Past." *American Quarterly* 43, no. 4 (December 1991): 602–624.

Finkelman, Paul. *An Imperfect Union: Slavery, Federalism, and Comity*. Chapel Hill: University of North Carolina Press, 1981.

Fisher, Philip. *Hard Facts: Setting and Form in the American Novel*. New York: Oxford University Press, 1985.

Fisk, Clinton B. *Plain Counsels for Freedmen*. Boston: American Tract Society, 1866.

Fisk University. *Unwritten History of Slavery: Autobiographical Accounts of Negro Ex-Slaves*. Nashville, TN: Fisk University Social Science Institute, 1945.

Fitzhugh, George. *Cannibals All! Or, Slaves without Masters*. Richmond, VA: A.

Morris, 1857. Reprint, Cambridge, MA: Belknap Press of Harvard University Press, 1971.

Fogel, Robert William, and Stanley L. Engerman. *Time on the Cross: The Economics of American Negro Slavery.* Boston: Little, Brown, 1974.

Foner, Eric. *Politics and Ideology in the Age of the Civil War.* New York: Oxford University Press, 1980.

———. *Reconstruction: America's Unfinished Revolution, 1863–1877.* New York: Harper and Row, 1988.

Foner, Philip S., and George E. Walker, eds. *Proceedings of the Black State Conventions, 1840–1863.* Philadelphia: Temple University Press, 1979.

Forbath, William E. "Free Labor Ideology in the Gilded Age." *Wisconsin Law Review* (1985), 767–817.

Forrester, John. *The Seduction of Psychoanalysis: Freud, Lacan and Derrida.* Cambridge: Cambridge University Press, 1990.

Forten Grimké, Charlotte. *The Journals of Charlotte Forten Grimké.* Edited by Brenda Stevenson. New York: Oxford University Press, 1988.

——— [as Charlotte Forten]. "Life on the Sea Islands." *Atlantic Monthly* (May 1864).

Foster, Stephen. *Minstrel Show Songs.* Edited by H. Wiley Hitchcock. New York: Da Capo Press, 1980.

Foster, Susan Leigh. *Reading Dancing: Bodies and Subjects in Contemporary American Dance.* Berkeley: University of California Press, 1986.

Foucault, Michel. *Discipline and Punish: The Birth of the Prison.* Translated by Alan Sheridan. New York: Vintage, 1979.

———. *The History of Sexuality.* Translated by Robert Hurley. New York: Vintage, 1980.

———. *Language, Counter-Memory, Practice: Selected Essays and Interviews.* Edited by Donald F. Bouchard. Translated by Donald F. Bouchard and Sherry Simon. Ithaca, NY: Cornell University Press, 1977.

———. *Power/Knowledge: Selected Interviews and Other Writings, 1972–1977.* Edited by Colin Gordon. Translated by Colin Gordon, Leo Marshall, John Mepham, and Kate Soper. New York: Pantheon, 1980.

———. "The Subject and Power." In *Michel Foucault: Beyond Structuralism and Hermeneutics,* edited by Hubert L. Dreyfus and Paul Rabinow. Chicago: University of Chicago Press, 1982.

Fox-Genovese, Elizabeth. *Within the Plantation Household: Black and White Women of the Old South.* Chapel Hill: University of North Carolina Press, 1988.

Fox-Genovese, Elizabeth, and Eugene D. Genovese. *The Fruits of Merchant Capitalism: Slavery and Bourgeois Property in the Rise and Expansion of Capitalism.* New York: Oxford University Press, 1983.

Franklin, John Hope. *The Emancipation Proclamation*. Edinburgh: Edinburgh University Press, 1963.

―――, ed. *Reminiscences of an Active Life: The Autobiography of John Roy Lynch*. Chicago: University of Chicago Press, 1970.

Fraser, Nancy. *Unruly Practices: Power, Discourse, and Gender in Contemporary Social Theory*. Minneapolis: University of Minnesota Press, 1989.

Fraser, Walter J., Jr., and Winfred B. Moore Jr., eds. *The Southern Enigma: Essays on Race, Class, and Folk Culture*. Westport, CT: Greenwood, 1983.

Frederickson, George M. *The Arrogance of Race: Historical Perspectives on Slavery, Racism, and Social Inequity*. Middletown, CT: Wesleyan University Press, 1988.

―――. *The Black Image in the White Mind: The Debate on Afro-American Character and Destiny, 1817–1914*. Middletown, CT: Wesleyan University Press, 1971.

Freeman, Alan. "Legitimizing Racial Discrimination through Antidiscrimination Law: A Critical Review of Supreme Court Doctrine." *Minnesota Law Review* 62 (1978): 1349–1369.

Freud, Sigmund. *Beyond the Pleasure Principle*. Translated by James Strachey. New York: W. W. Norton, 1961.

Friedman, Lawrence M. *Crime and Punishment in American History*. New York: Basic Books, 1993.

Furnas, J. C. *Goodbye to Uncle Tom*. New York: William Sloane Associates, 1956.

Gallop, Jane. *The Daughter's Seduction: Feminism and Psychoanalysis*. Ithaca, NY: Cornell University Press, 1982.

Gates, Henry Louis, Jr. *The Signifying Monkey: A Theory of African American Literary Criticism*. New York: Oxford University Press, 1988.

Geertz, Clifford. *The Interpretation of Cultures*. New York: Basic Books, 1973.

―――. *Negara: The Theatre State in Nineteenth-Century Bali*. Princeton, NJ: Princeton University Press, 1980.

Genovese, Eugene D. *From Rebellion to Revolution: Afro-American Slave Revolts in the Making of the New World*. Baton Rouge: Louisiana State University Press, 1979.

―――. *Roll, Jordan, Roll: The World the Slaves Made*. New York: Vintage, 1972.

George, Alexander L., ed. *Western State Terrorism*. New York: Routledge, 1991.

Georgia Writer's Project. *Drums and Shadows: Survival Studies among the Georgia Coastal Negroes*. Athens: University of Georgia Press, 1986.

Gillman, Howard. *The Constitution Besieged: The Rise and Demise of Lochner Era Police Powers Jurisprudence*. Durham, NC: Duke University Press, 1993.

Gilman, Sander L. *Difference and Pathology: Stereotypes of Sexuality, Race, and Madness*. Ithaca, NY: Cornell University Press, 1985.

Gilroy, Paul. *The Black Atlantic: Modernity and Double-Consciousness*. Cambridge: Harvard University Press, 1993.

———. "Sounds Authentic: Black Music, Ethnicity, and the Challenge of a Changing Same." *Black Music Research Journal* 13 (1991).

———. *There Ain't No Black in the Union Jack*. London: Hutchinson, 1987.

Glissant, Édouard. *Caribbean Discourse: Selected Essays*. Translated by J. Michael Dash. Charlottesville: University of Virginia Press, 1989.

Goldberg, David Theo. *Racist Culture: Philosophy and the Politics of Meaning*. Cambridge: Blackwell Publishers, 1993.

Goodell, William. *The American Slave Code*. New York: American and Foreign Anti-Slavery Society, 1853. Reprint, New York: Johnson Reprint Corporation, 1968.

Gordon, Katrina Hazzard. *Jookin': The Rise of Social Dance Formations in African American Culture*. Philadelphia: Temple University Press, 1990.

Gordon, Robert Winslow. "Negro 'Shouts' from Georgia." In *Motherwit from the Laughing Barrel: Readings in the Interpretation of Afro-American Folklore*, edited by Alan Dundes. Jackson: University Press of Mississippi, 1990.

Gossett, Thomas F. *Race: The History of an Idea in America*. New York: Schocken, 1963.

Graham, Howard Jay. *Everyman's Constitution: Historical Essays on the Fourteenth Amendment, the "Conspiracy Theory," and American Constitutionalism*. Madison: Wisconsin Historical Society of Press, 1968.

Gramsci, Antonio. *The Prison Notebooks*. Edited and translated by Quintin Hoare and Geoffrey Nowell Smith. New York: International Publishers, 1971.

———. *Selections from Cultural Writings*. Edited by David Forgacs and Geoffrey Nowell-Smith. Translated by William Boelhower. Cambridge, MA: Harvard University Press, 1985.

Griffin, Farah Jasmine. *"Who Set You Flowin'?": The African-American Migration Narrative*. New York: Oxford University Press, 1995.

Grimsted, David. *Melodrama Unveiled: American Theater and Culture*. Berkeley: University of California Press, 1987.

Grossberg, Lawrence. "On Postmodernism and Articulation: An Interview with Stuart Hall." *Journal of Communication Inquiry* 10, no. 2 (1986): 45–60.

Grossberg, Lawrence. *We Gotta Get Out of This Place: Popular Conservatism and Postmodern Culture*. New York: Routledge, 1992.

Guha, Ranajit. "Chandra's Death." In *Subaltern Studies*, vol. 5. Delhi: Oxford University Press, 1988.

Guha, Ranajit, and Gayatri Chakravorty Spivak, eds. *Selected Subaltern Studies*. New York: Oxford University Press, 1988.

Gutman, Herbert. *The Black Family in Slavery and Freedom, 1750–1925*. New York: Pantheon, 1976.

Habermas, Jürgen. *The Structural Transformation of the Public Sphere: An Inquiry into a Category of Bourgeois Society*. Translated by Thomas Burger. Cambridge, MA: MIT Press, 1991.

Hall, Stuart. "Cultural Identity and Diaspora." In *Identity: Community, Culture, Difference*, edited by Jonathan Rutherford. London: Lawrence and Wishart, 1990.

———. "Gramsci's Relevance for the Study of Race and Ethnicity." *Journal of Communication Inquiry* 10, no. 2 (1986): 5–27.

———. "Notes on Deconstructing 'the Popular.'" In *People's History and Socialist Theory*, edited by Raphael Samuel. London: Routledge and Kegan Paul, 1981.

Haller, John S., Jr. *Outcasts from Evolution: Scientific Attitudes of Racial Inferiority, 1859–1900*. Urbana: University of Illinois Press, 1971.

Haraway, Donna J. *Simians, Cyborgs, and Women: The Reinvention of Nature*. New York: Routledge, 1991.

Harding, Vincent. *There Is a River: The Black Struggle for Freedom in America*. New York: Harcourt, Brace, 1981.

Harris, Cheryl I. "Whiteness as Property." *Harvard Law Review* 106, no. 8 (June 1993): 1709–1791.

Harvey, David. *The Condition of Postmodernity: An Enquiry into the Origins of Cultural Change*. Oxford: Basil Blackwell, 1989.

Heilman, Robert Bechtold. *Tragedy and Melodrama: Versions of Experience*. Seattle: University of Washington Press, 1968.

Herbert, Christopher. *Culture and Anomie: Ethnographic Imagination in the Nineteenth Century*. Chicago: University of Chicago Press, 1991.

Herskovits, Melville J. *The Myth of the Negro Past*. Boston: Beacon Press, 1941.

Higginbotham, A. Leon, Jr. *In the Matter of Color: Race and the American Legal Process; The Colonial Period*. New York: Oxford University Press, 1978.

Higgins, Lynn A., and Brenda R. Silver, eds. *Rape and Representation*. New York: Columbia University Press, 1991.

Higginson, Thomas Wentworth. *Army Life in a Black Regiment*. Boston: Fields, Osgood and Co., 1870. Reprint, New York: W. W. Norton, 1984.

Hindess, Barry, and Paul Q. Hirst. *Pre-Capitalist Modes of Production*. London: Routledge and Kegan Paul, 1975.

Hine, Darlene Clark. "Rape and the Inner Lives of Black Women in the Middle West: Preliminary Thoughts on the Culture of Dissemblance." *Signs: Journal of Women in Culture and Society* 14, no. 4 (Summer 1989): 912–920.

Hirsch, H. N. *A Theory of Liberty: The Constitution and Minorities*. New York: Routledge, 1992.

Hirschman, Albert O. *The Passions and the Interests: Political Arguments for Capitalism before Its Triumph*. Princeton, NJ: Princeton University Press, 1977.

Hoff, Joan. *Law, Gender, and Injustice: A Legal History of U.S. Women*. New York: New York University Press, 1991.

Holloway, Joseph E., ed. *Africanisms in American Culture*. Bloomington: Indiana University Press, 1990.

Holt, Thomas C. *The Problem of Freedom: Race, Labor, and Politics in Jamaica and Britain, 1832–1938*. Baltimore: Johns Hopkins University Press, 1991.

Honig, Bonnie. "Nietzsche and the Recovery of Responsibility." In *Political Theory and the Displacement of Politics*. Ithaca, NY: Cornell University Press, 1993.

hooks, bell. *Ain't I a Woman: Black Women and Feminism*. Boston: South End Press, 1981.

Horsman, Reginald. *Race and Manifest Destiny: The Origins of American Racial Anglo-Saxonism*. Cambridge, MA: Harvard University Press, 1981.

Horwitz, Morton J. *The Transformation of American Law, 1870–1960: The Crisis of Legal Orthodoxy*. Vol. 2. New York: Oxford University Press, 1992.

Hountondji, Paulin J. *African Philosophy: Myth and Reality*. Translated by Henri Evans with Jonathan Rée. Bloomington: Indiana University Press, 1976.

Huggins, Nathan Irving. *Harlem Renaissance*. Oxford: Oxford University Press, 1971.

Hunter, Dianne, ed. *Seduction and Theory: Readings of Gender, Representation, and Rhetoric*. Urbana: University of Illinois Press, 1989.

Hurd, John Codman. *The Law of Freedom and Bondage in the United States*. 2 vols. Boston: Little, Brown, 1858–62.

Hurston, Zora Neale. *Mules and Men*. Bloomington: Indiana University Press, 1978. First published in 1935.

Inikori, Joseph E., and Stanley L. Engerman, eds. *The Atlantic Slave Trade: Effects on Economics, Societies, and Peoples in Africa, the Americas, and Europe*. Durham, NC: Duke University Press, 1992.

Jacobs, Harriet A. *Incidents in the Life of a Slave Girl, Written by Herself*. Boston: published by the author, 1861. Reprint, edited by Jean Fagan Yellin. Cambridge, MA: Harvard University Press, 1987.

Jameson, Fredric. *The Ideologies of Theory: Essays, 1971–1986*. Vol. 2. Minneapolis: University of Minnesota Press, 1988.

JanMohamed, Abdul R. "Sexuality on/of the Racial Border: Foucault, Wright, and the Articulation of 'Racialized Sexuality.'" In *Discourses of Sexuality: From Aristotle to AIDS*, edited by Domna C. Stanton. Ann Arbor: University of Michigan Press, 1992.

Jaynes, Gerald David. *Branches without Roots: Genesis of the Black Working Class in the American South, 1862–1882*. New York: Oxford University Press, 1986.

Jefferson, Thomas. *Notes on the State of Virginia*. London: John Stockdale, 1787. Reprint, New York: W. W. Norton, 1982.

Jenkins, William Sumner. *Pro-Slavery Thought in the Old South*. Chapel Hill: University of North Carolina Press, 1935. Reprint, Gloucester, MA: Peter Smith, 1960.

Johnson, Clifton H., ed. *God Struck Me Dead*. Philadelphia: Pilgrim Press, 1969.

Johnson, Guion Griffis. *A Social History of the Sea Islands, with Special Reference to St. Helena Island*. Chapel Hill: University of North Carolina Press, 1930.

Johnson, Roy F. *Supernaturals: Among Carolina Folk and Their Neighbors*. Murfreesboro, NC: Johnson Publishing Company, 1974.

Jones, Charles C. *The Religious Instruction of the Negro in the United States*. Savannah, GA: Thomas Purse, 1842. Reprint, Freeport, NY: Books for Libraries, 1971.

Jones, Jacqueline. *Labor of Love, Labor of Sorrow: Black Women, Work, and the Family, from Slavery to the Present*. New York: Basic Books, 1985.

Jones, LeRoi [Amiri Baraka]. *Blues People: Negro Music in White America*. New York: William Morrow, 1963.

Jones, Norrece T., Jr. *Born a Child of Freedom, Yet a Slave: Mechanism of Control and Strategies of Resistance in Antebellum South Carolina*. Hanover, NH: University Press of New England, for Wesleyan University Press, 1990.

Jordan, Winthrop D. *White over Black: American Attitudes toward the Negro, 1550–1812*. Chapel Hill: University of North Carolina Press, 1968. Reprint, New York: W. W. Norton, 1977.

Joyner, Charles. *Down by the Riverside: A South Carolina Slave Community*. Urbana: University of Illinois Press, 1984.

Kairys, David, ed. *The Politics of Law: A Progressive Critique*. New York: Pantheon Books, 1982.

Kammen, Michael. *Mystic Chords of Memory: The Transformation of Tradition in American Culture*. New York: Alfred A. Knopf, 1991. Reprint, New York: Vintage Books, 1993.

Kaplan, Amy, and Donald E. Pease, eds. *Culture of United States Imperialism*. Durham, NC: Duke University Press, 1993.

Karp, Ivan, and Steven D. Lavine, eds. *Exhibiting Culture: The Poetics and Politics of Museum Display*. Washington, DC: Smithsonian Institution Press, 1990.

Katz, Michael B. *In the Shadow of the Poorhouse: A Social History of Welfare in America*. New York: Basic Books, 1986.

Keckley, Elizabeth. *Behind the Scenes; or, Thirty Years a Slave, and Four Years in the White House*. New York: G. W. Carleton and Co., 1868. Reprint, New York: Oxford University Press, 1988.

Kemble, Fanny. *The American Journals*. Edited by Elizabeth Mavor. London: Weidenfeld and Nicolson, 1990.

Kendrick, Benjamin B. "The Journal of the Joint Committee of Fifteen on Reconstruction: 39th Congress, 1865–1867." PhD diss., Columbia University, 1914.

Kettner, James. *The Development of American Citizenship, 1608–1870*. Chapel Hill: University of North Carolina Press, 1978.

Kirshenblatt-Gimblett, Barbara. "Objects of Ethnography." In *Exhibiting Cultures: The Poetics and Politics of Museum Display*, edited by Ivan Karp and Steven D. Lavine. Washington, DC: Smithsonian Institution Press, 1990.

Kolchin, Peter. *American Slavery, 1619–1877*. New York: Hill and Wang, 1993.

Kousser, J. Morgan, and James M. McPherson, eds. *Region, Race, and Reconstruction: Essays in Honor of C. Vann Woodward*. New York: Oxford University Press, 1982.

Kovel, Joel. *White Racism: A Psychohistory*. New York: Columbia University Press, 1970.

Kristeva, Julia. *Powers of Horror: An Essay on Abjection*. Translated by Leon S. Roudiez. New York: Columbia University Press, 1982.

Kull, Andrew. *The Color-Blind Constitution*. Cambridge: Harvard University Press, 1992.

Laclau, Ernesto. *New Reflections on the Revolution of Our Time*. London: Verso, 1990.

Laclau, Ernesto, and Chantal Mouffe. *Hegemony and Socialist Strategy: Towards a Radical Democratic Politics*. London: Verso, 1985.

Lane, Lunsford. *The Narrative of Lunsford Lane*. Boston: published by the author, 1842. Reprint, Boston: Hewes S. Watson, 1848.

Lefebvre, Henri. *The Production of Space*. Translated by Donald Nicholson-Smith. Cambridge: Basil Blackwell, 1991.

Levine, Lawrence W. *Black Culture and Black Consciousness: Afro-American Folk Thought from Slavery to Freedom*. Oxford: Oxford University Press, 1977.

Levinson, Sanford, and Steve Mailloux, eds. *Interpreting Law and Literature: A Hermeneutic Reader*. Evanston, IL: Northwestern University Press, 1988.

Lincoln, Abraham. *Abraham Lincoln: Speeches and Writings, 1832–1858*. New York: Library of America, 1989.

Litwack, Leon F. *Been in the Storm So Long: The Aftermath of Slavery*. New York: Vintage Books, 1979.

Lomax, John A., and Alan Lomax. *Folk Song, USA: The 111 Best American Ballads*. New York: New American Library, 1966.

Lott, Eric. *Love and Theft: Blackface Minstrelsy and the American Working Class*. New York: Oxford University Press, 1992.

Lyotard, Jean-François. *The Postmodern Condition.* Translated by Geoff Bennington and Brian Massumi. Minneapolis: University of Minnesota Press, 1979.

MacKinnon, Catherine A. "Feminism, Marxism, Method and the State: Towards Feminist Jurisprudence." *Signs: Journal of Women in Culture and Society* 8, no. 4 (Summer 1983): 635–658.

Maclean, Marie. *Narrative as Performance: The Baudelairean Experiment.* London: Routledge, 1988.

MacPherson, C. B. *The Political Theory of Possessive Individualism: Hobbes to Locke.* New York: Oxford University Press, 1962.

Magriel, Paul, ed. *Chronicles of the American Dance: From the Shakers to Martha Graham.* New York: Dance Index, 1948. Reprint, New York: Da Capo, 1978.

Mahar, William J. "Black English in Early Blackface Minstrelsy: A New Interpretation of the Sources of Minstrel Show Dialect." *American Quarterly* 37, no. 2 (Summer 1985): 260–285.

Manning, Patrick. *Slavery and African Life: Occidental, Oriental and African Slave Trades.* New York: Cambridge University Press, 1990.

Marcus, George E., and Dick Cushman. "Ethnographies as Texts." *Annual Review of Anthropology* 11 (1982): 25–69.

Mars, James. *Life of James Mars, a Slave Born and Sold in Connecticut, Written by Himself.* Hartford, CT: Press of Case, Lockwood and Co. 1864.

Martin, Waldo E., Jr. *The Mind of Frederick Douglass.* Chapel Hill: University of North Carolina Press, 1984.

Marx, Karl. *Capital.* Vol. 1. Translated by Ben Fowkes. New York: Vintage, 1977.

———. "On the Jewish Question." In *The Marx-Engels Reader,* edited by Robert C. Tucker. New York: W. W. Norton, 1978.

Mauss, Marcel. *The Gift: Forms and Functions of Exchange in Archaic Societies.* Translated by Ian Cunnison. Glencoe, IL: Free Press, 1954.

McLaurin, Melton A. *Celia, A Slave: A True Story.* Athens: University of Georgia Press, 1991. Reprint, New York: Avon Books, 1993.

McClintock, Anne. *Imperial Leather: Race, Gender and Sexuality in the Colonial Contest.* New York: Routledge, 1995.

McConachie, Bruce A. *Melodramatic Formations: American Theatre and Society, 1820–1870.* Iowa City: University of Iowa Press, 1992.

McPherson, Edward. *The Political History of the United States of America during the Period of Reconstruction.* Washington, DC: Philip and Solomons, 1871.

Mehta, Uday S. "Liberal Strategies of Exclusion." *Politics and Society* 18, no. 4 (December 1990): 429–430.

Miles, Robert. *Capitalism and Unfree Labour: Anomaly or Necessity?* London: Tavistock Publications, 1987.

Miller, Jane. *Seductions: Studies in Reading and Culture.* New York: Columbia University Press, 1990.

Minson, Jeffrey. *Genealogies of Morals: Nietzsche, Foucault, Donzelot and the Eccentricity of Ethics.* New York: St. Martin's Press, 1985.

Mississippi Reports. Book 18, vols. 36 and 37. St. Paul, MN: West Publishing Company, 1908.

Montgomery, David. *Beyond Equality: Labor and the Radical Republicans, 1862–1872.* New York: Alfred A. Knopf, 1967.

———. *Citizen Worker: The Experience of Workers in the United States with Democracy and the Free Market During the Nineteenth Century.* New York: Cambridge University Press, 1993.

Morgan, Edmund S. *American Slavery, American Freedom: The Ordeal of Colonial Virginia.* New York: W. W. Norton, 1975.

Morris, David B. *The Culture of Pain.* Berkeley: University of California Press, 1991.

Morris, Robert C. *Reading, 'Riting, and Reconstruction: The Education of Freedmen in the South, 1861–1870.* Chicago: University of Chicago Press, 1976.

Morrison, Karl F. *"I Am You": The Hermeneutics of Empathy in Western Literature, Theology, and Art.* Princeton, NJ: Princeton University Press, 1988.

Morrison, Toni. *Beloved.* New York: Plume, 1988.

Morton, Patricia. *Disfigured Images: The Historical Assault on Afro-American Women.* New York: Praeger, 1991.

Mudimbe, V. Y., ed. *The Surreptitious Speech: Présence Africaine and the Politics of Otherness, 1947–1987.* Chicago: University of Chicago Press, 1992.

Mullin, Gerald W. *Flight and Rebellion: Slave Resistance in Eighteenth-Century Virginia.* New York: Oxford University Press, 1972.

Munzer, Stephen R. *A Theory of Property.* Cambridge: Cambridge University Press, 1990.

Myerson, Joel, ed. *Studies in the American Renaissance in New England.* Detroit: Gale Research Co., 1978.

Mykkeltvedt, Roald Y. *The Nationalization of the Bill of Rights: Fourteenth Amendment Due Process and the Procedural Rights.* Port Washington, NY: Associated Faculty Press, 1983.

Napier, A. David. *Masks, Transformation and Paradox.* Berkeley: University of California Press, 1986.

Nathan, Hans. *Dan Emmett and the Rise of Early Negro Minstrelsy.* Norman: University of Oklahoma Press, 1962.

Nathanson, Y. S. "Negro Minstrelsy, Ancient and Modern." *Putnam's Monthly* 5 (January 1855): 72–79.

Nedelsky, Jennifer. *Private Property and the Limits of American Constitutionalism: The Madisonian Framework and Its Legacy.* Chicago: University of Chicago Press, 1990.

"Negro Superstitions Concerning the Violin." *Journal of American Folklore* 5 (1892): 329–330.

Nelson, Bernard H. *The Fourteenth Amendment and the Negro since 1920.* Washington, DC: Catholic University of America Press, 1946.

Nelson, Cary, and Lawrence Grossberg, eds. *Marxism and the Interpretation of Culture.* Urbana: University of Illinois Press, 1988.

Nieman, Donald G., ed. *African American Life in the Post-Emancipation South, 1861–1900.* Vol. 2. New York: Garland, 1994.

———. *Black Southerners and the Law, 1865–1900.* New York: Garland, 1994.

———. *To Set the Law in Motion: The Freedmen's Bureau and the Legal Rights of Blacks, 1865–1868.* Millwood, NY: KTO Press, 1979.

Northup, Solomon. *Twelve Years a Slave.* In *Puttin' On Ole Massa: The slave narratives of Henry Bibb, William Wells Brown, and Solomon Northup,* edited by Gilbert Osofsky. Baton Rouge: Louisiana State University Press, 1968.

Oakes, James. *The Ruling Race: A History of American Slaveholders.* New York: Alfred A. Knopf, 1982.

Olmsted, Frederick Law. *A Journey in the Back Country.* New York: Mason Brothers, 1863. Reprint, New York: G. P. Putnam's Sons, 1907.

———. *A Journey in the Seaboard Slave States.* New York: Dix, Edwards, 1856.

———. *A Journey through Texas; or, A Saddle-Trip on the Southwestern Frontier; with a Statistical Appendix.* New York: Dix, Edwards, 1857.

Olsen, Otto H. *The Thin Disguise: Turning Point in Negro History; Plessy v. Ferguson, A Documentary Presentation.* New York: Humanities Press, 1967.

Omi, Michael, and Howard Winant. *Racial Formation in the United States.* New York: Routledge and Kegan Paul, 1986.

Ostendorf, Berndt. *Black Literature in White America.* Totowa, NJ: Harvester Press, 1982.

Parrish, Lydia. *Slave Songs of the Georgia Sea Islands.* New York: Creative Age Press, 1942. Reprint, Hatboro, PA: Folklore Associates, 1965.

Paskoff, Paul F., and Daniel J. Wilson, eds. *The Cause of the South: Selections from De Bow's Review, 1846–1867.* Baton Rouge: Louisiana State University Press, 1982.

Pateman, Carole. *The Sexual Contract.* Stanford, CA: Stanford University Press, 1988.

Patterson, Orlando. *Freedom in the Making of Western Culture*. New York: Basic Books, 1991.

——. *Slavery and Social Death: A Comparative Study*. Cambridge, MA: Harvard University Press, 1982.

Payne, Daniel Alexander. *Recollections of Seventy Years*. Nashville, TN: Publishing House of the AME Sunday School Union, 1888. Reprint, New York: Arno Press and New York Times, 1968.

Pearson, Elizabeth Ware, ed. *Letters from Port Royal Written at the Time of the Civil War*. Boston: W. B. Clarke Company, 1906.

Pennington, James W. C. *The Fugitive Blacksmith*. In *Five Slave Narratives: A Compendium*, edited by William Loren Katz. New York: Arno Press and New York Times, 1968.

Perdue, Charles, Jr., Thomas E. Barden, and Robert K. Philips, eds. *Weevils in the Wheat: Interviews with Virginia Ex-Slaves*. Charlottesville: University of Virginia Press, 1976. Reprint, Bloomington: Indiana University Press, 1980.

Peterson, Thomas Virgil. *Ham and Japheth: The Mythic World of Whites in the Antebellum South*. Metuchen, NJ: Scarecrow Press, 1978.

Phillips, Ulrich Bonnell. *American Negro Slavery: A Survey of the Supply, Employment and Control of Negro Labor as Determined by the Plantation Regime*. New York: D. Appleton, 1918. Reprint, New York: Vintage Books, 1972.

——. *Life and Labor in the Old South*. Boston: Little, Brown, 1929.

Picquet, Louisa. *The Octoroon: A Tale of Southern Slave Life*. Edited by Hiram Mattison, 1861. In *Collected Black Women's Narratives*, edited by Henry Louis Gates Jr. New York: Oxford University Press, 1988.

Pike, James S. *The Prostrate State: South Carolina Under Negro Government*. New York: D. Appleton, 1874. Reprint. New York: Harper Torch Books, 1968.

Piven, Frances Fox, and Richard A. Cloward. *Regulating the Poor: The Functions of Public Welfare*. 2nd ed. New York: Vintage Books, 1993.

Poovey, Mary. *Making a Social Body: British Cultural Formation, 1830–1864*. Chicago: University of Chicago Press, 1995.

Post, Robert, ed. *Law and the Order of Culture*. Berkeley: University of California Press, 1991.

Power, Tyrone. *Impressions of America during the Years 1833, 1834, and 1835*. Vol. 2. Philadelphia: Carey, Lea and Blanchard, 1836.

Prince, Mary. *The History of Mary Prince a West Indian Slave*. Originally edited by Thomas Pringle, 1831. In *Six Women's Slave Narratives*. New York: Oxford University Press, 1988.

Propp, Vladimir. *Theory and History of Folklore*. Edited by Anatoly Liberman.

Translated by Ariadna Y. Martin and Richard P. Martin. Theory and History of Literature, vol. 5. Minneapolis: University of Minnesota Press, 1984.

Puckett, Newbell Niles. *Folk Beliefs of the Southern Negro.* Chapel Hill: University of North Carolina Press, 1926.

Quadagno, Jill. *The Color of Welfare: How Racism Undermined the War on Poverty.* New York: Oxford University Press, 1994.

Rabinowitz, Howard N. "From Exclusion to Segregation: Southern Race Relations, 1865–1890." *Journal of American History* 63, no. 2 (September 1976): 325–350.

Raboteau, Albert J. *Slave Religion: The "Invisible Institution" in the Antebellum South.* Oxford: Oxford University Press, 1978.

Rankin, John. *Letters on American Slavery.* Boston: Garrison and Knapp, 1833. Reprint, Westport, CT: Negro Universities Press, 1970.

Ransom, Roger L., and Richard Sutch. *One Kind of Freedom: The Economic Consequences of Emancipation.* New York: Cambridge University Press, 1977.

Ravenel, Henry. "Recollections of Southern Plantation Life." *Yale Review* 25 (1935–36): 748–777.

Rawick, George P., ed. *The American Slave: A Composite Autobiography.* 41 vols. Westport, CT: Greenwood, 1973.

———. *From Sundown to Sunup: The Making of the Slave Community.* Westport, CT: Greenwood, 1973.

Richardson, Joel. *Christian Reconstruction: The American Missionary Association and Southern Blacks, 1861–1890.* Tuscaloosa: University of Alabama Press, 1986.

Riley, Denise. *Am I That Name?: Feminism and the Category of "Women" in History.* Minneapolis: University of Minnesota Press, 1988.

Ringer, Benjamin B. *We the People and Others: Duality and America's Treatment of Its Racial Minorities.* New York: Routledge, 1983.

Ripley, Peter C. *Slaves and Freedmen in Civil War Louisiana.* Baton Rouge: Louisiana State University Press, 1976.

Roark, James L. *Masters without Slaves: Southern Planters in the Civil War and Reconstruction.* New York: W. W. Norton, 1977.

Roberts, John Storm. *Black Music of Two Worlds.* Tivoli, NY: Original Music, 1972.

Roberts, John W. *From Trickster to Badman: The Black Folk Hero in Slavery and Freedom.* Philadelphia: University of Pennsylvania Press, 1989.

Robinson, Beverly J. "Africanisms and the Study of Folklore." In *Africanisms in American Culture,* edited by Joseph E. Holloway. Bloomington: Indiana University Press, 1990.

Robinson, Cedric. *Black Marxism: The Making of the Black Radical Tradition.* London: Zed, 1983.

Robinson, Donald L. *Slavery in the Structure of American Politics, 1765–1820*. New York: Harcourt Brace Jovanovich, 1971.

Rodney, Walter. *How Europe Underdeveloped Africa*. Washington, DC: Howard University Press, 1981.

Roediger, David R. *The Wages of Whiteness: Race and the Making of the American Working Class*. London: Verso, 1991.

Rogin, Michael. *Blackface, White Noise: Jewish Immigrants in the Hollywood Melting Pot*. Berkeley: University of California Press, 1996.

Rooney, Ellen. "'A Little More Than Persuading': Tess and the Subject of Sexual Violence." In *Rape and Representation*, edited by Lynn A. Higgins and Brenda R. Silver. New York: Columbia University Press, 1991.

Roper, Moses. *A Narrative of the Adventures and Escape of Moses Roper, from American Slavery*. London: Darton, Harvey and Darton, 1838.

Rosaldo, Renato. *Culture and Truth: The Remaking of Social Analysis*. Boston: Beacon Press, 1989.

———. "From the Door of His Tent: The Fieldworker and the Inquisitor." In *Writing Culture: The Poetics and Politics of Ethnography*, edited by James Clifford and George E. Marcus. Berkeley: University of California Press, 1986.

Rose, Willie Lee. *Rehearsal for Reconstruction: The Port Royal Experiment*. London: Oxford University Press, 1964.

Rourke, Constance. *American Humor: A Study of the National Character*. New York: Harcourt, Brace, 1931.

Ryan, Michael. "The Politics of Film: Discourse, Psychoanalysis, Ideology." In *Marxism and the Interpretation of Culture*, edited by Cary Nelson and Lawrence Grossberg. Urbana: University of Illinois Press, 1988.

Sacks, Howard L., and Judith Rose Sacks. *Way Up North in Dixie: Black Family's Claim to the Confederate Anthem*. Washington, DC: Smithsonian Institution Press, 1993.

Saks, Eva. "Representing Miscegenation Laws." *Raritan* 8, no. 2 (1988): 39–70.

Sanchez-Eppler, Karen. "Bodily Bonds: The Intersecting Rhetorics of Feminism and Abolition." *Representations* 24 (Fall 1988): 28–59.

Sandel, Michael J. *Liberalism and the Limits of Justice*. New York: Cambridge University Press, 1982.

Sarat, Austin, and Thomas R. Kearns, eds. *The Fate of Law*. Ann Arbor: University of Michigan Press, 1991.

Sassoon, Anne Showstack. *Gramsci's Politics*. Minneapolis: University of Minnesota Press, 1987.

———, ed. *Approaches to Gramsci*. London: Writers and Readers, 1982.

Saxton, Alexander. "Blackface Minstrelsy and Jacksonian Ideology." *American Quarterly* 27, no. 1 (March 1975): 3–28.

Scarry, Elaine. *The Body in Pain: The Making and Unmaking of the World.* New York: Oxford University Press, 1985.

Schafer, Judith. "Sexual Cruelty to Slaves." *Chicago-Kent Law Review* 68, no. 3 (1993).

Schechner, Richard. *Between Theatre and Anthropology.* Philadelphia: University of Pennsylvania Press, 1985.

———. *Performance Theory.* New York: Routledge, 1988. First published as *Essays on Performance Theory* by Ralph Pine, for Drama Book Specialists.

Schurz, Carl. *Report on the Condition of the South.* First published 1865. Reprint, New York: Arno Press, 1969.

Schwartz, Barnard, ed. *The Fourteenth Amendment.* New York: New York University Press, 1970.

Scott, James C. *Domination and the Arts of Resistance: Hidden Transcripts.* New Haven, CT: Yale University Press, 1990.

———. *Weapons of the Weak: Everyday Forms of Peasant Resistance.* New Haven, CT: Yale University Press, 1985.

Serequeberhan, Tsenay. *The Hermeneutics of African Philosophy: Horizon and Discourse.* New York: Routledge, 1994.

Shore, Laurence. *Southern Capitalists: The Ideological Leadership of an Elite, 1832–1885.* Chapel Hill: University of North Carolina Press, 1986.

Slaughter, Linda Warfel. *The Freedmen of the South.* Cincinnati: Elm Street Printing Company, 1869.

Sloterdijk, Peter. *Thinker on Stage: Nietzsche's Materialism.* Translated by Jamie Owen Daniel. Minneapolis: University of Minnesota Press, 1989.

Smart, Carol. *Feminism and the Power of Law.* London: Routledge, 1989.

Smith, James L. *Autobiography of James L. Smith.* Norwich: Press of the Bulletin Company, 1881.

Smith, Paul. *Discerning the Subject.* Minneapolis: University of Minnesota Press, 1988.

Smith, Valerie. *Self-Discovery and Authority in Afro-American Narrative.* Cambridge, MA: Harvard University Press, 1987.

Smith, Venture. *A Narrative of the Life and Adventures of Venture, a Native of Africa.* New London, CT: C. Holt, 1798.

Smith, William B. "The Persimmon Tree and the Beer Dance." *Farmer's Register* 6 (1838): 58–61.

Sobel, Mechal. *Trabelin' On: The Slave Journey to an Afro-Baptist Faith.* Princeton, NJ: Princeton University Press, 1988.

Southern, Eileen. *The Music of Black Americans: A History.* New York: W. W. Norton, 1971.

———. *Readings in Black American Music.* New York: W. W. Norton, 1972.

Spaulding, H. G. "Under the Palmetto." *Continental Monthly* 4 (1863): 188–203.

Spillers, Hortense. "Mama's Baby, Papa's Maybe: An American Grammar Book." *Diacritics* 17, no. 2 (Summer 1987): 65–81.

Spivak, Gayatri Chakravorty. "Can the Subaltern Speak?" In *Marxism and the Interpretation of Culture,* edited by Cary Nelson and Lawrence Grossberg. Urbana: University of Illinois Press, 1988.

———. *Outside in the Teaching Machine.* New York: Routledge, 1993.

Stallybrass, Peter, and Allon White. *The Politics and Poetics of Transgression.* Ithaca, NY: Cornell University Press, 1986.

Stampp, Kenneth. *The Peculiar Institution: Slavery in the Ante-Bellum South.* New York: Alfred A. Knopf, 1956.

Stanley, Amy Dru. "Beggars Can't Be Choosers: Compulsion and Contract in Postbellum America." *Journal of American History* 78, no. 4 (March 1992): 1265–1293.

Stearns, Marshall. *The Story of Jazz.* New York: Oxford University Press, 1956.

Stearns, Marshall, and Jean Stearns. *Jazz Dance: The Story of American Vernacular Dance.* New York: Schirmer, 1968.

Stephenson, Gilbert Thomas. *Race Distinctions in American Law.* New York, 1910.

Stepto, Robert B. *From Behind the Veil: A Study of Afro-American Narrative.* Urbana: University of Illinois Press, 1979.

Stocking, George W. *Race, Culture and Evolution: Essays in the History of Anthropology.* New York: Free Press, 1968.

Stoller, Anna Laura. *Race and the Education of Desire: Foucault's History of Sexuality and the Colonial Order of Things.* Durham, NC: Duke University Press, 1995.

Stowe, Harriet Beecher. *Palmetto-Leaves.* Boston: James R. Osgood, 1873.

———. *Uncle Tom's Cabin.* Boston: John P. Jewett, 1852. Reprint, New York: New American Library, 1966.

Stowe, William F., and David Grimsted. "White-Black Humor." *Journal of Ethnic Studies* 3 (Summer 1975): 78–96.

Stroud, George M. *A Sketch of the Laws Relating to American Slavery in the Several States of the United States of America.* Philadelphia: Kimber and Sharpless, 1827. Reprint, New York: Negro Universities Press, 1968.

Stroyer, Jacob. *My Life in the South.* In *Five Slave Narratives: A Compendium,* edited by William Loren Katz. New York: Arno Press and New York Times, 1968.

Stuckey, Sterling. *Slave Culture: Nationalist Theory and the Foundations of Black America*. Oxford: Oxford University Press, 1987.

Sundquist, Eric J. *To Wake the Nations: Race in the Making of American Literature*. Cambridge, MA: The Belknap Press of Harvard University Press, 1993.

Szwed, John F. "Race and the Embodiment of Culture." *Ethnicity* 2 (March 1975): 19–33.

Szwed, John F., and Morton Marks. "The Afro-American Transformation of European Set Dances and Dance Suites." *Dance Research Journal* 20/21 (Summer 1988): 29–36.

Tadman, Michael. *Speculators and Slave Traders: Masters, Traders, and Slaves in the Old South*. Madison: University of Wisconsin Press, 1989.

Takaki, Ronald. *Iron Cages: Race and Culture in 19th-Century America*. Seattle: University of Washington Press, 1979.

Tambiah, Stanley Jeyaraja. *Culture, Thought, and Social Action: An Anthropological Perspective*. Cambridge, MA: Harvard University Press, 1985.

Tansey, Richard. "Bernard Kendig and the New Orleans Slave Trade," *Louisiana History* 23, no.2 (Spring 1982): 160.

Tate, Claudia. *Domestic Allegories of Political Desire: The Black Heroine's Text at the Turn of the Century*. New York: Oxford University Press, 1992.

Taussig, Michael T. *The Devil and Commodity Fetishism in South America*. Chapel Hill: University of North Carolina Press, 1980.

———. *Shamanism, Colonialism, and the Wild Man: A Study in Terror and Healing*. Chicago: University of Chicago Press, 1987.

Taylor, Diana. "Transculturating Transculturation." *Performing Arts Journal: The Interculturalism Issue* 13.2 (May 1991): 90–104.

Taylor, William R. *Cavalier and Yankee: The Old South and American National Character*. New York: George Braziller, 1961.

ten Broek, Jacobus. *The Antislavery Origins of the Fourteenth Amendment*. Berkeley: University of California Press, 1951.

———. *Equal Under Law*. London: Collier, 1969.

Thomas, Emory M. *The Confederate Nation, 1861–1865*. New York: Harper and Row, 1979.

Thomas, Kendall. "Beyond the Privacy Principle." In *After Identity: A Reader in Law and Culture*, edited by Dan Danielsen and Karen Engle. New York: Routledge, 1995.

Thompson, John. *The Life of John Thompson, a Fugitive Slave*. Worcester, MA: published by the author, 1856.

Thompson, L. S. *The Story of Mattie Jackson*. In *Six Women's Slave Narratives*. Oxford: Oxford University Press, 1988. First published in 1866.

Thompson, Robert Farris. *African Art in Motion: Icon and Act.* Berkeley: University of California Press, 1974.

——. *Flash of the Spirit: African and Afro-American Art and Philosophy.* New York: Random House, 1984.

Thompson, Rose. *Hush, Child! Can't You Hear the Music?* Edited by Charles Beaumont. Athens: University of Georgia Press, 1982.

Thompson, Stith. *Motif-Index of Folk-Literature.* 6 vols. Bloomington: Indiana University Press, 1955–58.

Tiedeman, Christopher G. *A Treatise on the Limitations of Police Power in the United States, Considered from Both a Civil and Criminal Standpoint.* St. Louis: F. H. Thomas Law Book Co., 1886.

Toll, Robert C. *Blacking Up: The Minstrel Show in Nineteenth Century America.* New York: Oxford University Press, 1974.

Tompkins, Jane. *Sensational Designs: The Cultural Work of American Fiction, 1790–1860.* New York: Oxford University Press, 1985.

Tong, Rosemarie. *Women, Sex, and the Law.* Totowa, NJ: Rowman and Allanheld, 1984.

Torrey, Jesse. *American Slave Trade.* London: J. M. Cobbett, 1822. Reprint, Westport, CT: Negro Universities Press, 1971.

Trachtenberg, Alan. *The Incorporation of America: Culture and Society in the Gilded Age.* New York: Hill and Wang, 1982.

——. *Reading American Photographs: Images as History, Mathew Brady to Walker Evans.* New York: Hill and Wang, 1989.

Trelease, Allen W. *White Terror: The Ku Klux Klan Conspiracy and Southern Reconstruction.* New York: Harper and Row, 1971.

Tucker, George. *Letters from Virginia.* Translated by F. Lucas. Baltimore: J. Rubinson, 1816.

Tucker, Robert C., ed. *The Marx-Engels Reader.* New York: W. W. Norton, 1978.

Turner, Victor. *Dramas, Fields, and Metaphors: Symbolic Action in Human Society.* Ithaca, NY: Cornell University Press, 1974.

Turner, Victor W., and Edward M. Bruner, eds. *The Anthropology of Experience.* Urbana: University of Illinois Press, 1986.

——. *From Ritual to Theatre: The Human Seriousness of Play.* New York: PAJ Publications, 1982.

——. *The Ritual Process: Structure and Anti-Structure.* Ithaca, NY: Cornell University Press, 1969.

Tushnet, Mark. *The American Law of Slavery, 1810–1860: Considerations of Humanity and Interest.* Princeton, NJ: Princeton University Press, 1981.

U.S. Congress. *Report of the Joint Committee on Reconstruction.* Washington, DC: Government Printing Office, 1866.

————. *Testimony Taken by the Joint Select Committee to Inquire into the Condition of the Late Insurrectionary States.* Washington, DC: Government Printing Office, 1872.

Van Deburg, William L. *Slavery and Race in American Popular Culture.* Madison: University of Wisconsin Press, 1984.

Walker, Clarence Earl. *Deromanticizing Black History: Critical Essays and Reappraisals.* Knoxville: University of Tennessee Press, 1991.

Waterbury, Jared Bell. *Friendly Counsels for Freedmen.* New York: American Tract Society, 1864.

Waters, Donald J., ed. *Strange Ways and Sweet Dreams: Afro-American Folklore from the Hampton Institute.* Boston: G. K. Hall, 1983.

Watson, John F. *Methodist Error; or, Friendly, Christian Advice, to Those Methodists, Who Indulge in Extravagant Emotions and Bodily Exercises.* Trenton, NJ: D. and E. Fenton, 1819.

Weber, Max. *The Protestant Ethic and the Spirit of Capitalism.* New York: Charles Scribner's Sons, 1958.

Weiner, Jonathan M. *The Social Origins of the New South: Alabama, 1860–1885.* Baton Rouge: Louisiana State University Press, 1978.

Weld, Theodore D. *Slavery and the Internal Slave Trade in the United States.* London: Thomas Ward, 1841. Reprint, New York: Arno, 1969.

Wheeler, Jacob D. *A Practical Treatise on the Law of Slavery.* New York: Allan Pollock Jr., 1837.

White, Deborah Gray. *"Ar' n' t I a Woman": Female Slaves in the Plantation South.* New York: W. W. Norton, 1985.

White, E. Francis. "Africa on My Mind: Gender, Counter Discourse and African-American Nationalism." *Journal of Women's History* 2, no. 1 (Spring 1990): 73–97.

White, Hayden. *Metahistory: The Historical Imagination in Nineteenth-Century Europe.* Baltimore: Johns Hopkins University Press, 1973.

————. *Tropics of Discourse: Essays in Cultural Criticism.* Baltimore: Johns Hopkins University Press, 1978.

Wiecek, William M. *The Sources of Antislavery Constitutionalism, 1760–1848.* Ithaca, NY: Cornell University Press, 1977.

Wiegman, Robyn. *American Anatomies: Theorizing Race and Gender.* Durham, NC: Duke University Press, 1995.

Williams, Eric. *Capitalism and Slavery.* Reprint, London: Andre Deutsch, 1964. First published in 1944.

Williams, Patricia J. *The Alchemy of Race and Rights: Diary of a Law Professor.* Cambridge, MA: Harvard University Press, 1991.

Williams, Raymond. *The Country and the City*. New York: Oxford University Press, 1973.

———. *Keywords: A Vocabulary of Culture and Society*. New York: Oxford University Press, 1976.

———. *Marxism and Literature*. Oxford: Oxford University Press, 1977.

Wilson, Theodore Bratner. *The Black Codes of the South*. Southern Historical Publications, no. 6. Tuscaloosa: University of Alabama Press, 1965.

Winter, Marian Hannah. "Juba and American Minstrelsy." In *Chronicles of the American Dance*, edited by Paul Magriel. New York: Da Capo, 1978.

Wittke, Carl. *Tambo and Bones: A History of the American Minstrel Stage*. Durham, NC: Duke University Press, 1930.

Wood, Forrest G. *Black Scare: The Racist Response to Emancipation and Reconstruction*. Berkeley: University of California Press, 1968.

Woodward, C. Vann. *Origins of the New South, 1877–1913*. Baton Rouge: Louisiana State University Press, 1951.

Wynter, Sylvia. "Sambos and Minstrels." *Social Text* 1 (Winter 1979): 149–156.

Yetman, Norman R. *Life Under the "Peculiar Institution": Selections from the Slave Narrative Collection*. New York: Holt, Rinehart and Winston, 1970.

Young, Iris Marion. *Justice and the Politics of Difference*. Princeton, NJ: Princeton University Press, 1990.

Žižek, Slavoj. "Beyond Discourse Analysis." In Ernesto Laclau, *New Reflections on the Revolution of Our Time*. London: Verso, 1990.

———. *Looking Awry: An Introduction to Jacques Lacan through Popular Culture*. Cambridge, MA: MIT Press, 1991.

———. *The Sublime Object of Ideology*. London: Verso, 1989.

ANNOTATIONS

Transit in the Flesh / On Being the Object of Property

The notation is indebted to Patricia Williams, Hortense Spillers, Albert Raboteau and Sterling Stuckey and to the spirit guardians and defenders of the dead.

"Grave of Hackless Jenkins, 1878–1928, Sea Islands, Georgia, decorated with clocks, glassware, & other objects"
Sea Islands—1930–1940, Library of Congress
James Smillie after J. G. Chapman
The Lake of the Dismal Swamp, c. 1836
Mezzotint
Cameron Rowland
Out of sight, 2020
19th-century slave iron, 19th-century slave iron with missing rattle
Rental
Irons with rattles built into their handles, called slave irons, were designed to be used by the enslaved working inside the plantation house to iron the laundry of the masters. While out of sight, the rattle audibly signaled to the master that the slave was working continuously. Removing the rattle was a refusal of this oversight.
Nkisi Sarabanda, a Kongo cosmogram, or diagram of the shout
Robert Farris Thompson, *Flash of the Spirit*, 1984
Toni Morrison and Middleton A. Harris, *The Black Book*, 1974
"Utensils and a pot trammel, made by slave blacksmith"
Old Slave Mart Museum, Charleston, South Carolina

"Green Hill, Slave Auction Block, State Route 728, Long Island, Campbell
County, VA"
Historic American Buildings Survey, Library of Congress
Christina Sharpe, *In the Wake*, 2016

Black Antagonism

In homage to the sweetgrass basket makers of Edisto Island and what they are
owed. Sweetgrass basket made on Edisto Island, 2017
"An African trade passed down from Africa to South Carolina"

Cycles of Accumulation and Dispossession

The things understood inside the circle are expressed by way of counterclockwise
movement and the propulsive force of recursion and repetition. The diagram bears
the imprint of this movement and should be read in multiple directions at once.
The lines are divergent, permeable, shifting and charged and they advance a set of
propositions about slavery, accumulation, dispossession, and blackness that are
open to realignment and to other formulations.

Sylvia Wynter, *Black Metamorphoses* (n.d., unpublished manuscript)
Cedric Robinson, *Black Marxism*, 1983
Éduoard Glissant, *The Poetics of Relation*, 1990
Harriet Jacobs, *Incidents in the Life of a Slave Girl*, 1861
Frederick Douglass, *My Bondage and My Freedom*, 1855
Slyviane Diouf, *Slavery's Exiles: The Story of the American Maroons*, 2016
Katherine McKittrick, *Demonic Ground*, 2006
Denise Ferreira da Silva, *Toward a Global Idea of Race*, 2007
Zakiyyah Iman Jackson, *Becoming Human*, 2020
Karl Marx, *Capital*, volume 1, 1867
Fred Moten, *Stolen Life*, 2018
Stephanie Smallwood, *Saltwater Slavery*, 2007
Alexander Weheliye, *Habeas Viscus*, 2015
Achille Mbembe, *Critique of Black Reason*, 2019
Sarah Haley, *No Mercy Here*, 2016
Tina Campt, *Listening to Images*, 2017
Jennifer Morgan, "Partus Sequitur Ventrem," 2018
Lindon Barrett, *Blackness and Value*, 2008

Anthony Farley, "The Colorline as Capital Accumulation," 2008, & "The Apogee of the Commodity," 2004

Frank Wilderson, *Red, White & Black*, 2010

Jared Sexton, "The Social Life of Social Death," 2016, & "The *Vel* of Slavery: Tracking the Figure of the Unsovereign," 2014

Dennis Childs, *Slaves of the State*, 2015

Marisa Fuentes, *Dispossessed Lives*, 2016

Christina Sharpe, *In the Wake*, 2016

Theses on the Nonevent of Emancipation
or the Graphic Registers of a Moan

Ottobah Cugoano, *Thoughts and Sentiments on the Evil and Wicked Traffic of the Slavery and Commerce of the Human Species*, 1787

"where I heard the groans and cries of many"

Oxford English Dictionary: To breathe with a deep-toned murmur; to utter a low deep sound expressive of grief or pain.

To breathe (one's life, soul) *away* or *out* in groaning

To bewail, to lament.

Moan: To complain of, lament; to bemoan, bewail.

To lament, to grieve.

A long, low plaintive sound.

To make a long, low, inarticulate sound indicative of mental or physical suffering or (in later use also) pleasure; to utter a moan or moans. Of an animal: to produce a similar sound.

Moan gives way to mourning and morning.

W.E.B. Du Bois, *The Souls of Black Folk: Essays and Sketches*, 1903

"Of the Sorrow Songs"

W.E.B. Du Bois, *Black Reconstruction*, 1935

"The slave went free"

Ron Eglash, *African Fractals: Modern Computing and Indigenous Design*, 1999

"A nonlinear spiral of finite diameter can have an infinite number of turns, because even though there is less and lesss space remaining as one goes toward the center, the distance between each revolution can get smaller and smaller."

Jean Toomer, *Cane*, 1923

"Blood-Burning Moon"

Édouard Glissant, *Poetics of Relation*, 1990

"The Slave Trade came through the cramped doorway of the slave ship, leaving
     a wake like that of crawling desert caravans. It might be drawn like this:
        ⟩⸻⟨ African Countries to the East; the Lands of America to the West.
     This creature is in this image of a fibril."

Fred Moten, *In the Break*, 2003

"the resistance of the object" & "black moanin' "

Those who made a way

Black Compositional Thought / Notes on Redolent Space and Fugitive Architecture

In built and natural environments, each object helps define our conditions of movement. The design of our physical world informs the methods in which motion emerges and spatial energy is organized. For Black people, moving through a given environment comes with questions of belonging and self-determination, of visibility and semi-autonomy. This means for the systematically disenfranchised, compositional movement (ways in which the body unifies, balances, and arranges itself to move through space) is a skill used in the service of self-emancipation within hostile territories.

—Torkwase Dyson, "Black Interiority: Notes on Architecture, Infrastructure, Environmental Justice, and Abstract Drawing"

The drawings or compositions that open each chapter attend to the histories of forced migration, captivity, enclosure, and death, while tracing lines of fugitive and stealth movement, dwelling and maroonage, black ecologies of inhabitation. These abstract drawings register the scale and intensity of confinement, the violence of settlement and extraction, and the imposed grid of intelligibility that legitimates the order of property: the slave estate and the apprehension of earth as parcels of commodified land. At the same time, these spatial compositions orient us toward the swamps, rivers, forests, and hills. By exploring the properties of space and scale, the drawings imagine other spatial arrangements from the implicit perspective of figures in motion. These architectural renderings are always already inhabited and transformed by blackness, so the lines of confinement and enclosure expand and collapse, as those forced to stay put and those in flight inhabit and negotiate space and time in its manifold dimensions. These compositions offer provisional designs as to how we might live; they imagine an existence within and outside the hold and a blueprint for inhabiting earth that might yield other forms for existence.

INDEX

Monroe, Garland, 114–15
Moore, Fannie, 114
morality, 277
    debt and, 223
    grafted onto economics, 222–23
Morgan, Edmund, 104–5, 402n
Morrison, Toni, 8, 52, 386n
Moses, Charlie, 3, 4
motherhood
    commercial vitiation of, 146
    critical to reproduction of property and
        black subjection, 171–72
    negation of maternity, xxxvi, 128,
        171–72, 192
motivation, 253
movement, 259
    freedom of, 266–67
    of laborers, 250
    liberty and, 266–67
Munzer, Stephen, 389n
Murray, Ben, 71
mutuality, violence of, xxxviii, 8, 153–54,
    157, 232, 357
    debt and, 232
    rape and, 152
    separate but equal, 339, 349, 357
    submission and, 157
"My Old Kentucky Home," 43

narration, 423n
    seductiveness of, 187, 423n
natal alienation, 84, 94, 113, 122, 125,
    145, 172
National Freedman, 221
national identity, consolidation and
    remaking of, 301–2
national innocence
    fabrication of, 307–9
    individual culpability and, 234–36
national memory, political imperatives
    shaping construction of, 13
national prosperity, 275–76, 278, 280
natural rights, rights of man, 233, 243,
    265, 267, 268, 286
necessity, 250, 251
    liberty and, 224
need(s), 250, 358
    desire and, 82, 93, 94, 109, 117, 121, 361
    embodied, 118–21
    politics of, 405n
    runaway, 452–53n
negligible injury, xxxviii, 140, 146, 166,
    178, 375–76
"Negro question," 299, 300–301, 341

"negro's enjoyment," defamiliarization
    of, 98–102
New Deal, 299, 452n
New Orleans Daily Picayune, 58
Newsome, Robert, 141–45, 149–50. See
    also Celia; rape
Nietzsche, Friedrich, 222, 223
Nora, Pierre, 409n
normalization, 2, 3, 214, 229, 285, 447n
North Carolina, antimiscegenation laws
    in, 331–32
North Carolina Supreme Court, 158–60
Northern entrepreneurs, 225, 243, 256
Northup, Solomon, 119, 406n
    Twelve Years a Slave, 67–68
Norton, Anne, 425–26n

obeisance, demanded of formerly
    enslaved, 227, 228, 268
obligation, 221–88. See also duty;
    indebtedness
the obscene, the festive and, 50–54
obscurity blacker than poverty, 299–304
The Octoroon, 36, 41, 48
Oh, Hush! 45
"Old Folks at Home," 41, 43
"Old Virginia Never Tire," 49
Old Zip Coon, 45
Omi, Michael, 401n
opacity, slave song and, 54–55
    acts of resistance, 10
    blackness and, 26, 300
    lower frequencies and, 54
    rights to, 54
oppositional culture, Douglass's search
    for, 75–77
originary accumulation, violence of, 245
origin stories, 230–36
orisha tradition, 124

Pace v. Alabama, 333
pain
    as conduit of identification, 21–26
    denial of, 55–65
    disavowing claims of, 55–65
    redressing the pained body, 81–135
the panopticon, 243–44
Parker, Theodore, 74–75
particularity, universality and, 216
partus sequitur ventrem, 416n, 421n
Pasquino, Pasquale, 350–51, 453n
the past, 121–27. See also history; memory
the (plantation) pastoral, 13, 87–88, 127,
    247, 253, 399–400nn

Cameron Rowland
National Ex-Slave Mutual Relief, Bounty and Pension Association
Badges, 2016
Pot metal
1¼ × 1¼ inches and 1¼ × 1¼ inches

The National Ex-Slave Mutual Relief, Bounty and Pension Association was founded in 1898 by ex-slaves I. H. Dickerson and Callie House. It was one of the first organizations to advocate for ex-slave compensation. Members were provided with badges and certificates of membership. The certificate of membership read:

> Having paid the membership fee of 50 cents to aid the movement in securing the passage of the Ex-Slave Bounty and Pension Bill, as introduced February 17th, to the 57th House of Representatives of The United States by the Hon. E. S. Blackburn of N.C. The holder of this Certificate agrees to pay ten cents per month to the local Association to Aid the Sick and Bury the Dead. I hereby testify that I was born a slave in _____ and am entitled to all the benefits included in said Bill.

The badge on the left was dug in Faison, North Carolina. The badge on the right was dug in Vicksburg, Virginia. Both were sold in 2015 by Civil War memorabilia dealers.

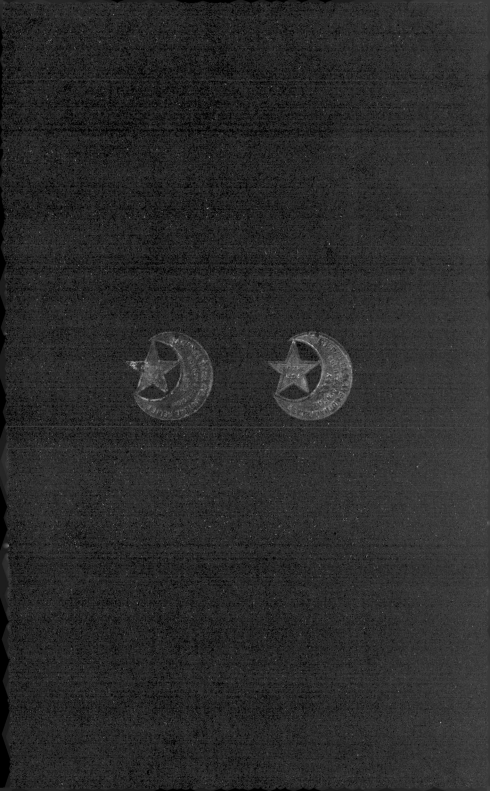